Middle English Legends
of Women Saints

Middle English Texts

General Editor

Russell A. Peck
University of Rochester

Associate Editor

Alan Lupack
University of Rochester

Assistant Editor

Dana M. Symons
University of Rochester

Advisory Board

Rita Copeland
University of Pennsylvania

Thomas G. Hahn
University of Rochester

Lisa Kiser
Ohio State University

R. A. Shoaf
University of Florida

Bonnie Wheeler
Southern Methodist University

The Middle English Texts Series is designed for classroom use. Its goal is to make available to teachers and students texts that occupy an important place in the literary and cultural canon but have not been readily available in student editions. The series does not include those authors, such as Chaucer, Langland, or Malory, whose English works are normally in print in good student editions. The focus is, instead, upon Middle English literature adjacent to those authors that teachers need in compiling the syllabuses they wish to teach. The editions maintain the linguistic integrity of the original work but within the parameters of modern reading conventions. The texts are printed in the modern alphabet and follow the practices of modern capitalization, word formation, and punctuation. Manuscript abbreviations are silently expanded, and *u/v* and *j/i* spellings are regularized according to modern orthography. Yogh is transcribed as *g*, *gh*, *y*, or *s*, according to the letter in modern English spelling to which it corresponds. Distinction between the second person pronoun and the definite article is made by spelling the one *thee* and the other *the*, and final *-e* that receives full syllabic value is accented (e.g., *charité*). Hard words, difficult phrases, and unusual idioms are glossed on the page, either in the right margin or at the foot of the page. Explanatory and textual notes appear at the end of the text, along with a glossary. The editions include short introductions on the history of the work, its merits and points of topical interest, and also contain briefly annotated bibliographies.

Middle English Legends of Women Saints

Edited by
Sherry L. Reames

with the assistance of
Martha G. Blalock
and
Wendy R. Larson

Published for TEAMS
(The Consortium for the Teaching of the Middle Ages)
in Association with the University of Rochester

by

Medieval Institute Publications

WESTERN MICHIGAN UNIVERSITY

Kalamazoo, Michigan — 2003

Library of Congress Cataloging-in-Publication Data

Middle English legends of women saints / edited by Sherry L. Reames with
the assistance of Martha G. Blalock and Wendy R. Larson.
     p. cm. -- (Middle English texts series)
Includes bibliographical references.
  ISBN 1-58044-046-0 (alk. paper)
 1. Christian literature, English (Middle) 2. Christian women
saints--Legends. 3. Christian hagiography. I. Reames, Sherry L. 1942-
II. Consortium for the Teaching of the Middle Ages. III. University of
Rochester. IV. Middle English texts (Kalamazoo, Mich.)
  PR1120 .M524 2003
  820.8'0382700922--dc21

                                    2002152808

ISBN 1-58044-046-0

Printed in the United States of America
P 5 4 3 2

Cover design by Linda K. Judy

Contents

Acknowledgments

Although many people helped in the preparation of this volume, the contributions which most need acknowledging are those of my two collaborators, Martha Blalock and Wendy Larson. Martha did most of the hard, unglamorous work of glossing and explicating the texts by Lydgate, Bokenham, and Mirk, working initially from the EETS editions because we assumed (erroneously) that those texts would not need any actual re-editing. Wendy helped enormously at a later stage in the process by drafting introductions to St. Margaret and St. Katherine that were good enough to serve as models for all the other introductions in this collection. Wendy also wrote many of the explanatory notes on those two legends.

I am grateful as well to Russell Peck, who generously offered encouragement and expert advice at every stage of this project; to Karen Saupe, who provided additional support and know-how; to John Sutton, who did the final formatting and checking with great care and prevented a number of errors; and to Dana Symons, who proofread the entire volume and prepared the final camera-ready copy. The Graduate School Research Committee of the University of Wisconsin-Madison provided financial support for two summers of research in England. I also wish to thank the gracious keepers of manuscripts at the British Library, Bodleian Library, Cambridge University Library, Durham University Library, and three Cambridge colleges, Gonville and Caius, Magdalene, and Trinity, all of whom made me welcome in their collections and facilitated my research by allowing the reproduction of the folios used for this edition. Finally I would thank the National Endowment for the Humanities for its generous support of the Middle English Texts Series.

Middle English Legends of Women Saints

General Introduction

Hagiography or saints' legends, writings that recount and celebrate the lives, deaths, and posthumous miracles of men and women recognized as saints, comprised one of the dominant literary genres in Europe from Late Antiquity to the end of the Middle Ages. From this long period, many thousands of hagiographical texts survive — a vast body of potential source material on the history and culture of the medieval church. Most of these texts are in Latin or Greek, and were clearly designed for monastic or clerical audiences; but an enormous number and variety of vernacular versions were produced in the later Middle Ages (thirteenth, fourteenth, and fifteenth centuries), suggesting that the legends eventually reached most segments of the lay public as well. Although the popular character of the legends has sometimes been exaggerated, there is no denying the strength of their influence on lay religious culture in the late Middle Ages. Favorite episodes were illustrated far and wide in church windows, frescoes, sculptures, and tapestries, many of them specifically commissioned by lay donors. Episodes from the legends also occupy a prominent place among the motifs chosen for illustration in books of hours and other devotional articles made for private use by laymen and women. Responses to the legends by less prosperous and literate laypeople cannot be gauged so directly, but a great deal of evidence suggests that the fabric of most people's lives was densely interwoven with beliefs and practices fostered by the legends — not just participation in the annual festivals of important saints, but also visits to shrines to seek healing or forgiveness, the knowledge of proverbs and folk customs that preserved bits of lore about the saints, the practice of giving children names that linked them with particular patron saints, the use of charms and talismans that supposedly conferred a given saint's protection, and so on.[1]

Despite the obvious cultural importance of saints' legends in the Middle Ages, modern readers have often been tempted to ignore or dismiss them — largely, I believe, because we have tended to approach them with the wrong expectations. For example, one will be continually frustrated if one expects the legends to provide sober, trustworthy biographies of

---

[1] For a good recent example of research on the popular, folkloric aspects of a saint's cult, see Francesca Sautman, "Saint Anne in Folk Tradition: Late Medieval France," in Ashley and Sheingorn, *Interpreting Cultural Symbols*, pp. 69–94.

individual saints.[2] Most hagiographers were not disinterested historians, but preachers and publicists. Their chief goal was to glorify the memory of a particular saint, generally for such practical purposes as strengthening the morale of the community to which the saint had belonged, driving home some point of doctrine or morality, winning new adherents to the saint's way of life, or drawing pilgrims to the saint's shrine. In this context, advocates of a new saint might go to some lengths to prove that he or she had surpassed or at least equaled the holiness and power of earlier heroes of the faith, and advocates of earlier saints might respond by improving their own legends. Hence the genre is full of conventional formulas, polemical exaggerations, and shameless borrowings from the Bible and earlier legends.

What can modern scholars and students hope to learn from sources like these? If we work cautiously enough, attempting to strip away all the conventional and polemical material in the legends, we may find nuggets of reliable historical detail. Donald Weinstein and Rudolph M. Bell give a large-scale demonstration of this procedure, with applications to medieval family history, in the first half of their 1982 book, *Saints and Society.* Alternatively and even more fruitfully, we can study the conventions and polemical elements themselves, seeking to understand what the traditional patterns can tell us about the assumptions and concerns of the people who used them or changed them in various ways. In the past few decades, students of medieval culture have begun to produce valuable and interesting work of this kind. Applying narrative theory to early hagiography, for example, Alison Goddard Elliott treats the genre quite seriously as a variety of folklore, or myth, analyzing the structural patterns that underlie it and the functions served by its conventions.[3] Elliott's book develops an important distinction suggested in 1975 by Charles F. Altman:[4] whereas the typical structure of a martyr's *passio* sets goodness in diametrical opposition to evil, the typical structure of a confessor's *vita* "presents a gradational view of the universe, in which *good* is opposed to *better* and *worse*" (Elliott, p. 17). To the former Altman and Elliott relate medieval epic; to the latter, romance.

Some important recent historical studies have shed light on other facets of hagiography by studying legends in relation to the particular cultural and historical contexts from which they came. In a series of seminal articles and books, Peter Brown has explored the psychological

---

[2] Even Hippolyte Delehaye, the world's greatest authority on saints' legends in the early twentieth century, seems sometimes to have fallen into this trap. In his well-known introduction to the genre, *Les Légendes hagiographiques* [*The Legends of the Saints*], he regretfully dismissed the majority of the legends as a kind of childish folklore that had substituted itself for authentic, valuable historical documents about the saints.

[3] Alison Goddard Elliott, *Roads to Paradise: Reading the Lives of the Early Saints* (Hanover: University Press of New England, 1987).

[4] Charles F. Altman, "Two Types of Opposition and the Structure of Latin Saints' Lives," *Medievalia et Humanistica* n.s. 6 (1975), 1–11.

and social needs that were met by the cult of the saints in Late Antiquity and the early Middle Ages, in the process revealing unexpected depths of meaning in many conventional features of the legends.[5] André Vauchez has done similarly ground-breaking research on the cult of the saints in the late Middle Ages, showing how the new spiritual movements and emphases that emerged during these centuries were reflected in the veneration of new kinds of saints.[6] One valuable contribution of such studies is the clarity with which they demonstrate that conceptions of sanctity are socially or institutionally constructed, rather than natural and inevitable, and that they vary not only in different chronological eras, but also in different regions, kinds of communities, and interest groups. During the later thirteenth and fourteenth centuries, for example, Vauchez found that urban Christians in Italy were spontaneously venerating local saints who exemplified one paradigm of sanctity while Christians north of the Alps continued to prefer aristocratic saints who conformed to an earlier paradigm and the popes were limiting the possibility of official canonization to candidates who fit a new, more selective paradigm of their own.

Studies of gender in saints' legends must begin with the uncomfortable recognition that female saints have been greatly outnumbered by male saints in every period of church history.[7] There is of course an easy explanation for this imbalance: the powers of official canonization were always in male hands, and so were most of the pens that recorded oral traditions for posterity.[8] But the issue of sanctity and gender is too complicated and interesting to be reduced to a mere case of sex discrimination by church authorities — as even a brief chronological survey suggests.

In Late Antiquity, the prevailing images of sanctity were unambiguously masculine. Women were included among the martyrs, of course, but even the martyr was envisaged as fulfilling

---

[5] See especially *The Cult of the Saints: Its Rise and Function in Latin Christianity* and two of Brown's articles, "The Rise and Function of the Holy Man in Late Antiquity" and "Relics and Social Status in the Age of Gregory of Tours" (Brown [1982], pp. 222–50).

[6] André Vauchez, *La Sainteté en Occident aux derniers siècles du Moyen Age* [*Sainthood in the Later Middle Ages*].

[7] On this issue, see Schulenburg (1978) and Herlihy, "Did Women Have a Renaissance?"

[8] Even in Late Antiquity and the early Middle Ages, when canonization was a relatively informal and localized matter, a community was not supposed to treat a deceased person's tomb as a shrine, or to add his or her name to the local catalog of saints, until the evidence for that person's sanctity had been approved by at least one appropriate representative of the church hierarchy, normally the diocesan bishop. As time went on, of course, the processes required to authorize a cult became increasingly formal and elaborate, reaching their apparent climax in the thirteenth century, when papal canonization became the official norm. On these developments, see Eric W. Kemp, *Canonization and Authority in the Western Church* (London: Oxford University Press, 1948) and the opening chapters of Vauchez's *La Sainteté en Occident*.

3

a prototypically male role, that of athlete or warrior, which was beyond the natural capacity of women. Thus the endurance of the female martyr Blandina, in the eyewitness account of the persecutions at Lyons in the second century, is depicted as miraculous: "Tiny, weak, and insignificant as she was she would give inspiration to her brothers, for she had put on Christ, that mighty and invincible athlete, and had overcome the Adversary in many contests, and through her conflict had won the crown of immortality."[9]

The second great model of sanctity in the early centuries of Christianity was the monastic ascetic who withdrew from the world, renouncing all earthly pleasures and possessions to seek God alone. Among the legendary ascetics were a few repentant female sinners like Mary of Egypt and Thais, former prostitutes who became saints by devoting the remainder of their lives to a penitential regime of total solitude and extreme privation.[10] But the conventional image of the ascetic saint, like that of the martyr, was male. The strength of this gender identification is suggested by the way Jerome praises his already saintly, ascetical friend Paula when he describes her visit to desert monks in Egypt: "Her endurance [was] scarcely credible in a woman. Forgetful of her sex and of her weakness she even desired to make her abode . . . among these thousands of monks."[11] There were also hagiographical romances about idealistic women who disguised themselves as men — casting off their own gender, in effect, so that they could join such communities of monks and achieve sainthood.[12]

From the sixth to the twelfth century, the western Christians most likely to become saints were bishops, abbots, monastic founders, and kings — individuals, that is, who wielded considerable power in society because of their high office and (usually) aristocratic birth. Given the emphasis on public power in this paradigm of sanctity, it is not surprising that women tended to be overshadowed by men, comprising only about 15% of the total number of new saints recognized during these centuries. There were some major interruptions in this pattern, however, especially in the early Middle Ages. The pre-Carolingian saints of France included such famous and influential women as Clothild, queen of the Franks (d. 544/5), who

---

[9] Translated by Herbert Musurillo in *The Acts of the Christian Martyrs*, p. 75.

[10] For a good introduction to these legends of female penitents, including translations of the key texts, see Benedicta Ward's *Harlots of the Desert: A Study of Repentance in Early Monastic Sources*.

[11] Jerome, letter 108, trans. W. H. Fremantle, in *Select Library of Nicene and Post-Nicene Fathers of the Christian Church*, ed. Philip Schaff et al., second series, vol. 6 (New York: The Christian Literature Company, 1893).

[12] On the early legends of transvestite saints, see John Anson, "The Female Transvestite in Early Monasticism: The Origin and Development of a Motif," *Viator* 5 (1974), 1–32. Paul Szarmach discusses an interesting Anglo-Saxon version of one such legend in "Aelfric's Women Saints: Eugenia," in *New Readings on Women in Old English Literature*, ed. Helen Damico and Alexandra Hennessey Olsen (Bloomington: Indiana University Press, 1990), pp. 146–57.

4

was credited with the conversion of her husband and his people; Radegund (d. 587), a later Frankish queen who left her husband to become a nun, establishing an important convent at Poitiers, but remained engaged in the public life of the kingdom; and Balthild (died c. 680), a Merovingian queen who became renowned both for her generosity in endowing monastic communities and her zeal in reforming their way of life.[13] Female saints also left their mark on the church in early medieval Ireland. The most famous example is Brigid (died c. 525), founder and ruler of the great double monastery at Kildare. St. Brigid wielded so much power in the Irish church that some accounts of her life portray her as the *de facto* bishop of her diocese, with the power to choose and supervise the man who nominally filled that office, and one legend claims that she herself was ordained as a bishop.[14] The monastic culture of Anglo-Saxon England seems for a time to have been similarly hospitable to the charisma and talents of saintly women. During the century between 650 and 750, in fact, nearly 40% of the new saints recognized in Britain were women,[15] and many of these women played major roles in the church of their day. Royal abbesses like Etheldreda [or Æthelthryth] of Ely (d. 679), Ethelburga [or Æthelburg] of Barking (d. 675), Ebba [or Æbbe] of Coldingham (d. 683), and Elfleda [or Ælffled] of Whitby (d. 714) governed important monastic foundations, presiding over communities of monks as well as nuns, and most of them also ministered to the laity, advised princes and bishops, and took part in the deliberations of councils and synods. The most influential of these abbesses may have been Hilda or Hild of Whitby (d. 680), whom Bede credits with having established one of the greatest educational centers in northern England, where she oversaw the educational and spiritual formation of a whole generation of monks, training them so well that five of her pupils went on to become bishops.[16] St. Hilda also hosted and participated in the famous synod at Whitby in 663/64, at which leaders of the Celtic and Roman parties in the British church met with King Oswy to resolve the conflicts between their traditions with regard to the dating of Easter and other issues. When St. Willibrord and later St. Boniface launched their missionary efforts among the Germanic peoples on the Continent, starting around 690, Anglo-Saxon nuns and abbesses became active participants in that work too, and some of them were also eventually recognized as saints. These early female saints of England were largely forgotten after the Norman Conquest, and many of their legends have been lost entirely.[17] Perhaps the best of the surviving sources from a

---

[13] Modern English versions of the early Lives of these three saints and fourteen more can be found in *Sainted Women of the Dark Ages,* a collection by Jo Ann McNamara et al.

[14] On this issue, see, for example, Schulenburg, *Forgetful of Their Sex*, pp. 93–95.

[15] Schulenburg, *Forgetful of Their Sex*, p. 65.

[16] Bede, *Ecclesiastical History of the English Nation*, 4.23.

[17] Bede preserves some information about them, of course, as do a number of other historical records. As Stephanie Hollis has shown, however, the surviving sources — and Bede more than most — tend

hagiographical perspective is the Life of the missionary abbess St. Leoba by Rudolf, a monk in St. Boniface's monastery at Fulda.[18] The accounts in this text of Leoba's learning, her influence as a teacher and adviser, and her miracles all testify rather memorably to the kind of benevolent, world-changing power which some early medieval monks were willing to credit to holy women as well as holy men.

As Jane Schulenburg and others have shown, the various ecclesiastical reform movements which began around 750 seem to have improved the discipline and status of priests and monks at the expense of religious women, who were more and more strictly confined to their cloisters. As a result, the opportunities for women to contribute to the work of the church declined steadily during the ninth, tenth, and eleventh centuries, and so did the proportion of new women saints.

When one turns to the hagiography of the late Middle Ages, on the other hand, a great change seems to have occurred, for female saints suddenly become much more common. Of all the new saints recognized in Europe from the thirteenth through the fifteenth century, in fact, nearly a third were women — an enormous rise from the overall percentage in the preceding centuries. In addition, the late Middle Ages saw the multiplication of stories about the Virgin Mary, especially in her role as the last resort of sinners, and a great importation from the Eastern church of romanticized legends about early virgin martyrs like Margaret of Antioch and Katherine of Alexandria. Some of these late-medieval images of female sanctity are credited with great wisdom and spiritual power, but rarely do they recall the androgynous public authority of an Anglo-Saxon abbess like Hilda or Leoba. Instead, their legends tend to dwell on virtues that sound quintessentially feminine — chastity, long suffering (whether from persecution, penitential asceticism, or illness), and compassion for unfortunates — and on such private supernatural experiences as spiritual marriage to Christ and visits from angels. Some late-medieval hagiographers go so far as to suggest that being female is actually an advantage, rather than a liability, in the quest for holiness.

The late-medieval emphasis on holy womanhood does not mean, of course, that some great feminist tide was sweeping through the church. Most hagiography was still written in Latin by and for celibate male members of the clergy and monastic orders. The paradoxical attachment of such men to feminine images of sanctity has been explored most notably by Caroline

---

to be heavily biased by the orthodoxy of a later period when all power in the church was supposed to be in the hands of ordained male clergy and religious women were supposed to be confined to their cloisters. One has to read against the grain of such sources in order to find the contributions actually made by women — as Hollis herself does in her fascinating study, *Anglo-Saxon Women and the Church*.

[18] For an English translation of this Life, see C. H. Talbot, *The Anglo-Saxon Missionaries in Germany*. Hollis gives a detailed analysis of its strengths and limitations in the final chapter of *Anglo-Saxon Women and the Church*.

Walker Bynum, who has systematically analyzed uses of pertinent imagery by spiritual writers of both sexes.[19] Bynum shows that late-medieval images of female sanctity were not developed specifically to inspire or indoctrinate women, as modern readers have often supposed; in fact, they seem at least initially to have mattered most to men who were ambivalent about their own privileges and power. Hence the recurrent emphasis on those aspects of women's experience which posed the sharpest contrast to the traditional male paradigm of earthly authority and public achievements. One can see something of the same pattern in contemporary Lives of male saints, a number of whom (like St. Francis of Assisi) were revered for having renounced the kinds of power which earlier medieval saints had used for the glory of God. When the Lives of the saints in question were translated into the vernacular or retold in sermons for the laity, of course, these feminized images of sanctity became available to large numbers of women, some of whom adopted them as models for imitation.

Vernacular Lives of Women Saints in Late-Medieval England

It is dangerous to generalize broadly about Middle English hagiography because it was written for a number of different audiences and includes a wide range of literary forms, purposes, and levels of sophistication. At one end of the spectrum are unassuming popularizations which place their emphasis on colorful, dramatic story-telling, sacrificing the layers of symbolic meaning in their Latin sources for an engaging narrative and some straightforward lessons about faith and conduct. Among the texts in this category are most chapters of the *South English Legendary (SEL)*, a well-known collection of versified legends and other material for church festivals that was apparently written for oral delivery to unlettered members of the laity, and a number of individual saints' legends that were retold in the style of secular verse romances and sometimes copied into the same manuscript anthologies with them. The *SEL* circulated widely, especially in the southwestern part of England, as attested by the surviving manuscripts, which number more than 60 (counting fragments), ranging in date from about 1300 to 1500. The exact contents of this collection vary considerably from manuscript to manuscript; but of the saints most often included, about 20% are female. Women saints are much more prominently represented among the romance-like verse legends that were transmitted separately. In fact, the six most popular legends in this subgenre seem to have included those of three men (Alexis, Eustace, and Gregory) and three women (Katherine, Margaret, and Mary Magdalen). These individual legends have not survived in nearly as many manuscripts as the *SEL*; but to judge from the amount of manuscript variation in terms of textual readings, dialect, and date, they too must have reached

---

[19] See especially *Jesus as Mother*, ch. 4, and the essays reprinted in *Fragmentation and Redemption*.

a fairly wide audience and maintained their popularity for most of the Middle English period. If they are associated with any particular region, it would seem to have been the East Midlands.[20]

At the opposite end of the stylistic spectrum, one finds some Middle English legends that were composed for an elite readership and display considerable literary ambition. A surprisingly large proportion of these "literary" legends have to do with female saints. The most obvious examples come from three members of the clergy in East Anglia in the fifteenth century: Osbern Bokenham's *Legends of Holy Women*, thirteen Lives of female saints in a variety of metrical forms which he dedicated to various noble patrons, most of them women; John Lydgate's elaborately rhetorical hagiographical poems, which include a massive *Life of Our Lady* and a reworking of the Life of St. Margaret; and John Capgrave's hagiographical works — most notably his courtly-epic version of the Life of Katherine of Alexandria.[21] But literary hagiography in Middle English was not limited to these examples from East Anglia. In late fourteenth-century London, even Chaucer occasionally turned his hand to legends of saints and quasi-saints, and virtually all of his saintly figures are female.[22] And the writing and transmission of the famous Katherine Group legends[23] — skillfully elaborated accounts, in vivid alliterative prose, of the virgin martyrs Juliana, Margaret, and Katherine — suggest that there must have been at least a few vernacular readers, as far back as the early thirteenth century, who could appreciate complex and demanding retellings of women saints' legends, rich in what Th. Wolpers called "monastic-mystical" content (Görlach, "Middle English Legends," p. 444).

Between the two extremes of noticeably popular and noticeably literary styles, and perhaps more typical of Middle English hagiography than either, are some rather utilitarian-looking

---

[20] Manfred Görlach, "Middle English Legends, 1220–1530," p. 445. Using recent research on the dialects of the various manuscripts, Görlach contends that the important hagiographical collections in Middle English were identified with different regions of the country; a map on p. 440 shows the approximate distribution of the major ones.

[21] See Karen A. Winstead, ed., Capgrave's *Life of Saint Katherine* (Kalamazoo: Medieval Institute Publications, 1999).

[22] Chaucer's only retelling of a genuine saint's legend is the account of St. Cecilia which he assigned to the Second Nun in *The Canterbury Tales*, but he expertly imitated the genre on a number of other occasions — most notably in The Prioress's Tale, The Man of Law's Tale, The Clerk's Tale, and *The Legend of Good Women*.

[23] Modern English translations of all three Katherine Group legends can be found in *Anchoritic Spirituality: Ancrene Wisse and Associated Works*, trans. Anne Savage and Nicholas Watson. See also the forthcoming edition in Middle English, edited for the Middle English Texts Series by Elizabeth Robertson.

collections of legends. Among these, women saints are prominent in just one: the so-called "Vernon Golden Legend," a group of nine legends rarely seen in other English sources, including four on saintly women (Paula, A Virgin of Antioch, Theodora, and Euphrosyne), which comprises one part of a famous manuscript originally owned by a community of nuns or monks. Roughly contemporary with Vernon (c. 1400) are two larger collections of verse legends: the *Scottish Legendary*, which survives in just one manuscript and consists of a prologue and 50 legends selected and arranged by the translator, who calls himself a retired "mynistere of haly kirke," and the series of some 30 legends in short couplets that in two manuscripts is added to the usual contents of the *Northern Homily Cycle*. A better-known collection produced around the same time is John Mirk's *Festial*, a prose compilation that includes 30 short accounts of saints among its homilies and narratives for church festivals, all ostensibly designed to provide parish priests with material for sermons; Mirk's collection must have filled a real need, since it remained popular enough, decades later, to warrant nearly 20 early printed editions. A later and obviously less successful prose collection for priests, the anonymous *Speculum Sacerdotale*, survives in just one known manuscript. The fifteenth century also produced two massive collections of prose legends that evidently found sizable readerships of their own. The anonymous *Gilte Legende* or 1438 *Golden Legend*, which has sometimes been attributed (on little evidence) to Bokenham, contains up to 178 legends and survives in at least seven complete manuscripts and some fragments. But even the *Gilte Legende* is overshadowed by the monumental size and success of Caxton's *Golden Legend,* half a century later. Caxton's collection, evidently designed for private reading by prosperous and well-educated laypeople, expanded the total to some 250 legends; and it was a perennial best-seller from its first publication in 1483 until well into the 1520s.

Notwithstanding the number and apparent variety of Middle English legends that have survived, they represent only a small part of the Latin corpus that was potentially available for vernacular translation. The hagiographical tradition in Middle English, that is, gives just a sample of the Latin tradition — and it is a selective sample rather than a representative one, showing a strong predilection for certain kinds of sources over other kinds and certain paradigms or models of sanctity over others. Let us begin with the sources.

The selectivity of Middle English hagiography can be understood in part as the displacement of local or regional sources, including the Lives of most Anglo-Saxon and Celtic saints, by more universal ones. Some early studies of the subject went so far as to credit a single "universal" collection of abridged legends, the *Legenda aurea* of Jacobus de Voragine, with having shaped virtually the whole tradition in Middle English from the *South English Legendary* to Caxton. This is a great over-simplification, but like many fallacies it contains enough truth to seem plausible. Jacobus's work, a handy compilation of material on saints and liturgical seasons first issued around 1260, was one of the most popular books in Western Europe from about 1300 to the Reformation, acquiring the honorific title *Legenda aurea*

[*Golden Legend*] because it was held in such high esteem. Although Jacobus probably designed his work specifically for preachers and students in his own Dominican Order, it was so frequently imitated, adapted, and translated in the ensuing centuries that its influence seems almost ubiquitous. If one hopes to find the exact source or sources of a given Middle English legend, however, one must usually look well beyond the *Legenda*.[24] Hundreds of other Latin books about the saints were available in late-medieval England, and many of them even had the same practical advantages that evidently commended the *Legenda* itself to potential translators: brief, efficiently abridged narratives; handy organization, following the liturgical year; emphasis on "universal" saints, whose area of patronage could be defined very broadly, rather than more localized saints who were closely connected with particular places and institutions.[25]

A second pattern that can be seen in Middle English hagiography is the tendency to ignore recent saints in favor of saints from the first few centuries of the Christian era. Instead of celebrating the virtues and visions of fourteenth-century lay saints like Birgitta of Sweden and Catherine of Siena, that is, most Middle English hagiographers chose to retell the legends of New Testament figures and early martyrs. One might surmise that legends of such long-ago, far-off saints could serve only as escapist entertainment, since they would have no practical relevance to the lives of late-medieval English men and women. But that would be wrong. As Karen Winstead and others have shown, the vernacular writers tend to refashion even the legends of early virgin martyrs in ways that respond to the current needs and concerns of their own envisioned audience. And the Middle English tradition as a whole presents a series of different paradigms of female sanctity — from royal nuns and founders of institutions to beleaguered virgins to holy matrons and mothers — that move steadily closer to the ordinary life experiences of the laity. The organization of the present collection follows that series of paradigms.

---

[24] Görlach provides a good overview of his own extensive research in this area, with regard to the sources of the *SEL*, in "Middle English Legends," pp. 449–56. David Mycoff, who studied the legend of Mary Magdalen in great detail, helpfully defines the particular characteristics that distinguish the *Legenda* account of this saint from more traditional ones (see William Caxton, *A Critical Edition*, ed. Mycoff, pp. 25–27, cited below in the introduction to the Mary Magdalen legend) and goes on to draw appropriately careful conclusions about the sources of the various Middle English versions.

[25] The most obvious candidates are liturgical manuscripts: the breviaries and office lectionaries that provided the lessons read at Matins on saints' days during the year. Although the vast majority of the liturgical books used in England were destroyed at the time of the Reformation, there are dozens of surviving Sarum, York, and monastic manuscripts which give abbreviated accounts of the saints that do not match the lessons in the printed editions and have never been compared with the Middle English retellings of the same saints' legends.

General Introduction

We begin with legends about two monastic women of royal (or supposedly royal) birth: Frideswide and Mary Magdalen. No surviving text in Middle English really captures the status and power of the great Anglo-Saxon abbesses as we see them in pre-Conquest sources like Rudolf's *Life of Leoba*. Glimpses of that kind of authority can be seen in the legend of Mary Magdalen's Provençal apostolate — at least in some retellings, including the one reproduced here from an early manuscript of the *SEL*. But little or nothing remains of it in the legend of Frideswide. Although the historical Frideswide was an Anglo-Saxon abbess and probably governed a community that included monks as well as nuns, even the earliest surviving Latin account of her life seems already to have been influenced by the imported conventions of the virgin martyr legend, so that she is presented primarily as a victim of male persecution rather than a female or androgynous figure of power. The popular legend of Mary Magdalen, which was imported from the Continent in the twelfth or thirteenth century, is much richer and more multi-faceted; in fact, its fullest late-medieval forms include three different paradigms of sanctity — the repentant sinner, the apostle, and the contemplative — which could easily be appropriated as models for either men or women.

Popular legends of virgin martyrs, a subgenre represented here by the legends of Margaret of Antioch, Christina of Tyre, and Katherine of Alexandria, must be distinguished at the outset from the historical accounts of martyrs, which tend to be much briefer, more sedate, and less gender-specific, as well as chronologically much older. The popular virgin martyr legends which flourished in the late Middle Ages have aroused a good deal of controversy among modern readers because of the frequency with which they involve the motifs of men lusting after a young and beautiful virgin saint, stripping her naked, torturing her body in various horrible ways, and eventually putting her to death. Some critics have seen this fundamental plot as pornographic, or nearly so, in the way it seems to objectify the woman, subjecting her to terrible male violence as punishment for resisting male desires.[26] From another perspective, however, these legends can be seen as celebrating the victories of very strong women, whose resolve is undaunted by any tactic or weapon their adversaries can devise. Moreover, if one attends to the particulars of the individual texts, instead of assuming that they are all telling the same story, one notices that many of them seem to be about issues other than sexual desire and sexual violence. In fact, the virgin's adversaries tend to be the authority figures in her family

---

[26] This issue has recently evoked a good deal of spirited debate among feminist critics of Middle English literature. Among those critics who have read virgin martyr legends as deeply misogynistic, some of the most sophisticated and interesting arguments have come from Elizabeth Robertson, in *Early English Devotional Prose and the Female Audience* and again in "The Corporeality of Female Sanctity in *The Life of Saint Margaret*," and Gayle Margherita, in the second chapter of *The Romance of Origins: Language and Sexual Difference in Middle English Literature*. Persuasive counter-arguments have been offered by Jocelyn Wogan-Browne, especially in "The Virgin's Tale," and Sarah Salih, in "Performing Virginity: Sex and Violence in the Katherine Group."

or state, or both, and they are characterized more often as tyrants, infuriated by any disobedience to their orders, than as would-be rapists. Hence another group of critics has emphasized the practical functions of these legends not only in encouraging young women to remain virgins, resisting their parents' pressure to marry, but also in calling more covertly on audiences of both sexes to resist various kinds of political tyranny.[27]

The final portion of this collection is devoted to St. Anne, mother of the Virgin Mary. Anne's legend was exceptionally influential in the late Middle Ages because it popularized a new paradigm of female sanctity: a holy motherhood that was not miraculously virginal, like Mary's, or even quasi-virginal, like that claimed for most of the medieval saints who had been married.[28] In some respects the paradigm of the holy mother represents a significant retreat from earlier medieval images of the female saint as a powerful independent woman, a woman whose identity did not require any relationship with a mortal man to complete it. From another vantage point, however, this paradigm can be seen as an outgrowth of the same devotional and reformist trends that caused the late-medieval Church to place an increasing emphasis on celebrations of the human life of Christ and His family. And its meteoric rise in popularity suggests that it must have responded to a strong desire among the laity for saints who suggested the possibility of sanctifying their own everyday experience as spouses and parents.

Besides reflecting the general trends in Middle English hagiography with regard to sources and paradigms of female sanctity, this collection is intended to suggest the diversity of possibilities beneath the supposedly fixed and predictable surfaces of the legends. Medieval readers and listeners did not just passively receive saints' legends; they continually appropriated them and reused them for their own purposes. Hence the preference here, whenever possible, for multiple retellings of the same legend, in order to illustrate some of the different meanings and uses that could be derived from a single story. We have also attempted to choose retellings that are complete, reasonably effective and interesting, not overly long, and not easily accessible in other editions. Thus our collection includes a number of relatively unknown texts that have not appeared in print since Horstmann's transcriptions in the nineteenth century and a few that have never been published at all, but makes room for only

---

[27] On the practical relevance of these legends to young medieval women, see Jocelyn Wogan-Browne, "Saints' Lives and the Female Reader." Recent interpretations that find political messages in particular Middle English versions have included Lynn Staley Johnson, "Chaucer's Tale of the Second Nun and Strategies of Dissent"; Sherry L. Reames, "Artistry, Decorum, and Purpose in Three Middle English Retellings of the Cecilia Legend"; Mary-Ann Stouck, "Saints and Rebels: Hagiography and Opposition to the King in Late Fourteenth-Century England"; and Karen A. Winstead, "Capgrave's Saint Katherine and the Perils of Gynecocracy" and the final chapter in her book, *Virgin Martyrs: Legends of Sainthood in Late Medieval England.*

[28] On this issue, see Dyan Elliott, *Spiritual Marriage: Sexual Abstinence in Medieval Wedlock* (Princeton: Princeton University Press, 1993).

one legend from Bokenham's collection and completely excludes such famous and important examples of Middle English hagiography as the Katherine Group, Chaucer's The Second Nun's Tale, Capgrave's *Life of St. Katherine*, the standard contents of the *South English Legendary*, and all of Caxton's *Golden Legend*. Interested readers are urged, of course, to find those texts for themselves and compare them with the less well-known selections included here. Even when one compares all the versions of a legend that got written down in Middle English and preserved for us, however, one will have seen only the tip of the iceberg. This point is vividly illustrated by such large multi-lingual and multi-disciplinary studies as that of Jansen on the late-medieval cult of Mary Magdalen, or that of Kathleen Ashley and Pamela Sheingorn on the cult of St. Anne. As a first step toward completing the picture, we would suggest that readers of the present collection ask not only what messages each text was designed to convey, but also what possibilities of interpretation it opened or tried to close for its original audience.

General Bibliography

Principal collections of saints' Lives in Latin

Bolland, Joannes, et al., eds. *Acta Sanctorum quotquot toto orbe coluntur*. Original edition. Antwerp: Apud Joannem Mevrsium, 1643–. Third ed. [jan. i to oct. x]. Paris: Victor Palmé, 1863–69. Rpt. of original vols. 1–60. Turnhout: Brepols, 1966–71. [Scholarly editions of original *vitae* and other important sources on the saints, with historical and textual commentary, following the order of the liturgical year.]

Horstmann, Carl, ed. *Nova Legenda Anglie, as collected by John of Tynemouth, John Capgrave, and others*. 2 vols. Oxford: Clarendon Press, 1901. [Rich collection of texts on English saints.]

Jacobus de Voragine. *Legenda aurea, vulgo Historia lombardica dicta*. Ed. Theodor Graesse. Third ed. Vratislaviae [Breslau]: Koebner, 1890. Rpt. Osnabruck: Zeller, 1969. [This was the standard Latin version for most of the twentieth century, and the basis of most modern translations.]

_____. *Legenda aurea: Edizione critica*. Ed. Giovanni Paolo Maggioni. 2 vols. Second ed., rev. Florence: SISMEL, Edizioni del Galluzzo, 1998. [The most famous medieval collection of abbreviated saints' legends, finally available in a critical edition with useful notes, which sets the new standard.]

Mombrizio, Bonino (Boninus Mombritius), ed. *Sanctuarium, seu Vitae sanctorum.* 2 vols. Milan, c. 1477. Rpt. Paris: Albert Fontemoing, 1910. [A handy collection of some of the best-known Latin *vitae* that circulated in the Middle Ages.]

Principal collections of saints' Lives in Middle English

Bokenham, Osbern. *Legendys of Hooly Wummen.* Ed. Mary S. Serjeantson. EETS o.s. 206. London: Oxford University Press, 1938.

Caxton, William. *The Golden Legend, or Lives of the Saints.* [Ed. F. S. Ellis.] 7 vols. in 4. London: J. M. Dent, 1900. Rpt. New York: AMS Press, 1973.

d'Ardenne, S. R. T. O., ed. *The Katherine Group, edited from MS Bodley 34.* Bibliothèque de la Faculté de philosophie et lettres de l'Université de Liège 215. Paris: Société d'Edition les Belles Lettres, 1977.

D'Evelyn, Charlotte, and Anna J. Mill, eds. *The South English Legendary, edited from Corpus Christi College Cambridge MS 145 and British Museum MS Harley 2277.* 3 vols. EETS o.s. 235, 236, 244. London: Oxford University Press, 1956–59.

Görlach, Manfred, ed. *The Kalendre of the Newe Legende of Englande.* Middle English Texts 27. Heidelberg: Universitätsverlag C. Winter, 1994.

Hamer, Richard, and Vida Russell, eds. *Supplementary Lives in Some Manuscripts of the Gilte Legende.* EETS o.s. 315. Oxford: Oxford University Press, 2000.

_____, eds. *The Gilte Legende* [standard contents]. Forthcoming from EETS and Oxford University Press.

Horstmann, Carl, ed. *Sammlung altenglischer Legenden.* Heilbronn: Henninger, 1878. [Includes items 1–7 and 9 from the "Vernon Golden Legend."]

_____, ed. *Altenglische Legenden. Neue Folge, mit Einleitung und Anmerkungen.* Heilbronn: Henninger, 1881. [Includes legends added to the *Northern Homily Cycle.*]

Metcalfe, W. M., ed. *Legends of the Saints in the Scottish Dialect of the Fourteenth Century.* 6 vols. in 3. Scottish Text Society 13, 18, 23, 25, 35, and 37. Edinburgh: W. Blackwood and Sons, 1896. [Vols. 1 (nos. 13, 18) and 2 (23, 25) comprise the texts, vol. 3 (35, 37) the notes.]

14

Mirk, John. *Mirk's Festial: A Collection of Homilies.* Ed. Theodor Erbe. EETS e.s. 96. London: Kegan Paul, Trench, Trübner and Co., 1905.

Robertson, Elizabeth, ed. *The Katherine Group.* Kalamazoo: Medieval Institute Publications, forthcoming.

Weatherly, Edward H., ed. *Speculum Sacerdotale.* EETS o.s. 200. London: Oxford University Press, 1936.

Collections of legends in modern English translation

Bokenham, Osbern. *A Legend of Holy Women: Osbern Bokenham, Legends of Holy Women.* Trans. and intro. Sheila Delany. Notre Dame: University of Notre Dame Press, 1992.

Cazelles, Brigitte, trans. *The Lady as Saint: A Collection of French Hagiographic Romances of the Thirteenth Century.* Philadelphia: University of Pennsylvania Press, 1991.

Donovan, Leslie A., trans. and intro. *Women Saints' Lives in Old English Prose.* Cambridge, UK: D. S. Brewer, 1999.

Head, Thomas, ed. *Medieval Hagiography: An Anthology.* New York: Garland Pub., 2000.

Jacobus de Voragine. *The Golden Legend: Readings on the Saints.* Trans. William Granger Ryan. 2 vols. Princeton: Princeton University Press, 1993.

McNamara, Jo Ann, and John E. Halborg, with E. Gordon Whatley, ed. and trans. *Sainted Women of the Dark Ages.* Durham: Duke University Press, 1992.

Musurillo, Herbert, texts, trans., and intro. *The Acts of the Christian Martyrs.* Oxford Early Christian Texts. Oxford: Clarendon Press, 1972.

Noble, Thomas F. X., and Thomas Head, eds. *Soldiers of Christ: Saints and Saints' Lives from Late Antiquity and the Early Middle Ages.* University Park: The Pennsylvania State University Press, 1995.

Petroff, Elizabeth Alvilda, ed. *Medieval Women's Visionary Literature.* Oxford: Oxford University Press, 1986.

Savage, Anne, and Nicholas Watson, trans. and intro. *Anchoritic Spirituality: Ancrene Wisse and Associated Works*. New York: Paulist Press, 1991.

Stouck, Mary-Ann, ed. *Medieval Saints: A Reader*. Peterborough, ON: Broadview Press, 1999.

Talbot, C. H., ed. and trans. *The Anglo-Saxon Missionaries in Germany*. New York: Sheed and Ward, 1954.

Ward, Benedicta, SLG. *Harlots of the Desert: A Study of Repentance in Early Monastic Sources*. Kalamazoo: Cistercian Publications, 1987.

Winstead, Karen A., ed. and trans. *Chaste Passions: Medieval English Virgin Martyr Legends*. Ithaca: Cornell University Press, 2000.

Wogan-Browne, Jocelyn, and Glyn S. Burgess, trans. *Virgin Lives and Holy Deaths: Two Exemplary Biographies for Anglo-Norman Women*. London: J. M. Dent, 1996.

Historical studies of saints' legends and their cultural setting

Ashley, Kathleen, and Pamela Sheingorn, eds. *Interpreting Cultural Symbols: Saint Anne in Late Medieval Society*. Athens: University of Georgia Press, 1990.

Atkinson, Clarissa. *The Oldest Vocation: Christian Motherhood in the Middle Ages*. Ithaca: Cornell University Press, 1991.

Brown, Peter. "The Rise and Function of the Holy Man in Late Antiquity." *Journal of Roman Studies* 61 (1971), 80–101.

_____. *The Cult of the Saints: Its Rise and Function in Latin Christianity*. Chicago: University of Chicago Press, 1981.

_____. *Society and the Holy in Late Antiquity*. Berkeley: University of California Press, 1982.

Bynum, Caroline Walker. *Jesus as Mother: Studies in the Spirituality of the High Middle Ages*. Berkeley: University of California Press, 1982.

_____. "Introduction: The Complexity of Symbols." In *Gender and Religion: On the Complexity of Symbols*. Ed. Caroline W. Bynum, Stevan Harrell, and Paula Richman. Boston: Beacon Press, 1986. Pp. 1–20.

_____. *Holy Feast and Holy Fast: The Religious Significance of Food to Medieval Women*. Berkeley: University of California Press, 1987.

_____. *Fragmentation and Redemption: Essays on Gender and the Human Body in Medieval Religion*. New York: Zone Books, 1991.

Delehaye, Hippolyte. *Les Légendes hagiographiques*. Brussels: Société des Bollandistes, 1905. English ed. *The Legends of the Saints*. Trans. Donald Attwater. New York: Fordham University Press, 1962.

Dor, Juliette, Lesley Johnson, and Jocelyn Wogan-Browne, eds. *New Trends in Feminine Spirituality: The Holy Women of Liège and Their Impact*. Medieval Women: Texts and Contexts 2. Turnhout: Brepols, 1999.

Duffy, Eamon. "Holy Maydens, Holy Wyfes: The Cult of Women Saints in Fifteenth- and Sixteenth-Century England." In *Women in the Church*. Ed. W. J. Sheils and Diana Wood. *Studies in Church History* 27 (1990), 175–96.

Elkins, Sharon K. *Holy Women of Twelfth-Century England*. Chapel Hill: University of North Carolina Press, 1988.

Goodich, Michael. *Vita Perfecta: The Ideal of Sainthood in the Thirteenth Century*. Monographien zur Geschichte des Mittelalters 25. Stuttgart: A. Hiersemann, 1982.

Head, Thomas. "Hagiography." In *Women in the Middle Ages: An Encyclopedia*. Ed. Katharina M. Wilson and Nadia Margolis. London: Routledge, 2002.

Herlihy, David. "Did Women Have a Renaissance? A Reconsideration." *Medievalia et Humanistica* n.s. 13 (1985), 1–22.

Hollis, Stephanie. *Anglo-Saxon Women and the Church: Sharing a Common Fate*. Woodbridge, Suffolk: Boydell Press, 1992.

Kieckhefer, Richard. *Unquiet Souls: Fourteenth-Century Saints and Their Religious Milieu*. Chicago: University of Chicago Press, 1984.

McNamara, Jo Ann. *Sisters in Arms: Catholic Nuns through Two Millennia.* Cambridge, MA: Harvard University Press, 1996.

Mooney, Catherine M., ed. *Gendered Voices: Medieval Saints and Their Interpreters.* Foreword by Caroline Walker Bynum. Philadelphia: University of Pennsylvania Press, 1999.

Mulder-Bakker, Anneke B., ed. *Sanctity and Motherhood: Essays on Holy Mothers in the Middle Ages.* New York: Garland Pub., 1995.

Newman, Barbara. *From Virile Woman to WomanChrist: Studies in Medieval Religion and Literature.* Philadelphia: University of Pennsylvania Press, 1995.

Reames, Sherry L. *The Legenda aurea: A Reexamination of Its Paradoxical History.* Madison: University of Wisconsin Press, 1985.

Riches, Samantha J. E., and Sarah Salih, eds. *Gender and Holiness: Men, Women, and Saints in Late Medieval Europe.* New York: Routledge, 2002.

Salih, Sarah. *Versions of Virginity in Late Medieval England.* Cambridge, UK: D. S. Brewer, 2001.

Salisbury, Joyce E. *Church Fathers, Independent Virgins.* London: Verso, 1991.

Schulenburg, Jane Tibbetts. "Sexism and the Celestial Gynaeceum — from 500 to 1200." *Journal of Medieval History* 4 (1978), 117–33.

_____. "Female Sanctity: Public and Private Roles, ca. 500–1100." In *Women and Power in the Middle Ages.* Ed. Mary Erler and Maryanne Kowaleski. Athens: University of Georgia Press, 1988. Pp. 102–25.

_____. *Forgetful of Their Sex: Female Sanctity and Society, ca. 500–1100.* Chicago: University of Chicago Press, 1998.

Vauchez, André. *La Sainteté en Occident aux derniers siècles du Moyen Age, d'après les procès de canonisation et les documents hagiographiques.* Rome: Ecole française de Rome, 1981; rev. ed., 1988. English ed. *Sainthood in the Later Middle Ages.* Trans. Jean Birrell. Cambridge, UK: Cambridge University Press, 1997.

Weinstein, Donald, and Rudolph M. Bell. *Saints and Society: The Two Worlds of Western Christendom, 1000–1700*. Chicago: University of Chicago Press, 1982.

Wilson, Stephen, ed. and intro. *Saints and Their Cults: Studies in Religious Sociology, Folklore, and History*. Cambridge, UK: Cambridge University Press, 1983.

Wolf, Kirsten. "The Severed Breast: A Topos in the Legends of Female Virgin Martyr Saints." *Arkiv for Nordisk Filologi* 112 (1997), 97–112.

Literary studies of Middle English saints' legends and their contexts

Delany, Sheila. *Impolitic Bodies: Poetry, Saints, and Society in Fifteenth-Century England: The Work of Osbern Bokenham*. New York: Oxford University Press, 1998.

D'Evelyn, Charlotte, and Frances A. Foster. "Saints' Legends." In *A Manual of the Writings in Middle English, 1050–1500*. Ed. J. Burke Severs. Vol. 2. New Haven: Connecticut Academy of Arts and Sciences, 1970. Pp. 410–40 and 556–635.

Edwards, A. S. G. "The Transmission and Audience of Osbern Bokenham's *Legendys of Hooly Wummen*." In *Late-Medieval Religious Texts and Their Transmission: Essays in Honour of A. I. Doyle*. Ed. A. J. Minnis. York Manuscripts Conferences: Proceedings 3. Cambridge, UK: D. S. Brewer, 1994. Pp. 157–67.

Fletcher, Alan J. "Unnoticed Sermons from John Mirk's *Festial*." *Speculum* 55 (1980), 514–22.

_____."John Mirk and the Lollards." *Medium Aevum* 56 (1987), 217–24.

Görlach, Manfred. *The Textual Tradition of the South English Legendary*. Leeds Texts and Monographs n.s. 6. Leeds: University of Leeds, 1974.

_____. "Middle English Legends, 1220–1530." In *Hagiographies: International History of the Latin and Vernacular Hagiographical Literature in the West from its Origins to 1550*. Ed. Guy Philippart. Turnhout: Brepols, 1994– . Vol. 1, pp. 429–85.

_____. *Studies in Middle English Saints' Legends*. Anglistische Forschungen 257. Heidelberg: Universitätsverlag C. Winter, 1998.

Jankofsky, Klaus P. "National Characteristics in the Portrayal of English Saints in the *South English Legendary*." In *Images of Sainthood in Medieval Europe*. Ed. Renate Blumenfeld-Kosinski and Timea Szell. Ithaca: Cornell University Press, 1991. Pp. 81–93.

_____, ed. *The South English Legendary: A Critical Assessment*. Tübingen: Francke, 1992.

Johnson, Lynn Staley. "Chaucer's Tale of the Second Nun and the Strategies of Dissent." *Studies in Philology* 89 (1992), 314–33.

Lewis, Katherine J. "Model Girls? Virgin-Martyrs and the Training of Young Women in Late Medieval England." In *Young Medieval Women*. Ed. Katherine J. Lewis, Noël James Menuge, and Kim M. Phillips. New York: St. Martin's Press, 1999. Pp. 25–46.

Liszka, Thomas R. "MS Laud Misc. 108 and the Early History of the *South English Legendary*." *Manuscripta* 33 (1989), 75–91.

_____. "The *South English Legendaries*." In *The North Sea World in the Middle Ages: Studies in the Cultural History of North-Western Europe*. Ed. Thomas R. Liszka and Lorna E. M. Walker. Dublin: Four Courts Press, 2001. Pp. 243–80.

Margherita, Gayle. "Body and Metaphor in the Middle English *Juliana*." In *The Romance of Origins: Language and Sexual Difference in Middle English Literature*. Philadelphia: University of Pennsylvania Press, 1994. Pp. 43–61.

Millett, Bella. "The Audience of the Saints' Lives of the Katherine Group." *Reading Medieval Studies* 16 (1990), 127–56.

Pickering, O[liver] S. "The Outspoken *South English Legendary* Poet." In *Late-Medieval Religious Texts and their Transmission: Essays in Honour of A. I. Doyle*. Ed. A. J. Minnis. Cambridge, UK: D. S. Brewer, 1994. Pp. 21–37.

Powell, Susan. "John Mirk's *Festial* and the Pastoral Programme." *Leeds Studies in English* n.s. 22 (1991), 85–102.

Reames, Sherry L. "Artistry, Decorum, and Purpose in Three Middle English Retellings of the Cecilia Legend." In *The Endless Knot: Essays on Old and Middle English in Honor of Marie Borroff*. Ed. M. Teresa Tavormina and R. F. Yeager. Cambridge: D. S. Brewer, 1995. Pp. 177–99.

Robertson, Elizabeth. *Early English Devotional Prose and the Female Audience.* Knoxville: University of Tennessee Press, 1990.

_____. "The Corporeality of Female Sanctity in *The Life of Saint Margaret.*" In *Images of Sainthood in Medieval Europe.* Ed. Renate Blumenfeld-Kosinski and Timea Szell. Ithaca: Cornell University Press, 1991. Pp. 268–87.

Roth, Francis. *The English Austin Friars, 1249–1538.* 2 vols. New York: Augustinian Historical Institute, 1961–66. [On Bokenham: vol. 1, pp. 421–24, 515–17.]

Salih, Sarah. "Performing Virginity: Sex and Violence in the Katherine Group." In *Constructions of Widowhood and Virginity in the Middle Ages.* Ed. Cindy L. Carlson and Angela Jane Weisl. New York: St. Martin's Press, 1999. Pp. 95–112.

Stouck, Mary-Ann. "Saints and Rebels: Hagiography and Opposition to the King in Late Fourteenth-Century England." *Medievalia et Humanistica* n.s. 24 (1997), 75–94.

Strohm, Paul. "*Passioun, Lyf, Miracle, Legende*: Some Generic Terms in Middle English Hagiographical Narrative." *Chaucer Review* 10 (1975), 62–75 and 154–71.

Wakelin, Martyn F. "The Manuscripts of John Mirk's *Festial.*" *Leeds Studies in English* n.s. 1 (1967), 93–118.

Winstead, Karen A. "Piety, Politics, and Social Commitment in Capgrave's *Life of St. Katherine.*" *Medievalia et Humanistica* n.s. 17 (1990), 59–80.

_____. "Capgrave's Saint Katherine and the Perils of Gynecocracy." *Viator* 25 (1994), 361–76.

_____. *Virgin Martyrs: Legends of Sainthood in Late Medieval England.* Ithaca: Cornell University Press, 1997.

Wogan-Browne, Jocelyn. "Saints' Lives and the Female Reader." *Forum for Modern Language Studies* 27 (1991), 314–32.

_____. "The Virgin's Tale." In *Feminist Readings in Middle English Literature: The Wife of Bath and All Her Sect.* Ed. Ruth Evans and Lesley Johnson. London: Routledge, 1994. Pp. 165–94.

Reference works

Bodleian Library. *A Summary Catalogue of Western Manuscripts in the Bodleian Library at Oxford*. Oxford: Clarendon Press, 1895–1953.

Brown, Carleton, and Rossell Hope Robbins, eds. *The Index of Middle English Verse*. New York: Columbia University Press, 1943.

Chaucer, Geoffrey. *The Riverside Chaucer*. Gen. Ed. Larry D. Benson. Third ed. Boston: Houghton Mifflin Company, 1987.

Cutler, John L., and Rossell Hope Robbins, eds. *Supplement to the Index of Middle English Verse*. Lexington: University of Kentucky Press, 1965.

Whiting, Bartlett Jere, with the collaboration of Helen Wescott Whiting. *Proverbs, Sentences, and Proverbial Phrases from English Writings Mainly before 1500*. Cambridge, MA: The Belknap Press of Harvard University Press, 1968.

Commonly used abbreviations

TC	*Troilus and Criseyde*
MED	*Middle English Dictionary*
OED	*Oxford English Dictionary*
CT	*The Canterbury Tales*

The Legend of Frideswide of Oxford,
an Anglo-Saxon Royal Abbess

Introduction

Little is known with certainty about the historical Frideswide except that she was the abbess of a well-endowed monastery at Oxford in Anglo-Saxon times and was being commemorated there as a saint at the beginning of the eleventh century. Although her legend says she lived in the early eighth century, the early history of her monastery is almost a total blank because a fire in 1002 destroyed most of the records. The nuns must have been displaced either before 1002 or by the fire itself, for the minster church was staffed for most of the eleventh century by secular canons, property-owning clerics who were not subject to any monastic rule. In 1122 the monastery was refounded as a priory of Austin Canons — a more disciplined community of clergy which followed the Rule of St. Augustine. In the ensuing decades these canons excavated the grave of St. Frideswide, rediscovered her relics, and revived her cult. In 1180 they had her relics solemnly translated to a new shrine within the church, in a great public ceremony performed by the Archbishop of Canterbury. Miracles followed — over 100 of them during the year after the translation — and were duly recorded and publicized, drawing new streams of pilgrims to the shrine.

Frideswide's cult retained some strength until the end of the Middle Ages, especially in Oxfordshire and a few other western counties. Some of her relics had apparently been distributed to other religious houses at the time of the translation, for her name appears in the inventories of relics claimed by Reading Abbey, Hyde Abbey (Winchester), Waltham Abbey, and the royal chapel at Windsor. These same institutions commemorated her in their liturgies from an early date, and so did Abingdon Abbey, Exeter Cathedral, and the diocese of Hereford. However, only two medieval English churches and a chapel are known to have been dedicated to her: the minster church itself, the parish church at Frilsham in Berkshire, about twenty miles away, and the chapel at Binsey, just two miles from Oxford, that is mentioned in her legend. She was so closely associated with the town of Oxford that Chaucer adds local color to The Miller's Tale by having John, the provincial Oxford carpenter, spontaneously invoke her as his patron saint (*CT* I[A]3459). Early in the fifteenth century Oxford University joined the town in claiming her officially as its patron. In 1434 Archbishop Chichele endorsed a petition from the clergy asking that her feast day (October 19) should be celebrated thenceforth throughout the Province of Canterbury; in most churches, however, this order seems to have elicited little more than the addition of her name to the calendar.

The Legend of Frideswide of Oxford, an Anglo-Saxon Royal Abbess

In 1525 Frideswide's monastery was closed by Cardinal Wolsey, who appropriated its buildings and revenues for his newly founded Cardinal College (now Christ Church) and rebuilt the minster church to serve as the college chapel. In 1546 it became the cathedral church of the newly founded diocese of Oxford. Frideswide's shrine, still located inside the church, was destroyed and desecrated during the Reformation but has been partly reconstructed in modern times.

Frideswide's legend has received conflicting verdicts from modern scholars. In 1935 F. N. Stenton dismissed it as a late fabrication which just embroidered the brief account in William of Malmesbury's *Gesta pontificum*, attempting, in Stenton's words, "to give some appearance of substance to one of the most nebulous of English monastic legends" (p. 226). In the 1980s John Blair reopened the case, identifying two Latin versions of the legend, one of them contemporary with Malmesbury (c. 1100–30) and evidently based on earlier sources. This version, which Blair calls Latin Life A, seems to have been composed for monastic reading and includes a number of authentic-sounding details about Frideswide and her historical context. Latin Life B is essentially a revised and elaborated version of Latin Life A, probably composed between 1140 and 1170 by Robert of Cricklade, a scholarly Austin canon who was prior of St. Frideswide's, Oxford, while the canons were attempting to revive the saint's cult. Prior Robert, who obviously knew more about Oxford and its surroundings than the author of Latin Life A, improves the narrative's references to local geography and traditions and also adapts it to a new audience by omitting some of the details about monastic life, placing more emphasis on Frideswide's dedication to the ideals of poverty and virginity, and paying more attention to the roles played by parents and by the recipients of the saint's miracles.

The two Middle English versions presented here are based, respectively, on the two Latin versions discussed by Blair. They are both found in manuscripts of the *South English Legendary* and share many features of that compilation, including its predominant verse form (septenary couplets), down-to-earth language, and fondness for humorous and satirical comments from the narrator. But the two versions seem to be quite independent of each other. The shorter *SEL* account follows Latin Life A, abbreviating and simplifying the narrative but retaining its generally monastic outlook, which takes for granted such values as literacy, asceticism, virginity, and marriage to God rather than an earthly king. The longer *SEL* account looks much more like a deliberate recasting of the legend for a lay audience. It departs from its source, Latin Life B, by deemphasizing virginity and provides clear lessons on good and bad conduct for laymen instead — most obviously in the cautionary tale about working on Sunday, but also in the way it presents Frideswide's father as a man who makes virtuous choices and the king as a man who yields to demonic temptation. Also interesting in the longer account are all the details which tie Frideswide specifically to Oxford and its vicinity, showing her as patron and protector of this place, recipient of the town's welcoming acclaim when she returns after an absence, and provider of healings that continue at particular local sites.

Among more than 40 surviving manuscripts of the *SEL*, the shorter account of Frideswide is found in just two, Trinity College, Cambridge MS 605 (c. 1400) and British Library MS Stowe 949 (late 14th century), plus a very fragmentary third copy. The edition here is based on Trinity, which tends to have the best readings. The longer account of Frideswide is found in four manuscripts, of which Bodleian Library MS Ashmole 43 (c. 1300–30) is the earliest and usually the most reliable. The other manuscripts, all of which have eccentricities, are Magdalene College, Cambridge MS Pepys 2344 (c. 1325–50); British Library MS Cotton Julius D.9 (early 15th cent.); and Bodleian Library MS Bodley 779 (c. 1400–50).

Select Bibliography

Indexed in

Brown-Robbins, #2900.

Manuscripts

[shorter Life]   Trinity College, Cambridge MS 605 [formerly R.3.25], fols. 247r–248v.

[longer Life]   Oxford, Bodleian Library MS Ashmole 43 (*SC* 6924), fols. 155v–157v.

Previous editions

None published.

Latin Sources

Saint Frideswide, Patron of Oxford: The Earliest Texts. Ed., trans., and intro. John Blair. Oxford: Perpetua Press, 1988.

Historical Background and Criticism of the Frideswide legend

Blair, John. "Saint Frideswide Reconsidered." *Oxoniensia* 52 (1987), 71–127.

Görlach, Manfred. *The Textual Tradition of the South English Legendary*. 1974.

Jankofsky, Klaus P. "National Characteristics in the Portrayal of English Saints in the *South English Legendary*." 1991. Pp. 81–93.

_____, ed. *The South English Legendary: A Critical Assessment.* 1992.

Mayr-Harting, Henry. "Functions of a Twelfth-Century Shrine: The Miracles of St. Frideswide." In *Studies in Medieval History Presented to R. H. C. Davis*. Ed. Henry Mayr-Harting and R. I. Moore. London: Hambledon Press, 1985. Pp. 193–206.

Pickering, O[liver] S. "The Outspoken *South English Legendary* Poet." 1994. Pp. 21–37.

Stenton, F. M. *St. Frideswide and Her Times.* The St. Frideswide Papers 2. Oxford: Oxford University Press, 1953. Rpt. in *Preparatory to Anglo-Saxon England: Being the Collected Papers of Frank Merry Stenton*. Ed. Doris Mary Stenton. Oxford: Clarendon Press, 1970. Pp. 224–33. [Originally a lecture given on 19 October 1935 at the chapter house, Christ Church, on the occasion of the 1200th anniversary of St. Frideswide's death.]

Thompson, Anne B. "Shaping a Saint's Life: Frideswide of Oxford." *Medium Aevum* 63 (1994), 34–52.

Shorter South English Legendary Life of St. Frideswide, from Trinity College, Cambridge MS 605, fols. 247r–248v

	Seint Fretheswyde, that holy mayde, was of Englonde;	*from*
	Atte Oxenford heo was ybore, as ich understonde.	*she*
	Hir fader hete Kyng Dydan, and Sefreth hete the quene —	*was called*
	This were hire eldren, that hure gotten hem bytwene.	
5	Fretheswyd, hure yonge doughter, to lettre hii setten in youthe;	
	So wel heo spedde in six monnthes that heo hure Sauter couthe.[1]	
	Swythe wel heo was byloved, of hey and of lowe;	*Very; by all classes in society*
	Alle hii hadde joie of hure that couthen hure knowe.	
	Of the hard here was hure nexte wede.	
10	The meste mete that heo ete was worten and barly brede,[2]	
	And the cold welle water — that was hure drynke.	
	Now wold a knyghtes doughter grete hoker of suche sondes thynke![3]	
	The maide bysoght hure fadere to make hure nonne	*a nun*
	In Seint Marie churche, that he hadde er bygonne.	*begun [to build] earlier*
15	Hire fadere was the furste man that lete the churche rere	*who had the church built*
	That bereth the nam now of that mayde that lyth yschryned ther.	*name; enshrined*
	The king was glad of this chyld, that to clene lyf drowe.	
	He sende after a byschop anon hasteliche ynowe	
	Of Lyncolne that was tho[4] — Edgar was his name —	
20	To maken his doughter nonne ne thoght hym no schame.	*seemed to him no disgrace*

---

[1] Lines 4–6: *These were her parents (elders), who begot her together (between them). / Frideswide, their young daughter, they set to reading and writing in [her] youth; / So well she succeeded that in six months she knew her Psalter*

[2] Lines 8–10: *She was a source of joy to everyone who knew her. / The nearest garment [to her skin] was made of harsh haircloth. / The main foods she ate were vegetables and barley bread*

[3] *Nowadays a knight's daughter [not to mention a king's] would regard such provisions with great scorn*

[4] Lines 17–19: *The king was pleased with this child who was drawn to a life of virginity. / At once in a great hurry he sent after a bishop / Who was then [the bishop] of Lincoln*

The byschop for the kynges heste thuder he cam hymsulf   *command; thither*
And schar hure in the nonnerie with hire felawes twelve.   *cut her [hair]; companions*
 A nyght, as this mayde was huresulf alon,   *One night; by herself*
In hire bedes with hire sustren slepen everechon,   *prayers; sisters all asleep*
25 The fende hadde envye therof to hire goudhede
And thoght myd som gynne of goud lyf hure lede.
To hire he cam hire to fonde, in one mannes lyche[1]
In goldbeten clothes that semed swythe ryche.   *clothes adorned with beaten gold*
"My derworth mayde," he sede, "ne thynke thee noght to longe.
30 Tyme hit is for thy travayle that thou thy mede afonge.[2]
Ich am thulke that thou byst to: take now goud hede.   *the one to whom you pray*
Honoure me here, and for thy servyse ich croune thee to mede."[3]
The fende hadde in his heved an croune of rede golde;   *on his head*
Another he that mayde bede, yif heo hym honoury wolde.   *promised; she; honor him*
35 "Fare fram me, thou foule fende with thyn byheste!"   *Go away; promise*
Heo made the croys, and he fley awey with noyse and grete cheste.[4]
 In the holy nonnerie so longe heo lyved ther
That hure fadere and hure modere both ded were.
Algar hete the king after the king Dydan;[5]
40 He was king at Oxenford ychose — a wonder luther man.   *chosen; amazingly wicked*
He ofsende Fretheswyth, to habben hure to wyve.   *sent for; as [his] wife*
Heo sede heo was to God ywedded, to hold by hure lyve.   *throughout her life*
The forward that heo hadde ymade, heo sede heo nolde breke;   *promise; would not*
If heo dude, wel heo wyste God wold be awreke.
45 "A foule," heo sede, "ich were the hey King of Hevene forsake[6]
For gyfte other for anythyng, and thee His hyne take."   *gift or; servant*
 The messageres with grete strengthe wolden hure habbe ynome   *force; seized*
And don the maide byfor the king anon to hym come.   *caused; soon*

---

[1] Lines 25–27: *The devil hated her for her goodness / And planned by some trick to lead her away from [her] good life. / He came to her to tempt her, in the likeness (body) of a man*

[2] Lines 29–30: *"My beloved maiden," he said, "don't worry yourself (ponder) too long." / It is time for you to receive your reward for your labor(s)*

[3] *Worship me here, and I [will] crown you as a reward for your service*

[4] *She made the [sign of the] cross, and he flew away with an outcry and great disturbance*

[5] *The king who succeeded King Dydan was named Algar*

[6] Lines 44–45: *If she did [break her promise], she knew well that God would be avenged. / She said, "I would be a fool to forsake the high King of Heaven"*

Alle that weren ther woxen starc blynde;   *became completely*
50   Bynome hem was the myght the mayde for to fynde!¹
The borgeys of Oxenford sore were agaste,   *citizens; sorely afraid*
And this holy maide for this men hii beden atte laste,   *they begged*
That heo thorw Godes grace geve hem here syght;   *would give; their*
And thennes to the king passe that hii mosten habbe myght.²
55   Anon hii hadden here syght thorw hire bysechyng;   *their; her prayer*
Thannes hii wende, and al that cas hii toldyn the king.³
The king therfor hym made wroth tho he herd this,   *acted angry when*
And in grete wrath swor his oth that he wold hire seche, ywys;   *seek [and find]*
And that he hure habbe wolde. Faste he gan to yelpe   *possess; Vigorously; boast*
60   And swor that hure wocchecrafte scholde hure lyte helpe.   *witchcraft; little*
An angel that sulf nyght to that mayde cam   *same*
And bad hire oute of the kinges syght wende, that was so grame.   *to go; furious*
The levedy wende by nyght fram hure sustren tho   *lady went; sisters then*
With somme that heo with hure toke — tweyne, witthoute mo.   *some; two; more*
65   To Temese heo yede and fonde a bote al preste, thorw Godes sonde,⁴
And therin heo fonde an angel that broght hem to the londe.
For dred of the king heo wende, as God hit wolde,
Ne dorste heo come at non toune, to dwelle at non holde.   *house*
In a wode that Benesy yclyped ys al day   *is always called*
70   Thre wynter in an hole woned, that seylde me hure say.⁵
A mayde that seve yere ne myght nothing yse   *for seven years; see*
Cam to hure in the wode, and felle adoun a kne.   *on [her] knees*
Hure eyghen that holy mayde wysche with water of hure honde,   *eyes; washed; from*
And as hole as any fysche that maide gan up stonde.   *whole*
75   The king hym cam to Oxenford, wroth and eke wode,   *furious*
And thoght to do the mayde other than goud.
So sone so he to toune cam, he thoghte for to fyght   *As soon as; intended*
And habbe this maide Fretheswythe with strengthe agenryght.⁶

---

¹ *Taken away from them was the power to find the maiden*

² *And that they might have the ability to return from there to the king*

³ *Then they went away and told the king the whole story*

⁴ *She went to the Thames and found a boat [there] all ready, provided by God*

⁵ *[She] lived for three years in a cave, so that she was seldom seen*

⁶ *And to have this maiden Frideswythe immediately taken with force*

He enquered ware heo was. Me told hym sone that cas: *where; Men told him; fact*
80 That heo in the wode of Benysye preveliche yhydde was. *secretly hidden*
  The king rod toward the wode with hauke and with racche, *hawk; hunting dog*
 For to enserchy after this mayde yf he myght cache. *seek for*
 Tho this maide this yherd, anon heo bygan to fle
 Priveliche toward Oxenford, that non scholde hure se;
85 So that heo was underyute that heo was fleynde.
 After hure me wende faste; the king rod ernyng.[1]
 The mayde scaped into the toune, as hit was Godes grace.
 The kinges hors spornde witthoute the gate in a wel faire place *stumbled outside*
 And felle and brake the kinges necke; and that he gan awynne.[2]
90 Nas ther non of his men tho that derst come withinne. *There was none; dared*
  The maide holde hure ther in pes fram alle hure fon. *herself; peace; enemies (foes)*
 Glad was that myght with hure speke other to hure gon.
 Of hure holy lyf me told fer and eke nere,
 Into alle Englonde that me wyste nas yholde hure pere.
95 A wel swythe wondere cas byfelle oppon a day
 Up a fyscher that in a bote with his felawes aslepe lay.[3]
 He bygan to ravien as he awoke of slepe. *began to rave*
 Up among his felawes, wod he gan to lepe, *insane*
 So that on that ther was among hem alle he slowe; *one; killed (slew)*
100 And wan he was afalle, with his teth on hym he gnowe. *when; collapsed; gnawed*
 Alle that myght to hym come on hym setten honde, *restrained him*
 And uneth with muche pyne hii teyghede hym and bonde. *not easily; effort; tied up*
 Al hii wer busie that foule goste to lede *careful; evil spirit*
 Toward that holy mayde, that heo for hym bede. *so that; would pray*
105 The maide fourmed that croys tofor on his heved;[4]
 The bounden body felle adoune, as hit were ded. *tied-up body; as though*
 The maide hete unbynd hym anon in al wyse, *told [them] to untie him*

---

[1] Lines 85–86: *As a result, she was seen when she was fleeing. / After her men pursued swiftly; the king rode at a gallop*

[2] *And fell and broke the king's neck; and that [is] what he accomplished*

[3] Lines 92–96: *Everyone who could speak with her or go to [see] her was glad. / Her holy life was recounted everywhere, / Until nobody known in England was considered to be her equal. / A very amazing thing happened one day / To a fisherman who lay asleep in a boat with his companions*

[4] *The virgin made [the sign of] the cross on his forehead*

And suth hym a Godes name hole and sounde to aryse.[1]

Hol and sounde the man aros and hered God almyght   *praised; almighty*

110   And that mayde that hym delyvered of that foule wyght.[2]

As heo yede a day in the toune, a mysel heo mette.   *walked once; leper*

To hure the mysel felle adoune, and on knes hure grette,   *greeted*

And bysoght that lady that heo hym cusse scholde.   *kiss*

Heo custe hym, and he was hole, ryght as God hit wolde.   *kissed; healed; just*

115   Fele miracles by hure lyve of hure weren ycude,

And suth after hure deth; hii neren noght yhud.[3]

Heo wend out of this world a morwe up Lukes day.   *on the day after; [St.] Luke's*

Now God ous bringe to the blysse that He broght that may![4] Amen.

---

[1] *And then [told] him in God's name to get up, healed and sound*

[2] *And [praised] that maiden who had delivered him from that foul creature*

[3] *Lines 115–16: Many miracles were known of her during her life, / And also after her death; they were not hidden*

[4] *Now may God bring us to the joy where He brought that maiden!*

Explanatory Notes to Shorter South English Legendary
Life of St. Frideswide

3   *Kyng Dydan.* Blair suggests that he was probably a local sub-king who ruled part of the Thames Valley under the great Mercian kings of the seventh century, and that his seat was probably not in Oxford itself but in a more important center like Eynsham ("Frideswide Reconsidered," pp. 87, 88). See also textual note to this line.

6   *in six monnthes that heo hure Sauter couthe.* That is, she had learned all 150 Psalms (in Latin, of course) within six months. This kind of knowledge was important in the lives of monks and nuns, who were expected not only to meditate on the Psalms but also to sing them all frequently in the liturgy of the Hours, but it would have meant relatively little to the laity. Significantly, although the longer *South English Legendary* account preserves the name of Frideswide's teacher, it does not mention the saint's learning anything more specific from her than "godnesse" (line 12).

10–11   Frideswide's diet — limited to vegetables, coarse bread, and water — would have seemed unusually austere even to a well-disciplined medieval monk or nun, since most monastic rules explicitly recommended a menu for much of the year that also included fruit, eggs, dairy products, fish, and wine or beer.

12   *Now wold a knyghtes doughter grete hoker of suche sondes thynke!* A bit of satirical commentary that sets the saint's values against those of well-born women in the narrator's own society. Such satirical asides, directed especially at the rich and powerful, are a distinguishing feature of the *SEL.*

14   *Seint Marie churche, that he hadde er bygonne.* Not just a church in the modern sense but a religious foundation, a monastery. The foundation built by Frideswide's father was probably a double monastery of the kind familiar from other Anglo-Saxon examples (i.e., a house with both monks and nuns, headed by an abbess). Latin Life A includes some specific details omitted from this Middle English retelling: "Didan then had a refectory, dormitory and cloister built for the nuns, assigned religious men to serve them, and gave the estates and villages of St. Mary and a third part of the city of Oxford to provide the nuns' food" (quoted from Blair,

"Frideswide Reconsidered," p. 75, col. 1). The first abbess was of course Frideswide herself.

18–19   *a byschop . . . Of Lyncolne that was tho — Edgar.* Latin Life A calls him "Orgar, bishop of Lincoln." The title sounds like a blatant anachronism, since the modern see of Lincoln seems not to have begun until 1092. As Blair comments, however, "it is just possible that this reference has substance after all; between the 690s and the 720s the bishop of the old Mercian see of Lindsey was one Eadgar, who may conceivably have exercised diocesan functions in the Oxford area" when the see of Leicester was vacant (p. 82).

20   *To maken his doughter nonne ne thoght hym no schame.* This sounds like another pointed comment on upper-class values in the time of the *SEL* itself.

22   *schar hure.* The same verb was used for tonsuring a monk as for cutting off a nun's hair. In both cases, the "shearing" symbolized departure from one's former status in lay society and reception into the monastic life.

23–36   The story of being tempted by a devil who comes disguised as Jesus himself, but is recognized as an impostor, is told of Martin of Tours and other saints. Often the story conveys a theological or spiritual lesson — for example, in the case of Martin, that Jesus can be recognized in this world by the marks of His suffering, not the trappings of royal power. In this narrative about Frideswide, however, the point just seems to be the saint's ability to stand up to the devil, see through his fraudulent claims, and force him to depart.

39   *Algar hete the king after the king Dydan.* Latin Life A identifies this miscreant as "a certain king of Leicester, a man who was very wicked and hateful to God, . . . named Algar." Blair points out that, despite the familiar plot conventions in the king's pursuit of Frideswide, there was at least one historical English king in the early eighth century, Æthelbald of Mercia, who was actually "accused of seducing nuns" (p. 90).

41–46   The pagan ruler's attempt to woo the virgin saint, who rejects him because she is already betrothed to a much nobler and more desirable king, was a favorite motif in virgin martyr legends. For the most fully developed example in this collection, see the stanzaic Life of Margaret, lines 39–114.

47–56   The miraculous disabling of persecutors, to prevent them from doing violence to the saints, is another familiar motif in hagiography, and the disabling miracle is often followed — as it is here — with a cure that shows the mercy of God and His saints even to those who have been their enemies. An unusually dramatic example occurs in the legend of St. Agnes, whose pagan suitor is struck dead when he tries to take her by force, but is then resurrected by her prayers and converted to her faith. The great prototype for such stories is the blinding of Saul on the road to Damascus (Acts 9:1–19) — the miracle that transformed a fierce persecutor of the early Christians into the great apostle, St. Paul. As those examples suggest, the king's messengers in the Frideswide legend must be converted when their sight is restored, though this point is not clear in either of the *SEL* accounts.

57–68   The furious anger of the king, who vows to find and seize Frideswide himself, and the angelic warning that sends her into exile would have been likely to remind a late-medieval audience not only of other saints' legends, but also of Herod's enraged pursuit of the baby Jesus and the flight of the Holy Family into Egypt in order to escape him. This part of the Gospel, first related in Matthew 2:13–18, became exceptionally familiar in the Middle Ages because it lent itself so well to dramatic representation, both in Latin liturgical plays and in popular vernacular versions.

71–74   This brief miracle story is omitted from the longer *SEL* account.

74   *hole as any fysche.* Although the logic behind the simile is not obvious to a modern reader, "healthy as a fish" or "fish-hale" was a common saying in Middle English.

75–87   The sequence of events here — with the king first pursuing the saint in Oxford, then out into the woods (when the citizens of Oxford reveal that she has hidden there), then back toward Oxford — is confusing and hard to follow. The problem stems at least in part from a misunderstanding about the location of her hiding place that Blair calls "the central crux" in Latin Life A (p. 83).

88–90   The king's horse suddenly stumbles, without any apparent cause, outside the city gate, and the king's neck is broken. This punishment is harsher than those in either of the surviving Latin Lives of Frideswide, but there are many villains in other legends who are suddenly struck dead, most often while they are trying to break a martyr's will (as in the legend of St. Christina, included in this collection) or right after the martyr's execution (for example, the legends of Saints George, Agatha, and Andrew the Apostle). Here again there are Biblical prototypes — including the destruction of Pharaoh's army as they pursued Moses and the Israelites (Exodus 14) and the striking down of the King Herod who persecutes the early Christians (Acts 12).

95–110   This colorful story of demonic possession and exorcism appears in both Latin Lives A and B, but the longer *SEL* account chooses to omit it, emphasizing the next miracle story instead.

111–14   The story of this leper's healing is developed much more fully in Latin Life B and the longer *SEL* account.

117   This is a surprisingly brief and matter-of-fact reference to the saint's death. Most legends pay considerable attention to the way in which a saint prepares for death, and in this case Latin Life A supplies plenty of material that finds its way into Latin Life B and eventually into the longer *SEL* account, but is completely skipped in this shorter one.

Textual Notes to Shorter South English Legendary
Life of St. Frideswide

Abbreviations: **S** = British Library MS Stowe 949, fols. 144r–145v; **T** = Trinity College, Cambridge MS 605, fols. 247r–248v [base text].

1   *Fretheswyde.* Latin Life A uses the form "Fritheswitha," which looks like a plausible Anglo-Saxon name that combines elements meaning "peace, safety" (*frithu*) and "strong" (*swith*). Most of the Middle English accounts change one or both of the *th*'s in this name to *d*'s, and one MS (Bodley 779) uses the reduced form "Friswide."

3   *Kyng Dydan.* Latin Life A calls him "Didan," king of Oxford. Latin Life B uses the term *subregulus* (sub-king). The name "Didan(us)" does not look very authentic, but Blair explains it as possibly "a rather corrupt Latinisation of [Anglo-Saxon] 'Dæda,' 'Dida,' or 'Dydda,' all evidenced by placenames" (p. 83). See also explanatory note to this line.

        Sefreth. The form in Latin Life A is "Sefrida"; in Latin Life B, "Safrida." Either way, the name is historically improbable, as Stenton pointed out, since "Sæfrith" was a masculine name in Old English.

22   *schar hure.* T omits the pronoun; S: *schare er.*

116   T has a canceled word, no longer completely legible, between *hii* and *neren.*

Longer South English Legendary Life of St. Frideswide, from Bodleian Library MS Ashmole 43, fols. 155v–157v

	Seynte Fredeswide was her of Engelonde.	*in this country*
	At Oxenford heo was ibore, as ic understonde.	*she; born*
	Aboute seve hondred yer and sevene and twenti right	*directly*
	After that God was an erthe in Is moder alight,	*on; His*
5	This holi womman was ibore — Seynte Fredeswide.	
	Didan was hire fader name; hire moder het Saffride.	*father's; was called*
	Cristene man hire fader was. This maide of hem tuo,	*from the two of them*
	Seynte Fredeswide, com and hor eir was also.	*their heir*
	Tho this child was vif yer old and somwat more,	*When; five*
10	Mid an holi womman iset heo was to lore.	*With; placed; for instruction*
	Ailgive het hire maistresse, that good womman was inough;[1]	
	This yonge child heo teighte wel and to godnesse hire drough.	*she taught; drew*
	Ar this child were vol woxe, hire moder let that lif.[2]	
	That child bed hire fader yerne that he ne nome no wif,	*asked her; eagerly; take*
15	Ac that he arerde an chirche and in Godes service were.	*But; should erect; should be*
	This gode mon at Oxenford an chirche let rere	*caused to be built*
	In honor of our Levedi and of the Trinité	*Lady*
	And eke of Alle Halwe, as the boc telleth me,	*also; All Saints*
	Theras of Seynte Fredeswide an chirche nouthe is	*Where; now*
20	And an hous of religion of blake canouns, iwis.	*religious community; truly*
	Tho this gode mon Sire Didan arered hadde this chirche,	*When; had built*
	He feffede is doughter therwith, Godes service to wurche.	*endowed his*
	This maide in this chirche bilevede in Godes service	*remained*
	And bilevede hire eritage and everiche marchaundise,	
25	And seththe in this chirche, our Loverd vor te paie,[3]	
	Heo bilevede night and dai after hire fader daie	*remained; father's time*

---

[1] *Her teacher was called Ailgive, who was a very good woman*

[2] *Before this child was fully grown, her mother departed from this life*

[3] Lines 24–25: *And abandoned her inheritance and all worldly business, / And afterward in this church, in order to please our Lord*

The Legend of Frideswide of Oxford, an Anglo-Saxon Royal Abbess

	In vasting and in orsouns and in other godnesse also.	*fasting; prayers*
	More godnesse then heo dude, me nuste no womman do.[1]	
	Thervore the devel hadde gret envie therto.	*enmity toward her*
30	He ne mighte wel tholie noght hire godnesse so.	*could hardly endure*
	To hire he com in a tyme, in vair abit inou,	*on one occasion; very fine-looking garb*
	With a company of develen that bihynde him drou.	*devils; went*
	He sede he was Godes sone Jhesus fram Hevene igon	*come*
	And the develen with him angles were echon.	*devils; angels; all*
35	"My lemman, com vorth," he sede, "com vorth here anon,	*darling; forth; at once*
	Vor tyme it is that thou avonge with virgines mony on	*should receive; many*
	The croune of joie, of blis that ilasteth ever bright,	*forever remains bright*
	That thou hast ofserved wel both dai and nyght.	*deserved; at all times*
	Com vorth and knele adoun, and honoure as ic fare	*go*
40	The stapes here of myne fet that thou iwilned hast yare."	
	Ne hure ye hou queynteliche the screwe it couthe bifynde?	
	Nou luther thrift on is heved and on the companye bihynde![2]	
	That maide hire bithoghte of this wonder cas;	*pondered; amazing occurrence*
	Hire inwit hire sede sone that it the devel was.	*reason told her soon*
45	"Wrecche," heo sede, "hou darstou bihote other men so	
	Thing that thou ne might noght thisulf come to?[3]	
	Ac that thou vorlore thoru thi sori prute,	
	And ic and alle other eke with thee were yute,	
	Sunvol womman as icham, yif our Loverd ous nadde iboght,	
50	To wan thou evenest thee! Ac thou luxt: thou nart it noght."[4]	
	The devel anon myd this word with wel sori bere	*very sad demeanor*
	And with strong stench wende awei, and ne com na more there.	*foul stink went; came*

---

[1] *More good deeds than she did, men knew no woman to do*

[2] Lines 40–42: *"... The prints (steps) here of my feet that you have desired for a long time." / Now, do you not hear how slyly the villain (rascal/devil) knew how to contrive [a lie]? / Now may miserable luck fall on his head and on the company [of devils] behind [him]!*

[3] Lines 45–46: *"Wretch," she said, "how dare you thus to promise other people / Something that you cannot reach yourself at all? ... "*

[4] Lines 47–50: *"... But you lost that through your sinful pride, / And I and everyone else would still be with you, / Sinful woman as I am, had not our Lord redeemed us, / To whom you [dare to] compare yourself! But you lie — you are no such thing"*

"Nou an alle devel wei, amen," seggeth alle,
"And ne come he never in gode stude in chirche ne in halle!"[1]

55   Tho the screwe was overcome, sori he was and wo.   *When; villain; miserable*
To the kyng he wende of Englond — Kyng Algar that was tho —   *went; then*
And ofte entised him in thoght and in metynge   *tempted (enticed); dream*
That he scholde this maide of hire holi lif bringe,   *from her holy life take away*
And ligge bi hire flescliche and bynyme hire also

60   Hire abit of nonne that heo was inome to.[2]
    Thoru the develes poer the kyng was in such mod   *power; such a state of mind*
That ar the dede were ido he was wel ny wod.   *until; done; nearly insane*
To Oxenford is messageris he sende, that hi soghte   *his messengers; [so] that they*
This maide ware heo were ifounde and sone to him broghte.   *wherever*

65   To this maide sone hi come, that ladde so good lif,   *they came*
And in vaire manere hire bisoghte to be the kynges wif.   *a courteous way*
"Certes," quath this holi maide, "ye spekketh al vor noght!   *Certainly; for nothing*
To the Kyng of Hevene icham ispoused. I ne breke my thoght."[3]
    Mid strengthe hi wolde hire nyme tho and to the kynge lede,

70   Ac hi ablende tho anon echon myd the dede.
Tho mighte hi somdel be itemed and bileve hor wildhede;
Hi nolde tho habbe icome ther, vor al hor prute wede![4]
    That folc hadde deol of hem, and Seynte Fredeswide bede   *The people; pity; asked*
Vorgeve hor folie and wissi hem and rede.   *[To] forgive; guide; instruct*

75   That maide bed vor hem anon, so that thoru Is grace   *maiden prayed for; His*
Our Lord hem sende agen anon hor sight in the place.   *restored soon their*
    Tho wende hi sone agen and tolde the kynge vore
In wuch manere vor hor dede hor sight was vorlore.[5]

---

[1] Lines: 53–54: *Let everyone say, "Now to hell with him, amen, / And may he never come in good circumstances into either church or hall!"*

[2] Lines 59–60: *And lie with her carnally and take away from her also / Her nun's habit that she had solemnly received*

[3] *I am betrothed to the King of Heaven. I will not violate my religious allegiance*

[4] Lines 69–72: *With force they wanted to seize her then, and take [her] to the king, / But they were all suddenly blinded, right then and there. / Then might they be somewhat tamed and leave their violence; / They wished then they hadn't come there, despite all their proud appearance*

[5] Lines 77–78: *Then they went back soon and reported before the king / How their sight was taken away because of their deed(s)*

The kyng verde as he were wod, and more oth suor therto[1]

80 That heo ne scholde noght ofscapie thoru wicchinge so. *escape; witchcraft*

"Vor heo me hath so vorsake, ichulle do bi hire folie;

And wen ichabbe bi hire ido my wille of lecherie,

Ichulle bitake hire hose wole, stronge lechors and store,

That wen heo vorsaketh me, heo schal be comun hore!"

85 He lupte up is palefray and vorth then wei nom;[2]

As a man that were wod, to Oxenford he com.

Ac this holi maide tofore myd two sostren wende *beforehand; sisters*

Into Temese in a scip as God the grace sende. *the Thames; ship*

As sone as hi were in this scip, sodeinliche hi were

90 Under the toun of Benteme — hi nuste hou hi come ther. *they knew not*

Tho wuste wel this holi maide that it was Godes wille *Then knew*

That heo bilevede ther. Heo wende hir up wel stille *should remain; very quietly*

And bilevede longe in Godes servise there *remained*

Mid hire felawes priveliche, that nonnon also were. *companions; nuns*

95 The kyng com into Oxenford as man that were wod.

He soghte vaste her and ther this maide that was so good. *eagerly here*

He mighte seche longe inou, ac ever he was bihinde!

And wroth he was inou, vor he nuste war hire fynde.[3]

He asked that folc after hire, ac non ne couthe him telle. *the people; none; could*

100 He suor bote hi tolde him other, mony mon to quelle, *swore unless; otherwise; kill*

And throwe al the toun up-to-doun and bringe al to wrechede. *upside-down; misery*

He earnde to the North Gate to bigynne ther this dede. *ran*

Anon he ablende ther, as he bigan this strif, *went blind*

And bilevede ther the sori wreche, blynd al his lif,

105 And wende hom tame inou. Is prowesse was bihynde! *chastened; fell short*

He mighte segge war he com, "War, her cometh the blynde!"[4]

---

[1] *The king behaved as if he were mad, and swore a very great oath*

[2] Lines 81–85: *"Since she has thus rejected me, I will commit a [sexual] wrong against her; / And when I have done all the lechery I desire with her, / I will give her to whoever wants her — [to] flagrant and bold lechers, / [So] that when she leaves me, she will be [a] common whore!" / He leaped upon his palfrey and took the way forward*

[3] Lines 97–98: *He could seek for a very long time, but he was always at a disadvantage! / And he was exceedingly angry, because he didn't know where to find her*

[4] *Wherever he went, he could say, "Watch out, here comes the blind [man]!"*

And, vor is eyen were so vor is folie bynome,[1]
Ther ne dar no kyng in Oxenford yut to this dai come.   *dares; still*
   That holi maide at Bentone bilevede in Godes lore.
110 Heo ne dradde nothing of the kyng, that he wolde hire seche more.   *seek further*
Seththe toward Oxenford then wei hamward heo nom,[2]
To the toun of Bunseie, as God wold heo com.   *willed that she should come*
Thre yer with hire felawes heo bilevede there,   *years*
And to servy Jhesu Crist a chapel heo let rere,   *serve; had built*
115 Ther is yut a vair court and a chirche vair and suete,   *[Where] there is still; courtyard*
Arered in honour of hire and of Seynte Margarete.   *Built*
   As this maide wonede ther in holi lif and clene,   *dwelled*
The maidens that with hire were gonne hire ofte bymene   *complain*
That water was somdel to ver to al hor nede   *somewhat too far away for*
120 And cride on Seynte Fredeswide that heo scholde hem therof rede.[3]
This maide Seinte Fredeswide bed our Lordes sonde   *asked; favor*
That He water thoru Is grace sende hem ner in londe.   *should send; nearby*
Tho sprong ther up a wel vair welle, cler inou and clene,
That fond hem alle water inough that hi ne dorste noght hem bymene.[4]
125 That biside the chirche yut is, a lute in the west side,   *still; little*
That mony mon hath bote ido and that mony mon seche wide.   *healed; from afar*
   A yong mon ther was in a tyme that was in fol thoght,   *once; foolish intention*
To wurche in a Soneday, ac he belou it noght.   *work; did not rejoice over it*
Vor as he heu with is ax, is ax clevede vaste   *hewed; stuck fast*
130 To is honden, that vor nothing he ne mighte hire awei caste.[5]
Ther was sorwe and deol inou among is frend echon,   *great lamentation; his friends*
So that he was sone irad to the holi maide gon.   *advised; to go*
To hire he com and cride vaste, with is frend mony on;   *cried earnestly*
This maide bad God vor him, and he was dilivered anon.   *prayed to God*
135 Ac he was iwar afterward then Sonedai worke to do.   *warned [against]*

---

[1] *And, since his eyes were lost in this way on account of his wrongdoing*

[2] *Afterward toward Oxford she took the path homeward*

[3] *And entreated Saint Frideswide that she should advise them about it*

[4] Lines 123–24: *Then sprang up a very beautiful spring, very clear and pure, / That provided them all sufficient water [so] that they dared not complain*

[5] *To his hands, so that he couldn't throw it away whatever he did*

Of hem that wurche Sonedai, to vewe me serveth so![1]

Ate laste this holi maide, tho heo then tyme isei,   *when she saw the opportunity*

Fram Bunseie wende to Oxenford, vor it was somdel nei.   *rather near*

That folc of Oxenford anon wel thicke agen hire drou[2]

140 And broghte hire to hire owe chirche with nobleie inou.   *great ceremony*

As vor te honoure hire that folc so thicke wende,   *in such a crowd*

Our Lord vor hire love a vair myracle sende.   *pleasing; granted (sent)*

A mesel com among that folc, swythe grisliche myd alle,   *leper; very hideous indeed*

That hadde yare sik ibe and ne mighte no bote valle.   *for a long time; remedy acquire*

145 Loude he gradde and ofte inough, "Levedi, bidde ic thee,   *cried out*

Vor the love of Jhesu Crist, have mercy of me

And cus me with thi suete mouth, yif it is thi wille!"   *kiss*

This maide was sore ofschame and eode evere vorth stille.   *ashamed; walked; quietly*

This mesel gradde evere on and cride "milce" and "ore,"[3]

150 So that this maide him custe and was ofscamed sore.   *kissed; sorely ashamed*

A suete cos it was to him, vor therwith anon   *kiss*

He bicom hol and sound, and is lymes echon,   *all his limbs*

And vair man and clene inou was, and of thulke cosse there   *with regard to that kiss*

Me thencth the maide nadde no sunne, of ordre thei heo were![4]

155 This maide wende in Oxenford to hire churche sone

And ladde ther holi lif, as heo was iwoned to done.   *accustomed to do*

Seththe tho heo hadde ilyved in holi lif yare,   *After; for a long time*

And oure Loverdes wille was that heo scholde henne vare,   *go hence (die)*

Heo bigon to febli, and an hevenesse hire nom.   *grow weak; numbness came over her*

160 And longe bivore hire deth an angel to hire com

And sede that heo deie scholde in the monthe of Octembre,

The fourtethe kalendes as vel of Novembre,   *fourteenth; occurred (fell)*

The nyght after Seynte Lukes Day, in an Sonenyght,   *on a Sunday night*

And wende after hire holi deth to the joie of Hevene right.   *directly*

165 Glad was this maide tho, as heo mighte wel ethe,   *with good reason*

That so longe was bivore iwarned of hire dethe.

So that somdel bivore a fevere hire gan take,   *somewhat before*

---

[1] *Among those who work on Sunday, too few are treated in this way!*

[2] *That people of Oxford soon in great numbers came to meet her*

[3] *This leper called out incessantly and cried for mercy and help*

[4] *It seems to me that the virgin committed no sin, even though she was in a religious order*

A Seynte Lukes Day, then Saterday, an put heo let make[1]

Right in hire owe churche, and an sepulcre also. *own*

170 Our Loverdes flesc and Is blod heo underveng therto. *received*

Tho caste heo up hire eien toward hevene an hei; *on high*

The maide Seynte Katerine and Seynte Cecile heo sei *saw*

With othere virgines mony on toward hire alight *descend*

Fram Hevene wel mildeliche — ther was a suete sight! *very graciously; sweet*

175 This holi maide with hem spac, as hurde mony on, *spoke; many people heard*

And sede, "In youre companye ichulle wende anon."

    Heo bed hem alle good day that aboute hire were ther, *farewell*

And deide right thulke tyme that the angel hire sede er,[2]

And to the joie of Hevene with this virgines wende. *these*

180 Aboute hire ther as heo deide, our suete Loverd sende

So gret suotnesse into al that hous that the folc that was there *sweetness (fragrance)*

In so gret joie stode in Parais as thei hi were. *as though they were in Paradise*

Into hire owe churche this maide was sone ibore *carried*

And bured in thulke stude that heo wilnede byvore,[3]

185 Theras nou arered is a vair chanorie *Where; established; community of canons*

And a churche in hire name, and priorie, *a priory*

Ther hath ibe vor hire love ofte gret botnynge.[4]

    Nou bidde we God, vor hire love, that He to Hevene ous bringe! *let us ask*

---

[1] *On St. Luke's Day, the Saturday, she had a grave (pit) made*

[2] *And died at the exact time that the angel had told her before*

[3] *And buried in the same place that she had chosen previously*

[4] *Where there has often been great healing (deliverance) for love of her*

Explanatory Notes to Longer South English Legendary
Life of St. Frideswide

3   *Aboute seve hondred yer and sevene and twenti.* This dating of her birth follows Latin Life B, but is presumably an error. Latin Life A actually gives 727 as the year of Frideswide's *death*, and most authorities accept this tradition.

6   *Didan . . . Saffride.* On the names, see explanatory and textual notes to line 3 of the shorter account. As Thompson points out, the version being edited here does not identify Frideswide's father as a king, but only as "Sire Didan" (21), a prosperous Christian gentleman who may be intended as a good example for fathers in general.

12–15   This account departs from both Latin Lives A and B, as well as from the shorter *SEL* account, by omitting the details about Frideswide's learning the Psalms and about the austerities of her daily life. In place of those monastic virtues, Frideswide is here credited with having exerted a holy influence on her father by persuading him to remain celibate after his wife's death (a decision not mentioned at all in the other accounts) and to devote much of the family inheritance to building a religious institution (a decision usually attributed elsewhere to his own initiative).

16   *an chirche.* See explanatory note to line 14 of the shorter account.

16–18   These lines can be read as saying either that the institution founded by Frideswide's father had a single church with a threefold dedication to the Virgin Mary, the Trinity, and All Saints, or that it had two or three separate churches with their own dedications. Blair claims that there were precedents for both patterns.

20   *blake canouns.* St. Frideswide's monastery was refounded in the early twelfth century as a house of Augustinian (or Austin) canons.

22   *He feffede is doughter therwith.* That is, he presented her with the lands that provided an annual income for the monastery. Latin Life A provides a little detail on these lands, quoted above in explanatory note to line 14 of the shorter account.

31–54   On the conventional aspects of this story, see explanatory note to lines 23–36 of the shorter account. The present account follows its source, Latin Life B, in giving an unusually extended and dramatic version of the debate between the saint and the devil. But it also adds some colorful touches of its own to the story — including the rhetorical question to the audience in line 41 and the curses on the devil in lines 42 and 53–54. This kind of exuberant story-telling, which invites listeners in effect to hiss the villains and cheer for the heroes, seems to have been a common feature in medieval popular literature. There are a number of additional examples in this text (see below, lines 71–72, 105–06, 136, 154, 174, and their notes) and more in some versions of the stanzaic Life of Margaret (see the explanatory notes to that text, lines 75, 243, 263, and 271–72).

41   *the screwe*. The noun *shrew* was used in Middle English to refer to a wide range of evil or injurious creatures and things, including devils, malignant planets, vices, and bad ideas, as well as wicked or troublesome human beings of either sex. According to the OED, it was not until the seventeenth century that the word came to be associated primarily with scolding women.

56   *To the kyng he wende of Englond.* By establishing this connection between the first two episodes in the legend, the longer *SEL* account makes it impossible to mistake the king for an ordinary suitor with whom a lay listener might sympathize. His desire for Frideswide is instigated by the devil, and what he has in mind is defined from the start not as marriage (as seems to be the case in the shorter account), but as the violation of the holy virgin. On the possible identity of this king, who cannot be the ruler of England as a whole, see explanatory note to line 39 of the shorter account.

63–78   For the conventions being used in this episode, see notes to lines 41–56 of the shorter account.

71–72   Like the curses against the devil earlier in this text, these lines seem designed to encourage a listening audience to participate emotionally in the narrative, deriving satisfaction from the villains' punishment and the lesson they were forced to learn.

87–90   In this text, as Thompson has noted, there is no angelic warning and no angelic boatman. Frideswide still escapes by the grace of God, but more can be attributed to her own initiative than in the shorter account.

90   *Benteme.* Also spelled "Bentone" (below in this text, line 109). Another town on the Thames, about 13 miles west of Oxford. The modern English form is "Bampton." Note the geographical difference from the shorter account, which had her supposedly hiding in Binsey woods.

95–108   This part of the narrative is noticeably clearer and more dramatic than in the shorter account. In this text the residents of Oxford either cannot or will not help the king find Frideswide, and he is about to retaliate against the city itself when he is miraculously struck blind. In short, Oxford has become identified with Frideswide. The miraculous punishment of the persecutor (who, unlike his messengers, is never healed) saves both the saint and her city, and no subsequent king dares to challenge her protection.

105–06   The colloquial exclamations in these lines seem to invite the audience to laugh at the sudden reversal of the king's fortunes.

108   *Ther ne dar no kyng in Oxenford . . . come.* There is at least one historical reference to this superstition: the chronicler Thomas Wykes reports that Edward I refused in 1275 to enter Oxford, although the city was already decorated in his honor and awaiting his arrival, because he was afraid of St. Frideswide's curse (*Annales monastici*, ed. H. R. Luard, vol. 4, pp. 263–64; cited by Michael Prestwich, *Edward I* [New Haven: Yale University Press, 1997], p. 101).

111–26   This episode, first found in Latin Life B, seems to have served at least two purposes for Robert of Cricklade and the Priory of St. Frideswide in Oxford. As Blair explains, it resolves an obvious geographical error in the earlier Latin life, which had placed Binsey wood in Bampton, by explaining Frideswide's travels to one from the other, and it also serves to buttress the Priory's claim that the chapel and well in Binsey had always belonged to their monastery (pp. 84–85).

112   *Bunseie.* Binsey is a village less than two miles from Oxford with the remains of what may have been a monastic settlement. Blair suggests that Frideswide's community in Oxford may have used it as a retreat house (pp. 91–92).

117–24   The miracle in which the saint provides water for her complaining followers by appealing to God closely resembles a story in the well-known Life of St. Benedict by Gregory the Great (Gregory's *Dialogues*, II.5). Gregory's version, in turn, was modelled after the Biblical story in which Moses miraculously produced water from a rock in the wilderness (Exodus 17:1–7, Numbers 20:2–13) when the people of Israel were complaining of thirst.

127–36   The miraculous punishment and later healing of the young man who was trying to work on Sunday, in violation of the commandment to keep the Sabbath day holy, is omitted from the shorter *SEL* account but appears in both Latin Lives of Frideswide. Its inclusion here suggests that the author of the longer *SEL* account, at least, regarded Sabbath-breaking as a problem that was still current in his own society. Indeed, line 136 places additional emphasis on this problem by inviting the audience to join in the wish that God would intervene more often to punish Sabbath-breakers.

141–53   Like Latin Life B, which it follows, this account gives a much longer and more dramatic narrative about the leper's healing than the version in the shorter *SEL* account and its source, Latin Life A. Here Frideswide encounters the leper in the context of her festive return to Oxford — a joyous occasion that is discordantly interrupted by his insistent cries for a kiss. The Latin version of this scene places great emphasis on the leper's repulsive appearance, explaining that his repulsiveness allows Frideswide to kiss him without any risk to her vow of chastity. The Middle English text chooses instead to emphasize the great modesty of the virgin saint and the embarrassment she feels at being thus publicly forced to kiss the man and to reveal her saintly power of healing at the same time.

160–64   Being given such advance notice of the date on which she will die places Frideswide in the privileged company of such earlier saints as John the Evangelist, Mary Magdalen, and Benedict. The date of her death, the fourteenth calends of November, falls on October 19.

168–69   Latin Lives A and B both explain that she had her grave prepared ahead of time because she knew she would die on Sunday and did not want anyone to be obliged to work on that day.

170   *Our Loverdes flesc and Is blod.* Medieval saints' legends rarely miss an opportunity to emphasize the importance of receiving the Eucharist as part of one's preparation for death.

172–76   Being escorted to heaven by a company of holy virgins, headed by two of her greatest predecessors in this vocation, is another privilege which the legend uses to suggest St. Frideswide's stature as a saint. Latin Life B explains the choice of

Katherine and Cecilia by calling them "the virgins whom she most venerated"; but this is an obvious anachronism in the case of Katherine, whose cult seems not to have been known at all in England until the eleventh century.

174   *ther was a suete sight!* Another exclamation that seems intended to encourage the audience to participate vicariously in the narrative.

180–82   The miraculous fragrance is of course another proof of Frideswide's sanctity. A similar phenomenon is reported at the time of Mary Magdalen's death; see the early *SEL* version of her legend below, lines 618–19 and 638–39, and the explanatory note on the former lines.

183–84   *Into hire owe churche . . . that heo wilnede byvore.* Like Latin Life B, which it follows, this account says nothing about the translations of Frideswide's relics, the first and most important of which occurred in 1180. Blair uses the omission as evidence that Latin Life B must have been written before that date, since Prior Robert or his successor would certainly have mentioned the translation if it had already taken place.

185–86   Since *chanorie* in this context probably means a community of canons and *priorie* means a house of regular canons, governed by a prior, the difference of meaning between these two rhyme words is not easy to see. Presumably one of them is intended to refer to the building or buildings in which the canons live, and the other either to the men themselves or to the form of religious life they are following.

Textual Notes to Longer South English Legendary
Life of St. Frideswide

Abbreviations: **A** = Bodleian Library MS Ashmole 43 (*SC* 6924), fols. 155v–157v [base text]; **B** = Bodleian Library MS Bodley 779 (*SC* 2567), fols. 280v–282r; **J** = British Library MS Cotton Julius D.9, fols. 273v–275v; **P** = Magdalene College, Cambridge MS Pepys 2344, pp. 430–34.

9   *vif.* "Five." In the Southern dialect of the *Legendary* spirants (f) at the head of morphemes are voiced (v). Thus we find *vif* for "fif" ("five"); "vol" for "fol" (fully, line 13); "vor" for "for" (lines 25, 36, 67, 75, 78, 81, 107, 129, 134, 138, 141, 142, 146, 151, 187, 188); "vaste" for "fast" and "vasting" for "fasting" (lines 27, 96, 129, 133); "thervore" for "therefore" (line 29); "vair" for "fair" (lines 31, 66, 115, 123, 153, 185); "vorth" for "forth" (lines 35, 39, 148); "vorgeve" for "forgive" (line 74); "vorlore" for "forelore" (lost, lines 47, 78); "verde," "vare" for "fared," "fare" (lines 79, 158); "vorsake" for "forsake" (line 81); "ver" for "far" (line 119); "bivore" for "before" (lines 160, 166, 167, 184); "vel" for "fel" (line 162); and "underveng" for "underfeng" ("received," line 170).

11   *Ailgive.* Latin Life A gives this name as "Ælfgiva," which sounds like an authentic Anglo-Saxon name, "Ælfgifu"; the later Latin Life simplifies it to "Algiva."

13   *that lif.* This text preserves some inflected forms of the definite article from Old English — including the neuter form *that* with the historically neuter nouns *lif*, "child" (line 14), "maide" (lines 43, 75, 111), "folc" (lines 73, 99, 139, 141, 143), and "hous" (line 181).

43   *maide.* A: *made.*

47   Emended from the reading in A, *Ac that thou vorlore were.* The line is much harder to construe with the inclusion of *were*, and none of the other MSS has it (B: omits; P: *while*; and J: *wolle.*).

84   *vorsaketh.* A: *vorsakth.*
      heo. A: *he.*

85   *then wei.* A more conspicuous relic of Old English grammar than the recurrent use of "that" with neuter nouns (see textual note to line 13). *Then*, a form of the definite article that preserves the distinctive *n* of the masculine singular accusative in Old English, is correctly used here to modify *wei*, a masculine noun that is the direct object of the verb *nom*. There are several similar examples below in this text: "then

wei" (line 111), "then Sonedai" (line 135), "then tyme" (line 137), "then Saterday" (line 168). Further examples occur in the early *SEL* version of the Mary Magdalen legend; see textual note to line 405 of that text, below.

93   A appears to have another word here, possibly *wel*.

95   *kyng.* A: *kyn.*

105   *tame.* A: *came.*

112   *Bunseie.* "Buneseia" in Latin Life B; "Bunsey," "Benseye," and "Biniseye" in other *SEL* MSS.

122   *hem.* Inserted in the margin in A.

123   *cler.* A: *crer.*

187   *botnynge.* Emended from *bonynge*, the reading in A, on the authority of B, J, and P.

The Legend of Mary Magdalen, Penitent and Apostle

Introduction

The Mary Magdalen of medieval legend was a composite figure who had her origins in the Biblical passages about three different women — not just the woman explicitly called Mary Magdalen in the Gospels, but also Mary of Bethany, sister of Martha and Lazarus, and the unnamed female sinner who washed Christ's feet with her tears. Biblical exegetes in the Latin West tended to equate the three from the time of Gregory the Great on, but the various New Testament passages about these women were first woven into a single narrative *vita* in a tenth-century sermon attributed to Odo of Cluny. Odo's sermon, which was subsequently used as a source of lessons in the liturgy for Mary Magdalen's feast day (July 22), relates her life up to the time of Christ's Ascension. The post-Ascension portion of the legend developed in a great variety of ways, but the dominant version in the West was clearly the one that claimed that she journeyed to Provence in a rudderless boat, had a successful career as an apostle in Marseilles and Aix-en-Provence, and then spent thirty years alone in the wilderness nearby as a contemplative hermit.

Victor Saxer, who did most of the pioneering work on both the cult and the legend, found that the legend of Mary Magdalen in Provence has four major components, which originated separately. (1) The *vita eremitica*, recounting her years of solitude in the wilderness and her death, was probably borrowed in the ninth century from the Greek legend of a reformed prostitute, Mary of Egypt. As Katherine Ludwig Jansen has pointed out, the Bible never actually specifies the nature of Mary Magdalen's sins, but medieval exegetes and preachers found it natural to connect female sinfulness with prostitution (*The Making of the Magdalen*, pp. 146 ff.). (2) The *vita apostolica*, recounting Mary Magdalen's apostolic work in Provence but not the story of the prince of Marseilles, dates from around the same time in the tenth century as Odo's sermon. (3) A translation story was added in the eleventh century to explain how her body had been rediscovered in Provence some 200 years earlier and brought north — with her consent — to the abbey of Vézelay in Burgundy. (4) The story of the prince of Marseilles, which bears close resemblances to secular romance and would become a favorite part of the vernacular legends of Mary Magdalen, was added even later — probably in the twelfth century. In addition to these major components, the Provençal legend in its fully developed form often includes two other kinds of relatively late additions: brief accounts of Martha, Lazarus, and other saints who supposedly accompanied Mary to Marseilles and participated in the evangelization of France, and stories about her miraculous intercessions for believers who have prayed to her or honored her memory in other ways.

As the additions to her legend suggest, the cult of Mary Magdalen was still strong and dynamic in the late Middle Ages. Her cult had special resonance in France, of course, because her principal shrines were located there. The Cluniac abbey of Vézelay, which had gained papal recognition in 1058 for its claim to possess her body, grew into one of the greatest pilgrimage centers in Europe — thanks to the prestige of its patron saint, the support of the French monarchy, and its perfect location, on a main route used by pilgrims from Germany to Santiago of Compostella. In Provence were the grotto at Sainte-Baume, widely believed to have served as the site of Mary Magdalen's thirty-year sojourn in the wilderness, and nearby the monastic church of St. Maximin, specifically mentioned in some versions of the legend as her original burial place. The relative status of the Provençal shrines improved considerably after 1279, when the monks of St. Maximin's and the Angevin prince Charles of Salerno miraculously discovered that her body was still there after all, hidden inside an ancient sarcophagus in the crypt of the church. Thus Charles and his allies attempted to reclaim the saint's patronage and protection, which had earlier been symbolically transferred to Burgundy, for the county of Provence and the house of Anjou. But the cult of Mary Magdalen in France was a larger phenomenon than the claims of any single region or ruling family. For one thing, the legend of her apostolate in Provence had been incorporated (along with the legends of St. Denis of Paris and St. Martial of Limoges) into the myth of origins which proved the antiquity and importance of the French church as a whole. The tradition that she and Lazarus had personally brought Christianity to Gaul in the first century had such deep patriotic appeal that it remained stubbornly lodged in French popular belief until the nineteenth century, despite the best efforts of historians to debunk it.

In England, the cult of Mary Magdalen must have begun in Anglo-Saxon times, as witnessed by the presence of her feast day in Bede's martyrology (c. 720) and in early monastic calendars. The entry for her in the *Old English Martyrology* (c. 900) already shows a knowledge of her *vita eremitica*, and Exeter Cathedral claimed to have one of her relics as early as the tenth century. The most striking evidence of growth postdates the Norman Conquest, but only a fraction of it can be ascribed to French influence. Where two or three churches had been dedicated to her by 1100 and some 35 a century later, the total had grown to nearly 200 by the end of the Middle Ages. The importance of her cult in late-medieval England is further suggested by the high ranking of her feast day in the summer calendar, her prominence among the saints chosen for visual depiction in churches and in manuscripts, and the fact that she was the first female saint to have a college dedicated to her at Oxford (where the students, of course, were all male). Even more telling than the number of such tributes, however, is the diversity of persons and groups from which they came. For the late-medieval Mary Magdalen was an exceptionally multi-faceted saint, who served many different functions for different segments of the population. She was the archetypal sinner who repented and was redeemed, supplying a powerful illustration of God's forgiveness and an example of reform that was potentially relevant to every Christian, although it could also be narrowed to provide lessons for female sinners or sexual sinners in particular. Because of her own transformation from sinner to saint, she was the patron saint of moral rebirth and regeneration and of institutions founded for that purpose, including convents for former prostitutes and hostels for pilgrims. Because of her loving care for Christ's body when she washed His feet and went to the tomb to anoint His body after death, she was often held up as a model of active charity; hence she became a favorite patron of hospitals and confraternities that engaged in works of corporal mercy. Since she was also believed to be the Mary whom Jesus praised for having "chosen the better part" (Luke 10:42) when she sat quietly at his feet instead of attending to the mundane chores of the household, she provided an appealing patron and model for cloistered nuns, monks, and others who had chosen lives of contemplation rather than worldly activity. At the opposite extreme, as David Mycoff has suggested, the legend of the prince of Marseilles invited rich laymen to invest in her cult as a form of family insurance: "Mary Magdalene, the harlot saint who twice renounced a great patrimony and the dynastic (i.e., reproductive) obligations of that inheritance — once to follow a life of sin in unbridled sexuality and once to follow holiness in negated sexuality — becomes a source of fecundity and dynastic stability. She procures children for the princes, in one instance serving as midwife and nurse."[1]

Given the wealth of possible themes and messages that could be derived from this legend in its late-medieval form, a good way of approaching its retellings is to notice which choices each has made. For example, which aspects of Mary Magdalen's sanctity have been chosen for emphasis? Is she being presented primarily as an exemplar of penitence, of loving service to Jesus, of active charity in the world, or of contemplative withdrawal into solitude? Is she actually being held up as a model for imitation, or is this retelling designed instead to encourage devotion to her as a patron and intercessor, or merely to provide some edifying entertainment? It is also instructive to notice how the various retellings of this legend deal with particular issues that had become controversial toward the end of the Middle Ages. The most obvious example is Mary Magdalen's career in Provence as a preacher and apostle. Since laymen and women were expressly forbidden to preach, a prohibition repeatedly attacked during this period by Waldensians on the Continent and Lollards in England, defenders of orthodoxy did not find it easy to explain away the apparent precedents set by women saints who had preached. In some cases they could simply ignore that aspect of a saint's example — as the *Speculum Sacerdotale* does in its account of Mary Magdalen (edited below). As Jansen has recently shown, however, Mary Magdalen's apostolic preaching had so much significance for the clergy themselves that they generally preferred less radical solutions. The early *SEL*

[1] See William Caxton, *A Critical Edition*, ed. Mycoff, p. 178.

account given below illustrates one such solution when it grants her power and efficacy as a preacher but insists on her subordination to the pope and Bishop Maximus whenever there is a sacrament to be administered (lines 312, 446–60, 527–30, and 627–31). Another controversial question was the extent to which Mary Magdalen's early loss of chastity was reversed thereafter by her perfect penance and love for Christ (Jansen, *The Making of the Magdalen*, pp. 287–94). Was it possible for her actually to become a virgin again, as her place among the virgins in the litany of saints seemed to suggest? Some late-medieval texts, including the Digby play *Mary Magdalene*, give strongly affirmative answers to this question, which was clearly an important one to contemporary women like Margery Kempe. Although none of the accounts given below takes an explicit stand on the matter, the *Speculum Sacerdotale* may be alluding to it in the very careful wording of lines 73–76, which connects Mary Magdalen to the virgins in the litany without quite calling her a virgin herself.

The account of Mary Magdalen here called the "early *SEL* account" is not really part of the *South English Legendary* itself, although it is found in Bodleian Library MS Laud Misc. 108 (c. 1300) and two later manuscripts of that work. According to Manfred Görlach, who has done the most authoritative research on the textual history of the *South English Legendary*, this account is probably a much earlier poem that was inserted "as an emergency measure of the 'L' compiler who, not finding a legend of the important saint in his defective exemplar, adapted the heterogeneous text to the style of the *SEL* collection" (*Textual Tradition of the South English Legendary*, pp. 181–82). Like the stanzaic accounts of Margaret and Katherine in the present edition, this version of the Mary Magdalen legend borrows frequently and sometimes conspicuously from the conventions of secular verse romances, suggesting that it was competing for the attention of a lay audience whose tastes and expectations had been formed by that genre. The nature of the intended audience in this case is further suggested by another striking feature of the stanzaic Mary Magdalen: the emphasis it places on the proper uses of wealth. Those who generously share their material possessions, especially by feeding the hungry and offering hospitality to Christ and his disciples, are defined from the outset as wise and good (e.g., lines 27–28 and 55–62), and the story of the prince of Marseilles dramatically suggests how God will bless those who practice such generosity and punish those who neglect or refuse to do so.

John Mirk was a canon at Lilleshall Abbey in Shropshire who wrote three extant books, *Instructions for Priests*, *Manual Sacerdotis*, and the *Festial* or *Liber Festivalis*, between about 1380 and 1410. The *Festial*, which includes this prose account of Mary Magdalen, is a collection of vernacular sermons for the major saints and festivals of the church year, for use by priests who were not learned or ambitious enough to find sermon materials for themselves. One notable feature of Mirk's sample sermons is the extent of their reliance on legends, exempla, and popular tales, most of them drawn from Latin collections like the *Legenda aurea* and the *Gesta Romanorum*. This style of preaching was harshly criticized by the Lollards and later by Protestant reformers, who charged that it substituted entertainment for wholesome teaching based on the Bible, but it must have been successful in holding the attention of unlearned congregations. The usefulness of the *Festial* is suggested by the fact that it circulated widely — often in versions that had been adapted, revised, or supplemented for other kinds of audiences — for well over a century. There are at least 40 extant manuscripts which include one or more of Mirk's sample sermons, and 18 editions of the *Festial* were printed between 1483 and 1532. Mirk's sermon on Mary Magdalen begins and ends with lessons about the connections between her experience and that of "alle synful [people]," who should be inspired to repent as she did in the certainty that God's grace will meet and surpass their needs. One question worth asking about his retelling of the legend is whether it actually encourages more identification with the saint than those in the early *SEL* and the *Speculum Sacerdotale*, or whether some other agenda can be glimpsed behind his choice of emphases and details.

The *Speculum Sacerdotale*, an anonymous collection of sermon material that survives in just one manuscript, is probably just a decade or two later in date than Mirk's *Festial*, and very similar to Mirk's work in sources, scope, and apparent purpose. In fact, Edward H. Weatherly suggests in his introduction to the EETS edition of the *Speculum* that the two works "are efforts . . . to do exactly the same thing — to furnish a book of instruction in matters of church observance and legend in the vernacular for the use of parish priests" (p. xl). Nonetheless, Weatherly himself points out several significant differences between the two. The author of the *Speculum Sacerdotale* seems relatively unconcerned with effective story-telling, apparently because his goal was to supply "a mass of material upon which priests might draw for sermons" (Weatherly, p. xxxvi), rather than chapters suitable for delivery as they stood. The *Speculum* includes more expository material than the *Festial* does, and some of it is clearly intended for the instruction of priests themselves — most notably a long treatise on the sacrament of penance that includes specific instructions on hearing confessions and assigning penances (pp. xli, xxxix). In addition, Weatherly notes one suggestive difference between the kinds of stories the two works tend to tell: "Most of the stories in the *Festial* teach a moral; those in the *S.S.* attempt to arouse devotion through wonder at the miraculous" (p. xli). One might also point out that the *Speculum* includes only two female saints other than the Virgin Mary, and makes very short work of their lives at that. In the case of Mary Magdalen, it takes her directly from Christ's Ascension to the desert, omitting the entire legend of her apostleship and concentrating instead on the priest's encounters with her just before she dies and a series of posthumous miracles in which she intervenes to save a child and two adult sinners.

Select Bibliography

Indexed in

[Early *SEL* Life]   Brown-Robbins, #3159.

Manuscripts

[Early *SEL* Life]   Oxford, Bodleian Library MS Laud Misc. 108 (*SC* 1486), fols. 190r–197r.

[Mirk]   London, British Library MS Cotton Claudius A.ii, fols. 91v–93v.

[*Spec. Sac.*]   London, British Library MS Additional 36791, fols. 96r–98r.

Previous editions

Early *South English Legendary* Life
Horstmann, Carl, ed. *Sammlung altenglischer Legenden*. 1878. Pp. 148–62.

Mirk
Mirk, John. *Mirk's Festial*. Ed. Theodor Erbe. EETS, e.s. 96. 1905. Pp. 203–08. [The EETS edition is based on Bodleian Library MS Gough Eccl. Top. 4 (*SC* 17680). I have chosen to follow Cotton Claudius instead because it is probably earlier than Gough Eccl. and often has fuller readings.]

Speculum Sacerdotale
Weatherly, Edward H., ed. *Speculum Sacerdotale*. EETS, o.s. 200. 1936. Pp. 170–74.

Important sources and analogues in English

Bokenham, Osbern. *Legendys of Hooly Wummen*. Ed. Mary S. Serjeantson. EETS o.s. 206. 1938. Pp. 136–72.

Caxton, William. *A Critical Edition of the Legend of Mary Magdalena from Caxton's Golden Legende of 1483*. Ed. David A. Mycoff. Salzburg Studies in English Literature, Elizabethan and Renaissance Studies 92:11. Salzburg: Institut für Anglistik und Amerikanistik, Universität Salzburg, 1985. [Analogue with comprehensive introduction and notes, including a discussion of the relationship between the three accounts edited here and the *Legenda aurea*.]

[The Digby] *Mary Magdalen*. In *Late Medieval Religious Plays of Bodleian MSS Digby 133 and E Museo 160*. Ed. Donald C. Baker, John L. Murphy, and Louis P. Hall, Jr. EETS o.s. 283. Oxford: Oxford University Press, 1982. Pp. 24–95.

Jacobus de Voragine. *The Golden Legend*. Trans. William Granger Ryan. 2 vols. Princeton: Princeton University Press, 1993. Vol. 1. Pp. 374–83.

The Life of Saint Mary Magdalene and of her Sister Saint Martha: A Medieval Biography. Trans. and ed. David Mycoff. Cistercian Studies Series 108. Kalamazoo: Cistercian Publications, 1989. [Analogue with helpful notes on particular details. Migne and the Library of Congress attribute this text to Rabanus Maurus (c. 780–856), but it is actually an anonymous work from the late twelfth century.]

Historical background and criticism

Haskins, Susan. *Mary Magdalen: Myth and Metaphor*. London: HarperCollins, 1993.

Jansen, Katherine Ludwig. "Maria Magdalena: *Apostolorum Apostola*." In *Women Preachers and Prophets through Two Millennia of Christianity*. Ed. Beverly Mayne Kienzle and Pamela J. Walker. Berkeley: University of California Press, 1998. Pp. 57–96.

_____. *The Making of the Magdalen: Preaching and Popular Devotion in the Later Middle Ages*. Princeton: Princeton University Press, 2000.

Saxer, Victor. *Le Culte de Marie Madeleine en Occident des origines à la fin du moyen âge*. 2 vols. Paris: Libr. Clavreuil, 1959.

Thompson, Anne B. "Narrative Art in the *South English Legendary*." *JEGP* 90 (1991), 20–30. [Essay on the later *SEL* account.]

Early South English Legendary Life of Mary Magdalen,
from Bodleian Library MS Laud Misc. 108, fols. 190r–197r

	Sleighe men and egleche, and of redes wise and bolde,	*Wise; brave; counsels*
	Lustniez nouthe to mi speche, wise and unwise, yongue and olde.	*Listen now*
	Nothing ich eou nelle rede ne teche of none wichche ne of none scolde,[1]	
	Bote of a lif that may beo leche to sunfule men of herte colde.	*healing to sinful*
5	Ich nelle eou nother rede ne rime of kyng ne of eorl, of knyght ne of swein,	
	Ake of a womman ich chulle ou telle that was sunful and forlein;[2]	
	A swythe fol wumman heo bicam, and thorugh Godes grace heo was ibrought ageyn,	*very foolish; she; restored*
	And nouthe heo is to Crist icome, the fayre Marie Maudeleyn.	*now*
	Of hire ichulle yeou telle nouthe al hou and hware heo was ibore,	*I shall; where*
10	Yif ye to me wullez iheore and habben of God thonk therefore.	
	This word "Marie" so is brightnesse and bitokne the steorre of the se,[3]	
	And soruwe also and biturnesse, ase the bok tellez me;	
	For hwane a man fielez in is heorte that he havez muche misdo,[4]	
	And him therefore biguynnez to smeorte, that is to him bitur and wo,	*feel pain*
15	He mournez and he sikez ofte. This ilke Marie fierde also,	*sighs; felt the same*
	That thing that was hire leof and softe was seththe hire fulle fo.[5]	
	In the Castel of Magdalé this faire wumman was ibore;	
	Heo was icleoped in propre name the Maudeleyne right therfore.	*called*
	To speken of hire ich am wel fous, and it likez me ful murie.	*eager; pleases*
20	Ire fader was hoten Sire Titus, and hire moder Dame Euchirie,	*Her; called*
	Hire brothur was cleoped Lazarus, and Martha was hire soster.	*called*

---

[1] *I will not tell or teach you anything about any witch or scold*

[2] Lines 5–6: *I will not speak or recite verses to you about a king or nobleman, a knight or retainer, / But I shall tell you of a woman who was sinful and unchaste*

[3] Lines 10–11: *If you will listen to me and have thanks from God as a result. / This word "Marie" stands for brightness and signifies the star of the sea*

[4] *For when a person feels in his heart that he has greatly sinned*

[5] *What had been dear and comfortable to her was afterwards her great enemy*

The Legend of Mary Magdalen, Penitent and Apostle

Heo was debonere and pitiuous, and heo was a seli foster.[1]

Heore fader and heore moder bothe comen of riche kunne, *from rich families*

Of bolde kyngus and of quienes, men of muchele wunne, *great wealth*

25 Of castles and of tounes, of londes and of theodes, *estates (properties)*

Of halles and of boures, of palefreighes and of stedes.

Large huy weren of heore metes to heom that hadden neode,

To men goinde and eke sittinde that heore bonene wolden heom beode.[2]

  Wyse men and sleyghe overal huy weren itolde. *prudent; they; considered*

30 Tho that huy scholden deighe, and so huy weren iholde, *When; die; afflicted*

Heore londes and heore leodes huy delden alle a-threo,[3]

Tounes and heore theodes, heore guod and heore feo, *estates; possessions; money*

To feoffen heore children tharewiz echon,

For huy ne scholden nought strive hwane huy heom weren atgon.[4]

35 Wel sone thereaftur, tho huy nede scholde, *when they must*

Deiden fader and moder, ase Jesu Crist it wolde. *Died; willed*

Bi heom men duden sone ase huy oughten to done[5]

And to heore longue home broughten heom ful sone. *their final resting place*

Jesu Crist of heovene of heom habbe merci *heaven; have mercy on them*

40 And for Is names seovene fram helle heom waraunti! *His; protect them*

  Huy dighten heore londes among heom alle threo, *disposed of; three*

And with heore hondene delden heore gold and heore feo.[6]

To Marie bilefde the castel Magdalé; *was left*

Tharefore Maudeleyne formest icleoped was heo. *she was first called "Magdalen"*

45 Lazarus hadde that halvendel of al Jerusalem, *half portion*

Of wodes and fieldes and of sart almest to Bedlehem. *cleared land; Bethlehem*

Martha was ifeoffed with the Betanie *endowed; Bethany*

And also with Genezarez, bote the bok us lie. *Gennesaret, unless*

  Marie heo ne tolde nought bote al of hire pruyde, *did not care for anything except*

---

[1] *She was courteous and compassionate, and she was a blessed child*

[2] Lines 26–28: *Of halls and of bedchambers, of saddle horses and of warhorses. / Generous they were with their food to them that had need, / To people of all kinds who would ask them for help*

[3] *They divided all their landed properties into three parts*

[4] Lines 33–34: *To endow each of their children therewith, / So that they would not quarrel when they (the parents) had departed from them*

[5] *People soon did their duty by them*

[6] *And with their hands divided their gold and their movable property*

50	Ake tharon was al hire thought, and faire hire to schruyde,[1]	
	And seththe for to walke aboute to don hire flechses wille,	*then; flesh's desire*
	To gon and eorne feor and neor, bothe loude and stille.[2]	
	For sothe, heo was riche inough, and so heo moste nede;	*she should have been*
	Manie riche men hire leighen bi and geven hire gret mede.	*lay by her; reward*
55	Lazarus spendede al is thought opon his chivalerie,	*his*
	Of othur thingus ne tok he no yeme, ne to housebondrie.	*heed; careful management*
	The selie Martha, that othur suster, heo was of redes guode,	*blessed; good counsels*
	Ase thei heo and hire soster neren nought of one blode.	*As though she*
	Martha nam hire brothur lond and hire sustres also,	*took; brother's*
60	And dude heom teolien wel inough, ase wys man scholde do;	*had them farmed*
	Tharewith heo fedde alle heore men and clothede heom also,	*all their people*
	Povere men and wummen, that weren neodfole and in wo.	*needy*
	So fair womman nas thare non in none kunnes londe[3]	
	Ase Marie was of bodie, and of fote and honde;	
65	So more fairore that heo bicam, the more of hire was prys,	*The more beautiful; praise*
	The more fol womman heo wax, and sunful and unwys.	*foolish; became; both sinful*
	Hire righte name Marie overal heo les tharefore;	*true; everywhere; lost*
	"Sunfole wumman" men cleopeden hire bihinde hire and bifore.[4]	
	Tho this wumman hadde iheord that hire name was ilore,	*When; heard; lost*
70	That heo was so bigyled and bicherd, wo was hire tharefore.	*led astray*
	Tho men hire cleopeden sunfule and lieten hire righte name,	*When; ceased to use*
	Heo wax kareful and dreori of thought and gan sore to schame.[5]	
	Tho nolde heo no more bifore the riche men come;	*she would not*
	Into hire castel for sorewe heo havez hire inome	*she betook herself*
75	For to ore Loverd cam and prechede overal in that londe.[6]	
	Martha hire suster ofte bifore opbraid hire schame and hire schonde	*disgrace*
	And chidde hire ful ofte for hire lecherie,	*scolded*
	Bothe fastinde and eke ful, that unnethe heo mighte it drie.[7]	

---

[1] *But upon [pride] was all her thought and to adorn herself beautifully*

[2] *To go and run far and near, both noisily and quietly (i.e., in every way, place, and time)*

[3] *There was no woman so beautiful in any land*

[4] *"Sinful woman" people called her behind her back and to her face*

[5] *She grew full of care and apprehensive and became sorely ashamed*

[6] *Until our Lord came and preached everywhere in that land*

[7] *Both [when] fasting and also [when] full (i.e., all the time), [so] that she might scarcely endure it*

The Legend of Mary Magdalen, Penitent and Apostle

	A man of that contreye that heighte Symond Leperous,	*was called; the Leper*
80	Also the bok us tellez, bad ore Loverd to is hous,	*As; invited our Lord; his*
	And Is deciples tweolve with Him, to the mete,	*His disciples; to dinner*
	For He ne mighte nought Himsulf fram heom alle ete.	*apart from them all*
	Marie this iheorde and tharof was ful glad,	*heard*
	A smeorieles to greithi tharto heo was ful rad.	*An ointment; prepare; quick*
85	Heo wende to Symundes hous, that no man hire ne bad,	*where no one had invited her*
	To ore Loverd Jesu Crist; and ful sore heo was ofdrad.	*afraid*
	For that heo was so sunful, bifore ore Loverd to come	
	Careful heo was and sore aferd forto beon inome.[1]	
	Heo ne dorste ore Loverd repie nought bihinde ne bifore,	*touch*
90	Ne no man hire nolde cleopie, and that hire grefde sore.	*address; grieved*
	Tho ore Loverd was isete in Symundes house there	*When; seated*
	And his apostles to the mete, that with him tho were,	*at dinner; then*
	Ore Loverd sat and thoughte muche, ake bote luyte He ne eet.	*but He ate little*
	Marie, that was so sunful, heo crep doun to Is fiet.	*crept; His feet*
95	Heo custe Is fiet and wusch also with hire wete teres,	*kissed; washed [them]*
	And wipede heom afturward with hire yeoluwe heres.	*yellow hair*
	Out of hire boxe heo nam oynement ful guod	*jar; took*
	And smeorede ore Loverdes heved with ful blisful mod.	*anointed; head*
	Judas was thare biside and smulde hit, and tharefore he was neigh wod;	
100	That swote smul him culde neigh and gremede is sorie blod,[2]	
	And bad don up that riche thing that heo ore Loverd gan with smeore;[2]	
	To spene it so in wasting, he seide, it was gret lure,	*use; to no purpose; a great loss*
	And seide, "It mai beon isold ful deore, to bugge with muchel mete,[3]	
	Povere men tharewith to freveri of drunch and of mete."	*comfort with drink; food*
105	Tho saide ore Loverd to Judas, "Lat thou this wumman beo!	
	Ful guod weork it was and is that heo wurchez in me;	*deed*
	For ai schulle ye povere with eou habbe, and so ne worth eou me.[4]	
	Thi toungue moste bien ischave; to speche heo is to freo."	*must be restrained; too free*
	Symund Leprous iheorde this; he thoughte wel manifold	*the Leper*

---

[1] *She was worried and very afraid of being seized (arrested)*

[2] Lines 99–101: *Judas was close by and smelled it, and on that account he was nearly insane; / That sweet smell nearly killed him and grieved his cursed blood, / And [he] said to put away that rich stuff with which she was anointing our Lord*

[3] *And [he] said, "It could be sold for a great sum, [and used] to buy a lot of food"*

[4] *For always you will have the poor with you, but you will not have me*

110   That, yif thes Profete were also wys ase He is fore itold,   *this Prophet; as wise*

        He nolde soffri this fole wumman His bodi enes to reppe,   *allow; even once; touch*

        For no weork that heo can do, or toward Him enes steppe.   *deed; take even one step*

          Ore Loverd wuste is luthere thought, ake tharof stod Him non eyghe:

        "Symund, thou thenchest muche for nought. Sumthing ichulle thee seighe."[1]

115   "Maister, seye," seide Symound, "ich it bidde thee!   *pray*

        For thou noldest for nothing segge onright to me."   *speak unjustly*

          "An usurer was hwilene that hadde dettores tweyne,   *There was once a money-lender*

        That swythe longue hwyle dette him scholden beyne:[2]

        That on him scholde fifti panes and twenti tharto,   *one; owed; pence; besides*

120   That othur him scholde of dette fifti panewes also,   *owed; pennies*

        And nothur of heom nadde hwareof the dette for to yelde.[3]

        Huy yolden, tho he it crevede, ase the bok us telde.   *They paid, when he asked for it*

        Hwethur of heom tweine cudde him more love tho?"

          "Maister, he that more gaf, me thinche, so mote I go."[4]

125   "For sothe, Symund Leperous, thou havest idemed aright.   *judged rightly*

        For seththe ich cam into thin hous, thou ne custest me no wight,[5]

        Ne thou ne wusche nought mine fiet with watur ne with teres,   *Nor; washed*

        Ne thou ne wypedest heom nought yuyt with clothe no with heres.   *yet; hair*

        Min heved on none halve with no manere oynement   *head; any side; kind of*

130   Ne smeordest, with none salve ne with no piement.   *anointed; ointment*

        Seththe ich cam into thin hous, this wumman nolde blinne   *Since; would not cease*

        Mine fiet to wasche and cusse withouten and withinne,   *kiss all over*

        And to wipen heom seththe afturward with hire faire here,   *then; hair*

        Min heved also to smeorien with riche oynement and dere.   *anoint; expensive*

135   "Op aris, thou wumman; thine sunnes thee beoth forgyve!   *Rise up; are forgiven you*

        Also ich nouthe can and may, of me thou art ischrive."   *As; by me; shriven (absolved)*

          Marie the Maudeleyne, ore swete Loverd hire schrof,   *absolved*

        Swete Jesu Crist out of hire seve develene He drof.   *seven devils*

---

[1] Lines 113–14: *Our Lord perceived his wicked thought, but felt no fear of it: / "Simon, you imagine much without good cause. I have something to say to you"*

[2] *Both of whom owed him payment for a very long time*

[3] *And neither of them had any means wherewith to repay the debt*

[4] Lines 123–24: *"Which of the two of them showed him the more love then?" / "Master, he who gave more, it seems to me, as I hope to live"*

[5] *For since I came into your house, you kissed me not at all*

	Ore Loverd makede hire Is procuratour, His leof and Is hostesse;	*spokesman; dear*
140	Heo lovede Him with gret honour in pays and in destresse.	*peace; need*
	Martha hire suster was ful sik, and so heo hadde ibeo ful yore;	*for a long time*
	At hire bihinde heo hadde ibled seven yer and more.	*bled*
	Heo ne mighte for nothing no lechecraft afonge,	*receive any healing*
	Are ore Loverd, Heovene King, among heom thare gan gongue,	*Until; began to walk*
145	And gaf hire Is swete blessingue and helde hire of hire sore	*healed; illness*
	And bad hire beon hol and sound; and so heo was evereft more.	*healthy; ever after*
	Heore beire brothur Lazarus was swythe sikel a man.	*The brother of them both; ill*
	Jesus hereborewede at heore hous hwane He bi heom cam,	*lodged; when; near them*
	And his apostles alle, hwane huy thare forth come:	
150	Heore in huy gonne cleopie and ase heore owene it nome;	
	Al swuch ase thareinne was huy eten and huy drounke — [1]	
	Men habbez ofte note of thing that luytel it habbut swounke.	*benefit; worked for*
	Tho Jesus hadde thare ibeo ase longue ase He wolde,	*wished*
	He wente to anothur contreye, for men iseon Him scholde.	*needed to see Him*
155	Marie He gaf Is blessingue and Martha and Lazarus,	
	Muchele and luttle, elde and yongue, that woneden in heore hous.[2]	
	Aftur that He was iwend, Marie wax egleche;	*had gone; grew brave*
	Crist hire havede aboute isent to sarmoni and to preche.	*had sent her out ; speak*
	To sunfole men heo was ful rad to wissi and to teche,	*ready; advise*
160	And to sike men heo was ful glad to beon heore soule leche.	*souls' physician*
	Mani on to Cristinedom heo broughte, and out of sunne,	
	Fram lecherie and horedom, thoru schrift, to joye and alle wunne.	*happiness*
	Aftur ore Loverdes passione in the thrittenthe yere,	
	Giwes weren proute and grimme, olme and of luthere chere:[3]	
165	Seint Stevene to dethe huy stenden, that was ore Loverd ful deore,	*stoned; [to]*
	And manie men huy flemden that Cristes limes were.[4]	
	Non apostle ne moste live in Giwene londe,	*could; the Jews'*
	Alle huy weren of londe idrive with wraththe and nythe and onde.[5]	

[1] Lines 150–51: *They called it their inn and used it as their own [dwelling]; / They ate and drank whatever was on hand there*

[2] *[And to everyone] great and small, old and young, that dwelled in their house*

[3] *[The] Jews were proud and stern, cruel and of wicked behavior*

[4] *And many people they put to flight who were members of Christ's body*

[5] *They all were driven from the land with wrath and malice and enmity (hatred)*

	Seint Maximus was tho with Godes apostles bicome;	*going about*
170	Sixti ant ten deciples togadere heom hadden inome.	*had joined themselves*
	Marie the Maudeleyne and hire brothur Lazarus	
	And heore suster Martha and the bischop Maximus,	
	Mani mo of Cristine men, wel mo thane I can nemne,	*name*
	Weren ihote fleme, and some to quelle and brenne.	*put to flight; be killed and burned*
175	Huy weren in a schip ipult withouten ster and ore,	*placed; tiller; oars*
	That huy scholden beon furfaren and ne libben no more;	*[So] that; killed; live*
	Thare nas nothur ido with heom nothur watur ne bred,	*was neither sent*
	For huy scholden ofhongrede beon and sone thareafturward ded.	*So that; starved*
	Huy schypeden in the salte se, ase Jesu Crist it wolde,	*sailed*
180	Forto that tyme scholde beo that huy arivi scholde.	*Until; come; reach land*
	To Marcile the wynd heom drof, a gret namecouth cité.	*Marseilles; drove; renowned*
	Everech of heom othur schrof are huy comen out of the se.	*shrove before*
	Huy ne founden thare no freond that wolde heom hereboruwe,	
	Cristine man ne no Giu, an eve nothur amoruwe,[1]	
185	Ne gyven heom mete ne drinke nothur ne lissen heore soruwe,	*alleviate*
	Ne no man, for love ne for swunch, that huy mighten of bugge ne borewe.[2]	
	In one olde porche huy stunten al that nyght,	*open-sided building; remained*
	Withoute light of torche, withoute fuyr and candle bright;	*fire*
	The porche was an old hous, of olde weorke iwrought,	*workmanship*
190	Thudere in huy weren alle wel vouse that of the se weren ibrought,[3]	
	For huy nusten ellehware that huy stunte mighte,	*did not know anywhere else; stay*
	Bote huy hadde gret schame and teone, and Giwes with heom to fighte.[4]	
	Thare huy duelden al that nyght forto it was day amoruwe.	*until; next morning*
	The Sarasins heom boden fight, to echen heore soruwe.[5]	
195	Alle the men that fram the se thuder weren icome,	*to that place (thither)*
	Huy nusten hwodere huy mighte fleo; forthi huy weren inome.[6]	

---

[1] Lines 183–84: *They found no friend (protector) there who would shelter them, / [Neither] Christian nor Jew, [neither] at night nor in the morning*

[2] *Nor anyone, for love or for hire, from whom they could beg or borrow*

[3] *Those who had been delivered from the sea were all very anxious to go into that place*

[4] *Unless they had great shame and sorrow, and Jews fighting with them*

[5] *The pagans challenged them to fight, to increase their grief*

[6] *They were not certain whither they might flee; because of this they were seized*

The Legend of Mary Magdalen, Penitent and Apostle

Huy weren ihote ope lyf and lime Jesu Crist fursake, *ordered at the risk of*

And, with thretningue and with strif, to heore false godus take.[1]

 The Marie Maudeleine heo saigh that folk arise, *saw*

200 Riche and povere, knyght and sweyn, to don that sacrefise;

Heo was anuyd and ofdrad, that hire bigan to grise; *displeased; afraid; feel horror*

To speken of God heo was ful rad, and so dude on hire wise. *ready; [she] did*

 Op heo stod with wordes bolde, with bright neb and glade chere, *Up; face*

And seide,"Herkniez to me, yunge and elde, that wullez beon Cristes *Listen; want to*

205 Ne bilievez nought opon Mahun, ne on Tervagaunt is fere, *his companion*

For huy beoth bothe deve and doumbe, and huy ne mouwen iseo ne ihere,

Ne huy ne mouwen eou helpe nought of none kunnes thingue,[2]

Thei men of heom yelpen ought, ne no guod to eu bringue. *Though; may boast; you*

For huy bez doumbe and deve, crokede and eke blinde; *lame*

210 Heore mighte is fallen to grounde biforen and bihinde. *power; i.e., everywhere*

Ake ye schulle lieven on Jesu Crist, oure heighe Heovene Kyng, *must believe*

That al this worldes Maister is, withoute ani ending, *Ruler*

For He may don Is wille of evereche cunnes thing *kind of*

That ye wilniez with righte and withouten suneguyng. *desire rightfully; sinning*

215 He is withoute biguynningue, and He is withouten ende,

Withoute fuylthe and sunegyng, so corteys and so hende *filth; sinning; gracious*

That al thing that man with skile Him biddez He wole him gyve and sende,

To man that goth and eke rit, that wole to him wende. *any kind of person; turn*

He is Wuryte of alle thing; He makede heovene and helle, *Creator (Wright)*

220 Ne may no kayser ne no kyng His vertues alle telle; *emperor; enumerate*

The man that Him servez wel ne may him no feond dwelle, *fiend deceive*

Ake huy that wullez agein Him fighte, to grounde He wole heom felle.

He makede day and eke nyght, steorrene and sonne and mone; *stars*

The man that trewe is and lovez Him aright, He wole graunti him is bone, *his boon*

225 And that he biddez Him with treouthe, He it grauntez him ful sone; *asks; integrity*

He helpez bothe king and knyght, the povere alle mididone." *all together*

 A riche prince of Sarazins thudere was icome, *thither*

With him is wyf and his mayné that with him he hadde inome. *retinue; taken*

To Maries prechingue he lustnede ful sone; *listened*

230 For that heo was so fair a thing, to hire huy token guod gome. *Because; good heed*

---

[1] *And, with threatening and with violence, to worship their (the attackers') false gods*

[2] Lines 206–07: *For they are both deaf and dumb, and they may not see nor hear, / Nor can they help you in any respect*

	The Sarazins onvele weren, fulle of nythe and hete.	*wicked; malice; hatred*
	Tho it was time of mele, huy wenden to heore mete;	*When; mealtime; food*
	Tho huy comen hom unsele and tharto weren isete,	*unblessed; seated*
	Cristes men to delen guod ful clene huy hadden forgete.[1]	
235	Thare weren of Cristine men mo thane sixti and tene;	
	No man nadde reuthe of heom, and that was thare isene:	*pity on; evident*
	Huy weren witoute mete and drunch, in gret hongur and in teone,	*suffering*
	Ne huy ne duden no weork ne swunch, ne nothing men nolde heom lene.[2]	
	Hit was in one nyghte aftur the thridde day	
240	That this riche princes wif in hire bedde lay.	
	Thare cam Marie Maudeleyne, and biforen hire heo stod:	
	"Dame, me thinchez thou art unhende, for thou hast muche guod.[3]	
	Of thee ich habbe gret feorlich, and muche me thinchez wunder	*surprise*
	That thou last Jesu Cristes folk thus steorve for hungur.	*allow (lettest); die*
245	Bote yif thou othur thi loverd lissi heore kare,	*Unless; or; lord relieve their*
	Wite ye mid iwisse, sorewe eou schal beon ful yare;[4]	
	Swuch a fierd schal opon eou come that schal eou so furfare	*army; destroy*
	And aquellen eou and eouwer folk; huy nellez eou nothing spare."	*kill; will not*
	This riche princes wif this word nolde hire loverd nought telle —	
250	For sothe, heo was puyrliche unwys, in sawe and in spelle.	*totally; speech; report*
	The othur nyght the Maudeleyne eftsone yeode hire to	*second; immediately went*
	And spak to hire wel stuyrneliche, and the thridde nyht also;	*very sternly*
	And yuyt heo nolde hire erinde to hire loverd do.	*still; message; deliver*
	Marie cam the feorthe nyght and bifore the prince heo stod:	
255	"Slepestou, tyraunt, thou develes knyght of Sathanasses blod?	*Satan's kin*
	Thi wif, the naddre, heo is amad; ich holde hire puyr wod.	*adder; insane; utterly mad*
	Heo nolde thee telle that ich bad, for uvele ne for guod.	*what I ordered; evil*
	Thou havest mete and drunch inough and luytel othur care,	*in abundance*
	And soffrest Cristes men with wough for hungur thus furfare!	*misery; to perish*
260	Bote thou amendi heore stat sone, thee is sorewe al yare:[5]	
	Thare schal so strong folk come thee agein that wollez thee luytel spare,	

---

[1] *They had completely forgotten to give anything to Christ's followers*

[2] *Neither did they have any kind of work [with which to earn food], nor would anyone lend them anything*

[3] *Lady, it seems to me you are ungracious, because you have much property*

[4] *Know with certainty that sorrow will afflict you very soon*

[5] *Unless you remedy their condition soon, sorrow is all prepared for you*

	With sweord and spere huy schullen thee sle and al thi folk furfare."	*destroy*
	The Maudeleyne yeode fram him and liet him ligge thare.	*went away; let; lie*
	The quiene awok and sighte sore and tolde hire loverd so;	*sighed*
265	Tho thoughte him that he iwarned was threo nyghtes and mo.	
	Heo tolde him that hire was iseid and also ihote to do —	*what she had been told*
	Feden Jesu Cristes men and lissi heom of heore wo,	*To feed; relieve*
	Othur heom scholde sorewe inough and kare comen heom to.	*Or else; great sorrow*
	Tho seide the prince, "Dame, hwat schulle we do	
270	Of thisse opene warningue that is icome us to?	*About; explicit*
	Betere is that we Cristes men swythe wel heom fiede and schruyde,	
	Thene we tellen luyte of heom in vilté othur in pruyde."[1]	
	Huy token Jesu Cristes men and ladden hom to heore inne;	*their own dwelling*
	Al that heom was neod huy founden heom with love and alle wunne.	
275	The Maudeleyne heom radde wel to witien heom fram sunne,[2]	
	So that heom ne thorte nevere drede of Sathanases kunne.	*they would never need fear*
	Opon a day heo bigan Godes word for to preche	*One day*
	And of Godes lawe, with gret wit, ase heo thar mighte areche;	*there could attain*
	To leden heore lyf in guod fey alle heo gan heom teche,	*faith*
280	And for to lovie God and don awey wraththe and onde and wreche.	*malice; revenge*
	The prince saide tho to hire with egleche wordes and bolde:	*fearless*
	"Might thou provi with treuthe that thou prechest may beo wel iholde?"[3]	
	The Maudeleyne saide, "Ye, ich am redi eou to teche,	*Yes*
	Bi ore maistres conseile and mid is holie speche —	*his*
285	That is Seinte Petre of Rome — hou ye schullen on take	*behave*
	The blisse of Heovene for to afongue and the feondes lore forsake."	*receive*
	Tho seide the prince anon and is wyf also:	
	"We beoz bothe redie anon thine wille for to do,	*are*
	So ase thi Loverd is of so muchel mighte	*Since*
290	That He may, hwane He wole, at Is wille alle thingus dighte.	*dispose*
	Bide thine Loverd, Heove King, that is us alle above,	*Ask; Heaven's*
	So ase He may don alle thing, and also for Is moder love,	*Since; mother's*
	And for thine bisechingue, that He gyve a child that beo a sone.	*give [us]*

---

[1] Lines 271–72: *It is better that we feed and clothe Christ's people very well, / Than [that] we disregard them because of iniquity or pride*

[2] Lines 274–75: *All that to them was needful they provided for them with love and all joy. / Then Magdalen taught them well to guard themselves from sin*

[3] *Can you prove truly that what you preach deserves to be believed?*

	And at thane forewarde we wollez with eou wone;	*with that agreement; dwell*
295	Ore kinedom also forth with us His owene we wollez bicome,	
	And we wollez yelden agein to Is men that we heom habbez binome."[1]	
	Tho seide Marie the Maudeleine,"That nelle ich nought bileve;	*cease*
	A preiere to mi Loverd to make nele me nothing greve.	
	Ich bidde thee, swete Jesu Crist, that makedest sonne and mone,	
300	That thou this prince siende a child, and that it beo a sone."	*send*
	Heo bad with guode heorte and milde; heo was iheord ful sone;	*heard*
	That ilke nyght huy geten a child, ase God heom gaf grace to done.	*conceived*
	Tho the prince wuste that is quiene was with childe,	*When; knew*
	Anon right toward Jesu Crist he wax meoke and milde.	*gentle*
305	Huy leten heore uvele dedes that weren so wikke and wilde,	*left; evil; ungoverned*
	And aftur Godes dedes huy wroughten and gonne buylde.	*according to; acted; live*
	Tho swor the prince and seide,"Bi heved min, wiende ichulle to Rome	*I shall go*
	And bicome a pilegrim and don aftur the holie dome,	*authority*
	And with Seint Petur ichulle speke and don aftur is redes,	*according to his counsels*
310	Yif it is so ase Marie seiz of Jesu Cristes dedes;	
	And yif that ich him finde at the court of Rome,	
	Of him ichulle underfongue fullouht and Cristendome."	*receive baptism*
	Tho seide the lavedi,"Ichulle wiende with thee,	*I shall go*
	And, thare thou art icristned, ichulle also beo;	*where*
315	And hwane thou comest hidere agein, ich may come with thee."	
	Tho seide the prince, leighinde, to is wif agame:	*laughing; playfully*
	"And beo nouthe ase thou seist, mi leove swete dame,	*let it be; dear*
	Bote in schipe wexez ofte soruwe, peril, and teone and grame;	*suffering; harm*
	And thou art nouthe with childe; couth is that guode fame.	*that good news is known*
320	In the se thou mightest ful sone hente schame —	*sea; receive injury*
	Yuyt hadde ich leovere ich were ihuld and evere to ligge lame!	
	Ake bilef thou at hom and reste thee wel and yem alle ore thingues.	
	At mine agein-come God siende me of thee guode tithingues!"[2]	
	Tho spak the lavedi, the quiene, and feol adoun to is fote:	*lady; fell; his feet*
325	"Leve loverd, thou let beo that, and graunte me that ich mote!	

---

[1] Lines 295–96: *Along with us we want our kingdom to become His own, / And we will repay to His people what we have deprived them of*

[2] Lines 321–23: *Rather than that I would even prefer to be skinned alive and remain disabled forever! / But stay you at home and rest yourself well and take charge of all our possessions. / At my home-coming may God send me good tidings about you!*

This ilke sorewe wole me aslen bote thou do me bote."[1]

Yeot seide the levedi, and weop wel swithe sore,   *The lady said more; wept*

Deolful and dreori heo ful adoun and seide ofte,"Sire, thin ore!

Hou mighte ich libbe and beon glad bote we togadere wore?

330   We loveden us so youngue, and nouthe we beoth sumdel hore."

     So longue and yeorne this lavedi bad hire loverd, that was so hende,[2]

That he hire grauntede, and was ful glad, with him for to wiende.   *to go (travel)*

For neodfole bisokne of heom and heore men   *eager petitions*

The holie blessingue with hire hond Marie makede on heom,

335   For no wickede gost bi the weye ne scholde hem derie,   *So that; spirit; harm*

The holie Rode tokningue fram sorowe heom scholde werie.[3]

     The Marie huy mauden wardein of heom and of heore schipe,   *made guardian*

The swete holie Maudeleyne, in Cristes wurthschipe,   *honor*

For heo was the Kingue of Heovene leof and deore and queme,

340   And bitoken hire ech del to witien and to yeme.[4]

     Huy nomen with heom into heore schip bred inough and wyn,   *took*

Venesun of heort and hynd and of wilde swyn;[5]

Huy nomen with heom in heore schip al that hem was leof,   *took; dear*

Gies and hennes, crannes, and swannes, and porc, motoun, and beof,

345   For huy scholden passi the Grickische Se,[6]

And for that huy nusten hou longue huy scholden thareinne be.   *did not know*

     Huy drowen op seil and ore and schipeden anon right,   *embarked*

Alle, the lasse and the more — eorl, baroun, and knyght.   *the lesser and the greater*

Huy nadden bote seve nyght iseiled in that flod,   *no more than seven*

350   That huy neren sore ofdradde; the se wax stuyrne and wod.   *Before they were; fierce*

---

[1] Lines 325–26: *Dear lord, put that [line of argument] aside and allow me [to accompany you]! / This sorrow itself will kill me unless you give me a remedy for it*

[2] Lines 328–31: *Full of grief and misery she fell down and often said, "Sire, have mercy! / How could I live and be glad unless we were together? / We loved each other [when we were] so young, and now we are getting old (lit., rather grey)." / So persistently and eagerly this lady begged her lord, who was so gracious*

[3] *The holy sign of the Cross should defend them from sorrow*

[4] Lines 339–40: *For she was beloved and dear and pleasing to the King of Heaven, / And entrusted everything to her to guard and take care of*

[5] *Meat of male and female deer and wild boar*

[6] Lines 344–45: *Geese and hens, cranes and swans, and pork, mutton, and beef, / Because they had to cross the Mediterranean ("Greek Sea")*

	The se bigan to flowen, and the wawes for to arise;	*surge; waves*
	Some bigonne to swounen, and heore heortene sore agrise.	*hearts; were afraid*
	The se bigan to ebbi, and the wynd ful stuyrne to blowe.	*ebb; fiercely*
	Ase the quiene on hire bedde lay, hire token ful strongue throwes.[1]	
355	Heo swounede ful ilomeliche and harde pinede tharefore,	*often; suffered*
	So forto that hire youngue sone were of hure ibore.	*To the point that*
	Tho that child ibore was, the moder bigan to deye.	
	That folk gradde, "Allas, allas!" and weopen with heore eye.	*cried; wept*
	Tho the levedi was ded, aftur that thet child was ibore,	
360	Huy ne mighten it bileve to make deol tharefore.	*cease; lamentation*
	That child wolde souke, and it nuste hwam;	*wanted to suck; knew not whom*
	Thare nas no milk aboute, ne no mielch wumman.	*wet nurse*
	"Allas," quath the prince, "that ich evere was ibore!	
	Wo is me for this yunge child, and for mi quien that ich habbe ilore!	*lost*
365	And nouthe it mot nede deye, for souke ne hath it non,	
	Ne I not in none halve hwat me is best to don."	
	The schipmen hieten with stuyrne mod that men ne schulden nought spare	
	The dede quien to casten in that flod, othur elles huy mosten furfare:[2]	
	"The hwyle that bodi is here with us, the stormes beoth so kete,	*So long as; violent*
370	To quellen us huy thenchez, and that huy nellez lete."	*kill; intend; leave off*
	Huy nomen up that dede bodi, into the se forto caste.	
	"Abidez yuyte and herkniez me!" the prince gradde faste.	*Wait; cried*
	"Yif ye nellez for mi love it lete, ne for love of mi wif,	
	Spariez for mi luytel sone, so that he mouwe habbe is lyf.	*little son; may*
375	For yif is moder mouwe yuyt of hire suoweningue awake,[3]	
	Thanne may mi luytel sone to hire tete take."	*make use of her breast(s)*
	Huy lokeden heom biside and seighen an heigh hurst	*high hill (island)*
	Swithe feor in the se, and the prince it isaigh furst.	*far; saw*
	Him thoughte that wel more wisdom to the bodie it were	
380	To burien it opon thet heighe hurst thane fisches it eten there.[4]	

[1] *As the queen lay on her bed, extremely strong [birth]pangs (contractions) overcame her*

[2] Lines 365–68: *"And now it must unavoidably die, for mother's milk it has none, / Nor do I know on any side what is best for me to do." / The shipmen ordered with stern countenance that people should not hesitate (delay) / To throw the dead queen into the sea, or else they must [all] perish*

[3] *For if his mother may still awaken from her swoon*

[4] Lines 379–80: *It seemed to him that it would be much more fitting to bury the body on that high hill than for fish to eat it there [in the water]*

71

	Tho huy comen thudere, huy ne mighten make no put:	*thither; grave (pit)*
	The hurst was al of harde stone, ech faste in othur iknut.	*hill; joined tightly together*
	Huy nomen the quiene and hire child and wounden in a mantel,	*wrapped [them]*
	And leide opon the heighe hurste in a grene cantel;	*laid [them] on; nook*
385	Huy leiden that childes mouth to the moder tete.	*mother's breast*
	Tho the prince that isaigh, with wepingue is neb he gan wete.	*his face*
	With gret deol the quiene and hire child thare huy gonne lete,	*lamentation; left*
	Opon thet hurst that was so heigh and hard and wilde and kete.	*rugged*
	The prince wep and wende forth with his schip in the se.	*wept*
390	"Marie Maudeleyne," quath the prince, "alas, that evere kneu ich thee!	*I knew*
	To don this pelrimage hwy raddest thou me?	*make; did you advise*
	Thou bede thi God a bone that mi wif with childe scholde be:	*asked; favor*
	And nouthe is ded thus sone bothe hire child and heo.	*so soon*
	Al mi lond and al mi thing ich habbe itake thee	*committed to*
395	To witen and to wardi; hwi schal it thanne thus be?	*protect; safeguard*
	Mi wif and mi yungue child, Marie, ich bitake	*entrust*
	To Jhesu Crist, thi owene Loverd, that alle thing of nought gan make,	
	That, yif He is so corteys and mightful ase thou seidest to me,	*So that; powerful*
	He save mi wif and mi child, furfare that ich ne be."[1]	
400	To his schyp he wende, and so forz in the se.	*forward*
	God hem to Rome sende, for thudere wolden he.[2]	
	Seinte Petur wuste wel that the prince cam	*knew*
	With milde mod, and fair compaygnie ageines him he nam.	*to meet him*
	Petur axede him fram hwanne he cam and hwodere he wiende wolde.	
405	"To Rome," he seide, "then wey ich take, and speke with thee I scholde."	*the road*
	He tolde of Marie Maudeleyne, hou he to hire cam,	
	And hou he Cristus sixti men and tene to him nam;	*ten; received*
	He tolde him of is child, he tolde him of is wif,	
	Hou he with milde heorte for heom tholede strif.	*suffered hardship*
410	Seinte Petur creoysede him opon is right scholder;	*marked him with a cross*
	Of that Marie havede iseid he havede game and wonder,	*what; had delight*
	And seide, "Prince, welcome thou be and thine knightes alle!	
	Pays and grace with thee beo, and joye thee mote on falle.	*Peace; may joy befall you*
	In bour and in halle, in field and in toun also,	*bedchamber; reception room*
415	In castel nothur in boure ne worthe thee nevere wo.	*may sorrow never come to you*

---

[1] *He [might] save my wife and my child, so that I will not be ruined*

[2] *May God send them to Rome, for that is where they wished to go*

In watur and in londe and in alle stude   *all places*
God thee fram harme schilde, and that ich habbe ibede.[1]
　"They thy wif slepe nouthe and thi sone him reste,   *Although your wife sleeps*
Loke that thou ne weope nought for hem ne make deol ne cheste!   *grief; strife*
420　Mi Loverd is swithe mighthful, He wole don Is wille,   *powerful*
And He is also quoynte and sley, bothe loude and stille. *crafty; ingenious; i.e., always*
He can gyven and binimen, borewi and eke yielde   *give; take away; borrow; repay*
For soruwe blisse, hwane His wille is, in toune, in watere, in fielde;   *joy for sorrow*
Hwane He is wroth He doth wreche, ake that fallez ful sielde;
425　Ake ofte gret fuyr and eke stuyrne wext of a luytel spielde."[2]
　　Petur ladde thene riche man agein to Jerusalem,   *the powerful man; back*
And fro thannes thene wey he nam with him to Bedlehem,   *the road; Bethlehem*
Fram thannes to the flym Jordan, an long bi the strem —   *thence; river*
I segge it ase ich ou telle can, in boke and nought in drem.[3]
430　He schewede him Calvarie, thare God was don on Rode,   *placed*
His fiet and Is hondene al hou huy ronnen on blode. *feet; hands; streamed with blood*
He tolde him of the thornes that on His heved stode,   *were fixed*
And of the nailes that in Is fiet and in His hondene wode,   *went*
And yet he tolde him of the spere that to the heorte Him stong,   *further; stabbed*
435　And hou He an heigh opon the Rode deide with muche wrong,   *on high; injustice*
Hou He into helle cam, with Sathanas to fighte,   *Satan*
And Is folk that thareinne was hou He it gan out dighte,   *removed*
Hou He aros, and to Heove steugh to Is Fader sete   *ascended; Father's throne*
And sat Him thareinne, for He was gleugh and was Him swythe imete.[4]
440　Tho the prince hadde iheord Seint Peteres lore,   *teaching*
He carede laste he were bicherd, for he hadde ibeo thare so yore;[5]
He hadde ileorned swithe wel al clanliche his Bileve,   *entirely; Creed (see note)*
His Oures and is Sauter ech del. Tho seide he, "God it geve *Hours; Psalter every bit*
That ich were sone in mine owene contreye,
445　And al mi folk with flechs and blod, right ase ich wolde, seighe!"   *i.e., in the flesh*
Seint Petur he bad par charité cristni him anon   *for charity's sake; baptize (christen)*

---

[1] *May God protect you from harm, and I have prayed for that*

[2] Lines 424–25: *When He is angry He takes vengeance, but that seldom happens; / But often a great and fierce fire grows from a little spark*

[3] *I recount it to you as best I can, in [a] book and not in [a] dream*

[4] *And placed Himself therein, for He was wise and [it] was very fitting for Him [so to do]*

[5] *He was worried that he might have erred in staying there so long*

	And al is othur mayné, and laten heom wende hom,	*retinue; let*
	And thanne habben guod day, "And gif us thine blessingue!	*say farewell*
	We wollez so blive so we mouwen don us to schipiingue."[1]	
450	"Thou schalt withouten cristndom wienden into thine londe —	*baptism go*
	Ne drede thee noughth, for thou might it don withoute schame and schonde![2]	
	The Maudeleyne schal beon with thee, and to thee heo schal fongue;	*act as sponsor*
	Lazarus and Martha, al thre, bi thee huy schullen stonde	
	Thare thou schalt icristned beo thoru Jesu Cristes sonde,	*Where; dispensation*
455	And muche folk also of thine contreye — ne thinche thee nought to longue!	
	An holi man schal cristni eou, the bischop Maximus,	
	That can is mester don swithe wel in Jesu Cristus hous.	*perform his office*
	He wole beo yep and eke rad, sley and eke vous;	*astute; discreet; eager*
	To cristni manie he wole beo glad to is Loverd Jesous —	
460	He were a fol and unwis that ne were of glad and blithe."[3]	
	The prince tok leve of Seint Petur and thonkede him fale sithe.	*many times*
	The prince saide, "Holie fader, have nou wel guod day!	
	Ichulle wienden hamward so blive so ich may."	*homeward as quickly as*
	He dude him into the salte flod. His schip bigan to go,	*betook himself to*
465	So blive — for the wind was guod — as swaluwe swift othur flo.[4]	
	Withinne the seven-nightte thudere he was icome	*a week thither*
	Thare he agein is wille bilefde is wif and is sone.	*Where he against his will had left*
	Huy iseighen bi the stronde a luytel child gon pleye	*saw; shore; playing*
	With publes on is honde bifore hem in the weye.	*pebbles in*
470	The prince stap out of the schipe — of hem alle he was the furste,	
	Opon the stronde he gaf a lupe, he highede him to the hurste.	*leap; hastened; hill*
	That child was swithe sore ofdrad, tho the prince cam,	*when*
	To his moder he was wel rad and about the necke hire nam.	*swift; embraced*
	The levedi lai wel stille and slep opon a grene cantel,	*slept; nook*
475	That child for fere orn to hire and crep under hire mantel.	*ran; crept*
	Tho saide that child, "Hiderward a thing, me thoughte I saigh come;	*something*
	Of him ich am ful sore adrad laste we beon inome."	*lest; seized*
	"Beo stille, mi sone, mi leove child! He is mi worldes fiere.	*spouse*
	For gladnesse wepe he wole that us findez here."	

---

[1] *We want to embark as soon as we can.*

[2] *Don't be afraid, for you can do it without injury or disgrace*

[3] *Anyone who was not glad and joyful [on such an occasion] would be a fool and unwise*

[4] *As swiftly — for the wind was favorable — as [a] fast swallow or [an] arrow*

480	The prince cam and fond hire ther, ligginde on the hurste,	
	Thare ase he bilefde hire er, and that child sek hire breste.	*left; before; sucked*
	For joye he weop and sat on is knen and heold up his honde:	*knees*
	"That ich evere moste this iseo, ich thonki ore Loverdes sonde.	*might; thank; sending*
	A, swete Marie Maudeleine, that me wolde nou right thinche murie	*seem joyful*
485	Mighte this wumman quikie agein and liven and hire sturie!"[1]	
	Tho he hadde that word iseid, his wif bigan to wake,	
	Of a swume heo schok and braid, and sone bigan awake	*swoon; trembled; started*
	And seide, "The hende Marie Maudeleyne, heo hath igive me space,	*a span of time*
	Fram dethe to live heo havez me ibrought thoru hire Loverdes grace.	*life*
490	Heo havez ifed me and mi sone and idon us alle guode;	*provided us with*
	To seggen it thee hwi scholde ich schone? That yelde hire the Rode![2]	
	Heo havez ibeon min houswif, mi mayde and mi norice,	
	And bote ich thee seide hou heo heold mi lif, for sothe ich were nice.[3]	
	"Al that Seint Petur hath seththe ischewed thee,	*since showed*
495	The swete Marie Maudeleyne it havez ischewed me.	
	Heo me havez on hire hond ilad over the salte strem	*led me by the hand; sea*
	And seththe fortheremore to Jerusalem;	*then*
	And seththe heo me ladde Bedlehem for to seo,	*to see Bethlehem*
	Thudere ase Seint Petur bifore ladde thee;	*To the same place*
500	And seththe to the flum Jordan heo ladde me ful rathe,	*river; soon*
	Withoute harme and sight of man and withoute schame and scathe.	*injury*
	And overal heo me ladde, mi loverd, thare thou were;	*everywhere*
	And, for thou scholdest joyful beo, nouthe right heo broughte me here."	*just now*
	Quath the prince, "Ich thonki God almighti that ich eou habbe alive.	*have you*
505	Arisez bothe, yif ye mouwen, and go we to schipe ful blive!"	*if you can; let us go*
	Huy duden heom to the watere and schipeden alle anon;	*took themselves*
	The wynd was blowinde swithe wel, and heore schip bigan to gon.	*blowing*
	Huy gonne to seili swithe in that salte fom,	*move very fast*
	And higheden heom ful blive, that huy weren at hom.	*hastened; [so] that*
510	Withinne a quartron of the yere huy comen to Marcilie.	*one fourth*
	Mani men of feor and ner of heom gonne speke and spilie;	*tell stories*
	Manie hem hadden togadere inome, eorl, baron, knyght and swein,	*assembled*
	Are huy weren to londe icomen for to wenden heom agein,	*turn their ship around*

---

[1] *If this woman could quicken again and live and move*

[2] *Why should I hesitate to tell you about it? May the Cross reward her for it!*

[3] *And I would be foolish indeed not to tell you how she has guarded my life*

Sarazins and the Giwes some, and the Marie Maudeleyn.
515   Martha cam and Lazarus — of heom huy weren ful glad,
And the holie bischop Maximus — to heom he was ful rad,   *eager*
And manie of Cristine men — huy neren nothing ofdrad   *not at all afraid*
To comen and gon ageinest him and don that he heom bad.[1]
     Tho the prince and is wyf weren icome to londe,   *When*
520   The Maudeleyne, withoute strif, irevested thare huy founde;[2]
And tho huy comen fram schipes bord, Marie huy founden stonde
For to prechen Godes word to heom that were on londe.
     The prince tok is wif and is sone with heorte guod and swete;
To the Maudeleyne huy comen and fellen doun to hire fete,
525   And tolden hire al heore liif that heom bifeol in that weye,   *befell them; journey*
Pays and love, harm and strif — al huy gonne hire seighe.   *Peace; struggle; told her*
Huy lieten thane Bischop Maximus cristni heom anon;   *caused; to christen*
Marie and Martha and Lazarus — huy broughten heom tharon.
The children and the wummen alle that weren in the londe,
530   Alle huy nomen Cristindom, and that was thoru Godes sonde.   *received; sending*
Ich wot huy nomen heore false godes and casten heom thare doune   *took*
And brenden al to poudre, feor fram everech toune;   *burned; powder, far*
Huy duden arere churches over al the contreies,   *had churches built; districts*
And priories wurche, and manie guode abbeies,   *constructed; abbeys*
535   And preostes huy gonne makien overal in the londe,   *had ordained everywhere*
Sudecknes and othur clerkus, to servi heom to honde.   *Subdeacons; available*
Huy mauden Lazarus bischop, the Maudeleynes brother;   *made*
The holie Bischop Maximus maude also mani anothur.
     Tho al that lond Cristine was and al that folc thareinne,   *Christianized*
540   Marie bithoughte a wonder cas and stal awey fram hire kunne.   *contrived; kindred*
Into wildernesse heo wende, al for to wonien there.   *dwell*
Swuch grace God hire sende, heo was thare thritti yeres.   *sent [that]; thirty*
Thare nas no watur aboute, ne thare ne wax no treo   *tree(s)*
That ani best mighte onder atroute, the betere an ayse to beo.[3]
545   For sothe ichulle yeou telle of a ferliche wonder: *marvellous*
Aungles comen evereche day right abouten ondern,   *Angels; mid-morning*
And nomen swithe softeliche the Marie Maudelein   *very gently*

---

[1] *To come and go in his (Maximus's) presence and do what he asked them*

[2] *The Magdalen, without difficulty, they found in ceremonial vestments there*

[3] *Under which any animal (beast) might take refuge, in order to rest better*

And beren hire op into the lofte, and broughten hire eft agein.   *carried; air; back*
Men nusten hou heo leovede, for no man ne saigh hire ete;   *lived; saw*
550   Ake some huy onderstoden that heo livede bi aungelene mete.   *But; angels' food*
A preost thare was in Marcilie that wilned swithe muche   *desired*
For to leden elinge lif, the betere fram sunne him wite.   *solitary; [to] guard himself*
He maude him a woniingue in that wildernesse   *dwelling*
Thare Marie, the swete Maudeleine, wonede in clennesse.   *purity*
555   He ne bulde nought fram Marie bote a wel luyte mile;   *only a scant mile*
For to quemen God he it dude, and He yeld wel is hwile.   *please; repaid; his effort*
He hadde wunder for that he saigh that the aungles comen ofte
Aboute onderne eche daye, ase he stod in is crofte,   *mid-morning; small garden*
And hou huy beren the Maudeleyne an hei opon lofte,   *carried; on high in the air*
560   And also hou huy broughten hire agein and setten hire adoun wel softe.   *gently*
The preost aros opon a day and wende neor the stude;   *near the place*
He wolde iwite hwat he isaigh, and tharefore he it dude.   *wanted to know; saw*
To thulke stude he cam so neigh, al bote a stones caste;   *stone's throw*
Tho bigonne hise theon to schrinke and to croki swithe faste;   *thighs; contract; bend*
565   Adrad he was and turnde agein, and so he moste nede —   *Afraid; back*
Ne kneu he nought the Maudeleyne ne hire guode dedes.
Eftsone he yeode him thudeward, is fiet bigonne folde,   *Again; in that direction; falter*
His heorte and his inneward him gonnen al to colde;   *turn cold*
He thoughte it was sum derne thing othur som holi priveté,   *hidden; secret*
570   Icomen fram the Hevene King, that he ne scholde it nought iseo.[1]
He sat adoun opon is kneon and bad ore Loverd there   *knees*
That he moste iwite and seon hwat that feorlich were.   *know; see; marvel*
He gradde on eornest and on game, "Thou best in thine celle,
Ich halsni thee a Godes name of thi stat that thou me telle!"[2]
575   Heo bigan to tellen wordes him agein:
"I segge it thee for sothe: ich am Marie Maudeleyn,
That to the Kingue of Heove of mine sunnes ich me schrof,   *made confession*
And foule develene seovene out of me He drof.   *seven foul devils*
Ich habbe iwoned nouthe here fulle thritti yer,   *dwelled; all of*
580   Ake I ne saigh nevere no man thus neigh bote thee nouthe her.   *so near; here*
Of nothing that ani man of the eorthe evere biswonk   *earthly man; prepared*

---

[1] *Come from the King of Heaven, that he was not supposed to see*

[2] Lines 573–74: *He cried seriously and playfully (i.e., in all ways), "You creature (beast) in your cell, / I adjure you in the name of God to tell me about your mode of existence"*

The Legend of Mary Magdalen, Penitent and Apostle

I ne et, seththe ich hidere cam, no mete, ne no drunch ne dronk; *ate; drink*
Godes aungles everech day habbe me here inome *angels*
An ibore me alnewey, hwane I scholde come, *every time*
585 An heigh to Heovene lofte, evere hwane I ete scholde, *needed to eat*
And hidere agein wel softe hwane ich misulf wolde. *myself wished*
   "Ich halsni thee a Godes name that thou wende to Marcilie, *adjure; in God's name*
And with mine freond withoute blame loke wel that thou spilie. *friends; talk*
Thou gret wel Martha, mi soster, ofte and mi brother Lazarus, *greet*
590 And also gret ofte swithe wel thene Bischop Maximus,
And seie hem wel ichulle comen a Sonenday at eve, *tell; on Sunday*
With heom for to wonie and evere with heom bileve — *dwell; remain*
For I schal to Paradis newene fram heom fare, *soon*
Ake mi bodi, for sothe iwis, bileve schal with heom thare.
595 Seighe heom that huy kepen me aftur the midnighte, *Say [to]; [should] await*
For thare ich hopie for to beo thoru Godes swete mighte." *hope*
   This holie preost him wende forth and dude hire herinde anon *errand*
To the Bischop Maximus, ase heo bad him don.
The holie Bischop Maximus was glad of that sonde, *message (sending)*
600 And for that tithingue he thonkede God and to Him heold up is honde. *news (tiding)*
Hire soster and hire brother weren tharof wel fayn: *very glad about it*
"Nou comez oure maister sone, the Marie Maudeleyn." *master*
   Of this ilke tythingues huy weren swithe glad
That huy hadden iheord, ake some weren ofdrad
605 That huy bitrayde weren; ake the bischop Maximus *deceived*
Wuste wel that hit was sothz; to seon hire he was joyous, *true; see*
And to witen hire stat everechdel he was wel corajous.[1]
For to seon thane messager thene Sonen-nyght he wakede *Sunday; kept watch*
And al nyght was in heore queor, and his oresones he makede; *their choir; prayers*
610 Bifore the heighe auter ore Loverd he bad that he moste iseo *altar; might*
The Maudeleynes face, that he the gladdore mighte beo. *the more glad*
   Sone aftur the midnight, are ani koc him creu, *before any cock crowed*
Thare cam a wonder muche light, ake no wynd thare ne bleu: *marvellously great*
The aungles comen fram Heovene and broughten the Marie,
615 Huy seiden the Salmus Seovene and the Letanie. *Seven Psalms; Litany*
Fram the eorthe huy gonne hire holden swithe longue stounde, *upheld; time*
The hwyle heo makede hire preyere, and seththe lieten hire to grounde. *lowered*

---

[1] *And he was very eager to know all about her way of life*

Tho cam wit hire swuch a smul among heom everechon,   *[sweet] smell*

In churche, in halle, and in bour, that swuch ne smulden huy never er non.[1]

620   The bischop for the muchele liight and for that swote smullingue   *great*

Sumdel tharefore he was aferd, and a luyte him drough bihinde.   *drew back*

Marie turnede, of wordes freo and of vilenie quiit and sker,

And seide, "Fader, hwy wolt thou thi doughter fleo? Abid, and cum me ner!"[2]

He saigh hire neb and turnde agein, so bright so sonnebem,   *face; as bright as*

625   Of that swete Maudeleine, so liight so ani leom.   *as light as any flame*

Heo saide, "Fader Maximus, par seinte charité,   *for holy charity*

Schrift and hosel ich yuyrne — sone thou graunte it me!"[3]

Huy cleopeden alle the preostes and the clerkus everechon   *called*

And alle the othur ministres, and duden hire wille anon.

630   Heo it aveng wepinde with guod devotion,   *received [the sacrament]; weeping*

And wel sore sichinde heo lay hiresulf adoun,   *sighing*

And seide, "Jhesu, that deidest opon the treo, al mi stat thou wost;   *condition; know*

Into thine hondene ich bitake thee mi liif and mi gost."   *commit to you; spirit*

Anon right heo gaf up hire liif and hire gost, iwis.   *spirit*

635   Heo was ilad withouten strif anon right to Paradys.   *taken; opposition*

The bischope thoughte murie and the clerkes echon,   *rejoiced*

And anon right gonne hire burien in a marbreston.   *marble casket/tomb*

Seve night thareafturward that day that heo ibured was,[4]

Night and day that smul was thare — it was a wonder cas.   *a marvelous event*

640   The bischop thoughte murie and bad, hwane he ded were,   *rejoiced; prayed*

That men him scholden burien bisiden hire right there.

Of the Maudeleine this is the righte endingue.   *proper conclusion*

God us schilde fram peyne and to Heovene us bringue! AMEN.   *protect; torment*

---

[1] *In church, in hall, and in chamber, that they had never smelled anything like it anywhere*

[2] Lines 622–23: *Mary turned, gracious in speech and without the least hint of discourtesy, / And said,*
"Father, why do you want to flee from your daughter? Stay, and come nearer to me!"

[3] *I long for absolution and the Eucharist — grant it to me soon!*

[4] *For seven days after her burial*

Explanatory Notes to Early South English Legendary
Life of Mary Magdalen

Abbreviations: **A** = Auchinleck (National Library of Scotland MS Advocates 19.2.1), fols. 62r–65v; **L** = Bodleian Library MS Laud Misc. 108 (*SC* 1486), fols. 190r–197r [base text]; **T** = Trinity College, Cambridge MS 605, fols. 127v–133r.

1–10   This opening uses the conventions of oral delivery, most obviously when it urges listeners to pay attention (lines 1–2 and 9–10). It also suggests that the audience it envisions is more accustomed to romances than to saints' legends — hence the mentions of typical romance subjects, such as the heroism of noblemen (line 5), which it is not going to treat.

11–16   *This word "Marie . . ."* This etymology of Mary's name derives, probably quite indirectly, from St. Jerome's *Liber de nominibus hebraicis*.

17   *the Castel of Magdalé.* Latin versions of this legend use the noun *castellum*, in this context probably meaning "town" or "village." But the anachronistic image of a late-medieval castle goes well with the other romance conventions in the ensuing account of Mary's family background: the titles given to her parents (line 20), the little catalog suggesting their royal lineage and landed wealth (lines 23–26), and their rich endowment of their children when they die (lines 30–34).

20   *Sire Titus . . . Dame Euchirie.* The name of Mary's father is generally given in medieval sources as "Syrus," perhaps because his supposed homeland was Syria. As David Mycoff points out, the name of Mary's mother, "Eucharia," probably comes from a Greek word for "thanksgiving" (Caxton, *A Critical Edition*, p. 155n51–55).

27   *Large huy weren.* The phrase introduces the ideal of generosity to those in need, an ideal that resembles the familiar aristocratic virtue of "noblesse" but will be extended much further in this text.

40   *Is names seovene.* The MED (*name* n. 2a. [c]) conjectures that this phrase might refer to the name "Jesus Christ" plus the six names in Isaiah 9: "Wonderful," "Counselor," etc.

47–48   *the Betanie.* Bethany, the town near Jerusalem mentioned in the Gospels as the home of Martha, Mary, and Lazarus. *Genezarez* is presumably Gennesaret, a narrow plain bordering the Sea of Galilee, which is mentioned in other versions of the legend only in reference to the location of Magdala. Taking it as part of the family property may be a misunderstanding peculiar to this Middle English version of the legend.

53–54   The narrative suggests that Mary added to her inherited wealth by becoming a kind of high-class prostitute, whose favors were reserved for rich men who gave her lavish gifts.

55–62   This version of the legend seems to be criticizing the youthful selfishness of Lazarus as well as Mary, setting their tendency to follow their own inclinations against the better example of Martha, who responsibly looks after the family property and uses the proceeds to feed and clothe the poor people who depend on them.

79–136   The Gospels give three different accounts of the dinner or dinners at which a woman anoints Jesus with precious ointment. In Luke 7:36–50 Jesus is dining in the house of Simon the Pharisee and the woman is a penitent who washes his feet with her tears before anointing them. Since she is a well-known sinner in this account, the issue is whether Jesus should tolerate the ministrations of such a person. In Matthew 26:6–13, on the other hand, Jesus's host is called Simon the Leper, the woman (who pours the ointment over his head) is not particularly sinful, and the issue is the extravagance of her gesture, which scandalizes the disciples. The version in John 12:2–8 is much like that in Matthew except that Simon is no longer mentioned, the anonymous woman is now identified as Martha's sister Mary, and the protest comes only from Judas, who pretends the money should have gone to the poor but actually just covets it for himself.

        This version of the legend follows the account in Luke for almost all the details in lines 79–98, switches to John for Judas's protest and Jesus's response (lines 99–108), and then returns to Luke for the dialogue between Jesus and Simon (lines 109–36).

117–24   This version of the parable about the money-lender and his two debtors is significantly different from the version in the Gospel (Luke 7:41–43). There the first debtor owed ten times as much as the second and the moneylender forgave both debts, allowing Jesus to point out that the debtor who was forgiven more should logically respond with more gratitude and love to the money-lender he once feared. In the Middle English retelling here, on the other hand, the debts are said to be nearly the same size, both debtors evidently pay up when required to do so, and the lesson seems to be that the measure of one's love for God is how much one repays Him rather than how much one has been forgiven by Him. Perhaps the poet or scribe has simply misunderstood the point of the story. But the emphasis on generous human repayment of debts to God is quite consistent with the unusual focus on almsgiving that runs throughout this text.

138   *seve develene.* The exorcism is mentioned in Luke 8:2: "And [with Jesus were] certain women who had been healed of evil spirits and infirmities; Mary, who is called Magdalen, out of whom seven devils were gone forth, [and others]" (Douay-Rheims, Challoner rev.; all Biblical citations come from this edition).

141–46   The source behind this tradition about the healing of Martha is the story of the woman with the hemorrhage in Mark 5:25–34, Matthew 9:20–22, and Luke 8:43–48. According to Mycoff, the identification of that woman with Mary's sister Martha seems first to have been made in a sermon that was once attributed (erroneously) to St. Ambrose (*Life of Saint Mary Magdalene*, p. 124).

147   *Lazarus was swythe sikel a man.* With this opening, one expects the passage to continue with the famous Biblical story of Lazarus's death and his resurrection by Jesus (John 11:1–44); but both L and its nearest relative, T, leave that story untold and proceed instead to discuss the siblings' exemplary hospitality to Jesus and his disciples. The transition is so abrupt that one assumes there must have been an error in their common exemplar — perhaps something as simple as writing "sike" instead of "riche" because the scribe was expecting another miracle story at this point.

157   *Aftur that He was iwend.* Although the chronology here is not very clear, the idea seems to be that Mary was sent out to preach even during Jesus' lifetime, as the male apostles were (Mark 6:7–13; Matthew 10:1, 5–15; Luke 10:1–20). This claim would have few if any precedents, according to Mycoff (see Caxton, *A Critical Edition*, p. 91).

163–68   The beginning of this persecution and the martyrdom of Stephen are related in Acts 6:8–8:4. An early tradition assigned the division of the apostles and the beginning of their individual journeys as missionaries to the fourteenth (not usually the thirteenth) year after the Crucifixion.

166   *that Cristes limes were.* An echo of Paul's description of the Church as the body of Christ, an idea developed most fully in 1 Corinthians 12:12–27.

169   *Seint Maximus.* St. Maximinus or Maximin, who supposedly became the first bishop of Aix, in Provence. This was an easy name for medieval scribes to misread or miswrite because of all the minims, and the alternative forms "Maximus" and "Maximius" are quite common.

170   *Sixti ant ten deciples.* Other versions of the legend, including the one in the *Legenda aurea*, clearly identify Maximinus as one of the seventy or seventy-two disciples personally chosen by Jesus (Luke 10:1). Here he seems to be the leader of that large a group.

182   *Everech of heom othur schrof.* That is, they heard each others' confessions — presumably to help each other prepare for the possibility of an imminent death.

187   *one olde porche.* In other versions of the legend, including the *Legenda aurea* and its adaptations, the place where they take shelter is specifically identified as the portico of an old temple. Hence it makes sense when pagans start arriving to offer sacrifices the next morning (lines 199–200, below).

194   *Sarasins.* The term *Saracen*, which originally designated Syrian or Arabian nomads who raided the borders of the Roman Empire, was used loosely and anachronistically in medieval and early modern literature to refer to almost any kind of pagan or infidel who had ever attacked Christians. There are many additional examples in the stanzaic lives of St. Margaret and St. Katherine, below.

205   *Mahun.* The name *Mahoun(d),* a corruption of "Mohammed," was often used as the name of a pagan god in medieval texts.

    Tervagaunt. The name of a fictitious deity, supposedly worshiped by pagans or Saracens.

230   Instead of attributing Mary's success as a preacher to her beauty, as this version does, her legend tends to credit her with a special kind of persuasiveness, rooted in her close, loving relationship with Jesus. The *Legenda aurea*, for example, gives

this explanation: "All who heard her were in admiration at her beauty, her eloquence, and the sweetness of her message . . . and no wonder, that the mouth which had pressed such pious and beautiful kisses on the Savior's feet should breathe forth the perfume of the word of God more profusely than others could" (Jacobus de Voragine, trans. Ryan, 1.376–77).

247–48   The specificity of the threats here and in lines 261–62 sets this version of the scene apart from those in most other versions of the legend. More typically, Mary Magdalen just warns the prince and his wife of God's anger, leaving the nature of the threatened punishment to their (and the readers') imaginations.

255–56   Mary's startling denunciations of the prince and his wife, calling them instruments and children of the devil, suggest the depth of her anger — and God's — at their continued selfishness when Christ's people are homeless and miserable.

283–86   Her deference to Peter at this point is expressed more clearly and emphatically in the *Legenda aurea* version: "I am ready indeed to defend [the faith I preach]," she replied, "because my faith is strengthened by the daily miracles and preaching of my teacher Peter, who presides in Rome" (Jacobus de Voragine, trans. Ryan, 1.377).

324–30   This speech portrays the queen's position much more fully and sympathetically than is customary in other retellings of the legend. The Auchinleck version (MS A), for example, neglects to explain why she is so upset: "'For al love, leman,' sche seyd, / 'Lete now that will be doun aleyd!' / Sche wepe and crid and prayd him so / That he graunt hir with him to go" (lines 265–68). And the *Legenda aurea* just gives a summary that sounds quite disapproving: "But she insisted, doing as women do. She threw herself at his feet, weeping the while, and in the end won him over" (Jacobus de Voragine, trans. Ryan, 1.378).

334–36   In some versions of the legend she places a visible emblem of the Cross on their shoulders, marking them in effect as pilgrims bound for the Holy Land. In this text Peter does that for the prince (see line 410, below).

341–44   The little catalog of aristocratic food in these lines is a distinctive feature of L. Even the retelling in MS A, which resembles it most closely at this point, refers only in general terms to how richly their ship was provisioned: "A schippe thai gun to purvayen, / And richelich within to laien / Of al thing that hem nede stode" (lines 269–71).

368   The superstition of the sea's refusal to hold a dead body is ancient. See the Latin *Historia Apolloni Regis Tyri*, in Elizabeth Archibald, *Apollonius of Tyre: Medieval and Renaissance Themes and Variations, Including the Text of Historia Apolloni Regis Tyri with an English Translation* (Cambridge, UK: D.S. Brewer, 1991), appendix 1. Gower picks up the detail in his telling of the tale in *CA* 8.1089 ff. The point seems to be that since the sea will cast ashore a dead body, a corpse must be cast out of a ship lest the ship itself be cast ashore as well. See *Confessio Amantis*, ed. Russell A. Peck (Kalamazoo: Medieval Institute Publications, 2000), vol. 1, pp. 222–23, and notes to lines 271 ff. (pp. 328–29) and 1089 ff. (p. 337).

401   The line can be translated in several different ways, since the verb *sende* may be either present subjunctive or preterite, and *wolden* (a plural verb form) seems to conflict with the pronoun subject *he*. Does it mean "May God send them to Rome, for that is where He wanted [them to go]," or "God sent them to Rome, for that is where they wanted — or He wanted them — [to go]"?

405   Since the prince is presumably already in Rome, it would seem more logical for him to identify his destination as Jerusalem.

410   *creoysede.* According to the MED, the taking of this emblem often signified a pledge either to engage in a crusade or to go on pilgrimage to the Holy Land.

436–37   A reference to the Harrowing of Hell: the traditional belief that Christ's soul descended into hell when He died, defeated Satan, and freed the souls of all the faithful people of Israel who died too soon to be saved by faith in Christ.

442   *his Bileve.* This term could refer either in general to a body of religious doctrine or more specifically to the Creed — a single text that summarizes the key tenets of the faith. Given the references to other texts in the next line, the latter possibility seems the more likely.

443   *His Oures and is Sauter.* Since the prince is a layman, the "Hours" he is credited with learning would probably be the Little Office of the Virgin Mary — a much briefer and simpler set of daily prayers and devotions than the Daily Office performed by monks and other members of the clergy. He would probably not learn the whole Psalter either, but just the psalms recited regularly as part of the Little Office.

451   Peter assures him that he will not be violating his earlier vow (line 312) if he delays baptism until his return to his own kingdom.

455   *ne thinche thee nought to longue!* Peter urges him not to be distressed at the delay.

478   *worldes fiere.* That is, the partner of her life in this world.

492   *houswif.* Mary Magdalen's role as "housewife" would have been to keep the queen and her child supplied with the necessities of daily life. Other versions of the legend, including that in MS A, credit her instead with serving as the queen's midwife when the child was born.

501   The idea may be that it would have been scandalous for the queen to be seen making this pilgrimage without her husband or another male protector.

516–18   The point seems to be that the Christians are no longer afraid of being persecuted by their pagan neighbors for publicly associating with the bishop.

528   That is, Mary, Martha, and Lazarus act as their baptismal sponsors or godparents, as foreseen by St. Peter in lines 452–54.

533–38   The process of conversion is envisioned here in institutional terms: building churches and monastic communities throughout the prince's kingdom, ordaining priests and other kinds of clerics to staff them, and consecrating bishops to oversee the local churches.

537   According to tradition, Lazarus became the first bishop of Marseilles.

539 ff.   The legend of Mary Magdalen's thirty years of contemplative solitude in the wilderness seems to have been adapted in the early Middle Ages from the legend of Mary of Egypt, a repentant prostitute who withdrew to the desert. Mycoff gives translations of both legends in *The Life of Saint Mary Magdalene*.

591   *Sonenday.* In other versions of the legend, including Mirk's, her promised return takes place specifically on Easter.

602   *oure maister.* In this context, the phrase could mean that they are acknowledging her as their leader, their spiritual guide and instructor, their model, and/or their superior in knowledge, skill, or courage. It is a dramatic moment in the text, since

the term *maister* was rarely applied in a positive sense to a woman; even the closest relative of L, T, does not include this line. After this line, however, Martha and Lazarus conspicuously disappear from the narrative, leaving Maximinus alone to welcome Mary back to the Christian community she helped to establish.

604–05   This reference to fear of betrayal or deception may just mean that some people could not believe she was returning, after a thirty-year absence, but it also hints at the possibility of some rupture between Maximinus (whose position is strengthened by Mary's return and affirmation of his pastoral authority) and other members of the community.

608–11   Maximinus waits for her in the sanctuary of the church, praying all night before the high altar.

615   *the Salmus Seovene and the Letanie.* Both the seven penitential Psalms — Vulgate nos. 6, 31, 37, 50, 101, 129, and 142 — and the Litany, a solemn prayer with set responses, were prescibed for recitation on behalf of the dying and the dead, as well as for regular church services on penitential occasions.

618–19   On the odor of sanctity, see 2 Corinthians 2:14–15, Revelation 5:8, Philippians 4:18, and Ephesians 5:2. Compare the miraculous fragrance of the roses and lilies in Chaucer's Second Nun's Tale, *CT* VII(G)246–52.

627   *Schrift and hosel.* That is, she asks Maximinus to give her the last rites of the Church before she dies.

633   Her final prayer closely echoes the last words of Jesus on the cross, as recorded in Luke 23:46.

638–39   See explanatory note for lines 618–19.

642   *the righte endingue.* As this assertion suggests, there were competing accounts of where and how Mary Magdalen died. This version explicitly and emphatically enfolds her within St. Maximin's monastic community at Aix, reinforcing the claim of that abbey that her relics belonged there, in the place she herself had chosen. See the *Speculum Sacerdotale*, below, lines 55–67, for a competing tradition which undercuts this claim, having her die in an anonymous church after receiving the sacrament from an anonymous priest.

Textual Notes to Early South English Legendary
Life of Mary Magdalen

Abbreviations: see explanatory notes.

[The scribe of L has the peculiar habit of writing *ȝh* (yogh + *h*), which I have transcribed throughout as *gh*.]

11	*brightnesse.* L: *brighnesse.*
43–44	These two lines are written as a single, extended line in the manuscript.
78	*heo.* Emended from *he*, the form used in L at this point (and also below in lines 84, 87, 159, and 541). The pronoun *he* could mean either "he" or "she" in some dialects of early Middle English, but the scribe who copied this manuscript generally prefers *heo* for the feminine — making a distinction that also clarifies the text for modern readers. At least once (at line 138, below) he over-corrects, writing "heo" for a masculine "he."
104	*of drunch and of mete.* An early correction in the margin of L suggests replacing these five words with *to drinke and to ete*. The replacement would avoid rhyming lines 103 and 104 on the same word, but at the expense of relatively unnatural syntax.
118	*beyne.* Corrected in L from *beye*.
124	*gaf.* Apparently corrected in L from *gat*.
128	*heres.* Corrected in L from *here*.
130	*smeordest.* L: *smeredest smeordest*, with the latter form presumably intended to replace the former.
138	*He.* L: *heo* — an obvious error which strengthens the likelihood that the scribe was copying from a version of the text which used *he* for both the masculine and feminine forms of the pronoun.
160	*was.* L: *wa.*
189	*old hous.* L: *hold hous*, with the first *h* dotted for omission.
192	*gret.* L: *gre.*
204	The scribe has omitted or completely erased the rhyme word, which must have been something like *here* ("heir" — or "army, host").
261	*strong.* L: *stronk.*
269–70	These two lines are written as a single, extended line in the manuscript.

279 *heo*. Corrected in L itself from *he*.

298 *nothing*. L: *nothinging*.

306 *and gonne*. L: *a gonne*.

309 *redes*. Corrected in L from *dedes*.

312 *fullouht*. L: *fulloutht*, with the first *t* dotted for omission.

329 *wore*. Corrected in L from *were*.

332 *hire*. Corrected in L from *him*.

336 *sorowe*. L: *seoruwe*, with the first *e* dotted for omission.

337 *huy*. Emended from L: *heo*, an obvious error.

359 *thet child*. This portion of the text uses a number of inflected forms of the definite article, preserved from Old English — including *that* or *thet* with the neuter nouns *child* (here and below at lines 361, 385), "flod" (line 368), and "bodi" (lines 369, 371).

365 *hath it*. Emended from L: *hath i*.

367 *hieten*. Corrected in L from *hiete*.

371 *that dede bodi*. Emended from L, which has *thad* for *that*. See textual note to line 359.

388 *thet*. Corrected in L from *the*.

405 *then wey*. Another relic of earlier English grammar. The noun *wey* was masculine in Old English, and *then(e)* preserves the ending of the masculine singular accusative form of the definite article. There are similar examples in lines 426 ("thene riche man") and 427 ("thene wey"). Compare textual note to line 85 of the longer *SEL* Life of St. Frideswide, above.

418 *They thy*. Emended from L, which omits *thy*.

425 *ofte*. Emended from L: *of*.

465 *as*. L: *a*.

466 *he*. Inserted between lines in L.

481 *child*. L: *chil*.

488 *seide*. Omitted from L, though the context demands such a verb.

   space. Corrected in L from *grace*.

492 *houswif*. L: *hou wif*.

493 *seide*. Omitted from L, though the context demands it.

523 *tok*. L: *tok tok*.

John Mirk, *Sermon on St. Mary Magdalen,*
from British Library MS Cotton Claudius A.ii, fols. 91v–93v

Gode men, suche a day [N] ye schul have the feste of Mary Magdalé, that was
so holy that oure Lorde Jhesu Criste aftur Hys modur He lovid hir moste of alle
wommen. Wherefore ye schal comyn to the chyrch that day to worchep God and
this holy womman, for scheo was the furste in tyme of grace that dud penaunce
5 for hyr synnes, and so recovred ageyne grace be doing of penaunce, and repentyng
that scheo hadde loste be luste of the flesse and so synnyng. The wyche is made
a myrroure to alle synful to schewon how alle that wollon levon hur synne, and
done penaunce for hur trespace, thei schul recovre grace ageyn that thei have
loste and ofte myche more. An so dude this womman, and how ye schul here.
10 This womman Mary Magdaleyne hadde a fadur that was a grete lorde and comyn
of kyngus blode, and hadde grete lordeschep in Jerusalem, the wyche he gaf at
hys dying to Lazarus hys sone. And the lordschep that he hadde in Betanye, he gaf
to Martha, hys doghtor. Magdaleyn Castele wyth alle the lordschep he gaf to
Mary, hys other doghtyr, of the whyche castel scheo was callyd Mary Magdaleyne,
15 for scheo was lady therof. Than, as many bokys tellyth, whan John Evangeliste
schulde have weddyd hyr, Criste hadde John sewond Hym, and lyvon in
maydenhed; and so he dud. Herfore Mary was wroth and gaf hyr al to synne and
namely to lechery, insomyche that scho loste the name of Magdaleyne and was
kallyd the synful womman. Than, for it was often seyne that Cryste of the gresteyste

1 **suche a day**, on such and such a day [to be inserted by the speaker]. 3 **comyn**, come.
4 **dud**, did. 5 **be**, by. 6 **that scheo hadde . . . flesse**, what she had lost by (following) the
desire(s) of the flesh; **The wyche**, who (that is, she). 7 **alle synful**, all sinful [people];
schewon, show; **levon**, desist from. 8 **done**, do. 9 **An**, And; **and how ye schul here**, and
you shall hear how (all this came about). 10–11 **comyn of**, descended from. 11–12 **the
wyche . . . dying**, which he gave at his death. 16 **sewond**, follow. 17 **maydenhed**, virginity; **dud**, did; **Herfore**, For this reason; **gaf hyr al**, gave herself entirely. 18 **namely**,
especially. 19 **kallyd**, called; **gresteyste**, greatest.

20 synnerres He made the moste holy aftyr, wherfore whan He seygh tyme, He gaf this womman grace to knowyn hyrself and repentaunce of hur mysdedus.

Then, whan scheo herde that Cryste was atte the mete in a mannus houce that was kalled Symond the Pharasen, scheo toke a boyste wyth oynement, such os men usenden in that cuntré for hete of the sonne, and yode thidur. But for scheo

25 durste note for schame gon before Cryste, scheo yode behynde Hym, and toke Hys fette in hyr handes; and for sorow that scheo hadde in hur herte, scheo wepte so tendurly, that the terus of hur heyen woschon Cristes fette; than wyth hyr fayre fax sche wypud hem aftur; and than wyth alle the love that was in hyr herte, scheo cussyd Hys fette and so wyth hyr box anoynted hem. Bot no worde spake scheo

30 that man myght here, bot softely in hyr herte heghly scheo cried to Criste of mercy, and made a vow to Hym that scheo wolde nevre trespace more. Than hadde Criste compassion of hur, an clensed hur of seven fendes the whyche scheo hadde wythinne hur, and forgaf hur alle hur gylte of synne in herryng of alle that there weron.

35 Than for joy that scheo was thus delyverhud of the devellys bondys, scheo toke suche a tendur love to Cryste, that evre aftur sche was gladde and fayne to leven alle hur ladyschep and sewon Hym ay forth wyth so fervent love, that in Hys passion thereas Hys disciplus flowen away from Hym for drede of the deth, scheo lafte Hym nevre tyl scheo wyth othyr hadde layde Hym in Hys tombe. And

40 whan no man durste go thyddur for the armyd knytus that kep the tombe, scheo spared for no drede of lyf ne deth, bot in the dark dawyng toke wyth hur swete bawmus and yod thidor to have bawmet Crystus body. Thus scheo lovid Criste bothe levyng and dede.

---

20 seygh, saw. **22 atte . . . houce that**, at dinner in the house of a man who. **23 Pharasen**, Pharisee; **boyste wyth oynement**, jar of ointment; **os**, as. **24 usenden**, used; **for₁**, because of; **yode**, went. **25 durste note**, dared not. **26 fette**, feet. **27 terus**, tears; **heyen**, eyes; **woschon**, washed. **28 fax**, hair; **wypud**, dried. **29 cussyd**, kissed; **box**, jar [of ointment]. **30 heghly**, earnestly. **32 an**, and; **fendes**, devils (fiends). **33 herryng**, the hearing. **33–34 there weron**, were present. **35 delyverhud**, delivered. **36 fayne**, eager. **37 sewon**, follow; **ay forth**, from then on. **38 flowen**, fled. **39 othyr**, others. **40 durste**, dared; **for**, for fear of; **kep**, guarded. **41 spared**, held back; **dawyng**, dawn. **42 bawmus**, balms; **yod**, went; **bawmet**, embalmed. **43 levyng**, living.

45   Wherefore He, yytte in Hys lyve, for love of hur He helyd Martha, hur systur, of the rede flux that payned hur seven yere, and also reysyd hur brother Lazar from deth to lyfe, aftur he hadde layne foure dayes stynkyng in hys grave. And whan He rosse from deth to lyfe, He aperud to hur bodyly furste of alle othyr and suffred hur to touche Hym an cussyn Hys fette.

50   Than, for it was knowen to Jewes that Cryste schewod hur so many synus of love before many othyr, aftur that Cryste was steyed up to Heven, the Jewes tokon Mary Magdaleyne, Martha hur systur, and Lazarus and Sent Maximius, a byschop, and many othur, and dyden hem alle in an old schyppe, and putthyn hem into the see, hopyng so to a drowned hem alle. Bot God that ordeneth for alle aftur Hys lust, He broght hem alle holle and sounde to the londe of Marcile. There, undyr a

55   bonke that was nygh a tempul, thei tokyn here reste. Than see Magdaleyn grete pepul comyng towarde this tempul and the lorde of that cuntré to han done offering and sacrifice to here mawmentis. But Magdaleyne was so ful of grace of the Holy Goste, that scheo be hur gracious wordys turned hem alle ageyne hom. And for this lorde sethe hyr ful of alle swetnesse and gentryes, he had grete luste to

60   heren hyr spekyn and sayde thus to hur, "If thi God that thou prechyst of is so grete of mythe as thou sayste, pray to Hym that I may have a chylde be my wyf that is bareyne, and I wyl leven on Hym." Than graunted Magdaleyne; and so wythinne a schorte tyme the lady conseyvid and was wyth chylde.

      Than schappode this lorde to gone to Jerusalem, to speke wyth Seynte Petur

65   and wytte whether it where sothe that Magdaleyne prechud othour no. And whanne he hadde vytaylyd schyppus and made alle redy, than come the lady hys wyfe, praying wepyng that scheo moste wende wyth hym, thogh scheo were grete

---

44 yytte in Hys lyve, while He was still alive; **helyd**, healed. **45 rede flux**, flow of blood; **payned**, afflicted; **reysyd**, raised. **47 rosse**, arose; **bodyly**, in the flesh. **48 suffred**, allowed; **an cussyn**, and kiss. **49 schewod**, showed; **synus**, signs/proofs. **50 steyed up**, ascended. **52 dyden hem**, put them. **53 to a drowned**, to have drowned; **ordeneth**, ordains; **aftur**, according to. **54 lust**, pleasure; **holle**, whole. **55 bonke**, bank; **see**, saw. **55–56 grete pepul**, a great crowd. **57 mawmentis**, idols. **58 ageyne hom**, against them (the idols). **59 sethe**, saw (lit., sees); **gentryes**, nobility; **luste**, pleasure. **61 grete of mythe**, powerful. **62 leven**, believe. **64 schappode**, planned. **65 whether . . . othour no**, whether what Magdalen preached was true or not. **66 vytaylyd**, provisioned [with food]. **67 moste wende**, be allowed to go.

wyth schylde. And so wyth grete strenth of praying scheo gate graunte. Than, wyth bothe assente, thei betokyn alle hor godys to Magdaleyne to kepon; and

70 scheo sette on eyther of hyr schyldyr a crosse, and badde hem wende forth in the name of God. Bot whan thei hadde ryved a day and a nyght, than gan the see to swellen, and the wynde sternely to blowen, and suche a tempeste to ryson that thei wendon alle to han ben spylled. Wherefore this lady was so afryght that scheo began to travayle of chylde, and so anone was delyvered of a knave schylde. And

75 scheo in the burthe fel doun and dyod.

Than, whan the fadyr saw hys wyf dedde and the chylde borne and graspyng towarde the modur pappes, he began to wepe and wrynggyd hys handys and was so sore and so woo on uche syde that he ne wyste whatte he mythe done. Wondyr sory he was for hys wyfes deth, and nedys he moste sene hys schylde dyen, for

80 ther was no wommanus sokur for to helpon hym. And than cryed he to Mary Magdaleyne and sayde, "Allas, Mary Magdeleyne, why duste thou thus harde wyth me? Thou behettyst me a chylde, bot now is his modyr ded and it moste nedys dyen, for it hath no helpe, and I myselvyn am redy to be drowned. Help now, lady, and have compassyon of me, and namely of the chylde that is borne!"

85 Than toke the schypmen the dede body, and wolde han caste hyr into see, and saydon thei schuldon have no rest whyl the cors was in the schyppe. Than seyde he ful helte, "Scheo is not dede bot swowned for drede. Wherefore bryngge the schyppe to yondur schare for of myne cost, that I may rather gravyn hyr than caste hur into the watur to be drownyd and devowred of cursyd bestys." Than toke he

90 this cors and bare it up. And for ther was none erthe to makyn a grave, he leyde it

68 **schylde**, child; **graunte**, permission. 69 **bothe assente**, mutual agreement; **betokyn**, entrusted; **godys**, possessions. 70 **eyther**, each; **schyldyr**, shoulders. 71 **ryved**, journeyed. 73 **wendon . . . spylled**, all expected to be killed. 74 **began to travayle**, went into labor; **knave schylde**, baby boy. 75 **dyod**, died. 77 **modur pappes**, mother's breasts; **wrynggyd**, wrung. 78 **on uche syde**, on both accounts; **mythe done**, could do; **Wondyr**, Terribly. 79 **nedys . . . dyen**, he must inevitably see his child die. 80 **wommanus sokur**, woman's assistance. 81 **duste thou thus harde**, do you deal so cruelly. 82 **behettyst**, promised. 82–83 **moste nedys dyen**, must inevitably die. 84 **namely**, especially. 85 **wolde han caste**, wanted to throw. 86 **cors**, corpse. 87 **helte**, confidently. 88 **schare for of myne cost**, projecting rock before us, at my expense; **gravyn**, bury. 90 **for ther was none erthe**, since there was no dirt.

undir a hongyng skare and the schylde wyth, and hylled hem wyth a mantyl that
he betoke Mary Mawdeleyne to kepon, and yode ageyne to the scheppe wyth
wrngyng hys handys and wondur sore herte.

Than, whan he cam to Jerusalem, Seynt Petur was redy and welcomyd hym and
95   bad he schulde not ben hevy nor discounforded, thof hys wyf were dede; for God
was of myght to makyn hym another tyme as glad os he was than sory. And so lad
hym forth and schewed hym alle the places of Crystes doing in erthe, of Cristes
nativité, of Hys passyon, of Hys sepulture, and of Hys ascencion; and so evre
formyd hym in the feyth fully. And whan he hadde ben ther too yere, Sent Petur
100   sent hym home agayne and bad hym ben in ful beleve of Criste, and gaf hym hys
blessyng and bad hym grete wel Mary Magdaleyne and alle hyre ferus.

Than, whan this lorde cam ridyng in the see, he sagh the skyrre there he lafte
hys wyfe and hys chylde. And than ther felle suche longyng in hys herte to go
thydor that hym thoght he schuld dye bot he yode thydyr. Than made he the
105   schypmen to setton the schypp thidur; and whan he cam thidur, than sawe he a
schylde syttyngge on the see-sonde, pleying wyth smale stonys as schyldron wyllon.
But whan the chylde saghe hym, he ran forth into the skyrre. Than sued the fadur
aftur and cam ther he lafte hys wyf dede, and lyft up the mantyl and fond the
schylde sokyng the modur pappes. Than thankyd he Mary Magdaleyn wyth alle
110   hys mythe and sayde, "O Mary Magdaleyne, thou arte of grete myght wyth God
that thus haste kept and fede this schylde of this dede body now too yere in grete
comforde and joy to me! Woldest thou nogh of thi godenesse reyse my wyfe to
lyfe, than were I bondon evre to be thi servaunde, and wyl wyth a ful gode wille!"

91 hongyng skare, overhanging cliff; **the schylde wyth**, the child with [it]; **hylled**,
covered. **95 discounforded, thof**, discouraged, although. **96 os**, as; **so lad**, so [Peter] led.
99 formyd hym in the feyth, instructed and strengthened him in the faith; **too**, two. **101
grete**, greet; **ferus**, companions. **102 skyrre there he lafte**, projecting rock where he
had left. **104 bot**, unless. **105 setton**, steer. **106 see-sonde**, sea shore; **as schyldron
wyllon**, as children like to do. **107 sued**, followed. **108 fond**, found. **109 sokyng the
modur pappes**, sucking the mother's breasts. **110 mythe**, strength (might). **111 fede**, fed;
of, from; **too**, two. **112 nogh**, now. **113 were I bondon**, I would be obliged (bound); **wyl**,
will [be].

Than, wyth that worde, the lady satte up and sayde, "Mary Magdaleyne, yblessyd mote thou be that was mydwyf to me in my bythe-tyme, and sythen hast norised my chylde wel and sounde whyl I have ben in my pylgrymage!"

Than sayde he, "My wyf, lyvest thou?"

And scheo answerod and sayde, "Ye, syr, I lyf, and now com oute of my pylgrymage, as ye don. For as Seynte Petur hath ladde thee abowton, so hath Mary Magdaleyne ladde me the same gate," and tolde hym alle thyng and fayled in no poynte. Than heven thei her handys up to God, and thankyd Hym and Mary Magdaleyne of that grete miracul that thei schewed in hem.

And whan thei comyn hom, thei foundon Magdaleyne prechyng the pepul. And than anone thei fellon doun to hur fette and thankud hyr wyth alle here mythe and prayd hur to telle hem whatte thei schulde done, and thei wolde wyth glade herte. Than Magdaleyn bad hem distroy the tempulles of that londe and make ther schyrches, and reron fontes that the pepul myghte be cristened. And so in schorte tyme alle the londe was turnyd to Cristen feyth.

Than, for Magdaleyne wolde gef hyr alle to contemplacion, scheo yode prively fer into wyldernesse and was ther thirty yere unknowon of alle men wythoute mete or drynke. Than, uche day seven sythes, angelus beron hyr up into the ayre, and there sche was fullud wyth melody of angellus, that hur nedud none othyr bodyly fode. Bot whan God wolde that scheo schulde passon oute of this worlde, He made an holy preste to sene how angelus beron hur up and doune. And he, for to wytton the sothe whate that was, he yode to the place and halsodde yyf there were any Cristyn creature that he schulde speken and tellyn hym whatte he were.

Than answerid Magdaleyne and sayde that scheo was a synful womman that the Gospel spake of, that whesse Crystes fette, and badde hym gone to Maxcencius

115 **mote**, may; **bythe-tyme**, delivery; **norised**, fed (nourished). 118 **Ye, syr, I lyf**, Yes, sir, I am alive. 120 **gate**, way. 120–21 **fayled in no poynte**, recounted it all accurately. 121 **heven**, raise(d). 123 **prechyng**, preaching [to]. 124 **mythe**, strength (might). 125 **schulde done**, ought to do [from then on]. 126 **tempulles**, [pagan] temples. 127 **schyrches**, churches; **reron fontes that**, build baptismal fonts so that. 129 **wolde gef hyr alle**, wanted to devote herself completely. 131 **sythes**, times. 132 **fullud**, filled. 132–33 **that hur . . . fode**, so that she needed no other bodily nourishment. 134 **sene**, see. 134–35 **for to wytton the sothe**, in order to know the truth [about]. 135 **halsodde**, called out [in greeting]. 138 **whesse**, washed; **badde hym gone**, asked him to go.

140 the byschoppe, byddyng hym that he come on Astur morowon to chyrch, "for there I wyl meton hym."

Thus whan this byschop harde this, he was ful gladde; and whan he com to chyrch, than sawe he Magdaleyne borne up wyth angelus too cubitus fro the erthe, and than he was agaste. Than Mary callyd to hym and bad hym to hyr, and gone and sayne a masse, that scheo mythe ben uselled. So in syght of alle the pepul, 145 whan masse was done, scheo wyth hye devocion reseyvid Goddys body; and anone therwyth scheo gaf up the goste. Than toke the byschop hyr body and leyde it in a tombe of stone and makyd for to graven alle aboghtyn the lyf of hur, in worchep of God, that dud so goddely be hur, and in honour of hyre and alse in heygh comforde to alle synful.

Wherefore ye schul knelon adoun etc.

139 **Astur morowon**, Easter morning. **140 meton**, meet. **142 too cubitus**, two cubits (about 3 feet). **143 agaste**, afraid; **to hyr**, to [approach] her; **gone**, to go. **144 ben uselled**, be houseled (receive the Eucharist). **147 makyd . . . lyf of hur**, had it carved on all sides with [scenes from] her life. **148 that dud so goddely be hur**, who had dealt so graciously with her; **alse**, also; **heygh**, great.

Explanatory Notes to Mirk's Sermon on St. Mary Magdalen

Abbreviations: **C** = British Library MS Cotton Claudius A.ii, fols. 91v–93v [base text]; **D** = Durham University Library MS Cosin V.III.5, fols. 118r–121v; **Dd** = Cambridge University Library MS Dd.X.50, fols. 126r–129v; **G** = Bodleian Library MS Gough Eccl. Top. 4 (*SC* 17680), fols. 116r–119r; **H 2403** = British Library MS Harley 2403, fols. 130r–133v; **H 2417** = British Library MS Harley 2417, fols. 53v–56v; **U** = University College, Oxford MS 102, pp. 195–200 (on deposit in the Bodleian Library, Oxford).

1   *Gode men.* This opening does not imply a single-sex audience. Other manuscripts make that explicit, beginning with such terms of address as *Dere frendes* (Dd), *Gode men and women* (H 2403 and H 2417), and *Crystyn men and woymen* (G).

       suche a day [N]. Evidently Mirk expected sermons for saints' days to be given on the preceding Sunday, rather than on the actual day of the saint's feast. A number of the manuscripts insert the abbreviation "N" to remind the preacher where to insert the name of the appropriate weekday.

4   *in tyme of grace.* That is, Mary is the first repentant sinner mentioned in the New Testament. The era of the law was understood to have given way to the era of grace with the birth of Jesus.

10–15   For the properties left to Mary and her siblings, see explanatory notes to lines 17 and 47–48 of the early *SEL* version.

15–17   This traditional explanation of Mary's fall is explicitly rejected by the *Legenda aurea* (Jacobus de Voragine, trans. Ryan, 1.382), partly on the grounds that Albert the Great supplied a different identity for John's intended bride.

22–34   For the Biblical sources of this scene, see the note to lines 79–136 of the early *SEL* version. Notice that Mirk retells only the narrative of Mary's repentance and forgiveness, omitting both the issue of her extravagance, raised by the apostles, and the issue of her daring to touch Jesus (and His tolerating her ministrations) when she is so flagrant a sinner.

32   *clensed hur of seven fendes.* By incorporating the exorcism from seven devils into the scene in which Jesus declares Mary forgiven, Mirk suggests a figurative reading of those seven devils as sins.

35–43   Mirk says more about Mary's courage and faithfulness at the time of the Crucifixion than either the early *SEL* or the *Speculum Sacerdotale.* This theme, suggested more strongly in John 20:1–2, 11–18 than in the other Gospels, was extensively developed in the larger medieval tradition surrounding Mary Magdalen, including sermons and commentaries; see Caxton *A Critical Edition*, ed. Mycoff, pp. 164–65, 168–70.

44–45   On the healing of Martha, see explanatory note to lines 141–46 of the early *SEL* version.

45–46   The resurrection of Lazarus is recounted in John 11:1–44. Although the story in John suggests a good deal about the relationship between Jesus and Mary Magdalen, the prose retellings of her legend in this collection mention it only in passing, and the early *SEL* omits it entirely.

47   *He aperud to hur bodyly furste of alle othyr.* The Gospels do not suggest any kind of post-Resurrection appearance by Jesus before he greeted Mary in the garden, but there is at least one MS of Mirk's sermon (H 2417) which inserts "after His moder" after "first" — thus explaining the qualification *bodyly* by reminding us that there was a medieval tradition which claimed that the Virgin Mary saw her resurrected Son in a vision even before Mary Magdalen encountered him in the flesh.

51   *Maximius.* That is, Maximinus. On the various forms of his name, see explanatory note to line 169 of the early *SEL* version.

57   *mawmentis.* As the OED explains, the terms "maumet" or "mawment" ("idol") and "maumetrie" or "mawmentry" ("idolatry") were derived from the name "Mahomet," due to the erroneous belief among medieval Christians that the followers of Mohammed worshiped him as a god.

58–63   Notice that Mirk omits all the dramatic appearances of Mary Magdalen at the prince's bedside (lines 239–72 in the early *SEL* version). In this account the poverty of the apostles is not mentioned and the prince's conversion sounds easy and almost instantaneous.

70   *scheo sette on eyther of hyr schyldyr a crosse.* See explanatory note to lines 334–36 of the early *SEL* version.

85–86   On the shipmen's superstitious fear, see explanatory note to line 368 of the early *SEL* version.

87   *helte.* This adverb, meaning "confidently," is surprising in this context, and some of the MSS replace it with alternatives that suggest the prince is speaking heedlessly or by chance: *lyghtly* (H 2403), *happis* (D), or *happely* (U).

150   *etc.* In C the sermon ends here. Other MSS continue: *and pray to God as he foryaf Mary Maudelen hur synnys, soo he forgeve you your synnys, and grawnt you the blys that he boght you to. Amen* (quoted from G [EETS]. H 2403, H 2417, and Dd all have the first two clauses of the same closing formula, ending with "your synnys.").

Textual Notes to Mirk's Sermon on St. Mary Magdalen

Abbreviations: see explanatory notes.

12   *Betanye.* C: *Betayn(e)*.

15   *as many bokys.* Emended from C: *as many as bokys.*

17   *and so he dud.* C: omits the *he* found in most MSS.

20   *wherfore.* C: *whefore.*

27   *the terus.* Emended from C, which has combined the two words into *therus.*

52   *an old schyppe.* This is the reading in most MSS. C: *a holde schyppe.*

54   *Marcile.* "Marseilles." C: *Martile.*

55   *nygh a tempul.* This is the reading in most MSS. C: *nyght* for *nygh.*

69   *hor godys.* This is the reading in most MSS. C: *his godys.*

85   *the dede body.* This is the reading in most MSS. C: omits *body.*

88   *for of myne cost.* This is the reading in some MSS, including G [EETS]. C: omits *cost.* Other MSS substitute a much easier interjection, *I praie thee* (D) or *I pray yow* (Dd).

97   *Crystes.* C: *crytes.*

108   *lyft.* C: *lyf.*

111   *too yere.* Most MSS have the *too* (or *two*) omitted by C.

113   *were.* C: *where.*

Mary Magdalen, from *Speculum Sacerdotale,*
from British Library MS Addit. 36791, fols. 96r–98r

In syche a day ye schull have the feste of Seynt Marye Magdalene, whiche was
the synneful womman and servyd to hure fleschely desires, and to whome God
afterward gafe siche grace that sche servyd forgevenes of here synnes.

For when Crist was in the hous of Symon the Leprous, as sone as Marye herde
5   telle of Hym, sche thought in hireself by dyvyne aspiracion and grace that it were
then covenable tyme for to converte and make sorowe and penaunce of hure lyf
that sche hadde ladde afore. And sche toke an oynement in a vessel and yede into
the hous of Symon where Jhesu was and yede to the feet of Jhesu and wasshid
hem with here teris of hure yghen and then dide wipe hem with the heeres of hire
10   heed and anoyntyd hem then with hire oynement.

And seeynge Crist that the Pharasye Symon hadde indignacion that Crist lete
siche a synful womman come so nye hym, he seide to hym thus: "Symon, sethen
I come into thyn hows thou nether kyssid my feet ne wasshid hem ne anoyntid
hem, but this womman hath done al this sethen sche come." And therefore seide
15   Crist to Symon, "*Propterea dimittuntur ei peccata multa quoniam dilexit multum.*
Therfore for hure myche love is the multitude of hure synnes forgeven." And then
he seide to the womman, "*Remittuntur tibi peccata tua quoniam dilexisti me.*
Woman, for thou hast shewyd to me love, thi synnes are forgeven. *Vade, fides tua
te salvam fecit.* Go, thi feith hath made thee safe."
20   Joseph telleth us that Marie Magdalein for the grete brennyng love that sche
loved God wold never have housbonde ne se man with hire yghen after the ascension of Crist. But sche yede into deserte and there sche dwellyd the space of

---

1 In syche a day, On such and such a day [to be inserted by the speaker]; **whiche**, who.
2 servyd to, was obedient to. **3 gafe**, gave; **servyd**, deserved. **5 aspiracion**, inspiration.
6 covenable, suitable (fitting). **7 yede**, went. **9 yghen**, eyes. **11 seeynge Crist**, when
Christ saw; **Pharasye**, Pharisee. **12 nye**, near; **sethen**, since. **16 myche**, great. **18 for**,
because. **19 safe**, delivered from sin, saved. **20 Joseph**, Josephus (see note). **20–21
that sche loved**, with which she loved. **22 yede into deserte**, went into the wilderness.

thirty yere unknowyn to alle maner of men, ne never ete mete of man ne dronke drynke. But in yche tyme and in yche houre when that men worschipid here God, then the aungels of Hevene come to hyre and reysed hure up betwene hem into the eyre, and there sche made hire prayer with hem to God.

So it happened after the space of the thirty yere that there was an holy preste, mayster of a serteyne bretherhede. And this preste usyd in yche tyme of the Quadragesime for to go and dwelle in the deserte in prayingis and fastyngis by hymself fro his bretheren. And in a tyme he sawe with his yghen howe the angels of God come downe fro Hevene and there toke a thynge and bare it up betwene hem and after brought it ageyn and left it where they toke it. At the laste this preste thought in hymself that there was some seynt in that coste that was so often tyme ivisit with angels. And atte the excitacion of the Holy Gost he yede to the place where the angels went to, and there he fonde a denne iclosid, and there he knelyd and cryed, seyinge, "I conjure thee by vertu of the Fader and Sone and the Holy Goste that whether thou be man or what creature that thou be that is in this place, that thou speke with me, and yif thou be a spirit that thou answere to me."

And then a voyce spake unto hym out of the denne and seide, "For that thou haste so conjured me by the holy Trinité, therfore I shall answere and speke to thee and schewe to thee what I am. Ne herdest thou never in the Gospel ne redde never of Marie the grete synner, that wateryd the feet of hire Savyoure and wypid hem with here heeres and deserved so to have forgevenes of hire synnes?"

And he answerd and seid, "Yis, I have herde it and redde it, and nowe it is the holy Gospel over alle the world."

And then Marie seide to hym ageyn, "Sire, I am the same Marie; and for the grete love that I have to my Lord, I may se no man. And therfore anone after His ascencion I come into this wyldernes and have dwellyd here thirty yere, and in al

---

23–24 ete mete of man ne dronke drynke, consumed human food or drink. **24 houre,** canonical hour (see note). **26 eyre,** air. **28 mayster . . . bretherhede,** superior of a certain monastery or other religious community. **28–29 tyme of the Quadragesime,** season of Lent (see note). **30 fro,** apart from; **in a tyme,** on a certain occasion. **31 a thynge,** something; **bare,** lifted. **33 coste,** borderland. **34 ivisit with,** visited by; **excitacion,** instigation. **35 denne iclosid,** secluded lair or cave. **36 conjure,** solemnly call upon; **vertu,** the power. **37 what,** whatever. **47 anone after,** immediately after.

50 this tyme I sawe never man ne herde man but thee nowe. And in yche houre commeth to me angels of my Lord God and ledeth me to my prayinge place to-ward Hevene. And there they schewe to me swetnes of the blisse, and then they brynge me ageyn unto this denne. And for this swetnes of Hevene and fayrenes of angels, I never covetyd mete ne drynke of man ne hunguryd ne thyrstid this thirty yere. And, sire, nowe I knowe well that the day of my passynge out of this world

55 commeth nye, that I may dwelle in the sight of my Lord for evermore. And therfore I praye thee, do nowe at my prayere, as I have done at thyne: *scilicet*, go home and come ageyn at the seventhe day hens, and brynge with thee a wyndynge clothe. For I wol ende in the same maner as othir men doth."

And then the preste yede and brought afterward syche a clothe and cast it at the

60 dore of the denne. And then Marie prayed hym that he schuld brynge hire to some place of men, where that hymself wold, that sche myght ende ther hire lyf. And he brought hire home to his bretheren, and there Marie was comonyd with the body and blode of oure Lord Jhesu Crist. And sche then lyfte up hire yghen and hire handes to God, and so passid the spirit.

65 And after tyme of hire passynge there was ther syche a smelle and a savoure that it was felyd by five dayes after. And then the preste beriede worschipfully hire holy body, and after his deth he made hym to be beriede with hire.

And this Marie was the suster of Lazar, that Crist rerede fro his sepulcre, and also sustre of Martha, the whiche did myche mynystracion to Crist, as is redde in

70 the Gospel. But the Marie aforesaid chese the beste parte, for sche sete by the feete of oure Lord and herde his holy wordes, and sche folowyd hym to the crosse, and sche yede in the day of Paske to his sepulcre for to anoynte hym. And after that he was up resyn, sche was the firste that sawe hym. And therfore in

---

49 houre, canonical hour (see note to line 24). **51 the blisse**, Paradise (the place of perfect joy). **53 covetyd . . . man**, desired human food or drink. **55 nye**, near. **56** *scilicet*, namely. **57 hens**, from now (hence); **wyndynge clothe**, shroud [to wrap her body for burial]. **58 ende**, die. **61 where . . . wold, that**, wherever he chose, [so] that. **62 was comonyd**, received the sacrament of Holy Communion. **64 passid the spirit**, she died (the soul departed). **65 savoure**, fragrance. **66 felyd . . . after**, perceived for five days afterward; **worschipfully**, honorably. **67 hym**, himself. **68 Lazar**, Lazarus; **rerede**, raised (see note). **69 mynystracion**, service (see explanatory note to lines 69–71). **70 sete**, sat. **72 Paske**, Easter.

75 oure Letanie we take hure before alle virgines except the moder of God, the whiche noght onely is set and prayede afore virgines, but also afore alle other seyntis after hire Sone.

And oure Lord hath shewyd for Marie aforeseide syche a myracle. In the flode that is callyd *Flumen Ligeris* was a schip chargyd with men and wymmen. So it happenyd that there rose up a wynde and siche a storme that the schip perischid

80 and was fillyd with the water and isonkyn. And then alle that were in the schipp were so trowbulyd with the drede of deth that they nolde triste in no prayere ne behotynge to God or to eny other good seyntis. But as the mayny were in drenchynge, it sterde into the mynde of a certeyn womman of hem that sche schuld crie and speke with as hye a voyce as she myght, in these wordes: "O Seynt Marie

85 Magdalen, so wele beloved with Crist, I praye thee by thy byttre terys that thou wettest Cristis feet with, for to delyver me fro this peril of deth."

And this same womman was grete with childe, and she made a vowe to God for to geve hure childe, yif that he schuld be a man, to be made a monke in an abbey therebeside. And anone there aperyd to hire a womman of gentel schap, and put

90 hire hande unto the womman, and toke hire by the chynne, and brought hire up saf and sownde unto the banke. And so was the womman delyvered through help of God and of Mary Magdaleyn, and alle the tother pereschid ychone. So afterward when the womman hadde conceyved and was avised of hire vowe that sche hadde made, sche offrid the childe to God and to Seynt Marie Magdaleyn, and he

95 evermore in alle his lyf was here servaunt.

Also ther was a knyght slawe in a batell, the whiche hadde used every yere to come to the sepulcre of Marie Magdalen. And as his frendis wepte and sorowed for hym, beholdyng hym on the beere, they were wrothe to Marie Magdaleyn and seide why that sche suffred hire servant for to dye sodeynly withoute confession,

74 Letanie, Litany (see note). **77 syche a myracle**, the following miracle; **flode**, river. **78** *Flumen Ligeris*, the Loire River [in France]; **chargyd**, loaded. **79 perischid**, was destroyed. **80 isonkyn**, sunk. **81 trowbulyd**, disturbed (troubled); **triste**, trust. **82 behotynge**, promise (vow); **mayny**, company. **82–83 in drenchynge**, being drowned. **83 sterde**, came suddenly. **84 hye**, loud. **85 with**, by. **88 a man**, a male child. **89 gentel schap**, noble appearance. **89–90 put hire hande unto**, reached out to. **92 alle . . . ychone**, every one of the others died. **93 avised**, aware. **96 slawe**, slain. **98 beere**, bier; **wrothe to**, angry toward. **99 seide why that**, asked why.

100   doynge of penaunce, and contricion. And sodeynly the dede body in grete mervayle
to alle men rose fro deth and made a preste to come to hym. And anoon when he
hadde confessid hym and receyvyd Goddis body, he passyd ageyn to reste.

     Also there was a clerk of Flaundres and felle into siche a multitude of crymes,
and so he usid syche grete vicis and crymes that he wolde nether do that good was
105   ne yit heere it. Nevertheles he hadde in Marie Magdaleyn grete devocion, and
worschepid hire feste and fastid for hire devoutly. So in a tyme as he had visit hire
sepulcre, as he lay in his devocion and hadde fallen into a slomerynge, *scilicet*,
half slepyng, half wakyng, Marie Magdaleyn come to hym, havynge as hym thought
sterne yghen, and in a faire semely schape and borne betwene two aungels, and
110   seide to hym, "Stevene, answere nowe to me. Why and wherfore dost thou so
wickydly ageinst the prayers and the merites that I make for thee? I make for thee
grete instaunce and stere my lippes for thee to my Lord, that thou schuldest noght
be perischid, and thou wolt noght amende; for I have evermore prayede for thee
to God, for the grete devocion that thou haste hadde for me. And therefore ryse
115   and amende it, and I shal nevere leve thee til thou be reconselyd to God." And
anone this clerke felid this grace of God and Marie Magdaleyn, that he forsoke
the world and enteryd into religion and was of a passynge parfite lyf. And in the
tyme of his deth, Marie Magdaleyn was seen stondyng with angels beside his
beere, takyng and berynge up his sowle like a white dowve to heven, with lovyng
120   and songes, *et cetera*.

100–101 in grete mervayle to, to the great amazement of. **102 confessid hym,** made his
confession; **Goddis body,** the Eucharist. **103 siche a multitude,** a great multitude. **104
usid,** practiced; **that good was,** what was good. **105 yit,** even. **106 worschepid hire
feste,** honored her feast day; **in a tyme,** once. **107 devocion,** act of worship; **slomerynge,
scilicet,** a light sleep, that is. **108 as hym thought,** as it seemed to him. **109 semely
schape,** comely appearance. **110 dost,** behave. **111 merites . . . thee,** spiritual benefits
that I confer on you (see note). **112 grete instaunce,** urgent entreaties; **stere,** vigorously move. **113 perischid,** lost, destroyed. **115 reconselyd,** reconciled. **117 religion,**
a religious order (see note); **passynge parfite,** surpassingly perfect. **119 beere,** bier;
dowve, dove (see note); **lovyng,** praise.

Notes to Mary Magdalen, from Speculum Sacerdotale

Abbreviation: **Ad** = British Library MS Addit. 36791, fols. 96r–98r [base text].

1   *In.* Initial capital never added to Ad.

         ye schull. Ad: *ye ye schull.*

4   *Symon the Leprous.* Although the Pharisee's name is derived from Matthew 26:6, the ensuing lines here retell just part of the story from Luke 7:36–50, omitting both the apostles' reaction (from Matthew and John) and the parable in Luke about the money-lender and his two debtors.

20   *Joseph.* The ascription to the Jewish historian Josephus, who lived during the first century of the Christian era, is traditional but spurious. The story of Mary Magdalen's thirty years in the desert was actually borrowed many centuries later from the legend of Mary of Egypt.

24   *houre.* There were seven canonical hours of prayer, traditionally observed in monastic communities: Matins, Prime, Sext, Terce, Nones, Vespers, and Compline.

29   *Quadragesime.* The Latin term for Lent, the forty-day season of fasting and self-discipline before Easter, was derived from the adjective meaning "forty."

55–67   Compare this account of her death with the more complicated and wonder-filled narrative given by the early *SEL* account and Mirk. One noteworthy difference is that the same anonymous priest discovers her secret abode and presides over the final events that welcome her back into the human community of the church: giving her the last sacraments, taking charge of her burial, and arranging for his own eventual burial next to her tomb. Bishop Maximinus, whose role was so prominent at the end of the other accounts and so useful as publicity for Mary's shrine at the Abbey of St. Maximin in Aix, is conspicuously missing.

60   *some.* Ad: *somee.*

65   *syche a smelle and a savoure.* This sign of her sanctity is mentioned also in the early *SEL* account, lines 618–19 and 638–39; see explanatory note to lines 618–19.

68   *Lazar, that Crist rerede fro his sepulcre.* See explanatory note to lines 45–46 of Mirk's account.

69   *did.* Ad: omits.

69–71   The story of Martha, who busied herself with the practical work of hospitality when Jesus came to visit while her sister Mary just sat at his feet and listened to his words, is found in Luke 10:38–42.

72–73   Mary Magdalen's visit to Christ's tomb on Easter morning is mentioned in all four gospels, but her individual role receives the most emphasis in John 20.

74   *oure Letanie.* The Litany of saints, a long prayer that was chanted in procession on Rogation Days and other solemn occasions, included petitions for assistance from the Virgin Mary, the apostles, and a large number of martyrs, confessors, and virgins, all invoked by name. Although both the order and selection of names varied somewhat from place to place, the Virgin Mary always preceded all the other saints and Mary Magdalen headed the list of virgins.

87–95   It was common in the early Middle Ages for monastic communities to include child oblates — children given as an offering by their parents, to be brought up as monks or nuns. In the twelfth century, however, the laws of the church were changed to stipulate that no one could be permanently committed to the monastic life without freely taking the necessary vows for themselves after reaching the age of adulthood (usually 18). The custom of child oblation died out almost completely after this time.

93   *conceyved.* Presumably this is an error; since the woman is already pregnant, one would expect "given birth" or "been delivered" [of the child].

96–97   *hadde used . . . Marie Magdalen.* That is, the knight had made an annual pilgrimage to one of the shrines that claimed to house the relics of the saint.

99–100   *to dye . . . contricion.* The risk of damnation, or at least a prolonged period in Purgatory, was believed to be greatly increased if one died suddenly, without time to repent and be absolved of all one's sins. Hence the mercy of the saints was frequently illustrated with stories, like this one, in which a deceased person was restored to life just long enough to complete the recommended spiritual preparations for death.

110   *Stevene.* The clerk's name.

111   *the merites that I make for thee.* The underlying idea is that Mary and other saints could vicariously bestow on their needy followers some of the spiritual benefits that were due to the saints themselves because of their great virtues, or merits.

116–17 *forsoke the world and enteryd into religion.* That is, he abandoned secular life and its temptations for the more austere and disciplined life of a monk or a friar.

119   *like a white dowve to heven.* Like the presence of the patron saint and a company of angels, the image of the soul ascending to Heaven like a white dove, amid songs of praise and thanksgiving to God, is part of the standard iconography for a holy death.

120   *et cetera.* At this point a preacher using this text would insert one of the standard closing formulas and a blessing. See for example the endings of Mirk's sermons in this collection.

Margaret of Antioch

Introduction

St. Margaret of Antioch was one of the most popular saints among the laity in medieval England, primarily because of her association with childbirth. Many churches housed side altars or images of this saint and had guilds dedicated to her. St. Margaret is also one of the most common subjects for wall paintings in England; some churches have her entire life — as many as twenty scenes — adorning their walls. When hearing the story of Margaret retold on her feast day (July 20), many people could have followed along by looking at the images painted on the walls of their own church. Because of the promises made just before Margaret's death to assist anyone — especially women in childbirth — who has her life written down, reads it, or has it read to them, extant copies of her legend are quite common, some of them written on long strips of parchment which were fastened around the abdomens of women in labor.

The cult of St. Margaret first developed in the eastern Church (the first extant Lives in Greek date from the ninth century), where she was known as Marina and usually portrayed as seizing a demon, about to strike him with a hammer. Her victory over the demon caused Marina to be regarded as a protector against demonic powers generally. Once her cult became established in the West, her intercessory power became more specific and included protection for newborns against demonic possession and other birth defects. Eventually she came to be identified as a protector of both mother and child during and immediately after birth, although (as will be seen in the two later Middle English texts) the petitions for undeformed children are sometimes omitted and the prayer focuses primarily on the mother's welfare.

As early as the tenth century there was concern about the authenticity of the most spectacular elements in the Margaret legend, her victories over the dragon and the demon. When reading different versions, these are important sites to compare. Some writers were uncomfortable with the idea that Margaret had actually been swallowed by the dragon; for instance, Jacobus de Voragine, the author of the *Legenda aurea*, called the scene "apocryphal and not to be taken seriously" (trans. Ryan, 1.369), and other writers found alternative ways of presenting the episode. In this selection, the stanzaic Life attributes Margaret's escape not to her own gesture of making the sign of the cross, but to the actual cross on which Christ was crucified. Mirk says that the dragon took Margaret into his mouth, but not that he swallowed her. Lydgate's dragon gets only as far as Margaret's head before he splits open. Despite clerical discomfort with the dragon scene, it could not be dropped completely from vernacular lives of Margaret

111

because it served as the source for the familiar iconography of this saint, who is traditionally shown either as emerging from the dragon or standing atop it in triumph. Mirk specifically calls his audience's attention to this moment as the image of Margaret that they know.

Another notable feature of the Lives of St. Margaret is the way they seem to reflect the needs of particular audiences by means of the particular petitions in Margaret's final prayer. Petitions for the preservation of chastity, safe childbirth and healthy offspring, protection from other kinds of danger, and forgiveness of sins suggest the wide range of believers who might turn to this saint in times of trouble. The claims for Margaret's power as an intercessor also became a matter of concern for some reform-minded clergy; and later versions of her legend sometimes water down the contents of her final prayer — as may be seen by comparing the bold promises in the stanzaic account below with the more general assurances of comfort and grace in the retellings by Mirk and especially Lydgate.

Although the present edition is based on a fifteenth-century copy (Cambridge University Library MS Addit. 4122), the anonymous stanzaic Life dates to the second half of the thirteenth century, making it approximately contemporary with the *South English Legendary*. The rhymes would have made this version of the saint's life easy to memorize, as well as entertaining for those who heard it read or recited aloud. The text's strong emphasis on childbirth highlights the importance of St. Margaret for laywomen, and it is easy to imagine this version being utilized as a means of comfort during labor. The text is lively but decorous; in comparison with some earlier manuscripts of the stanzaic Life, in fact, this fifteenth-century copy seems remarkably polite and restrained. The narrative contains some details rarely found in other versions, such as the story of Margaret's parents and especially her mother, who is barely mentioned in most accounts.

Mirk's version is presented as a sermon that a priest could adapt or simply read aloud from the pulpit on the appropriate Sunday in July. Although it is obviously designed with lay hearers in mind, it seems intent on reminding them that the cult of St. Margaret should be connected with the sacraments of the church, not turned into a matter of private observances at home. Thus the sermon begins rather tellingly with the priest admonishing his parishioners to attend mass on the saint's feast day if they want the full benefits of commemorating her. Mirk's retelling of the legend itself places unusual emphasis on baptism. In fact, he makes a point of explaining how both Margaret herself and her thousands of converts manage to satisfy this requirement for entering the kingdom of heaven, and he has the devil confess to Margaret that his favorite evil deed is to make Christians forget their baptismal vows; in most versions of the legend, the devil's main target is chastity.

John Lydgate, born around 1370, was a Benedictine monk at St. Edmund's monastery in Bury. He was a prolific author and had an enormous reputation during his lifetime, receiving commissions for poems from many notable patrons, including the future king Henry V. Anne Mortimer, Countess of March, commissioned his *Life of St. Margaret* sometime between 1415 (the year of her marriage to Edmund Mortimer) and 1426 — that is, during the period of her life when she was likeliest to be concerned with childbearing and with Margaret's special focus as an intercessor. Lydgate wrote eight saints' lives altogether, as well as an additional miracle of the Virgin Mary. His style may be contrasted with that of the two earlier texts, and reflects the tastes and concerns of his aristocratic audience.

Select Bibliography

Indexed in

[stanzaic Life]   Brown-Robbins, #203 and #2672.

Manuscripts

[Lydgate]   Durham University Library MS Cosin V.II.14, fols. 97v–106r.

[Mirk]   London, British Library MS Cotton Claudius A.ii, fols. 90v–91v.

[stanzaic Life]   Cambridge University Library MS Additional 4122, fols. 6r–38v.

Previous editions

Lydgate
Lydgate, John. *The Minor Poems of John Lydgate*. Ed. Henry Noble MacCracken. Part 1. EETS, e.s. 107. London: Kegan Paul, Trench, Trübner and Co., 1911 (for 1910). Rpt. London: Oxford University Press, 1961. Pp. 173–92.

Mirk
Mirk, John. *Mirk's Festial*. Ed. Theodor Erbe. EETS e.s. 96. 1905. Pp. 19–22.

Stanzaic Life
Religiöse Dichtung im englischen Hochmittelalter: Untersuchung und Edition der Handschrift B.14.39 des Trinity College in Cambridge. Ed. Karl Reichl. Munich: Wilhelm Fink Verlag, 1973. Pp. 163–249. [Gives the text from all six known manuscripts of the stanzaic version.]

Three Popular Legends of Virgin Martyrs

Important sources and analogues in English

Bokenham, Osbern. *Legendys of Hooly Wummen*. Ed. Mary S. Serjeantson. EETS o.s. 206. 1938. Pp. 7–38.

Clayton, Mary, and Hugh Magennis. *The Old English Lives of St. Margaret*. Cambridge Studies in Anglo-Saxon England 9. Cambridge: Cambridge University Press, 1994. [Includes two Old English versions and two Latin ones, both with facing-page translations in modern English, with extensive introductions and notes.]

Jacobus de Voragine. *The Golden Legend*. Trans. William Granger Ryan. 1993. Vol. 1. Pp. 368–70.

Medieval English Prose for Women: Selections from the Katherine Group and Ancrene Wisse. Ed. Bella Millett and Jocelyn Wogan-Browne. Oxford: Clarendon Press, 1990. Pp. 44–85. [Gives the thirteenth-century prose *Seinte Margarete* both in the original Middle English and in modern English translation on facing pages.]

Historical background and criticism

Larson, Wendy R. "The Role of Patronage and Audience in the Cults of Sts Margaret and Marina of Antioch." In Riches and Salih, *Gender and Holiness*. Pp. 23–35.

Lewis, Katherine J. "The Life of St. Margaret of Antioch in Late Medieval England: A Gendered Reading." In *Gender and Christian Religion*. Ed. R. N. Swanson. *Studies in Church History* 34 (1998), 129–41.

_____. "'Lete me suffre': Reading the Torture of St Margaret of Antioch in Late Medieval England." In *Medieval Women: Texts and Contexts in Late Medieval Britain. Essays for Felicity Riddy*. Ed. Jocelyn Wogan-Browne et al. Turnhout: Brepols, 2000. Pp. 69–82.

Price, Jocelyn. "The Virgin and the Dragon: The Demonology of *Seinte Margarete*." In *Sources and Relations: Studies in Honour of J. E. Cross*. Ed. Marie Collins, Jocelyn Price, and Andrew Hamer. *Leeds Studies in English* n.s. 16 (1985), 337–57.

Winstead, Karen A. *Virgin Martyrs*. 1997. Pp. 23–63, 89–97, 122–33, et passim.

Stanzaic Life of Margaret,
from Cambridge University Library MS Addit. 4122, fols. 6r–38v

Here begynnes the lyfe of saynte Margarete

Olde and younge, I you praye youre folyes for to lette	*cease*
And byleve on Jhesu Cryste, that gave you wytte youre synnes for to bette.	*atone*
Lystenys, I wylle you tellen wordys fayre and swete —	
The lyfe of a mayden that hyghte Margarete.	*was called*

5	Her fader was a patryarke, as I telle you may.	*pagan chief priest*
	In Antioche a wyfe he chees in that false laye.	*chose; religion*
	Febylle was his herte and false was hys faye;	*faith*
	The fendys oute of helle, thei servyd hym both nyghte and day.	

	Theodosy it was his name. One God loved he noghte;	
10	He beleved in false goddys that were with hondys wroghte.	*made by [human] hands*
	They had a chylde schulde crystened be, it ranne hym welle in thoughte.[1]	
	He comaunded whann hit was borne it schulde be broghte to noughte.	*killed*

	Her moder was an hethen wyfe that her to this uorld bare.	
	As sone as the chylde was borne, sche wolde it schulde not forfare.	*perish*
15	Sche it sente into Asye with massyngeres fulle yare,	*messengers; ready*
	To a noryse that her fedde and sette her to lare.	*nurse; learning*

	The noryse that this mayden toke, sche kepte her with wynne.	*pleasure*
	Alle thei her loved, as seyes the boke, in house that sche was ynne.	
	Sone sche coude grete wysdome, and mykel sche dredde synne;	*knew; abhorred*
20	Sche gave herre herte to Jhesu Cryste and lefte alle her kynne.	

The noryse that her kepte hadde chyldren sevyn;
The eyghte was Margarete, Crystys mayde of hevyne.

---

[1] *He had a premonition that their child would be baptized as a Christian*

115

Talys sche herde manye one, moo than I can neven,　　　　　*name (tell)*
Howe the Jewes dydde martirdome to Saynte Laurence and Stevyn.

25　As sone as this mayde was of fyftene wynter elde,
　　Sche kepte her noryscys schepe on dayes in the felde.　　　　*nurse's sheep*
　　Her felowes that satten her by, fulle faste thei her behelde
　　Whenne sche maade her preyers to Jhesu, that alle doth welde.　　　*govern*

　　Sche bytoke her maydenhede as Jhesu wolde her deme.　　　*committed*
30　Sche loved Him with herte and gladlye wolde Hym queme.　　　*please*
　　Fulle welle He herde her preyer, I telle you at a worde.
　　As bokes dose us telle, Olibrius than was lord

　　Of Asye and Antioche, to geven and to selle.　　　*with absolute power*
　　He served both nyghthe and daye the foule fendys of helle.
35　And alle that beleved on Jhesu Cryste, he fondes hem to qwelle.　　*tries to kill them*
　　From Antioche to Asye were myles tenne and twelve.

　　For to dystroye Crysten peple he hastyd hym belyve.　　　*hurried eagerly*
　　He sawe Mayde Margarete the schepe before her dryve.
　　Sone sayd that Sarasyne he wolde have her to wyfe:
40　"Goo, summe of my men, and brynge her me belyve.　　　*at once*

　　"Bye my lay, if sche be comen of kynrede free,　　　*law; from a free-born family*
　　Of alle women that I knowe beste thanne schalle sche be.

　　"For her fayre bewté, if sche be come of thral,　　　*descended from slaves or serfs*
　　By Mahound, her maryage schalle sche not lese alle.　　　*lose entirely*
45　Fulle fayre I wylle her clothen, in purpylle and in palle;　*rich fabrics/splendid clothing*
　　Sche schal be my lemman, I telle you nowe alle."　　　*mistress*

　　The Saryssones dydde as he hem badde to mayden Margarete,
　　There sche kepte her noryscys schepe so fayre in the strete.
　　Mykel was it that thei her boden and more thei here behete;[1]
50　The trowthe of her herte ne wolde sche not lette.　　　*abandon*

---

[1] Lines 48–49: *Where she kept her nurse's sheep gently (honorably) in public. / They offered her much and promised her more*

The Saryssones, her erande to done, forthe thei gunne stryke.[1]
"Damysel," thei sayden, "we wolle thee not smyte.
Olibryus oure lord of Antioche so ryche,
He desyres thee to wynne; fulle welle it maye thee lyke."   *please you*

55   Than answered mayden Margarete, as bryghte as onye levyn.   *any lightning flash*
     Sche them sadlye answered with fulle mylde stevyn: *soberly; voice*
     "I have geve my maydenhed to Jhesu Cryste of heven,   *given*
     To kepe it, if His wylle be, for His names seven.   *preserve*

     "Jhesu Cryste my Lord, that dydeste for us alle,   *died*
60   Hyghe Kynge of heven, to Thee I clepe and calle.
     Of my steedfaste herte ne latte me never falle,   *From*
     And of my stabylle corage not turne for hem alle.   *firm intention; despite them*

     "Jhesu Cryste my Lord, to Thee I me wende,   *turn*
     That never hadde begynnynge nor never schalle have ende.
65   If Thi swete wylle were, an angel me Thou sende,
     From this foule gostys I may me defende.[2]

     "Alle my kynne I have forsake; to Thee, knelynge on my knee,
     Jhesu Cryste, my good Lord, to Thee I betake me.   *commit myself*
     Gladlye I wylle for Thi love in erthe a martyre for to be,
70   Nowe has he his houndys on me sette, that I ne may not flee."   *dogs; [so] that*

     The Saryssones to hym wenten and seyden alle her sawe: *words*
     "Lord, of alle thi posté sche gevys not a hawe![3]
     Sche belevys on Jhesu Cryste, to her warant sche Hym dos make;   *protector*
     For alle the payne thou mayest her done, sche wylle Hym not forsake." *inflict on her*

75   Than bespake Olibryous. He waryed both sonne and moone.   *spoke up; cursed*
     For this virgyne glorious his wittys was nere goone.   *nearly*

---

[1] *The Saracens went forward to do their errand*

[2] *[So that] I may defend myself from these evil spirits*

[3] *Lord, she does not give a hawthorn berry (a type of something worthless) for all your power*

"Brynge her me byforne," he sayde. "I wylle turne her mode fulle sone.[1]
I schalle her make me to love longe or hit be none." *before; midday*

Tho Saryssonnes agayne wentyn to that mayde Margarete.
80   Thei leydenne handes her uppon and leddyn her into the strete. *road*
Sche come befor Olibryous; fulle fayre sche gan hym grete. *courteously; greet*
He asked her what sche hyghte, and sche sayd, "Margarete." *was called*

"Mayde Margarete," he sayde, "my lemman thou schalte be, *sweetheart; must*
And I thee wylle wedde if thou be comen of free. *of gentle birth*
85   If thou be of thral born, I geve thee gold and fee. *possessions*
Thou schalte be my lemman so longe as it schal bee."

That mayde hym answered fulle sone and anoone:
"I am a Crysten woman, baptised in the funtestone. *font*
Blessed be my Lord that I beleve uppon.
90   I wylle not lese His love for noon erthelye man." *lose*

"Beleveste thou," he sayde, "on Jhesu Cryste, that done was uppon the Rode? *Cross*
Longeous thirled His syde — the stremys ranne on blode. *pierced*
The crowne was of thornes that on His hede stode.
If thou troweste that He levyth, I holde thee but wode." *consider; mad*

95   Thanne bespake that mayde as an angel hir kende: *spoke up; taught*
"He dyed on the Rode oure soules to amende,
And sythen into helle His holy goste He sente
To take us oute of prysone to joye withowten ende."

Thanne bespake Olibryus. He sawe it was no bote *was useless*
100   To stryve with that mayden, so stedfastely sche stode. *argue*
He baad men schulde bynde her, both honde and fote, *commanded*
And sithen don her in preson — "that ye mowe turne her mode." *put; may change*

Mayde Margarete alle nyghte in pryson laye.
Sche come befor Olybryus uppon that other day. *the second day*

---

[1] *"Bring her before me," he said. "I will change her mind very soon"*

105   "Mayde Margarete," he sayde, "truste uppon my laye;   *religion (law)*
       Jhesu that thou beleveste on, forsake Him nowe for aye.   *forever*

       "Truste on me and be my wyfe — fulle welle than thou schalte spede.   *then; prosper*
       Antioche and Asye thou schalte have to mede;   *as a reward*
       Syclaton, purpel and palle, that schalle be thi wede;   *expensive/rich fabrics; clothing*
110   With the beste metys of the londe we schalle thee noryse and feede."   *foods; nourish*

       "Alle thi counselle," sche sayde, "it turnes not my thought.   *advice*
       I betake me to Jhesu Cryste, whiche that has me bought.   *commit myself*
       And alle this myddel erthe, forsothe He maade of noughte,   *from nothing*
       And sythen with His precyos bloode oute of helle us broughte."   *then*

115   Thanne bespake Olybryous, "Nowe it schalle be seen   *spoke up*
       Who it is that thou leveste on and why thou arte so keene.   *believe in; bold*
       Honge her uppe by the here, her Lord for to tene!   *hair; to anger her Lord*
       Bete her with scorgys tyl ye her dede wene!"   *until you believe her dead*

       The Saryssones dydde as he hem badde and to her gunne dryve;   *went*
120   Thei beten her with scorges and with her gan stryve.   *contend*
       The blode ranne from her bodye as watyr dos of schyve   *from a sieve*
       Tylle that thei alle wendyn sche hadde departed the lyve.

       Than bespake Olybryus, bye her as he stode:
       "Mayde Margarete," he sayde, "is this payne good?
125   Beleve on my goddys and turne nowe thi mode.
       Have mercye on thi whyte flesshe and spyllynge of thi bloode."

       "Blessed be my Lord," sche sayde, "that borne was in Bethleem,
       Of Marye that mayden, as bryte as the sunne beme.
       Thou doyste as thou kenneste after Sathanas thin eme.[1]
130   Me thinketh thise paynes swetter then mylkes reeme."   *sweeter than cream*

       Than bespake Olybryus: "Ne geveth sche not an hawe;   *hawthorn berry*
       For alle the peyne that ye her doon, sche sette not bye a strawe! *does not care a straw*

---

[1] *You act as you know how in the manner of Satan your uncle*

With youre scharpe nayles the fleshe of her ye drawe,
Also cleene from the boone as houndys had it gnawe."[1]

135   Thise turmentoures dydde as he hem bade; to hir thei gunne goo.   *torturers*
     With her scharpe nayles thei dydde her moche wo.   *their; caused*
     Of her fayre whyghte flesshe thei drowe ever froo,
     That the bloode from her heede ranne doune to her too.   *So that; toe*

     Summe that stode beforne her, fulle sorye that thei were
140   Of that maydens whyte flesshe and of her yelowe here.
     "Fayre Margarete," thei sayde, "of thee we have grete care.
     Have mercye on thiselfe and on thi bodyes welfare."

     "A, ye wreched counselloures, why rede ye me soo?   *advise*
     With bysynes ne with scourgys ye doo me no woo.[2]
145   My Lordys angeles comyn me to and froo.
     Alle is to me grete joye that ye wene is woo.[3]

     "Jhesu Cryste my Lord, if it Thy wylle ware,   *were*
     Have mercy on thyse synefulle that wolde myne evel fare.[4]
     Hye Kynge of hevenne, I praye Thee me here;   *hear*
150   I sofer this paynes for Thi love, Thou boughteste me ful dere."   *suffer these*

     Than spake Olybryus: "Mayden," he sayde, "this is my posté.   *power*
     Haste thou nou yghen, that thou mayste hit see?   *Have; now; eyes*
     Beleve on my goddys, yit I rede thee,   *still; advise*
     Or for thi God that thou leveste on martyred schalte thou bee."   *believe in*

155   "Thye goddys," sche sayde, "ar made of stoone.
     Of my Lordys joye telle may ther noone.[5]

---

[1] Lines 133–34: *With your sharp instruments tear the flesh from her bones as completely as if dogs had chewed it off*

[2] *Neither your concern nor your whips cause me any grief*

[3] *Everything that you consider misery is a great joy to me*

[4] *Have mercy on these sinful [people] who wish me ill*

[5] *My joy in the Lord none [of your gods]/no [human being] can express*

Though thou have posté of my flesshe and boon,   *power over*
To take from Cryste my soule power haste thou noone."

"Thou schalte," he sayde, "into pryson, there thou schalte lyke ylle[1]
160   To be bounden with yren bondes. Thi flesshe schalle I spylle."   *destroy*
"Jhesu Cryste my Lorde, to whom is that I telle;   *the one whom I proclaim*
He maye me delyver whan it is His wylle."

Fayre mayden Margarete was than in pryson doone.   *put*
The Holye Gooste to her sente a bryte angelle swythe anoone,
165   Schynynge bryghte as the sunne evyn aboute mydde noen.   *midday*
The Rode was in his honde that Cryste was on doen.   *on which Christ was placed*

"Mayde Margarete," he sayde, "herke that I thee telle: *hear what*
In hevenryche blysse thou schalte ever dwelle.   *the joy of heaven*
Jhesu Cryste that is my Lord, He hathe herde thi spele;   *story*
170   He sente thee this holye Crosse the foule dragon to qwelle.

"Thou, mayde Margarete, drede thou not it:
Thi sete is made in heven before my Lord so bryghte.   *place; prepared*
There is nothinge in erthe nor no erthelye wyghte   *creature*
That maye telle the joye that was made of thee this nyghte.

175   "Iblessed be my Lord," sche seyde, "that me this word sente,
For this holye angel that to me is wente.   *has come*
Fader and Sone and Holye Goste, Lord of alle this warde,   *world*
Ne late never the foule gooste my stable harte wende."[2]

Holye mayde Margarete loked her besyde.   *beside her*
180   There sche sawe a lothelye dragon in a corner glyde,   *hideous (loathsome)*
Brennynge as the blake fyre. His mouthe he gaped wyde.   *Burning; pale*
That mayde wexed alle greene as the gresse in someres tyde.   *grass*

The lowe fleye oute from his tonge as the fyre of brymeston.   *flame flew*
That mayde felle to grounde tylle sche craked everye boone.   *rattled*

---

[1] *"You must go to prison," he said, "where you will be displeased (sad)"*

[2] *Do not ever permit the evil spirit to change my steadfast heart*

185   He toke her up in his mowthe; he swalowed her anoon;
      Thorugh vertue of her he braste, that harme hadde sche noon.   *burst; [so] that*

      Holye mayde Margarete uppon that dragon stoode;
      Blysfulle was her herte and glad was her mode.
      "Iblessed be Thou, Jhesu Cryste; Thi myghte is fulle good.
190   Now slayne is this dragon thorugh vertu of the Roode."

      Thanne mayde Margarete wente the dragone froo.
      Yit was there in a corner another devil moo.   *in addition*
      He hadde hondys, fete, and nayles on everye too;   *toe*
      If he toke, never so lytylle, a thynge uppon the erthe, it schulde goo.[1]

195   Sche wente to that foule thinge with the crosse in her honde.
      By the vertue of Jhesu Cryste with her wympylle sche him bonde. *head-dress; bound*
      Sche toke hym bye the heede, and doun sche him slonge;   *threw (slung)*
      Sche sette her foote in his necke and to the erthe hym wronge.   *forced*

      "Sey me nowe," sche seyde, "thou lothelye thynge,   *hideous*
200   Who that is thi lord and who is thi kynge
      And who that thee hyder sente to make me ferynge,   *hither; afraid*
      For sawe I never in erthe yit so foule a thynge."

      "Ladye," he sayde, "for thi Lordys love, Lord of alle londys,
      Lyfte a lytyl thi foote that on my bodye stondys.
205   Wyde have I walkyd by water and by sondys,   *by water and lands (i.e., everywhere)*
      Yit was I nevyr bounden in so harde bondes.

      "Ruffyn that was my brother was the dragon that thou slowe.   *killed*
      Whanne he was alyve, he wroughte sorowe inowe.
      He made men on nyghte to stele, so thereto he hem drove;
210   He qwytte them her servyse, were thei never so lothe.[2]

      "In a dragones forme I hym sente to thee,
      To reve thee of thi memorye or make thee wode to bee.   *deprive*

---

[1] *If he seized anything on earth, no matter how lightly, it would have to die*

[2] *He repaid them for their service [to him], however much that displeased them*

Thou brakest hym in peces, and bounden thou haste me.   *broke; hast*
A mayden us so to overcome, lytyl is oure posté!¹

215   "Belsabub it is my name. No bote is me to sure;   *It will not help me to surrender*
This peynes that I have I maye not longe endure.
My myghte is not in erthe, but with wynde I flye.
Alle I wolde do qwelle that I may see with ye.   *Everyone; cause to die; eye*

"There I wyste ony wyfe unborn was her barne,²
220   Thedyr wolde I come belyve, in childyng to do her harme.   *at once; childbirth*
If it were unblessed, I brake it foote or arme,
Or the woman herselfe in some wyse I dydde harme.

"Salamon the wyse kynge, whyle he was on lyve,   *alive*
He closed us in a bras fat and dalfe us in a clyve.   *brass vessel; buried; cliffside*
225   The men of Babylon that bras fat gunne ryve;   *split open*
And whanne that broken was, oute we gan dryve.   *went*

"To have founde golde thei wenden; oute thei leten us goo —   *imagined*
Soth it is to sayne ten thousand and moo —
Some swyfter then the wynde and some as swyfte as roo,   *deer*
230   And alle that byleve on Jhesu Cryste we werke hem mychel woo.

"If thou wylte wytte what I am, as thou mayste wete welle,   *know*
Loke uppon thi bokys and thou schalte wyte everydele.
I praye thee for thi Lordys love, thou bynde me with stele,   *steel*
That I may no man in erthe nor no woman with chylde do ylle."

235   "Be stylle!" sche sayde. "Thou art so lothelye thou schalte goo into helle,
Be thou never so hardye, no man for to qwelle.   *bold; harm*
I praye my Lorde that in heven doth dwelle thi power for to felle."   *destroy*
And than he sanke into helle as stone dos into welle.

It was uppon the thridde day, at the hye mydde noone,   *noon precisely*
240   Olybryus comaunded that may out of pryson schulde come.   *maiden*

---

¹ *If a mere girl can overcome us like this, our power is minuscule!*

² *Where I knew any woman whose child was not yet born*

The turmentoures were fulle wylde and fette her ful sone.   *violent; fetched*
Sche helde the crosse in her honde that Cryste was on doon.   *put on*

Than bespake Olybryus, there he was fulle wrothe.   *called out*
He sayde to mayde Margarete, "Haste thou turned thi othe?   *changed; vow*
245   Beleve on my goddys too, I geve thee bothe golde and clothe,   *will give*
And if thou wylte not do soo, thi lyfe it schalle be fulle loth."   *hateful*

"Cursed be thi goddys that thou beleveste ynne!
Thei come oute of helle and been of Sathanas kynne.
They be alle togedyre fulle of lothelye synne.
250   Whan thou trustyste hem beste, thei wylle brynge thee in synne.

"But do thou welle and beleve on Hym that maade thee to man,   *as a man*
Fader, Sone, and Holye Goste that alle this worlde wanne,   *redeemed*
And do thee baptysyn today in a funtestoone,   *baptismal font*
As was Jhesu Cryste hymselfe in the flome of Jordon."   *river*

255   "Do away!" sayde Olybryous. "Bale my men schalle thee brewe.[1]
Thi Lorde schalle thee turne to payne grevous, and to no nother sewe.   *do homage*
Myne goddys be verry good, and thyn is untrewe.
For thou wylte not turne thi moode, sore it schalle thee rewe.[2]

"Where are my turmentoures? A payne I wolde kenne: *I want to teach [you]*
260   Welland lampes of oyle on her ye latte renne.   *Boiling*
From the necke to the foote scalde her as an henne.   *chicken*
But sche turne her mode, loke ye do her brenne."   *Unless; burn*

The Saressones dyde as he hem baade, lampys for to wellyn   *boil*
And uppon her hede oyle thei lete fellyn.   *fall*
265   The oyle ranne down by her hede as water doth fro welle;
The angel her kepte, they myghte her note qwelle.   *guarded; not harm*

"Wylte thou," he seyde, "mayde Margarete, yit thyn herte wende?   *turn*
Truste uppon me and be my wyfe, and thi payne schalle amende."

---

[1] *"Cut it out!" said Olibrius. "My men will prepare suffering for you"*

[2] *Since you will not change your disposition, you will bitterly regret it*

Sche answered him fulle sone: "Cryste it me defende.   *forbid*
270 I beleve on Hym that maade me, His joye has noone ende."

Icursed be thi Saryssones! God geve hem yvel endynge, *give them a bad end*
And alle the same dayes that clerkys reede or synge. *days of judgment or wrath*
In a grete fatte fulle of water he baade thei schulde her brynge. *vat*
But sche wolde turne her herte, to dethe thei schulde her slynge. *Unless; throw*

275 Sche sayde, "Lorde, if Thi wyl be, with this water that I see
I may be baptysed this daye in the name of Thee."
The thundyre byganne to breste, the folke gunne to flee; *burst*
The angeles her toke oute of the water that alle men myghte see.

Manye for that myracle turned ther moode fulle swythe *quickly*
280 And byleved on Jhesu Cryste, both men, chyldren, and wyfe —
Forsoth for to telle, ten thousand and fyve.
For the love of Hym men broughte hem o lyve. *out of*

Ful welle sawe that Sarysyne that he myghte not her stere. *budge*
He clepyd forth Malcus, that was his manqweller. *executioner (man-killer)*
285 "Lede," he sayde, "oute of the towne — or elles I schalle her bere —
And brynge her oute of lyve with swerde or with spere."

They come withoute the towne, there men schulde her sloo. *outside; kill (slay)*
Alle folowed up and downe that myghte ryde or goo.[1]
The thunder began to brestyn, the sunne wexed alle bloo, *burst; grew; lead-colored*
290 The folke felle down to grounde — thei wyste of welle nor woo.[2]

Jhesu with his aungeles He sente hir a fayre steven — *voice*
To mayden Margarete, Crystes mayde of heven:
"Blessed be thou todaye with alle that I canne nevene. *name*
Todaye schalte thou wende into the blysse of heven."

295 Malcus sawe the angeles. He sette hym on his knee. *knelt down*
"Mayde Margarete," he seyde, "thi Lorde has grete thee, *greeted*

---

[1] *All followed from everywhere who could ride or walk (i.e., all classes)*

[2] *I.e., they were too dazed to tell joy from sorrow*

125

| | And alle this angeles that been aboute thee. | *these* |
| | Streche thi necke, reseyve my swerde, and have mercye on mee." | *receive* |

Than spake that mayden, holye Saynte Margarete:

300	"Brother, if thi wylle it bee, yit a lytel byde for me	*wait*
	Whyle I make my prayers. I schalle have doon fulle sone."	*finish*
	"Bydde," he sayde, "what thou wylte. I falle to thee anoone."	*Pray; prostrate myself*

	"Fader, Sone, and Holye Gooste, Lord of alle weldande,	*governing*
	Thou madeste alle this worlde of noughte, and Adam with Thin honde.	*from nothing*
305	Of mayde Marye thou was borne, that was floure in londe;	*the virgin*
	And alle men that to me callen, louse hem, Lord, oute of bonde.	*release*

	"Alle that to my passyon wylle herken or reede,	*listen or read*
	Or settes chirche or chapel, or geveth ony almysdede,	*establish; give any*
	Jhesu Cryste mye Lorde, with honoure Thou hem feede.	*nourish*
310	The joye that is in heven graunte hem to her meede.	*as their reward*

	"Jhesu Cryste, if ony woman that schal delyvered be,	
	That Thou helpe than, if sche cale to me,	*[I pray] that; then*
	And unbynde her anoone[1] thorugh the vertue of that Tree	
	That thou dyedeste uppon to make us alle free.	

315	"Lord God, I praye thee, for Thi grete myghte,	
	As Thou madeste sonne and moone here in erthe to geve a lyghte,	
	So graunte her that her chylde be borne with alle the lymmes aryghte,	*intact*
	And not to be dumme, nor nothynge broken, nor blynde withouten syghte.	

	"Also tho that have this day of my dethe in memorye,	*those who*
320	Or with good devocyon doth me worshipe or praye,	*do me honor or pray to me*
	Jhesu Cryste my Lord, the maydens Sonne Marye,	*the Virgin Mary's Son*
	Have mercye on tho soules, where ever the bodye lye."	*those*

| | Than spake oure Lorde Jhesu Cryste, Saynte Maryes Sone: | |
| | "By heven and by erthe, by sonne and by moone, | |

---

[1] *I.e., open her womb, so that the child can be born safely*

325   Mayde Margarete, I graunte thee thi bone —   *prayer*
      To cume to that joye that thou haste wonne."

      Than bespake mayde Margarete; her prayers gan sche blynne.   *spoke up; ceased*
      "Malcus," sche sayde, "smyte of myn hede. Forgeven is thee that synne."   *off; to thee*
      "That wylle I not doo," he sayde, "for alle this worlde to wynne.
330   Thi Lord has grette thee, that thou beleveste ynne."   *greeted*

      "But if thou do," sche sayde, "elles schalte thou never have   *Unless*
      That joye that is in paradyse, that thou after doeste crave."
      Malcus herde this wordys; his swerde than dydde he drawe
      And smote of her hede with drede and mykel awe.   *off; great*

335   Mycael and Gabryel and Raphael in fere,   *together*
      Cherubyn with ten thousand that there were,
      With senserys and taperys to heven thei her bere,   *censers; tapers*
      Fulle hyghe tofore Jhesu Cryste; sche is to Hym fulle dere.

      Theophyle the good clerke, he wrote her vye,   *life (vita)*
340   And the noryshe that her feede in the cytee of Asye,   *nurse; brought up (fed)*
      They bare her bodye to Antioche, and nowe in golde dos lye.   *golden [shrine]*
      Thei settyn a chirche in her name, ever to be had in memorye.   *established; kept*

      Alle that seke were and thedyr wolde goo,   *sick; thither*
      Jhesu hem delyvered or thei come therefroo.   *before; returned*
345   Jhesu Cryste of heven, latte us lyve soo
      To have that joye that lastes evermoo.

      Of that swete mayde this is her vye,   *life (vita)*
      The twenteuthe daye of her in the moneth of Julye.
      Jhesu Cryste, that was yborne of the virgyne Marye,
350   For Saynte Margaretes love on us have mercye. Amen.

Explanatory Notes to Stanzaic Life of Margaret

Abbreviations: **A** = Auchinleck (National Library of Scotland MS Advocates 19.2.1), fols. 16v–21r; **Bl** = Blackburn, Public Library MS (formerly Petworth 3), fols. 167r–183r; **Bo** = Bodleian Library MS Bodley 779 (*SC* 2567), fols. 204v–208r; **C** = Cambridge University Library MS Addit. 4122, fols. 6r–38v [base text]; **R** = Bodleian Library MS Rawlinson poet. 34 (*SC* 14528), fols. 1r–4r; **T** = Trinity College, Cambridge MS 323, fols. 20r–24r.

1–4   The poem's formulaic opening, a general call for the audience's attention, reminds us that it was probably designed to be read aloud.

5–16   Compared with other versions of the legend, the stanzaic Life pays unusual attention to Margaret's parents, emphasizing her father's powerful position among the enemies of Christianity and presenting a narrative of subterfuge in which Margaret's pagan mother plays a positive role, secretly sending the infant away to preserve her life. In more typical versions Margaret is sent away to a nurse because her mother has died, and her father does not reject her until he learns of her conversion in the nurse's household; for example, see Mirk's retelling, lines 14–23, and Lydgate's retelling, lines 85–91.

8   This line sounds very much like a later description of the saint's main persecutor, Olibrius (line 34, below). A, Bl, Bo, R, and T all describe Margaret's father as a worshiper of insensate idols ("Deve thinges and doumbe he served night and day" [A]) instead of a priest-magician who conjures up demons, but the anticipation of Olibrius here suggests the power and unity of the pagan culture that persecutes the saint. It also foreshadows the legend's later emphasis on demons as the real enemies that are confronted and ultimately overcome by Margaret.

17–24   The role of the nurse sounds almost like a metaphor for the Church, which was often personified as a nurturing mother of many children. Here she is just given general credit for Margaret's education and subsequent conversion; it is in the nurse's home that she hears the stories of earlier martyrs and commits herself to Christ. In other versions of the legend, including MSS T and R of the stanzaic Life, the nurse plays a more explicit role in Margaret's education as a Christian.

24   St. Stephen, a deacon and the first Christian martyr, was stoned to death in Jerusalem around the year 35 (see Acts 6–7). St. Lawrence (d. 285), also a deacon, was martyred in Rome under the Emperor Valerian by being roasted on a gridiron, according to his famous legend. He and Stephen are often paired — probably because both were deacons as well as martyrs, and both had major feast days in early August. The error of blaming the Jews for both deaths seems not to have been widespread, however. Among the six surviving manuscripts of the stanzaic *Life of Margaret*, only the present text has this reading. A lacks the whole stanza, and the other four MSS just have Margaret learning "How they tholid [suffered] martirdom, Seint Laurens and Seint Steven" (Bo).

27–28   The idea in these lines seems to be that Margaret sets an example of piety that influences her fellow shepherds. The point is clearest in Bo, which reads, "And alle the other herdis wel yerne [eagerly/intently] here behelde, / Hou ofte she made here preyere to Jhesu that al may welde." This theme is developed much further in some versions of the legend than it will be in this one, however. For example, see Lydgate's version, lines 99–109.

39   *Sarasyne*. On the use of this term to describe pagan adversaries of the saints, see explanatory note to line 194 of the early *SEL* account of Mary Magdalen, above.

44   Like the term "Sarasyne" (line 39), swearing by *Mahound* (a corruption of the name "Mohammed") was part of the generic vocabulary used to characterize villains who were pagans, idolaters, or adherents of other false religions. The rest of this line seems to be promising to pay the equivalent of a marriage settlement for Margaret's virginity, if she turns out to be too low-born for him actually to marry.

47   An infinitive verb of motion is implied here, completing the sense of *dydde*.

58   *names seven*. Medieval commentators sometimes listed and discussed various names of Christ (as, e.g., in *Piers Plowman* B.19 and C.21), but the only apparent purpose of the phrase here is to complete the rhyme.

66   *foule gostys*. "Evil spirits." By using this wording C again suggests the demonic nature of Margaret's enemies. The other MSS just refer to them again as *Saracens*.

70   Margaret's words echo Psalm 21:17 (22:16 in Protestant translations): "For many dogs have encompassed me: the council of the malignant hath besieged me."

72   *sche gevys not a hawe!* Proverbial. See Whiting H190.

75   T, A, and Bo preserve a version of this line in which the curse is an interjection, directed at Olibrius by the narrator: *awarie/acorsse him sonne ant mone!* This kind of exuberant story-telling, which can also be seen in the longer *SEL* account of Frideswide in this collection, has been suppressed almost entirely in C, presumably for the sake of decorum. For other instances, see below, explanatory notes to lines 243, 263, and 271–72.

81   Only C and R make Margaret such a model of politeness that she graciously initiates the conversation with the pagan persecutor whose men have just arrested her. More logically, the other four manuscripts have it be Olibrius who greets Margaret politely (Bo) or — more often — eagerly.

92   *Longeous.* Longinus. The name traditionally given to the Roman soldier who pierced Christ's side while He hung on the cross in order to confirm His death (John 19:34). In some legends he was a blind man, led by others to this act, whose sight was mercifully restored by the water and blood which came from Christ's wound.

98   In four of the other five MSS this line ends, *and thider thou shalt wende!* or *that thou schalt in ende* — an explicit prediction or threat by Margaret, that is, that Olibrius will end up in the same hell from which Christ's followers have been freed. As usual, the reading in C is more polite.

131   *Ne geveth sche not an hawe.* See explanatory note to line 72.

132   *sche sette not bye a strawe!* Proverbial. See Whiting S813.

137   The sense is clearer in some of the other MSS, which have them flaying the skin from her flesh (T, R) or her bones (Bl).

139–46 The pity of onlookers and the saints' rejection of their advice are standard features of a virgin martyr legend, serving to emphasize the martyr's heroism. The onlookers focus on her tormented body, while she is concerned only for the state of her soul.

164–78 This account of the angelic visit before Margaret confronts the dragon may suggest some nervousness about the scene to follow. The angel not only assures her that she has nothing to fear, since her place in heaven is already assured, but also provides her with Christ's cross to use as a weapon. In other versions of the legend she herself initiates the confrontation by asking for the sight of her adversary and is able to protect herself just by making the sign of the cross as the dragon tries to swallow her. See Lydgate's account, e.g., lines 277–82 and 288–94.

182   *alle greene as the gresse.* Middle English writers often use "green" or even "green as grass" to describe a complexion that has become deathly pale. Compare, e.g., Chaucer's description of the grief-stricken Criseyde: "And thus she lith with hewes pale and grene, / That whilom fressh and fairest was to sene" (*TC* 4.1154–55).

187   Margaret's most common iconographic symbols portray her either as emerging from within the dragon or (especially from the mid fourteenth century on) standing triumphantly on top of it. Mirk comments explicitly on this iconography in lines 49–51 of his account, given below.

193   The standard Latin version just says his hands were fastened to his knees, perhaps an echo of Mark 3:27. But the MSS of the stanzaic Life tend to describe him as a monstrous creature having (variously) spikes on his feet and knees (Bo), or hands or heads on his knees and eyes on every toe (A, Bl), or extra eyes on his claws and also on his toes (T), or many horns on his head and eyes more than two (R).

195–96   In Eastern iconography, Marina is often shown grabbing the demon by the head with one hand and holding a hammer in the other. In the stanzaic Life of Margaret, the cross of Christ has evidently replaced the hammer as her weapon. The detail of her binding the demon with her wimple reinforces his later lament about his humiliation at the hands of a weak female (line 214). Images of Margaret with a leash-like cloth around the demon's neck are fairly common.

207   *Ruffyn.* The demon says the dragon destroyed by Margaret was his brother Ruffinus (or *Rufo, Rufonis* in the standard Latin version of the legend). The name, presumably derived from the word for "reddish" or "red-haired," is also used for a devil in the Chester Cycle (*Fall of Lucifer*, line 271, in *The Chester Mystery Cycle: A New Edition with Modernised Spelling*, ed. David Mills [East Lansing, MI: Colleagues Press, 1992]) and in *The Poems of John Audelay* (ed. Ella Keats Whiting, EETS o.s. 184 [London: Oxford University Press, 1931; rpt. 1971], pp. 75, lines 298–300).

210   Other MSS of the stanzaic Life say more directly that he repaid these human followers with great sorrow (T, A) or by having them hanged (R).

212   In the standard Latin version he says the goal was to swallow Margaret and obliterate her memory from the earth. In C and other MSS of the stanzaic Life, this has become a mental rather than a physical attack, attempting to rob Margaret of her sanity and her ability to remember and remain faithful to God.

215   *Belsabub.* The name "Beelzebub," which means "lord of the flies" in Hebrew, first appears in 2 Kings 1:6 (4 Kings 1:6 in Vulgate and Douay) as a distortion of the name of a Canaanite god. Later the name came to be used for a ruler of the demons opposed to God (see Matthew 10:25, 12:24; Mark 3:22; Luke 11:15–19), and sometimes as another name for Satan himself.

217   *with wynde I flye.* An allusion to Ephesians 2:2, where the devil is "the prince of the power of this air, of the spirit that now worketh on the children of unbelief."

218   *Alle I wolde do qwelle.* His expression of enmity to all living creatures is typical demonic discourse, since the devils were understood to be envious of the earth and its inhabitants, who were made to replace them after their fall from heaven. (See, e.g., lines 351–71 of Lydgate's account.)

219–22   Here the devil confesses his particular attacks on pregnant women (a point that will be mentioned again in line 234) and on newborn children who have not yet been baptized. Since the legend ordinarily either has him describe his assaults on the chastity of celibate men and women (as in the standard Latin version and the Katherine Group) or omits all such specifics, this unusual addition supports the hypothesis that the stanzaic Life was designed specifically for a lay audience. In this connection, see also explanatory note to lines 311–18, below, on Margaret's final prayer.

223–32   King Solomon of Israel built the first temple and was credited with writing three books of the Hebrew Bible — Proverbs, Ecclesiastes, and Song of Songs. The apocryphal *Testament of Solomon* records Jewish tradition about Solomon's power over demons, which is the source for this story about how the demons were locked in a vessel and buried by Solomon but later escaped when greedy men opened it, assuming it was filled with treasure. For an English translation of the *Testament*, see D. C. Durling and J. Charlesworth, *The Old Testament Pseudepigrapha*, vol. 1 (Garden City, NY: Doubleday, 1983), pp. 935–97.

239   Margaret emerges from prison and her victories over the devil on the third day, recalling Christ's emergence from the tomb and the Harrowing of Hell on the third

day. Most other versions of Margaret's legend, including the other MSS of the stanzaic Life, say she was in the cell just overnight.

243   Some MSS have the narrator curse Olibrius at the end of this line: *Crist yive him ivel dede!* (A), *that Criste worthe hym wrothe!* (Bl). On such interjections, which C nearly always omits, see explanatory note to line 75 above.

254   Jesus' baptism in the Jordan River is recounted in Matthew 3:13–17 and Mark 1:9–11.

260–66   This is an unusual version of Margaret's torments. More typically, she is burned with torches and then tied up and thrown into a vat of water, either to drown or just to increase her suffering. Here the tormentors are ordered to scald her with boiling oil; but instead of harming her, the oil anoints her head and runs down in plentiful streams — an image that would remind a Christian audience of Psalm 23:5 [Vulgate 22:5].

263   MS A curses the torturers at this point: *sorwe hem mot bitide!*

271–72   This curse may be spoken by Margaret herself, but it seems out of keeping with the mildness of her other speeches, especially in C, to everyone except the devil. Three other MSS of the stanzaic Life have the narrator calling down curses at this point on Olibrius (Bo), his men (A), or both (Bl), and that may be the most plausible interpretation here too.

275–76   As with the oil, the elements of Margaret's ordeal are transformed into positive Christian symbols. Margaret, who has just recommended baptism to Olibrius (lines 253–54), is now baptized in the water that was intended for her destruction.

279–81   The number of Margaret's converts at this point is usually given as five thousand, not counting women and children — echoing the wording used in Matthew 14:21 to describe the multitude miraculously fed with a few loaves and fishes by Jesus and his disciples. Mirk retains that traditional wording (lines 82–83), but the MSS of the stanzaic Life give numbers ranging from 1005 to 10,005.

284   Malchus is the name of the high priest's slave in John 18:10, who comes with other men to arrest Jesus. Peter cuts off his ear with a sword, but Jesus restores it.

287–90   The scene of Margaret's execution is reminiscent of Christ's: she is led out of town, escorted by a crowd, and the occasion is marked by fearful omens. See Matthew 27:31–54, Mark 15:20–39, Luke 23:26–48.

303–22   Margaret's final prayer is the main source of her power as an intercessor. Note the different ways in which she says her memory and assistance may be invoked: by reading or hearing the story of her passion, building a church or chapel, giving any alms, or (lines 319–20) just honoring the day of her death or devoutly praying to her. The list is broad enough to cover the whole economic and educational spectrum of believers.

311–18   The Auchinleck MS (A) of the stanzaic Life places further emphasis on Margaret's specific role as an intercessor for women in childbirth by omitting most of the other petitions and introducing her final prayer with these lines:

> Mergrete the milde that was Godes mayde
> Thought upon the wordes the dragoun in prisoun seyd:
> that devels yede in erthe women for to breyd
> that were traveland of child or doun in childebed leyd.
> Than bad Mergrete to Jhesu that was so fre:
> "Yif ani woman travayl and hard clepeth to me,
> Deliver hir, Lord, with joie thurch vertu of the Tre
> That thou dest thi body on to make ous al fre."

Among MSS of the stanzaic Life, however, only C includes the stanza which extends the petitions specifically to the condition of the newborn child, asking that it be delivered with all its limbs and senses intact.

313   In a house where a woman was giving birth, it was customary for all knots to be unfastened in hopes that the "unbinding" would carry over to the delivery.

322   Here Margaret's general efficacy as an intercessor for the forgiveness of sins seems to be extended to those who cannot be buried in consecrated ground. If this promise was interpreted as applying to sinners who died without being shriven, it might have raised objections from church authorities.

323–26   The Rawlinson MS (R) reinforces and extends the promise to Margaret's devotees by adding another stanza after this one:

> "More to thee ys grauntede off allemyghty Godde in Trynité,
> Off thinge that thou nameste noughte, and worde is sente be me.

In what hous thi lyffe ys redde and a childe yborene schalle be,
Off the womane ne of the childe the ffynde getethe no postee."

328–34   See Jesus' words to the thief on the cross who confesses faith in Him: "This day thou shalt be with me in paradise" (Luke 23:43). In many versions of the Margaret legend, the executioner Malchus, converted by Margaret's prayer and the answering voice from heaven, falls dead at her side after striking the fatal blow.

335–36   It is unusual to name the angels who come to fetch a saint's soul, but Margaret's sanctity is emphasized in this version by the importance of her chief escorts, the three great archangels, as well as the great number of lesser angels in the retinue (a thousand in T, R, and Bl, and ten thousand here). Michael is a particularly appropriate escort for Margaret because he too fought great battles against demons and a dragon; in the eastern church, he and Marina were often paired as guardians of church doors.

337   Most MSS of the stanzaic Life say specifically that it is Margaret's soul that is borne to heaven by the angels. Her body remains on earth as a source of relics, of course, but some early versions of the legend say that the angels took her head to heaven immediately.

348   Margaret's feastday is July 20. This line says so a bit more clearly in T: *The twenteuthe dai is hire in the time of Julie.*

Textual Notes to Stanzaic Life of Margaret

Abbreviations: see explanatory notes.

29–32   As the broken rhyme scheme in this stanza suggests, there is a textual problem at this point. Bo, R, and Bl all have a full quatrain describing Margaret's relationship with Jesus which uses the rhyme words *yeme*, *deme*, and *queme* in its first, second, and final lines. But these MSS all have different readings — and different rhyme words — for the second half of the third line, suggesting that this part of the stanza was missing in their common ancestor. The same gap must have existed in the ancestor behind C. Instead of filling the gap as the other three MSS do, however, C changes the rhyme in line 31 and for line 32 borrows a line from the next stanza, where other MSS have *Olibrius was loverd, ase the boc us tellet* (T) or *Olibrius was tho lord, so ich you may telle* (Bo).

36   Having used the line which originally rhymed on "telle" to complete the preceding stanza, C has to supply something else for the fourth rhyme in this one. Again the solution is to borrow and slightly revise the first line from the next stanza, which in all other MSS gives the distance as "miles ten and five."

41–42   The other five MSS of the stanzaic Life have a full quatrain at this point, rhyming *see*, *me*, *free*, and *be*, which begins with Olibrius calling his men's attention to the maiden he has seen and sending them to fetch her. C, which has borrowed these lines to complete the preceding quatrain, settles for a mere couplet here and finally gets back in step with the other MSS.

43   *thral.* A correction in C, written by a later hand over what seems originally to have been *iral.*

52   *smyte.* The other MSS preserve the rhyme more exactly by using the verbs *(bi)swike* (A, Bl, Bo, R) or *fike* (T), both of which mean "to flatter or deceive."

54   *wynne.* In the other five MSS, Olibrius' men say explicitly at this point that he wants to marry [*wyve*] her. C's use of *wynne* creates more ambiguity.

68   *Cryste.* Corrected in C from *Cryste Cryste.*

73–74   The other MSS maintain the rhyme on "-awe" to the end of this quatrain, but only with difficulty. The most satisfactory version (found in T and Bo), which may preserve the original rhyme words, ends these last two lines with *drawe* and *plawe* — the latter, a variant form of the noun "play" that would have been completely unfamiliar in some Middle English dialects.

77   *he sayde.* No other MS of the stanzaic Life includes these words, which make the line too long and would have been unnecessary in an oral performance that dramatized changes of speaker. C has an added "he said" or "she said" or "they said" in a number of other lines as well, including 91, 124, 127, 151, 155, 159, 167, 175, 199, 203, 235, 275, 285, and 328.

78   The other MSS of the stanzaic Life all have Olibrius vowing at this point to make her change her religion rather than to love him.

85   *thral.* C: *ryal.*

86   *so longe as it schal bee.* Instead of this vague phrase, at least one MS of the stanzaic Life (T) has *so long so Ic be,* "as long as I live." The words *it* and *ic* look so similar in late-medieval handwriting that one could easily be mistaken for the other.

91   This line is obviously too long in C. See textual note to line 77, above.

106   *forsake Him nowe for aye.* The other MSS all use more colloquial wording: *thou do him al awei* (T, A, Bl), *thou lete him al away* (Bo), or *do him alle clene away* (R).

114   *oute.* Corrected in C from *oute oute.*

117   *by the here.* The other five MSS all have him ordering her to be hung up by the feet instead.

171   *dred thou not it.* Other MSS have the angel telling her to fear *no wight,* "no creature," or *nowid* "nothing (nought)."

177   *warde.* The rhyme in C is obviously defective. The other MSS have *that alle us mai amende* (T), or something similar, all with *amende* as the rhyme word.

184   *sche craked everye boone.* Other MSS of the stanzaic Life say she was so afraid that she *quakede* (T, Bl) or *schok* (Bo) in every bone.

192   The reading in C is *another dragon moo;* but the other five MSS all refer to it either specifically as a devil (T, Bo), as in the Latin, or more generally as a foul or hateful creature (A, Bl, R).

194   In place of this line, the other five MSS just say that he was the foulest or most hateful or most grisly creature that ever walked on the earth.

224–25   C has *fraffate,* which looks like a corruption of *bras fat,* the reading found in A and Bo. R and Bl have *fatte of bras* and *tonne of brasse* respectively. T omits this stanza and the next one.

241   Other MSS portray Olibrius's officers more neutrally at this point, referring to them as "sergeants" rather than torturers and describing them as *snelle* (T) or *fulle redy* (R) — that is, quick to obey, rather than sadistic.

250   Other MSS have less anticlimactic versions of this line which warn Olibrius that his gods are leading him to death (Bo, R) or to hell (T, A).

282   Unemended, this line in C says they were all brought *on lyve,* which might suggest a mass baptism. But other texts of the legend, including the other MSS of the

stanzaic Life, make it clear that all these converts were put to death (brought *of lyve* or *o live*) by Olibrius's men.

285–86   Olibrius threatens to carry Margaret out of town and kill her himself, if Malchus will not do it. C has the spear paired with a *schelde*, a familiar formula that does not suit the context here; the other MSS all have the more logical *swerde*.

299–300   The defective rhyme is not easily emended, since all the MSS of the stanzaic Life have different readings at this point.

339   *Theophyle.* Other MSS of the stanzaic Life name her biographer "Theophole" (Bl), "Theodius" (T), or "Theodocius" (R, A), all corruptions of "Theotimus," whose name derives from the Greek for "God" and "honor." He is a fictional character who first appears in the Mombritius recension of the Latin legend, claiming to have witnessed her trials and collected all the writings about her.

    her vye. C: *her bye* ("about her"), which is probably just a misreading of *her vye* ("her *vita*, or life"), the reading in T and Bl, which looks almost the same in a late-medieval English hand.

347   *vye.* In C this line ends with *weye*, another scribal substitute for the French word *vie*, preserved in T and Bl, which makes better sense and a better rhyme.

John Mirk, *Sermon on St. Margaret,*
from British Library MS Cotton Claudius A.ii, fols. 90v–91v

Gode men, suche a day [N] ye schal have the fest of Seynt Margrete. And thagh it be a lyght halyday, save theras the schyrch is edyfyed in hur name, yitte I warne yow, for as I suppose ther ben somme that have suche love to hure, that he wyl fasten hur evon. Bot than ye that faste hur evyn, ye quyte yow not to hyr

5   os ye schulde bot if ye comon to chyrch on morowun and heren a masse of hure; for scheo wyl cun yow more thank to makyn a masse isayde in worchep of hur than to faston many evenes brede and watur wythoute masse. For the masse joyeth alle the angellys of Heven, it fedeth and comfordeth the soules in purcatorie, and sokoreth alle that leveth in erthe in scharité. And he that fasteth the evyn, he

10   helpyth hymselfe, and no forthur. Than to styrron youre devocion the more to this holy maydon, I wil schewen in party of hyr lyfe, and whate scheo suffred for Goddys love.

[Narracio] I rede in hir lyf that scheo hadde a grete man to hir fadur, and he was a paynym and leved on falce goddys and mawmentrye. Bot whan that Margarete

15   was borne, the fadur sente hyr into the cuntré to a norys. So whyl scheo was longe there among othyr maydenys, sche harde spekon of God and of oure Lorde Jhesu Criste, how He boght mankynde wyth Hys deth oute of thraldam of the fende, and how He lovid specialy alle that woldon leven in chastité and servon

---

1 suche a day [N], on such and such a day [to be inserted by the speaker]. **2 thagh . . . hur name,** although it is just a minor holiday, except where the church is dedicated to her. **3–4 that he wyl fasten hur evon,** that he wishes (or, they wish) to fast on the evening before her feast day. **4–5 ye quyte yow not . . . a masse of hure,** you do not behave to her as you should unless you [also] come to church the next day and hear a mass in her honor. **6 cun yow more thank to makyn a masse isayde,** offer you more thanks for having a mass said. **8 joyeth,** gladdens. **9 sokoreth,** helps (succors); **scharité,** charity. **10 and no forthur,** and no one else. **11 I wil schewen in party of hyr lyfe,** I will tell a little of her life story. **14 leved on falce goddys and mawmentrye,** believed in false gods and idolatry. **16 harde spekon,** heard [people] speak. **17–18 thraldam of the fende,** slavery to the devil (fiend).

139

Hym in sympulnesse and poverté. Than, whan that Margarete harde this, scheo
20   toke suche a love to Jhesu Cryste, that scheo made a vow in hir herte, that scheo
wolde nevre have parte of mannus body, but lyven in hur maydonhedde alle hur
lyve-dayes aftur. But whan hyr fadur harde how Margarete, hys doghtyr, was
levyng in Criste, he forsoke hur for hys doghtyr and despysid hur to the utmaste.
Than dwellyd scheo wyth hyr noryce til scheo was fyftene yere holde, and than
25   scheo sette hyr to kepe hyr scheppe wyth other maydonys of hyr age.

    Than os scheo satte be the way, com the justyce of the cuntré rydyng that way
that was callyd Olybryus, and sagh Margrete that scheo was fayre passyng alle
othyr. Anone he caght suche a love to hyre for hur bewté that he badde hys men
bryngon hyr to hym, and if scheo were gentyl of kynde, he wolde weddon hyr,
30   and if scheo were a servaunde, he wolde han hyr to lemman. Bot whan scheo was
broght beforyn hym, and he wyst that scheo was of Criston fayth, than was he
neygh wode for wrothe. And for scheo wolde not assent to hym, he made to
henggyn hyr up, and so beton hyr wyth scorges, and to rason hyr fayre body
wyth euelys, that it was wondur to sene the grete plenté of blode that com oute of
35   hyr body, and aftyr made to caston hyr in prison til on the morowgh, that he
myght bethenkyn hym what were best to don wyth hyr.

    Than preyed Margrete to God that scheo moste sene the fende bodyly that so
reysyd so strong enemys ageynus hur. Than anone com there oute of a herne of
the prison a grete horrybul dragon and yonyd on hur, so that hys mowth was on
40   hyr heved, and wolde han swalowod hyr, and hys tong laste doun to hur hele. And
whan he hadde hyr alle in hys mowth, Margrete made a syne of the cros, and
anone the dragon braste on-sondyr. Than Margrete lokyd abowte hur and seygh

---

19 harde, heard. **21 have parte of**, have anything to do with; **lyven in hur maydonhedde**, would live in virginity. **23 forsoke hur**, disowned her; **despysid hur to the utmaste**, scorned her entirely. **24 fyftene yere holde**, fifteen years old. **26 os scheo satte be the way**, as she sat beside the road. **29 gentyl of kynde**, of gentle birth. **30 to lemman**, as his mistress. **32–33 he made to henggyn hyr up**, he ordered [his men] to hang her up. **33–34 rason hyr fayre body wyth euelys**, tear her lovely body with hooks (awls). **35 til on the morowgh**, until the next day. **37–38 that scheo moste sene . . . enemys ageynus hur**, that she might see in bodily form the devil (fiend) that aroused such strong enemies against her. **38 herne**, corner. **39 yonyd**, opened his mouth wide (yawned). **40 laste doun to hur hele**, reached down to her heel(s).

the fende standyn in a hurne, alle matyd, wyth hys handys boundyn behynd hym. Scheo styrte to hym, and pullyd hym downe undyr hyr fete, and sette hyr fette on hys nek, and thrust hym doun to the grounde wyth alle hyr mythe. Than cryed the fende and sayde, "Allas, I am undone for ever, and alle my myght is lorne, now suche a yong wenche hath ovrecome me! Many a byggar man and stronger I have ovrecomen, and nogh suche a noghtyng hath geton the maystry over me and put me undur hur fotte!" Herefore where that Margrete is peyntyd oythur corvon, scheo hath a dragon undyr hur fette and a cros in hur hande, schewing how be the vertu of the Cros scheo gate the victory of the fende.

Than seyde Margrete, "Holde thi janglyng, fende, and telle me anone whate ys thine lynage, and what ben thin werkys?"

Than answerid he and sayde: "My fadur is Lucifer that was furste the fayrest angel in Hevne, and now he is the fowlest fende in helle. And of my werkys I telle thee that be my techyng the Jewes slowen Cryste on the crosse and hys apostelys and alle hys dysciplus aftur, and many a martyr I have made to do to deth. I have made many on to slee othyr, and to synnon in letchery and in avowtry, and so leson here soules; and most levest me is to makon a Criston man to brekon that vow that he made at the fonte whan he toke hys cristondam." And he say he was on of the fendys that Salomon closyd in a vessel and hud in the erthe. "But aftyr Salomons deth, for men sen smok comen oute of the erthe ther we weron, thei wendon for to a fowndon grete plenté of tresour, and dyggon to oure vessel that

43 **standyn in a hurne, alle matyd,** standing in a corner, all defeated. 44 **styrte,** moved quickly. 45 **alle hyr mythe,** all her power (might). 46 **lorne, now,** lost, now [that]. 48 **nogh suche a noghtyng,** now such an insignificant person. 49 **Herefore where that Margrete is peyntyd oythur corvon,** For this reason, wherever Margaret is painted or sculpted (carved). 50–51 **be the vertu of the Cros scheo gate the victory of the fende,** by the power of the Cross she vanquished the devil. 52 **Holde thi janglyng,** Stop your noisy chatter. 53 **lynage,** ancestry. 56 **slowen,** killed (slew). 57 **made to do to deth,** caused to be put to death. 58 **made many on to slee othyr,** caused many a person to kill another; **avowtry,** adultery. 59 **leson here soules,** to lose their souls; **most levest me is,** what pleases me best is. 60 **whan he toke hys cristondam,** when he received baptism. 60–61 **say he was on of,** said he was one of. 61 **closyd,** enclosed; **hud,** hid. 62 **for men sen smok,** since people saw smoke. 62–63 **thei wendon for to a fowndon,** they supposed they had found. 63 **dyggon,** dug down.

we weron inne wythoute noumbur, and so brekyn the vesel, and leton us oute.
65 And so we fylleth the eyre and don Cristen men the gref that we connyn and mowne."

Than, whan Margrete herde this, scheo prayed to God that thilke fende most synkon into helle, and nevre greve more Criston bodyus. Than anone the erthe oponyd and swellowod hym into helle.

70 Than, on the morowen, Olybrius sende aftyr Margrete; bot for he myght be no way ovrecome hur, he made to fyllyn a grete fatte ful of watur, and byndon hyr hand and fette, and castyn hir therinne, to have drownyd hyr ther. Than scheo besoght God that fatte moste ben hyr fonte, and the watur the lavyr and wassyng of alle hur synnes, and so ben fowlowod in the noumbur of Cristen men. And 75 whan scheo was in the watyr and prayed thus, anone the bondus brekon, and scheo com oute saf and sounde. And the erthe quakyd so grysly, that alle the pepul was grevesly aferde. And therwyth com a mylk-qwyte colvyr from Hevne, bering a crowne of brygh golde in hyr bylle, and lygh on Margretes hed. And therwyth a voys spake fro Hevne and seyde, "Margrete, myn owen derling, be 80 studfaste in thine turnent, for alle the cumpany of Heven abydyth thi commyng."

Then, whan the pepul seygh and herde this, anone thei cryedon and seydon, "Ther is no God bot He that Margrete belevyth on!" And so fyve thousand of the pepul, wythoute wommen and chyldren, turnyd to Cristes fayth. The wyche Olibrius made anone to be hedon, and so thei weryn fulwode in hur owne blode 85 and yodon to Heven holy martyres. Than Olibrius commaunded to leden Margrete

---

64 brekyn, broke. **65–66 don Cristen men the gref that we connyn and mowne**, cause Christian people as much trouble (grief) as we know how and are permitted. **67–68 most synkon**, might sink. **68 bodyus**, people (bodies). **69 oponyd**, opened; **swellowod**, swallowed. **70 the morowen**, the next day. **70–71 for he myght be no way ovrecome hur**, since he could not defeat her by any means. **71 made to fyllyn a grete fatte**, had a great vessel filled. **73 that fatte moste ben hyr fonte**, that vessel might be her baptismal font; **lavyr and wassyng**, [spiritual] cleansing and washing. **74 fowlowod in the noumbur**, baptized into the company. **77 mylk-qwyte colvyr**, milk-white dove. **78 brygh**, bright; **lygh**, alighted. **80 turnent**, torment. **83 wythoute wommen and chyldren**, not counting women and children. **84 made anone to be hedon**, caused to be beheaded immediately; **fulwode in hur owne blode**, baptized in their own blood. **85 yodon**, went; **commaunded to leden Margrete**, ordered that Margaret be led.

to a certeyne place, and ther to be beheded. Bot whan scheo com to the place, scheo knelud doun, and prayde to God that evry man that made a chyrch in hur name or fond any lyght therinne in worchep of hur, and alle that wryteth hure passyon or reduth hyt or callyth to hur in grete distresse, that God schulde don

90 hem sokur radly, and graunte hem the joy that evre schal laston, and uche womman that calleth to hyre in travayle of chylde, that scheo muste be delivered sounde and the chylde come to cristyndom. Than com ther a voyse from Heven and sayde, "Margrete, thi bone is graunted, and schal lastyn for evremore." Than scheo putte forthe hur nekke, and the turmentoures smotte hur hed of at one

95 stroke. So that thei that stodon abowton seyne here soule comyn oute of hure body as a mylke-qwyte colvyr; and angelys comen and toke it, and beron itte into Hevne. Than, in the nyghte aftur, a Criston man stel the body and beryed itte, etc.

87 made a chyrch, built a church. **88 fond any lyght**, provided a lamp or set of candles. **89–90 don hem sokur radly**, give them help quickly. **91 in travayle of chylde**, in the pains of childbirth; **muste**, might. **92 come to cristyndom**, live long enough to be baptized. **93 bone**, request (boon). **94 turmentoures smotte hur hed of**, executioner(s) struck off her head. **95 thei that stodon abowton seyne**, they who stood nearby saw. **96 mylke-qwyte colvyr**, milk-white dove; **beron**, carried.

Explanatory Notes to Mirk's Sermon on St. Margaret

Abbreviations: **C** = British Library MS Cotton Claudius A.ii, fols. 90v–91v [base text]; **E** = Theodor Erbe [EETS edition]; **H 2391** = British Library MS Harley 2391, fols. 149r–150r; **H 2403** = British Library MS Harley 2403, fols. 127v–130r; **H 2417** = British Library MS Harley 2417, fols. 52r–53v.

60–66   For this tradition about Solomon, see explanatory note to the stanzaic life of Margaret, lines 223–32.

97   *etc.* Some MSS specify the call to prayer with which the sermon is to end: *Now schal ye knele adowne and pray Saynt Margret to kepe you from al myschevys and from the fyndys comburment [enticement to sin] so that ye may lyve and ende that ye may have the blysse that Jhesu boght you to. Amen* (quoted from E; H 2403 and H 2417 have *comburance* in place of *comburment*, and end there). H 2391 has a different closing formula: *Now trewly, frendes, sen it es so that this blessyd saynt, Saynt Margaret, askyd slyke a boon of God, me thynke that everylke Cristyn man and woman sulde have gret devocion to worschyp Saynt Margaret, that thurgh the wylke worschypyng we myght come to that blyse that never schall have end. Amen.*

Textual Notes to Mirk's Sermon on St. Margaret

Abbreviations: see explanatory notes.

1   *Gode men.* Some MSS have *Good men and women*, or no salutation at all.

2   *edyfyed.* Other MSS have *dedicated* or *deynt* instead.

5   *schulde.* C has the form *schuldo*, presumably an error for either *schulde* or *schulde do*.

30   *wolde.* C: omits.

31   *he wyst.* C and most other MSS omit *he*.

33   Some MSS specify that he hung her up by the hair.

54   *and.* C: *an.*

60   *he say.* C: omits *he*. A few MSS have the fuller reading *yeet he sayd more*, which also appears in E's EETS edition.

64   *leton.* The reading is found in E's EETS edition and most of the MSS. C: *beton.*

71   C: *bydon*, which I have emended to *byndon* on the basis of other MSS' *bynd* or *bonde*.

77   *pepul.* C has the peculiar form *pepully*, perhaps by contamination from one of the nearby adverbs.

81   *cryedon.* C: *cryened*, which is presumably just an error for *cryed* or *cryeden*.

84   *thei.* C: *the*, an obvious slip.

86   *to be beheded.* C: *to be heded hyre*, which looks like a mixture of the idioms "to be beheaded" and "to behead her."

90   *graunte.* C: *graunted*, but the syntax obviously demands either an infinitive or present subjunctive.

96   *and₁.* C: *an.*

John Lydgate, *"The Lyfe of Seynt Margarete,"*
from Durham University Library MS Cosin V.II.14, fols. 97v–106r

Here begynneth the prolog of the holy seynt, Seynt Margarete, compendyously compiled in balade by Lidgate dan Johan, Monk of Bury, A° VIII° h VI ¹.

	At the reverence of Seynt Margarete	*In honor of*
	My purpos is hir lyfe to compile;	
	Though I have no rethorikes swete	
	Nor colour noon t'enbelisshe with my style	*Nor any; to embellish*
5	Yet dar I seyn, it happeth so somen while,	*sometimes*
	Under writyng rude of apparence	*of rough appearance*
	Mater is hid of grete intellygence.	*knowledge*
	Ful ofte falleth, in this chestys blake	*[it] happens; these [ordinary] black chests*
	Golde and perlys and stones of grete prys	*pearls; value*
10	Ben ylooke and into warde ytake;	*locked [up]; guardianship*
	And by sentence and the prudent avys	*counsel*
	Of philosoffres, that holden were so wys,	*were considered*
	A royal ruby in whiche ther is no lak	*fault*
	May closed ben in a ful pore sak.	*be enclosed; very poor bag (sack)*
15	And though that I have noon eloquence	
	For to discryve hir parfit holynesse	*describe her (Margaret's)*
	Hir chaste lyf, hir tendre innocence,	
	Hir martirdam wrought by grete duresse,—	*hardship*
	Ay unmutable in hir stablenesse,	*Always unchangeable; resolution*
20	Unto the dethe ay one in hir suffraunce,	*always the same; patience*
	So was hir herte roted on constaunce.	*rooted in constancy*
	In Crystes feith she gan hir so delyte,	
	For whom she lyste despyse al worldly glorye,	*chose to despise*
	This daysye, with leves rede and white,	
25	Purpul hewed, as maked is memorye,	*Crimson colored*
	Whan that hir blode was shad oute by victorye,	*shed*

147

	The chaste lely of whos maydenhede	*lily; virginity*
	Thorough martyrdam was spreynt with roses rede.	*covered*
	Margarete, the storye dothe hir calle,	
30	After a stone ynamed "margarite,"	
	A precyous gemme amonge these stones alle,	
	In there bokes as clerkys liste to write;	*choose*
	For of nature perlys echone ben white,	*pearls are all*
	Right vertuous of kynde, rounde and smalle —	*powerful by nature*
35	Whiche propurtees resemblen hir at alle.	*properties; wholly*
	She was first white by virginyté,	
	In al hir lyvyng prevyde vertuous,	*proved*
	And smal she was by humylité;	*humility*
	Right strong in God, this maide glorious;	
40	And for she was thurgh deth victoryous,	*because*
	Thurgh her triumphe she gate the palme in hevene,	*earned; palm*
	With laurer crowned above the sterres sevene.	*laurel; seven stars*
	This stone in vertu is a cordyal,	*power; stimulant*
	To the spirit a grete confortatyf;	*something that restores and strengthens*
45	Right so hir herte was imperyal —	*majestic*
	I mene, in vertu duryng al hir lyf;	*virtue (power)*
	For she venquesshed with al hir mortal stryf	*overcame*
	The devel, the worlde, her storye dothe devyse,	*tell*
	And of hir flesshe she made a sacryfice	*flesh*
50	Unto the Lorde, that starf upon the Rode,	*died; Cross*
	Whan He liste deye for oure redempcyoun;	*chose [to]*
	So this virgine, t'aquyte Him, shad hir blode	*to repay; shed*
	Ful benygnely in her passyoun.	*graciously; martyrdom*
	O gemme of gemmes, vyrgyn of most renoun,	*virgin of greatest fame*
55	Thy lif to write be thou my socoure,	*help*
	And shede of grace the aureat lycoure	*golden liquid*
	Into my penne, quakyng of verray drede,	*[which is] quaking for very fear*
	Of retoryke for I have no muse	*rhetoric; because*
	Duely to write thi martirdom; in dede,	*Properly*
60	Ne were oo thyng, I wolde me excuse —	*except for one thing*

That thou of grace wylt me not refuse   *will not refuse me*
But dyrectyn, O blysful lode-sterre,   *guide; guiding star*
Me and my penne to conveye, whan I erre.   *to lead; wander*

Lat thi lyght in derkenesse be my guyde   *Let; guide*
65   Tochyng this processe whiche I have undertake.   *Concerning*
Remembre, O virgyne, upon that other side
On hir that caused, oonly for thi sake,   *exclusively*
Thyn holy lyf me to compile and make, —   *your holy life; write*
My Lady Marche I mene, whiche of entent   *who deliberately*
70   Gafe firste to me in commaundement   *Gave*

That I shulde considre welle and see
In Frensshe and Latyne thyn holy passyoun,   *suffering*
Thi martirdam and thi virginité,
And therof make a compilacyoun;   *from those sources; compilation*
75   So, as I cowde, under correccioun,   *as best I could, subject to correction*
And under supporte of alle that shal it rede,   *of everyone; read*
Upon this storye thus I wylle procede.

Here endeth the prolog of Seynt Margarete, and next folwyng begynneth the storye of hir.

In Anthiochye, a famous grete citee,   *Antioch*
This blyssed mayde, this martir gloryous
80   Whilom was born, hire legende ye may see, —   *Some time ago*
Hir fader callid Theodosius;   *father*
And as the storye playnly telleth us,
A patryark he was of paynym lawes   *chief priest; pagan religion*
After the ryghtes used in tho dawes.   *rites; those days*

85   To a noryce this mayde was ytake,   *nurse; taken*
Right gracious of shape and of visage.   *face*
The paynym lawe of herte she hath forsake   *pagan; from her heart; forsaken*
And was baptised in hir tendre age,   *young age*
For whiche hir fader gan fallen in a rage   *fell into*
90   And to hirward bare ful grete haterede,   *toward her; hatred*
Whan that he knewe she crystened was in dede.   *christened*

149

	And whan that she by processe dede atteyne	*passage of time; did attain*
	Unto the age of fiftene yere,	
	With othir maydnes of beauté sovereyne,	*outstanding beauty*
95	This holy virgyne, benygne and glad of chere,	*expression*
	Flouryng in vertu, moste goodly and entere,	*Flowering; complete*
	Humble of hir porte, this gracyous creature	*bearing*
	Kepte of hir noryce the shepe in theire pasture.	*sheep*

	Devoyde of pride, of rancour and of ire,	*ill humor; anger*
100	She called was a mirrour of mekenesse.	*gentleness*
	The Holy Gost hir herte so dede enspire	*inspire*
	That wille and thought were sette on parfitnesse;	*perfection*
	To thynke on Criste was holy hir gladnesse,	*wholly her joy*
	And chere benygne to alle she dede shewe,	*gracious bearing*
105	Softe of hir speche, and but of wordys fewe.	*few words*

	She gat hir love upon every syde	*was loved by all around her*
	By cause she was so inly vertuous,	*spiritually virtuous*
	For God and grace with hir dide abide —	
	Al thyng eschewyng that was vycious —	*avoiding everything*
110	Til that the Prefette, called Olibrius,	*Prefect*
	Of aventure rode on his pleyng,	*By chance; enjoying himself*
	Where he sawe first this mayde, hir shepe kepyng.	*tending her sheep*

	He was ravesshede anoon with hir beauté,	*overwhelmed*
	Hir grete fairnesse whan he dide adverte,	*beauty; perceive*
115	Hir fresshe face eke whan he dide see;	*also*
	Hir hevenly iyen perced thurgh his herte,	*eyes*
	Brent in his corage with importable smerte.	*Burned; heart; unbearable pain*
	This cruel wolfe, for love inpacyent,	
	Cast him devowre this cely innocent.	*Decided to; blessed*

	Firste to himself thus he spake and sayde:	
120	"What is she, this? Where doth this goodely duelle?"	*beautiful [person]*
	Who sawe ever toforn so faire a maide,	*before*
	Whiche alle othir in beauté dothe excelle?	
	Of wommanhede she is the verray welle,	*source*
125	For me semeth myn herte in every weyne	*vein*
	Is thurgh perced with hir iyen tweyne."	*pierced; two eyes*

150

	And with that thought he made for to gone	*had go to her*
	His servauntes to hir innocence,	
	Bad thei sholde enquere of hir anone,	*Ordered; ask*
130	What that she was, with al hir diligence,	*their effort*
	And reporte unto his presence	
	Of hir lynage playnly how it stode	*ancestry*
	And where she were born of gentil blode;	*whether; noble blood*
	"And of hir birthe if that she be fre,	*free born (noble)*
135	I wille hir have sothely to my wyfe,	*honestly*
	Love and cherysshe for her grete beauté,	*cherish [her]*
	As it is skyle, duryng al my lyfe,	*fitting*
	That atwene us ther shal be no strife;	*between*
	And if she be born of foreyne lyne,	*inferior blood*
140	I wille hir take to myn concubyne."	*as my concubine*
	Whan she was brought unto his presence,	
	First he enquerede of hir condicyoun,	*inquired*
	Bad hir declare platly in sentence	*Ordered; frankly in truth*
	Of hir lawe and hir religioun,	
145	And of hir kyn, by short conclusyoun,	*family*
	Clerly dyscure, and the trouthe attame,	*disclose; reveal*
	Hooly hir purpos, and what was hir name.	*intention*
	She, not to rekel for noon hastynesse,	*too rash; any*
	But ful demure and sobre of contenaunce,	*quiet; serious of conduct*
150	Gan looke on him by grete avisenesse,	*deliberation*
	Dressyng to God hir hertes remembraunce;	*Directing*
	Of chere nor colour ther was no variaunce.	*expression*
	Constaunt of herte, this holy blyssed mayde	
	To the Prefecte evene thus she saide:	
155	"Touchynge my lynage, by successyoun	*Concerning; lineage*
	My bloide conveied is fro grete noblesse,	*descent; nobility*
	My name Margarete; and of religioun	
	I am Cristen, in verray sothfastnesse;	*truthfulness*
	And in that lawe, withoute doublenesse,	*religion; duplicity*
160	For lyf or dethe playnly I wille abide,	
	Persevere stable, and varien on no side."	*steadfastly; change*

151

Wherof the juge in manere gan disdeyne,   *became indignant*
  To hir saide, for short conclusioun,
"Margarete, ther ben thynges tweyne   *two*
165   Ful covenable to thi condicyoun: *suitable*
  And this the first, to myn oppinioun,
Of thi byrthe the grete nobilité,
And the seconde is thi grete beauté,

"Whiche in thi persone joyned ben yfere,   *together*
170   Worthi to be called a Margarite,   *a pearl*
Of fairnesse of shape and eke of chere,   *face*
  A chose gemme among these perles white;   *choice; pearls*
  And in this tweyne for I me delite,   *two; because I delight*
Sewyng my counsaille thou mustest condiscende   *Following; consent*
175   Better avysed the thride to amende.   *advised to amend the third*

"To thi beauté it were a ful grete loos,   *loss*
  To thi youthe and to thi maydenhede,   *virginity*
To leve on him that deide on a croos.   *believe in; cross*
  I holde it foly; wherfore take goode hede,   *folly; heed*
180   Forsake his feithe, and do as I thee rede: *counsel*
First lat that god of thee be denyed   *let; yours*
Whiche on a tre was hange and crucified."   *a tree*

"Certes," quod she, "whatever that thou seye,
  He wilfully suffred passioun   *voluntarily*
185   And humbely liste for mankynde deye,   *chose; to die*
  And sched His blode for oure redempcioun
  To make us fre, and payen oure raunsoun,   *ransom*
Of His joye that we ne sholde mysse   *[so] that; lose*
Where now He regneth eternaly in blysse."   *reigns*

190   The juge, wrothe, sent hir to prisoun,
  There to abide tille on the next day;
Makyng as thoo no dilacioun,   *then no delay*
  Bad she sholde in al the haste thei may   *[He] ordered*
  Be brought aforn him, to seyn yee or nay   *before; yes or no*
195   Touchyng hir creaunce, what was hir lawe or feith.   *Concerning her belief*
And to hir evenne thus he seithe:

"Margarete," quod he, "have pité on thyne age,
   And have eke mercy on thi grete fairnesse.
   Spille not thi thought of foly ne of rage,   *Waste; mind with*
200   But tourn thyn herte, and thi wittes dresse   *turn; direct*
     To oure goddes, and do thi besynesse   *diligence*
   Hem to honour and plese her deyeté,   *deity*
   As thou desirest to lyve in prosperité."

   Quod she ageyn: "With hert, wille and thoughte
205   I worship Him verrayly in dede
   That made man, and after hath him bought,
     Whom hevene and erthe and the see dothe drede.
   Alle elementes He dothe conveie and lede,   *guide; lead*
   For wynde, nor weder, nor no creature
210 Withoute His mercy may no while endure."

   Quod the juge: "Anoon but thou consente   *unless*
     To my desire as thou hast herde devyse,   *tell*
   Truste fully that thou shalt repente.
     For first I shall in ful cruel wyse   *manner*
215   Mercyles thy body so chastyse —   *merciless; punish*
   Trust me welle, this is no feyned tale —   *feigned*
   Thi flesshe assonder kerve on peces smale."   *cut into small pieces*

   Quod Margarete, "While that me lastethe brethe,   *breath remains in me*
     I shal abide in this oppinioun.
220 Sytthe Criste for me suffred peyne and dethe,   *Since*
     Shad al His blode for my redempcyoun,   *Shed*
     So for His sake, of hole affeccyoun,   *complete*
   Be assured that I have no drede   *fear*
   To deye for Him, and al my blode to shede."   *die; shed*

225 The juge thanne upon a galowe tre
     Lete hangen up this holy pure virgyne,   *caused to be hung up*
   Hir flesshe be rente in his cruelté,   *torn*
     Whos blode ran doun right as eny lyne;   *in a straight line*
     Lyke a quyke this mayden in hir pyne   *Like a spring; pain*
230 Shad oute hir blode, hir veynes al torent,   *Shed; lacerated*
   Til of hir body the lycour was al spent.   *liquid*

Allas the while! Thei that stode beside
   Ful sore wepten of compassyoun.   *sorrowfully; out of compassion*
Allas! For doole thei myght unnethe abide   *sorrow; hardly remain*
235   To sene hir blode so renne and rayle doun.   *see; run and flow*
   So importable was hir passyoun   *unbearable*
For Cristes feithe that the peple abraide   *broke their silence*
And of pité thus to hir thei saide:

"O Margareta, allas, whan we take hede
240   Hou thou whilom were faireste on to see,   *once; to look at*
But now, allas! Thi body is al rede,   *red*
   Steyned with blode, whereof we han pité.   *stained*
   Allas! allas! Hou myght it evere be
To sene a mayde yonge, fresshe, and tendre of age   *unspoiled; young*
245   Mighty to endure of tourment suche a rage?   *Strong enough*

"Whi hast thou lost thyn excellent fairenesse?
   Whi hast thou lost thi shape and thy beauté?
And fynal cause of thi mortal distresse   *the ultimate*
   Is thi wilful incredulité.   *disbelief*
250   Lete fantasies oute of thyn herte fle   *flee*
Now at the last, that thou maist in eese   *ease*
Of thi turment the bitternesse appese."   *alleviate*

Quod she: "Goth hens, ye fals counsaylirys,   *go hence; counselors*
   Ye worldly peple, unsad and ever untrewe,   *unreliable; false*
255   Flesshely, chaungeable, and in youre desirys
   Delityng evere in thinges that be newe;
   Amonge remembreth — and wolde God ye knewe —   *Always; if*
That of my flesshe the mortal tourmentrie   *torment*
Is to my soule chief salve and remedie."   *medicine*

260   And to the juge thus she saide and spake:
   "O gredy hounde, lyoun insaciable,   *greedy dog; lion*
On my body thou maiste welle taken wrake,   *vengeance*
   But the soule shal persevere stable,   *steadfast*
   For Cristes feith abiden immutable.
265   For thilke Lorde Crist Jhesu, whom I serve,   *the same*
From al myschief my spirit shal preserve."   *harm*

154

The juge, confuse sittyng in the place,   *frustrated*
   To beholde myght not sustene
The rede blode rayle aboute hir face,   *run down*
270   Lyke a ryver rennyng on the grene;
Toke his mantel in his mortal tene,   *vexation*
Hid his visage, whanne that he toke hede,   *face*
In herte astoned to sene hir sydes blede;   *astonished*

Made hir in hast to be take doun   *taken*
275   Myd of hir peyne cruel and horrible,   *[In the] midst of*
And efte ageyne putte hir in prisoun,   *afterwards*
   Where she prayde: if it were possible,
   Hir mortal foo, dredful and odible,   *hateful*
The Lorde besechynge that she myght him see,   *beseeching*
280   Whiche cause was of hir adversité,   *hardship*

Hir impugnynge thurgh his mortal fight   *opposing (resisting)*
   That man first brought to destruccyoun.   *That first brought man to*
And sodeynly appered in hir sight,
   Where as she lay bounden in prisoun,
285   In the lykenesse of a felle dragoun   *fierce dragon*
The olde serpent, whiche called is Sathan,
And hastyly to assayle hir he began.   *attack*

With open mouthe, the virgyne to devour,
   First of alle, he swolwed in hir hede,   *swallowed; head*
290 And she devoutly, hirself to socoure,   *save*
   Gan crosse hirself, in hir mortal drede;   *fear*
   And by grace, anoon or she toke hede,   *before*
The horrible beste, in relees of hir peyne,   *relief*
Brast assondre and partyd was on tweyne.   *Burst; in two*

295 And efte ageyne to assayl hir he began,   *afterwards again; attack*
   The story seith, and after dothe appeere
By gret disceit in lykenesse of a man;   *deceit; form*
   And she devoutly, with hir yen clere   *eyes*
   Lyfte up to God, gan maken hir prayere.   *lifted*
300 And as she lay in hir orisoun,   *prayer*
Under hir fete lyggyng the dragoun,   *lying*

The devel, venquysshed, toke hir by the honde,   *defeated*
  Spake thes wordes, as I shal devyse:
"Thou hast me bounde with invisible bonde,
305   Whiche victorie ought ynogh suffice!
Cese of thy power, and lat me now aryse,   *Abate*
For I may not abiden thi constreynt,   *remain [in]*
In this batayle thou hast me made so feynt."   *weak*

And she aroos withoute fere or drede,
310   This cely maide, this tendre creature,   *innocent*
By grace of God hent him by the hede   *seized; head*
  And cast him doun, for al his felle armure,   *despite; fierce armor*
  Under hir fete — he myghte not recure;   *recover*
And on this serpent for to do more wrake,   *vengeance*
315   Hir ryght fote she sette upon his bake.   *back*

"Oo feende," quod she, "of malys serpentyne,   *treacherous malice*
  Remembre of thee how I have victorye,
A clene mayde, by powere femynyne,
  Whiche shal be rad to myn encrees of glorye.   *retold*
320   Perpetuelly putte eke in memorie,   *also remember*
How a mayde hath put under fote
Sathan, that is of synne crope and roote."   *head; source*

With that the serpent lowde gan to crie,
  "Thou hast me brought shortly to uttraunce!   *destruction*
325 I am venquysshed, I may it not denye;
  Ageyns thee ful feble is my puyssaunce.   *power*
  Thyn innocence hath brought me to myschaunce,   *misfortune*
And a mayde, but of yeeres tendre,   *merely*
Hath me outrayed with hir lymmes sklendre.   *overcome; slender limbs*

330 "Yif that a man, whiche had force and myght,
Had me venquysshed, I myght it welle sustene;   *bear*
But now, allas, ageyn al skele and ryght,   *reason; custom*
  A cely virgyne, a mayde pure and clene,   *innocent (harmless)*
  Hath me bore doun in al my felle tene;   *fierce vexation*
335 And this, allas, bothe atte eve and morowe
Is grettest cause of my dedly sorowe.   *mortal anguish*

"This encreseth grete party of my peyne,   *[to a] great extent*
   Whan I consydre withynne myself and see
How thi fader and moder bothe tweyne
340   Were in there tyme frendly unto me;
   But thou allone, thurgh thi virginité,
Thi chaste lyf, thy parfyt holynesse
Han me venquysshed and outrayed in distresse."   *overcome; ruined*

Whan she bigan the serpent to constreyne
345   To discure, and no thinge to hyde   *reveal*
By what mene and what manere treyne,   *means; trickery*
   Outher by malys, outher by envye and pryde *Either by malice, or*
   That he assailed man on any syde,
"The kynde of man, telle on anoon," quod she,   *nature*
350   "And be welle ware thou lye nat to me."   *careful; not to lie*

"Sothely," quod he, "I may it not denye —
To seyn the trouthe playnly, and not spare —
My nature is of custume for to lye,   *accustomed to lie*
   As I that am of trouthe and vertue bare,   *bereft*
355   Lyggynge awayte agenste the welfare   *Lying in wait against*
Of folkes goode, and alway envyous
To alle that ben parfite and vertuous.

"Naturelly to hem I have envye,
   Though thei thurgh vertu me ofte put abak, *strength (virtue); hinder*
360   And whan it falleth thei have of me mastrie, *happens; control over me*
   Ageyn to me resorteth al the wrak;   *returns; suffering*
   Of charité I have so grete a lak,
So grete sorowe only for lak of grace
That man in hevene sholde occupye my place.

365   "Yet, wote I welle, I may it not recure,   *recover*
   Nor in that place shal I never abide,   *live*
But in helle sorowe and peyne endure,
   From hevene caste for my grete pryde.   *thrown*
   This foule vice fro thennes was my guyde,
370   Yet of malys, the trouthe for to telle,
Envye I have that man ther sholde duelle.   *dwell*

	"This eke trouthe that whilom Salamon,	*same; once*
	As bookes olde recorden and conclude,	
	Closed in a vesselle fendes many on	*many devils*
375	And of spirites a grete multitude,	
	Whiche innocentes ful often can delude;	*very often can delude*
	But after dethe of that prudent kynge	
	Fro that vessel thei caste oute fire sparklynge.	*emitted*
	"Men supposyng in theire oppinioun	
380	There was closed grete tresour and rychesse,	*enclosed*
	Brak the vessel of entencyoun,	*on purpose*
	And sodeynly the fendes gan hem dresse	*turn themselves*
	Oute of that holde fer fro that distresse,	*confinement far*
	At her oute-goyng enfectyng al th'ayre,	*departure infecting; the air*
385	Where thei abiden and have theire repaire;	*live; dwelling place*
	"Whiche to mankynde do ful grete damage	
	By ther malys and ther temptacions,	*malice*
	To olde and yonge and every manere age,	*sort of*
	By ther conspired fals illusyouns;	*their malicious*
390	But fynally alle ther collusyons	*trickery*
	Goth unto nought, and al ther violence,	*for nothing*
	Whan ther is made myghty resistence."	
	Whan the serpent malicyous and olde	
	To the mayde, whos fote dede him oppresse,	
395	Had his processe and his tale tolde,	*narrative*
	She withedrowe to done him more duresse;	*forbore to do; harm*
	And the dragoun upwarde gan him dresse,	*turn himself*
	Disapered, and forth his wey is goo;	*Disappeared; is gone*
	And she, assured of hir gostly foo,	*certain about her spiritual enemy*
400	Venquysshed hath the prynce of al derkenesse,	
	And sitthe she hathe overcome the hede,	*since; head*
	It faylethe nat she nedes moste oppresse	*defeat*
	His cruel mynystre, and have of him no drede.	*servant; fear*
	And sewyng on, this floure of goodelyhede	*following; flower*
405	The nexte day, voyde of al refuge	*deprived of all help*
	Save of the Lorde, was brought afore the juge,	*Except*

Ful moche peple beynge in presence.   *many; in the court*
  And for she wolde do no sacryfice
The fals goddes, by mortal violence
410   She was dispoiled in ful cruel wyse   *stripped*
  And naked stode, that folke myght hir despise;
And after that this gemme of maydenhede
Was brent with brondus bright as eny glede.   *burned; brands; burning coal*

Hir sydes skorched, whilom white as melke,   *formerly white as milk*
415   The cruel mynystres liste hir nat to spare;   *chose*
For Crystes sake hir body, softe as selke,   *silk*
  Mercyles, naked stode and bare,   *Unpitied*
  And to aument and encrese hir care   *augment*
In boylyng water she was caste and bounde,
420   The wawys burblyng with bolles grete and round.   *waves; bubbles*

The folkes alle, that stonden enviroun   *stood in the vicinity*
  Of doolful pité, that sawe this aventure,   *sorrowful; event*
Gan wepe and pleyne, and of compassyoun   *complain*
  Merveyled sore a tendre creature   *Wondered*
425   Sustene myght suche tourment and endure;
For the tyraunt, to make hir peynes strange,   *extraordinary*
In fire and water gan hir tourment change.   *varied her torture*

And sodeynly there fille an erthequave.   *came an earthquake*
  The peple, in drede, dempte it was vengeaunce;   *thought*
430   And fyve thousand, for God wolde hem save,
  Converted weren from there myscreaunce,   *misbelief*
  For Cristes sake heveded by vengeaunce.   *beheaded*
Se how a mayde in al hir tourmentrie
The feith of Crist coude magnifie!

435   The blynde juge, al voyde of happe and grace,   *luck*
  Last that othre converted wolde be   *Lest; others*
To Cristes feith, withoute lenger space
  Commaunded hath that this mayde fre,   *gracious (noble)*
  In youthe flourynge and virginité,
440   To ben heveded, withoute more tarying,   *beheaded; delay*
In hir praier as she lay knelynge.

But first she praied of humble affeccyoun *desire*
 To the juge, to graunten hir leysere *opportunity*
That she myght make hir orisoun, *prayer*
445 And have a space to lyve in hir praiere. *to remain*
 And ful devoutly with hert hole and entere *perfect; sincere*
Upon the poynte whan she sholde deye, *At the time*
The blessed virgyne thus bygan to preye.

First she praide of parfite charité
450 For hir enemys and hir tourmentours,
For hem that caused hir adversité
 And had hir pursued with mony sharpe shours. *attacks*
 Of parfit love she gadrid oute the flours, *amassed the flowers*
Praying also for thoo folkes alle *all those people*
455 That after helpe unto hir grace calle, *call on her grace for aid*

And for alle thoo that have hir in memorie, *those*
 And swiche as truste in hir helpe at nede:
That God hem graunte, sittinge in His glorie,
Of His grace that thei may welle spede, *prosper*
460 And ageyn right that no man hem myslede, *lead them astray*
"And Lorde," quod she, "to alle be socoure *comfort*
That for thi sake done to me honoure. *pay their respects to me*

"And specyally to thee I beseche
 To alle wymmen whiche of childe travayle, *labor in childbirth*
465 For my sake, oo Lorde, be thou her leche; *their physician*
 Lat my prayere unto hem availe. *benefit them*
 Suffre no myschief tho wymmen, Lorde, assaile,
That calle to me for helpe in theire grevaunce, *suffering*
But for my sake save hem fro myschaunce. *misfortune*

470 "Lat hem, Lorde, not perisshe in theire childynge; *childbirth*
 Be thou her comforte and consolacyoun,
To be delivered thurgh grace of thyn helpynge;
 Socoure hem, Lorde, in theire tribulacyoun.
 This is my praier, this is myn orisoun, *prayer*
475 And specially do alle folkes grace
That calle to me for helpe in any place!"

	And fro that highe hevenly mansyoun	*mansion*
	Was herde a voys in open audience	*publicly*
	That God had herde hir peticioun,	
480	To be parfourmed withoute resistence.	
	And than this maide, moste of excellence,	*greatest*
	Roos up devoutly, and no thynge afferde	*rose; afraid of nothing*
	Seide unto him whiche that helde the swerde:	

	"Come nere," quod she, "myn oune brother dere,	
485	Smyte with the swerde, and loke thou spare nought.	*Strike*
	My body shal behynde abiden here,	*remain*
	But my soule to hevene shal be brought."	
	Hir hede enclynynge with an humble thought;	*head bowing*
	The mynystre with al his myght and peyne	*servant; effort*
490	Lefte up his swerde and smote hir necke on tweyne.	*struck; in two*

	The peple of pité gan to crie and sowne	*swoon*
	That stode and sawe hir bitter passioun;	
	Of martirdam thus she toke the crowne	*received*
	For Cristes feithe, with hole affeccyoun.	
495	Threttene kalendes, the boke maketh mencyoun,	*Thirteen*
	Of Jul this maide, a merour of constaunce,	*July; mirror (model)*
	Was laureat thurgh hir parfit suffraunce.	*honored; patience (endurance)*

	An holy seynt writeth of this maide, and seithe:	
	"This Margareta, parfyt of hir creaunce,	*perfect in; belief*
500	With drede of God moste stable in hir feythe,	
	Unto the deth havyng perseveraunce	
	Sette hoole to God with thought and remembraunce,	*devoted wholly*
	In herte ay compunt, she was so vertuous,	*always devout*
	Everything eschewyng that was vicious.	*avoiding*

505	"Hir blessed lyf, hir conversacioun	*conduct*
	Were example of parfite pacience,	
	Of grounded clennesse and of religioun,	*purity*
	Of chastité founded on prudence;	
	God gaf to hir soverayn excellence	
510	In hir tyme that she sholde be	
	To alle a maisterasse of virginité.	*model*

"Hir fadir, modir, hir kynred she forsoke;
　Hir holy lyvynge was to hem odious.　　　　　　　　*hateful*
To Cristes lawe al holy she hir toke,
515　　This blissed mayde, this virgyn glorious;
　Of alle hir enemyes she was victorious,
Til at the laste, in vertu complet goode,　　　　　*good with perfect virtue*
For Cristes sake she shad hir chaste bloode."　　　　　　　　*shed*

Explicit vita sancte Margarete.

Lenvoy

Noble princesses and ladyes of estate,
520　　And gentilwomen lower of degré,
　Lefte up your hertes, calle to your advocate
　　Seynt Margarete, gemme of chastité.
　　And alle wymmen that have necessité,
　Praye this mayde ageyn sykenesse and dissese,　　　　　*against*
525　　In trayvalynge for to do yow ese.　　　*childbirth; give you comfort*

And folkes alle that be disconsolat
　In your myschief and grete adversité,　　　　　　　*misfortune*
And alle that stonde of helpe desolate,　　　　　　　　*bereft*
　With devout hert and with humylité
530　　Of ful trust, knelyng on your kne,
Pray this mayde in trouble and alle dissese
Yow to releve and to do yow ese.　　　　*relieve; give you comfort*

Now, blissed virgyne, in hevene hy exaltat,　　　　　*exalted high*
　With other martirs in the celestialle se,　　　　*dwelling place*
535　Styntith werre, the dredfulle fel debat　　　*Stop; cruel conflict*
　　That us assailith of oure enemyes thre,　　　　　　　*from*
　　From whos assaute inpossible is to fle,　　*it is impossible to flee*
But, chaste gemme, thi servauntes sette at ese
And be her shelde in myschief and dissese.　　*their; misfortune; distress*

Explicit.

162

Explanatory Notes to Lydgate's "Lyfe of Seynt Margarete"

1–77   Lydgate's Prologue elaborately defines his account as a literary text based on other texts within a long rhetorical tradition. Note the difference from the openings of those narratives designed for a listening audience.

24–28   *daysye*. Daisy; also called a "margarita"; hence Lydgate's use of it in his stanza developing flower images in connection with Margaret. The white lily traditionally symbolizes chastity; red roses, the shed blood of a martyr.

29–53   *Margarete* is also a name for the pearl, which Lydgate describes and compares with St. Margaret in these stanzas. This passage closely parallels the prologue to Margaret's legend in the *Golden Legend* (or *Legenda aurea*) of Jacobus de Voragine.

41   *palme*. A symbol of martyrdom in western iconography.

43–44   *cordyal*. Lydgate is listing some of the medicinal properties attributed to pearls. They were also ground up and used as a coagulant, to stop blood flow — making them useful in connection with childbirth, as well as other medical emergencies.

56–57   *aureat lycoure/ Into my penne*. A figure for poetic inspiration.

69   *Lady Marche*. Anne Mortimer, countess of March (d.1432), who requested that Lydgate write this Life. Daughter of Anne of Woodstock and Edmund, earl of Stafford, she married Edmund Mortimer, earl of March, in 1415. Anne might have become queen, since Mortimer was considered the legitimate heir of Richard II, but Henry V was chosen instead.

72   *Frensshe and Latyne*. The languages of the court and the church, respectively.

120–26   Lydgate's account places unusual emphasis on Olibrius' inner feelings when he first sees Margaret. For a moment he sounds almost like a courtly lover.

139   *of foreyne lyne.* Other versions of the legend have him explicitly consider the possibility that she might be a mere serf.

164–82   Olibrius begins by being much politer and more complimentary to Margaret than he sounds in most other retellings. Compare this passage, e.g., with lines 81–94 in the stanzaic version.

232–59   Lydgate places unusual emphasis on the onlookers' pitying response to Margaret's ordeal. Compare this passage, e.g., with lines 139–50 in the stanzaic version.

283–398   Lydgate compresses the critical scenes of the dragon and the demon, making them the same demonic figure in two different forms, both of whom Margaret apparently defeats while lying bound in her prison cell. Rather than a vigorous fight with the demon in human form, here her prayer accomplishes the task and placing her foot on his back seems purely symbolic. In lines 298–301 Lydgate offers a well-known image of Margaret: her hands together in prayer as she stands on the defeated dragon. In lines 314–15 her two foes are again conflated: she stands on the human-shaped demon, but he is described as a serpent. In line 397 the demon is again called a dragon, and in lines 316, 323, 344, and 393 he is again linked with serpents.

316–22   See Luke 10:19, "Behold, I have given you power to tread upon serpents and scorpions, and upon all the power of the enemy: and nothing shall hurt you"; and Genesis 3:15, "I will put enmities between thee and the woman, and thy seed and her seed: she shall crush thy head, and thou shalt lie in wait for her heel." Margaret also alludes to the fact that her deed will be recorded and remembered, which was in fact an important part of her cult. (See below, especially lines 454–62.)

351–71   The demon's hatred for people stems from his envy that God created humankind to replace those angels who followed Satan and fell from heaven to hell. Therefore, humans will have the place in heaven which the demons know was once theirs.

372   *Salamon.* King Solomon. See explanatory note to lines 223–32 of the stanzaic Life.

396   *withedrowe.* I.e., she removed her foot from his back rather than cause him more duress.

401–03   This kind of explicit connection between the dragon/demon and Olibrius is also made in the *Legenda aurea* (Jacobus de Voragine, trans. Ryan, 1.370).

419   *boylyng water.* This touch may be original with Lydgate. Other versions of the legend suggest that the torturers sought to increase her suffering by plunging her alternately into fire and cold water.

432   *heveded by vengeaunce.* Beheaded for vengeance. That is, the 5000 new converts are executed immediately after their conversion. The next stanza suggests that Olibrius wants to have her killed before there are any more conversions.

463–73 Lydgate's version of Margaret's prayer for women in childbirth carefully makes God, rather than Margaret, the agent (literally, the physician). Unlike the version in MS C of the stanzaic Life (lines 315–18), Lydgate's version also makes no explicit mention of the infant's health.

495–96 *Threttene kalendes . . . / Of Jul.* Thirteen of the calends of July. This is July 20, Margaret's feast day in the western church. In the eastern church her feast is celebrated on July 17.

498–518 This passage is borrowed from the end of the chapter on Margaret in the *Legenda aurea.* Neither MacCracken nor editors of the *Legenda* have identified the "holy saint" being quoted.

511   *maisterasse.* Margaret's example during her lifetime makes her a model to be revered and imitated by everyone.

Lenvoy "The Envoy." A direct address to the reader or hearer at the end of a poem.

519–32 Although the poem was written at the request of Anne, countess of March (named in line 69), here Lydgate extends his audience to all gentlewomen, and then to all women who have need of the saint's assistance in childbirth, and finally to all people who need her help because of any kind of trouble.

533–39 The final stanza prays for the protection of Margaret and other martyr saints to help Lydgate and his readers resist the relentless attacks of the three enemies — the world, the flesh, and the devil. (See also the Prologue, lines 47–53). Margaret's particular efficacy is in protection against demons, but because she resisted the temptation to accept Olibrius' offer of marriage and endured torture, she has triumphed over the other two enemies as well. Note that "disease" is mentioned in all three stanzas of the Envoy, becoming broader and broader in its implications.

Textual Notes to Lydgate's "Lyfe of Seynt Margarete"

Abbreviations: **B** = Bodleian Library MS Bodley 686 (*SC* 2527), fols. 193v–200v; **D** = Durham University Library MS Cosin V.II.14, fols. 97v–106v [base text]; **H** = British Library MS Harley 367, fols. 80r–83v; **L** = Cambridge University Library MS Ll.5.18, fols. 29v–41v; **M** = Henry Noble MacCracken [EETS edition].

Here begynneth . . . According to M, this rubric is found in MSS B and H as well as D. The abbreviation at the end is a dating formula, meaning "in year 8 of the reign of Henry VI."

9	*Golde.* D's reading. M: *Gold.*
34	*smalle.* M lacks the final -e, indicated in D by crossing the double *l.*
41	*her.* D's reading. M: *hir.*
59	*thi.* D's reading. M: *this.*
74	*therof.* D's reading. M: *thereof.*
122	*sawe.* D's reading. M: *saw.*
129	*anone.* D's reading. M: *anoon.*
135	*sothely.* D's reading. M: *sothly.*
136	*her.* D's reading. M: *hir.*
138	*strife.* D's reading. M: *stryfe.*
164	*thynges.* D's reading. M: *thinges.*
171	*fairnesse.* D's reading. M: *fairenesse.*
174	*mustest.* D's reading, an unusual form. The other MSS cited in M all have commoner alternatives: *must* (H), *maist* (L), or *myghtest* (B).
175	*the thride.* M's emendation. D: *the the thride*, followed by an erased word, possibly *day.*
178	*deide.* D's reading. M: *deied.*
182	*Whiche.* D's reading. M: *Which.*
195	*feith.* D's reading. M: *feithe.*
201	*oure.* D's reading. M: *our.*
216	*this is.* My emendation. Both D and M omit *is*, which I have supplied on the basis of B and L.
229	*hir.* D's reading. M: *her.*
233	*Ful.* D's reading. M: *Full.*

240   *on to.* My emendation. M retains D's reading, *unto,* without comment, presumably because M construed *see* as a noun ("sea"). But the MED confirms that the phrase is much likelier to be the infinitive "to see on," "gaze on."

247   *thi.* D's reading. M: *this.*

250   *oute.* D's reading. M: *out.*

252   *thi.* D's reading. M: *thy.*

254   *worldly.* My emendation. M retains *worlde,* the reading in D, but H and L both have *worldly.* B has an odder adjectival form, *worldles.*

266   *myschief.* D's reading. M: *mischief.*

270   *Lyke.* D's reading. M: *Like.*

274   *take.* D's reading. M: *taken.*

280   *hir.* D's reading. M: *her.*

282   *destruccyoun.* D's reading. M: *distruccyoun.*

287   *hir.* D's reading. M: *her.*

292   *anoon.* D's reading. M: *anoone.*

310   *maide.* M's emendation. D: *made.*

313   *myghte.* M's emendation. D: *myght.*

316   *malys.* D's reading. M: *malyse.*

319   *shal.* D's reading. M: *shall.*

325   *venquysshed.* M's emendation. D: *vequysshed.*

334   *doun.* D's reading. M: *down.*

335   *atte.* D's reading. M: *at.*

340   *there.* D's reading. M: *their.*
        frendly. D's reading. M: *friendly.*

341   *thi.* D's reading. M: *thy.*

342   *chaste.* M's emendation. D: *chast.*

343   *distresse.* D's reading. M: *distress.*

370   *the.* D's reading. M: *thye.*

375   *spirites.* My emendation based on B, H and L. M retains the odd form in D, *spiritus.*

378   *oute.* D's reading. M: *out.*

386   *Whiche.* D's reading. M: *Which.*

387   *ther.* D's reading. M: *their.*

390   *alle.* D's reading. M: *all.*

396   *withedrowe.* D's reading. M: *with-drowe.*

400   *Venquysshed.* My emendation. D: *Wenquysshed,* which M retains.

405   *nexte.* M's emendation. D: *next.*
        al. D's reading. M: *all.*

407   *beynge.* D's reading. M: *beyng.*

408–09 *do no sacryfice / The fals goddes.* The idiom seems to demand a preposition after *sacryfice*, but there is nothing in M to suggest that any of the MSS inserts one.

420 Reconstruction from M. The line was evidently corrupt at an early stage of transmission. According to M, H has only the same fragment found in D: *The water blowyng.* B and L have complete lines, but significantly different ones: *The watter boilyng with bollys grete and rounde* (B); *The wawys burbyllyng bothe large and rounde* (L).

421 *enviroun.* D's reading. M: *enviroune.*

422 *doolful.* M's emendation. D: *dooful.*

426 *strange.* D's reading. M: *straunge.*

429 *peple.* D's reading. M: *people.*

435 *al.* D's reading. M: *all.*

439 *youthe.* D's reading. M: *youth.*

447 *whan.* D's reading. M: *when.*

449–55 D calls attention to this stanza with a prominent note beside it in the margin, apparently in the hand of the original scribe, which says, *primo oravit pro suis persecutoribus* ("First she prayed for those who persecuted her").

456–62 This stanza is marked with another prominent marginal note, in the same hand, saying, *Peticio et pro eius memoriam agentibus et se invocantibus* ("There was also a request for those who would honor her memory and call on her").

463–69 This stanza has another prominent marginal note, in the same hand, saying, *Etiam devote oravit ad Deum ut quecumque in partu parielitans se invocaverit illesam prolem emitteret* ("She also prayed devoutly to God that any woman who called on her in childbirth should deliver an uninjured child"). This note sounds more traditional than Lydgate's version of the prayer, where the emphasis actually falls on the safety of the mother.

477 *highe.* M's emendation. D: *high.*

487 *shal.* D's reading. M: *shall.*

488 *Hir.* D's reading. M: *Her.*

491–93 *sowne . . . crowne.* My emendations, based on B, H, and L. M retains the odder form, *soun*, from D, but emends D's *croun* to *croune.*

510 *sholde.* D's reading. M: *shulde.*

511 *alle.* D's reading. M: *all.*

515 *virgyn.* D's reading. M: *virgin.*

519–39 This ending is found in D and H but not in the other two MSS collated by M.

524 *sykenesse.* D's reading. M: *syknesse.*

534 *other.* D's reading. M: *othir.*

Katherine of Alexandria

Introduction

Although her legend would place Katherine's martyrdom in the early fourth century, she is not mentioned in any document written before the ninth or tenth century, when the earliest known accounts of her life appeared in Greek. Given the long gap, modern authorities have concluded not only that the legend is fictitious, but that the saint herself may never have existed. Her name, which comes from the Greek *katharos*, "pure," is suspiciously apt for a virgin martyr, raising the possibility that her legend (like that of Christopher, "Christ-bearer") may have originated as an allegory. Her feast — along with those of some other favorite medieval saints, including Christopher and Margaret — was abolished by the Vatican in 1969.

The main center of Katherine's cult in the Middle Ages was an Orthodox monastery at the foot of Mount Sinai, which claimed to have acquired her tomb and her relics by miraculous means. Since Katherine's tomb exuded an oil with healing powers that could be sold to pilgrims, it became a major source of fame and revenue for the monastery — aided by the advertisements for this pilgrimage site that ended many retellings of her legend. Some medieval readers were skeptical about the miracles that supposedly occurred at Mount Sinai (see Mirk's account, for example), but the rest of Katherine's legend was widely accepted, and by the end of the Middle Ages she had become one of the most popular saints in Europe. The main impetus for her cult in the west came not from Sinai itself, but from the abbey of the Holy Trinity and Saint Katherine at Rouen, in Normandy, which had acquired some of her relics by the end of the eleventh century. From Normandy, of course, her cult easily spread across the English Channel. Her great subsequent popularity in England is suggested by such facts as these: her name appears in the dedications of 62 medieval English churches, countless side altars, and many parish guilds; at least 56 churches had wall paintings with scenes from her life; and over 170 bells with inscriptions in her honor have survived until recent times. She was also one of the saints most frequently portrayed on church screens, in stained glass windows, and in small works of art for private use.

Katherine's appeal was even broader than Margaret's because her legend cast her in a wide range of roles, inviting different kinds of people to take her as their patron saint. For example, she was considered a suitable patron for aristocratic women because she was a princess who had been brought up to rule a kingdom. She was a good patron for nuns and other women with religious vocations because, like them, she was a consecrated virgin, a faithful bride of Christ. Her courage and outspokenness were clearly important to some exceptional women, including

Catherine of Siena and Margery Kempe, who emulated her example when they spoke out against abuses of power in their own society. More surprisingly, she was a favorite patron and role model for (male) university students and preachers, since she was such a brilliant scholar and debater that she had once defeated the arguments of fifty pagan philosophers at once. Her legend also made her an advocate for women with evil husbands, a patron for nursing mothers (because milk flowed from her neck when she was beheaded), and a powerful intercessor for those who invoke her when they are dying or in great need (because of her final prayer and its answer). Since the climactic instrument of torture devised by her persecutor was a diabolical set of wheels, she was often portrayed with a wheel as her emblem — with the paradoxical result that she even became the patron saint of wheelwrights, millers, and other craftsmen who worked with wheels.

Because Katherine served so many different purposes for various subgroups within medieval society, retellings of her legend vary enormously in their emphases. The eloquent and theologically learned speeches with which she converts the philosophers, for example, might be illustrated at length in retellings for clerics but were usually minimized for lay audiences — especially when it was feared that such audiences might try to imitate her, violating the rules against any public preaching by women or laymen. Some retellings for the laity skip most of the dialogue and concentrate on the most entertaining aspects of the story, including all the failures and reversals that drive Katherine's persecutor to the brink of insanity. More ambitious retellings for laymen and women, on the other hand, often emphasize the prayers and private visions that show the mutually loving relationship between Katherine and Christ. In some late-medieval versions (not including the three given here) this theme was greatly elaborated by adding a long introductory narrative that explained how she had converted to Christianity in her youth, rejected all earthly suitors, and entered into a mystical marriage to Christ.

Like the stanzaic Lives of Mary Magdalen and Margaret, the anonymous stanzaic Life of Katherine was probably composed during the thirteenth century, in part as an answer to the popularity of secular romances. Although Auchinleck (National Library of Scotland MS Advocates 19.2.1, c.1330) is the earliest of the three surviving manuscripts, only Gonville and Caius MS 175/96 (c. 1400), the one edited here, gives the complete text. One noteworthy feature of this version is the way it emphasizes the enlightenment and courage of Katherine's converts. Like Katherine herself, the converts are all shown as choosing to serve God instead of the tyrannical emperor, no matter what earthly rewards the emperor promises or what dire physical punishments he inflicts. There is a good deal of comedy here too, with Katherine and the converts given some wonderfully bold speeches of defiance against the emperor, who practically melts down in his impotent rage against them. But the text clearly invites its audience to follow Katherine's example instead of just enjoying the story and remembering the final promises of intercession.

Mirk's sermon offers a fairly detailed summary of the legend which shows Katherine's own courage and allegiance to God but otherwise differs quite noticeably from the emphases of the stanzaic Life. Katherine's converts receive relatively little space, and the confrontations with the emperor are all so muted and discreet that not even Katherine herself sounds like a rebel against his authority. Mirk's selectivity at the end of the sermon is more interesting still. He says not a word about Katherine's final prayer and its answer, which were usually stressed because they provided a strong incentive to call on her as an intercessor, but substitutes an *exemplum* that seems designed just to encourage faithfulness in observing her feast day. Some manuscripts of Mirk's sermon cycle also include an account of miracles at Mount Sinai (inserted here in brackets) which departs significantly from the more usual promises of healing at Katherine's tomb.

The brief chapter from the *Speculum Sacerdotale* retells most of the legend as briefly and efficiently as possible, but singles out two parts for detailed presentation: the design of the wheels (the visual emblem that generally served to identify Katherine) and her final prayer and its answer. There is not much ambiguity about the purposes of this account, then. It does not encourage its readers or listeners to imitate Katherine in any way, but only to understand and remember her emblem and rely on her as an intercessor.

Select Bibliography

Indexed in

[stanzaic Life]   Brown-Robbins, #1158 and #1159.

Manuscripts

[stanzaic Life]   Gonville and Caius College, Cambridge MS 175/96, pp. 107–118.

[Mirk]   London, British Library MS Cotton Claudius A.ii, fols. 116r–117r.

[*Spec. Sac.*]   London, British Library MS Additional 36791, fols. 137r–137v.

Previous editions

Stanzaic Life

Horstmann, Carl, ed. *Altenglische Legenden. Neue Folge, mit Einleitung und Anmerkungen.* 1881. Pp. 242–59.

Mirk

Mirk, John. *Mirk's Festial.* Ed. Theodor Erbe. EETS e.s. 96. 1905. Pp. 275–77.

Speculum Sacerdotale

Weatherly, Edward H., ed. *Speculum Sacerdotale.* EETS o.s. 200. 1936. Pp. 243–44.

Important sources and analogues in English

Bokenham, Osbern. *Legendys of Hooly Wummen.* Ed. Mary S. Serjeantson. EETS o.s. 206. 1938. Pp. 172–201.

Capgrave, John. *Life of Saint Katherine.* Ed. Karen A. Winstead. Kalamazoo: Medieval Institute Publications, 1999.

Clemence of Barking. "Life of Saint Catherine." In Wogan-Browne and Burgess, *Virgin Lives and Holy Deaths.* Pp. 3–43

Jacobus de Voragine. *The Golden Legend.* Trans. William Granger Ryan. 1993. Vol. 2, pp. 334–41.

"The Life of Saint Katherine" Ed. and trans. Karen A. Winstead. [Early fifteenth-century prose version from Harvard University, Houghton Library MS Richardson 44.] In Winstead, *Chaste Passions.* Pp. 115–63. [Modern English translation.] Pp. 184–201. [Original Middle English version of chs. 1–9.]

St. Katherine of Alexandria: The Late Middle English Prose Legend in Southwell Minster MS 7. Ed. Saara Nevanlinna and Irma Taavitsainen. Cambridge: D. S. Brewer, 1993.

Savage, Anne, and Nicholas Watson, trans. and intro. *Anchoritic Spirituality: Ancrene Wisse and Associated Works.* 1991. Pp. 259–84. [Modern English translation of the early thirteenth-century prose *Seinte Katerine.*]

Seinte Katerine. Ed. S. R. T. O. d'Ardenne and E. J. Dobson. EETS s.s. 7. Oxford: Oxford University Press, 1981. [Early thirteenth-century version in alliterative prose. Includes an edition of the Vulgate Latin Life, pp. 132–203.]

Historical background and criticism

Görlach, Manfred. "The Auchinleck *Katerine*." In *So Meny People Longages and Tonges: Philological essays in Scots and mediaeval English presented to Angus McIntosh.* Ed. Michael Benskin and M. L. Samuels. Edinburgh: Middle English Dialect Project, 1981. Pp. 211–27.

Jenkins, Jacqueline. "Popular Devotion and the Legend of St. Katherine of Alexandria in Late Medieval England." Ph.D. Diss. University of Western Ontario, 1996.

Jones, Charles W. "The Norman Cults of Sts. Catherine and Nicholas, saec. xi." In *Hommages à André Boutemy.* Ed. Guy Cambier. Collection Latomus 145. Brussels: Latomus, 1976. Rpt. in *Saint Nicholas of Myra, Bari, and Manhattan: Biography of a Legend.* Chicago: University of Chicago Press, 1978. Pp. 144–54.

Kurvinen, Auvo. "The Life of St. Catharine of Alexandria in Middle English Prose." D.Phil Diss. University of Oxford, 1960.

Lewis, Katherine J. *The Cult of St Katherine of Alexandria in Late Medieval England.* Woodbridge, Suffolk: Boydell Press, 2000.

Winstead, Karen A. *Virgin Martyrs.* 1997. Pp. 15–18, 147–77, et passim.

Stanzaic Life of Katherine,
from Gonville and Caius College, Cambridge MS 175/96, pp. 107–18

Incipit vita sancte Katerine virginis.

	He that made bothe sunne and mone	
	In hevene and erthe for to schyne,	
	Brynge us to Hevene with Hym to wone	*dwell*
	And schylde us from helle pyne!	*[the] pain(s) of hell*
5	Lystnys and I schal yow telle	*Listen*
	The lyf of an holy virgyne	
	That trewely Jhesu lovede wel —	
	Here name was callyd Katerine.	
	I undyrstonde, it betydde soo:	*happened*
10	In Grece ther was an emperour;	
	He was kyng of landes moo,	*many*
	Of casteles grete and many a tour.	
	The ryche men of that land	
	They servyd hym with mekyl honour.	*great*
15	Maxenceus was his name hotand,	*called*
	A man he was ful sterne and stour.	*harsh and cruel*
	Mahoun heeld he for hys god:	
	He trowyd in the false lay;	*believed; religion*
	On Jhesu Cryst levede he not,	
20	That Lord is and God verray.	*true God*
	He was a Sarezyn ful tryst,	*bold*
	With Crystyndom he werrede ay,	*always made war*
	For alle that trowyd on Jhesu Cryst	
	He stroyyd bothe be nyght and day.	*destroyed*
25	Whenne he hadde fyve and fyfty yer	
	Ben emperour and born the corown,	
	Thorwgh al the land hys messanger	

He sente aboute fro toun to toun;

To Alisaundyr he sente hys sawe *Alexandria; message*

30 And bad tho folk scholde come wel sone,

Ryche and pore, heyghe and lawe,

With here offryng to seke Mahone. *visit [the shrine or altar of]*

He bad the ryche men scholde brynge

Neet and scheep to here offerande, *Cattle; as their offering*

35 And pore men up alle thynge *above all other considerations*

Quyke foulys in here hande; *Live birds*

And as they wolde here lyvys hente, *to save their [own] lives*

For nothyng ne scholde they wonde. *hesitate*

This was the kyngys comaundement

40 That he sente thorwgh al hys londe.

The folk upon this manere yood — *went for this reason*

To wraththe the kyng they weren adrad. *make angry*

Beforn hys goddys hymselven stood, *[he] himself*

In ryche clothyng was he clad.

45 Glemen were there, bothe false and fykil, *Minstrels*

He bad that they scholde be ful glad;

Noyse they maden wundyr mekyl,[1]

As here emperour hem bad.

Another kyng in that lande was thoo:

50 Costus was hys name calde.

A doughtyr he hadde — chyldryn no moo —

Of eightene wyntyr was sche of alde: *She had reached the age of eighteen*

Kateryne was here ryghte name,

Of wyt and wysdom was sche bolde. *In; strong/confident*

55 Sche lovyd Jhesu, though sche bar blame — *even if that brought disgrace/danger*

For Hys love was here lyf solde. *given*

As sche stood in here fadyr coort,

Glemen herde sche lowde synge, *Minstrels*

With pypys and trumpys they maden desport, *entertained*

---

[1] *They made an amazing amount of noise*

176

60	And bellys herde sche lowde rynge.	
	Sche fraynyd of here fadir men	*asked; father's servants*
	What was that noyse and that pypyng.	
	They tolde here of that offryng then	
	That Maxeens garte his folk to bryng.	*caused*
65	Sche hoof up here hand, that mayden yungge,	*raised*
	And blyssyd here fol wyttyrly,	*herself very certainly*
	Ferst here brest and thanne here tungge —	
	So says the book of here story.	
	Thedyr sche sayde, alone sche thoughte,[1]	
70	For to se that melody.	
	But al alone wente sche noughte:	
	They wente with here, that stood here by.	
	Whenne sche com to hys palayse,	*(Maxentius's) palace*
	Sum sche sawgh make game and glee.	*enjoying the festivities*
75	That levyd on Jhesu weren evele at ayse.[2]	
	Sory men sche dede hem see:	*Sorrowful*
	For eythir they scholde don sacrefyse	*they either had to*
	To hys mawmettys imaad of tree,	*idols made of wood*
	Of ston and bras, on alle wyse,	*at all costs*
80	Eythir they scholde imartyryd be.	*Or*
	Sche com before the emperour there,	
	There as he made hys sacrefyze,	*Where*
	And grette hym al on this manere —	*greeted*
	Wordys sche spak bothe bolde and wyse:	
85	"Jhesu Cryst be with thee then,	
	Ryghtwyse Kyng and heyghe Justyse,	*Righteous*
	That tholyd deth for synful men	*suffered*
	And hadde pousty for to ryse.	*power*
	"I speke of Jhesu of Hevene within.	
90	Of alle kyngys He is flour,	*the most excellent*

---

[1] *She said [she would go] there, and she thought [she would be] alone*

[2] *Those who believed in Jesus were upset (ill at ease)*

That suffryd deth for alle mankyn,
He is oure alle Creatour.   *Creator of us all*
Behold Jhesu, the welle of wyt,   *wellspring of wisdom*
Sere Maxence, kyng and emperour!   *Sir*
95   This sacrefyse — to Hym doo it   *offer*
And seke Hym with thus mekyl honour!   *such great*

"But now me thynkith doost thou so nought.
Thou wyrkyst on a werse wyse:
This folk that thou hast hedyr brought,
100   Thou doost hem make the devyl servyse.[1]
Al that they doo, withouten were,   *doubt*
To these mawmettys upon this gyse,   *idols; in this manner*
A dysseyvaunce is to hem here,   *deception (MED deceivaunce)*
Fykyl and fals and al fayntyse."   *treachery*

105   This emperour awondryd was   *astonished*
Of this maydyn, fayr of vyse;   *At; face*
Here stedefastnesse in herte he has,
And sayde to here wurdys ful nyse: *foolish*
"Why dyspraysyst thou oure goddys so   *dispraise*
110   And holdyst hem of so lytyl pryse?   *consider; value*
Iwis, so scholdyst thou nought doo,   *Truly*
Me thynkith thou art nothyng wyse.

"Yyf thou were leryd of oure lay lel   *educated in our excellent religion*
And to oure scoles were entendaunte,   *attentive*
115   Thou woldyst saye we deden ful wel,
And with thy tungge thou woldist it graunte.
To myghteful goddes thou thee take,   *powerful; betake yourself*
Swylk as Mahoun and Termagaunt,   *Such as*
And Jhesu Cryst look thou forsake
120   The whylke thou holdyst thy waraunt![2]

---

[1] *You make them do service to the devil*

[2] *Whom you consider to be your protector*

"And for we have now on hande   *in progress*
This ryche feste, as thou mayst see,
Come now forth with thyn offerande,   *offering*
And holde it for no vanyté!
125   For to oure goddes, so good at nede,
Yif that thou wylt buxum be,   *obedient*
Ryche gyftys schal be thy mede   *reward*
And that thou sayde forgeve I thee."   *what; I [will] forgive*

Thenne bespak here Kateryne —
130   God of Hevene forgat sche nought;
That schoop here wymman and virgyne,   *[He] who created her [as]*
Sente grace intyl here thought: *into*
"These aren quyke develys to calle   *to be called living devils*
That this peple have here sought;   *come to visit*
135   Ther is no god but On of alle,   *One [Lord] of all*
That thee and me and al hath wrought."   *Who*

This emperour with woo gan wake,   *was stirred*
And thoughte on wylys and queynte crokes.   *stratagems; clever tricks*
Lettres gart he swythe make   *caused; to be written rapidly*
140   And prevyly, as saith the bookes,
Ou a maydyn was come ful yyng,   *[Saying] how; very young*
That here goddys alle forsook.   *their*
He selyd hem with hys owne ryng   *sealed*
That he of hys fyngyr took.

145   He took the messanger in hande   *gave*
The lettrys selyd for gret tokenyng   *sealed; proof of authenticity*
To alle the wyse men of hys lande,
And bad hem come withouten dwellyng.   *delay*
Ful gret honour he hyghte hem yyt,   *promised them moreover*
150   As he was trewe knyght and kyng,
Yyf they with here wysdam and here wyt
Myghten ovyrcome that maydyn yyng.

That maydyn was in presoun done,
Soone as the messanger was went.   *[As] soon; gone*
155   An aungyl com to here fol sone

That Jhesu Cryst here hadde isent.
He sayde, "My Lord gretes thee weel
That wyt and wysdam has thee lent —   *Who; given*
And that thyn herte be strong as steel   *[bids] that*
160   And thynk on Hym with good entent!

"Maxence hath isent hys sonde   *messenger*
Ovyral aboute in this cuntree
Aftyr men wysest in londe,
With thee to stryve, as thou schalt see.   *debate*
165   Be that thy wurdys they have herd tel   *By [the time] that*
As Jhesu Cryst schal wysse thee,   *teach*
Here trowthe schal ben in God ful wel,   *trust (faith)*
And for Hym schole they martyryd be."

Over al the world that was so wyde
170   Hys messanger wente ful yare.   *readily*
Fyfty men he broughte that tyde,   *time*
Grettest clerkys and wys of lare: *wise in knowledge*
In al wysdom and eke Latyne
Men sayde that they ryght redy wore
175   For to dysspute with Kateryne,
That Maxcense hadde withholden thore.   *kept [imprisoned] there*

Amonges hem was that mayden anon.
They desputyd with here of many matere,   *subjects*
Here resouns sayde they on be on,   *Their arguments; one by one*
180   Ylkon on hys beste manere.   *Each*
This maydyn, that I have of tolde,
Sche stood with a stedefast chere,
In herte here resouns gan beholde —   *She found her arguments in her heart*
Goddys aungyl was here fere.   *companion*

185   Whenne they hadden here resouns sayde,
Everylkone bothe more and lesse,   *Everyone*
To ylke a poynt withinne a brayde   *each moment*
Sche answerde with wol gret mekenesse.   *very great modesty*
Al here devys thenne sayde sche   *ideas (devices)*
190   Of God of hevene, that oure Lord ysse,   *is*

Is and was and evere schal be —
The Gospel took sche to wytnysse.

Of Holy Wryt sche taughte hem thore   *there*
And of Crystys Incarnacyoun,
195   And of a maydyn hou He was bore,
And hou He suffrede passyoun,
And hou He sente Hys postelys wyde   *apostles far and wide*
To brynge men to salvacyoun —
And Crystene trowthe sche tolde that tyde   *truth*
200   And prevyd it hem with pure resoun.   *to them by argument alone*

Whenne this mayden hadde isayde
Alle here resouns that were so goode,
Fol weel were these maystrys payde,   *scholars satisfied*
And they begunne to chaunge here moode.
205   But there Maxcence sat, in fay,   *(see note)*
For yre of herte he wax nygh wood   *anger; grew nearly insane*
And askyd, or they cowde ought say   *whether they could say anything*
Agayn that maydyn that there stood.   *Against*

Thenne bespak a maystyr anon
210   (Of ryche kynrede was he bore):
"Sere kyng, I wene we have mysgon;   *Sir; think; been mistaken*
Othere resouns beth betere us fore.   *are better for us*
For we scholen trowe on Jhesu Cryst   *believe*
That bar the corowne maad of thorn,   *Who bore*
215   As Kateryne hath itold fol tryst —   *courageously*
Ful loth us were to be forelorn."   *We would be very unwilling to be lost (damned)*

Alle togedere hem askyd he
Whether they wolde here thought ought wende.   *change at all*
They sayden, on Jhesu that deyde on tree
220   They wolde beleve withouten ende.
He wax agrevyd, that stoute syre,   *angered; fierce lord*
He bad hem bynden feet and hande;   *ordered them to be bound*
He swoor he scholde quyte here hyre —   *pay them as they deserved*
They scholde be brend as brennyng brande.   *burned; torch*

225   He garte hem caste al in gret feer.   *caused; fire*
       Gret myracle men myght ther see:
       Here fax, here clothis and here her   *hair*
       Of wem were they quyt and free.   *injury; completely free*
       Martyrdom they suffryd thore   *there*
230   For Hym that deyde upon the tree;
       To hevene were here soulys bore,
       In Goddys frayry for to be.   *brotherhood*

       Thoo bad the emperour hys men,
       "Bryngys forth that fayre may!"
235   And whanne sche com beforn hym then,
       "Welcome," he sayde, "par ma fay!   *by my faith*
       Hast thou yit thy counseyl tan   *decided*
       For to turne upon my lay?   *To convert to my religion*
       Have mercy on thy fayre pan!   *head*
240   Me longis nought don it away.   *I have no desire to take it away*

       "Thou schalt be menskyd as a qwene,   *honored*
       Bothe in boure and eke in halle;   *in private and in public*
       And in thy name I schal do clene
       An ymage make, ryght fayr withalle,[1]
245   And in this burgh thenne schal it stande,   *city*
       And heyghe and lowe schole loute it alle.   *i.e., everyone; pay homage to it*
       Of alle the nedys of this land
       We schole thee unto counseyl calle.[2]

       "Heyghe and lowe schal serve thee soo.
250   Kateryne, doo as I thee bede!
       And yit I wole thee more doo,   *do even more for you*
       Yyf thou wylt doo aftyr my rede: *as I advise*
       Of marbylston schal I do make   *marble*
       A ryche temple whenne thou art ded;
255   Among oure goddys thou schalt be take   *received*
       And layde in sylvyr and gold so red."   *enclosed*

---

[1] Lines 243–44: *And in your name I will have a statue splendidly made, a very beautiful one*

[2] Lines 247–48: *[And] on all matters of public importance / We will consult you*

"Be stylle, thou fool! I saye to thee,
Thou redes me to ful mekyl synne!
What man wolde idampnyd be
260   In helle for ony worldys wynne?   *any worldly joy*
I have to Jhesu Cryst my love:
He is my spouse, bothe oute and inne;   *everywhere (always)*
I hope to come to His hevene above,
There joye and blysse schal nevere blynne.   *cease*

265   "He is myn hope, my joye mest,   *greatest*
My Lord, my God in Trynyté,
My leef, my lyf, my love best —   *darling*
To swylke a lemman take I me.   *such a lover*
And yyf me were boote to speke,
270   Of thy counseyl now wolde I be
Thy goddys for to brenne and breke[1] —
For thou madyst hem, and they nought thee."

Be that sche hadde here wurdys sayde,   *By the time*
Hym thoughte hys herte scholde breke on fyve;   *into five pieces*
275   For yre and wraththe he styrte and brayde   *trembled and twisted*
And bad hys men hastely and blyve: *quickly*
"With whyppys and scourgys doth here sterte!   *make her jump*
Byndith and betith, whyl sche is on lyve,[2]
And in presoun then doth here smerte!   *make her suffer*
280   What boote is thusgate for to stryve?"   *What good does it do to argue like this?*

They maden here body al red blood ren   *run [with] red blood*
That fyrst was whyt as whales bon,
And aftyr sayde he to hys men:
"Prysouns here now swythe anon!   *Imprison her*
285   Hungyr schal sche hastely feel:
Mete ne drynk ne gevith here non,

---

[1] Lines 269–71: *And if it would do me any good to speak, / I would now advise you / To burn and destroy your gods*

[2] *Tie [her] up and beat [her], as long as she is alive*

Lytyl ne mekyl — now wete thou weel — [1]
Tyl twelve dayes be comen and gon!

"Out of this land I wole, for sothe —   *will [go]*
290   Me behoves nought longe dwelle,
To grete men and wyse bothe
Of these auntrys for to telle.[2]
Counseyl I have withouten dred   *I [must] have advice; doubt*
Hou I schal this maydyn quelle;
295   But sche take another red,   *Unless she decide differently*
Sche schal wete of woo ful welle."   *know a lot about misery*

Whenne the emperour was iwent,   *gone*
The qwene sayde untyl a knyghte —   *to*
Of knyghtys he was cheef and gent: *leader; nobly born*
300   Porphurye, seys the book, he hyghte —   *was called*
The qwene sayde: "With Kateryne
Doo me speke, yyf that thou myght!   *Arrange for me to speak*
Longyng I have in herte myne
To speke with here this ylke nyght."

305   That ylke nyght forgat he nought
To doo the qwenys comaundemente:
Unto presoun tho he here brought
And prevyly with here he wente.   *secretly*
They sawgh therinne ful mekyl lyght:
310   Goddys aungelys thedyr were sent,
That seten aboute that swete wyght,   *surrounded; person*
Anoyntyd here with oynement.

Aungelys they seen here cors anoynte,   *saw; body*
Ylke a wem and ylke a wounde.   *Each mark of injury*
315   Thorwgh Jhesu myght in every joynte   *Jesus'*
They maden here bothe heyl and sounde.   *well*

---

[1] Lines 286–87: *Do not give her any food or drink, / Not even a little — now understand this well*

[2] Lines 290–92: *It behooves me not to wait long / Before relating these events to great and wise men*

184

They hadde nought at the presoun dore
Istonden but a lytyl stounde,   *short time*
Of the lyght they were adred so sore
320   In swownyng fel they to the grounde.

The maydyn ros and to hem came
And spak to hem with mylde mood:
"Rysys up in Goddys name,   *Rise*
And loke ye ben of counfort good!"   *be of good courage*
325   On Jhesu Cryst sche bad hem leve,   *believe*
That for mankynde schedde Hys blood.
And whanne sche hadde this counseyl geve, *given this advice*
Up they resen and by here stood.   *rose*

Thenne spak the qwene sone anon: *spontaneously*
330   "Kateryne, fol weel is thee!   *you are very fortunate*
With Jhesu Cryst meche mayst thou don,   *much*
We have seen al thy prevyté."   *secret(s)*
"Looke thou," sche sayde, "upon Hym trowe
That Lord is of swylke pousté!   *such power*
335   He nele forgete, He wole hem knowe   *will not; acknowledge*
That serve Hym with herte free.

"I rede thee, dame, for thy behove,   *advise; benefit*
Forsake Maxence and al hys myght
For that ylke Kyngys love   *same*
340   That made bothe day and nyght,
Hevene and erthe, beste and man,   *animal*
Sunne and mone that schynys bryght.
The joye of Hevene schalt thou han,
And thou alsoo, I say, sere knyght!"   *sir*

345   Thenne spak that knyght to Kateryne:
"What kyn joye may that be?"   *kind [of]*
Kateryne sayde weel and fyne:
"Porphyrye, I wole telle it thee:
It is the joye withouten ende
350   That eeren ne eyghen may here ne see,   *ears nor eyes; hear*

185

No tungge of speke, herte thynke in mende —   *mind*
That lovith God lel, this ordeynith He.[1]

"Ther is non in that ryche empere   *great kingdom*
That hungyr has, cold, ne threste;   *thirst*
355 Drede ne wraththe is ther non there,
But love and lykyng, joye and reste."   *pleasure*
Thorwgh the wurdys that sche spake
Or mydnyght they were ful preste   *Before; prepared*
To suffre deth for Goddys sake;
360 They levyd in Jhesu alther beste.   *best of all*

They here betaughte Jhesu, oure Lord,   *committed her to*
And siththen wenten bothe away.   *then*
Two hundryd knyghtys servyd here at bord.   *her (i.e., the queen); at the table*
Whan sche tolde hem that othir day   *the next day*
365 Hou Goddys aungelys here servyd had
In presoun, that fayre may,
They levyd on Jhesu, as sche hem bad,
And forsoken here false lay.   *their; law*

For sche ne moste have neyther mete ne drynk   *Since*
370 Thorwgh comaundement of the emperour,
Twelve dayes, nevere a pynk,   *not even a bit*
Sche hadde a betere vyaundour: *provider of food*
Cryst sente to here goostly foode   *spiritual*
Fro Hevene, that is oure Saveour.
375 Aungelys that broughten here lyflode   *ration to live on*
Ther sche sat presounnyd in a tour.   *imprisoned*

And whenne the twelve dayes were gon,
Thenne com Jhesu, hevene Kyng,
With aungelys and maydenys many on,
380 For to speke with Hys derelyng.
He sayde, "For me thou hast ben led
In ful gret stryf and gret fandyng.   *conflict; temptation*

---

[1] *For those who love God faithfully, He ordains this [reward]*

Looke that thou be nought adred.   *afraid*
I geve thee, doughtyr, my blessyng.

385   "Often I have thy prayers herde,
Whenne that thou hast me besought;
I schal nought fayle thee — be nought aferde —
To jugement whenne thou art brought.
Looke thou be stedefast, trewe and sekyr!   *confident*
390   Of alle here peynys geve thou nought.   *their tortures*
For of the blysse thou may be sekyr   *sure*
That I have to myn handwerk wrought."   *for my creatures*

Whenne He hadde sayde these wurdis thoo,
Out of the presoun gan He glyde
395   To Hevene blysse, ther He com froo,
Hys aungelys upon ylke a syde.
Whenne Maxcense hadde idon his dede,
Hom he come with mekyl pryde;
With dukes, eerlys, and knyghtys he yede,   *went*
400   And pagys rennyng be here syde.   *by their*

Upon that other day ful sone   *the next*
He askyd of the maydenys staat,
Yif that sche were on lyve or none:[1]
"Sche is ful feble, weel I waat.
405   Fette here forth now, my gayler!   *Fetch; jailer*
For hungyr and thyrst sche is ful mate."   *defeated*
The gayler broughte here to hym ther,
Ther as he sat in ryal sate.

Whenne sche was before hym led,
410   He sayde, "Welcome, damyseel!
Thou hast ben ful harde isted   *afflicted*
Bothe in yryn and in steel;
But yit me thynkith that thou leve may   *survive (live)*

---

[1] Lines 402–03: *He inquired about the virgin's condition, / [Asking] whether she were alive or not*

	And that me lykith swythe wel.	
415	Jhesu, that thou hast spoken of ay,	*always*
	Thee behovith forsaken every del.	*It behooves you; completely*

"For I wolde nought do thee to dede,   *Since I did not want to put you to death*
To my presoun I dede thee goo.
But sertys now thou mostyst nede   *certainly; must necessarily*
420   To chese thee on of thyngys twoo: *To choose for yourself one of [these] two things*
Oyther upon my goddys leve   *Either*
And Cryst forsake for everemoo,
Or we schal thynke bothe morwe and eve   *plan*
With stronge paynys thee to sloo."   *tortures; kill*

425   Thenne spak the maydyn there sche stood   *where*
Among the Sarezynys so blak,
As Jhesu here taughte, that is so good,
With mylde wurdys withouten lak: *without fault*
"Though I schole deye, thou may me trest:
430   Jhesu ne schal I nevere forsake;[1]
For Jhesu love I am ful prest   *prepared*
Gladly here my deth to take.

"For though that thou bethynke thee
Aftyr peynys grete and sare   *tortures*
435   And doo hem alle to pyne me,   *afflict*
To suffre hem I wil be yare.   *ready*
Nevere in my lyf, be God above,   *by*
My flesch, my blood ne wole I spare   *hold back*
To spende hem for that Lordys love;
440   For me He suffryd mekyl mare.   *much more*

"Blely wole I martyryd be   *Gladly*
For Hym with peynys grete and smale:
He has me callyd to Hys frayré,   *brotherhood*
That schal be boote of al my bale."   *remedy; suffering*
445   Sche stood with a ful blythe mood

---

[1] Lines 429–30: *Even if I must die [for it], you can believe me: / I will never renounce Jesus*

Before Maxence, to tellen here tale.
But there he sat he wex nygh wood;   *where*
For tene and angyr he was al pale.   *anger and rage*

He skypte and styrte and sore gan grame.   *jerked; trembled; was vexed*
450   Ther com a Sarezyn forth anon —
Cursates, the book saith, was his name.
"Sere kyng," he sayde, "I am thy mon.
Yit I can a turnement make: *an instrument of torture*
Of swylke on herdyst thou nevere er telle;[1]
455   Whanne sche it seeth, I undyrtake,   *I assure you*
Another lessoun sche wole spelle.   *figure out*

"Foure wheles make schal I,
The twoo schole turne agayn the twoo,   *against the [other] two*
Ful thykke idreven by and by
460   With wythir-hokes, here to sloo.[2]
Among the foure sche schal be went.   *perish*
Here body schal have meche woo:
In smale peses sche schal be rent,   *pieces; torn*
On erthe schal sche nevere eft goo."   *She will never walk on earth again*

465   Thenne bad Maxcence hys gayler   *jailer*
That he scholde the mayden take
And leden here into presoun ther,
The whyles he scholde the wheles make.   *While; wheels*
And or the thrydde day were gon,
470   They weren iwrought al for here sake.
So grym they were to loke upon
That many a man they garte quake.   *caused to tremble*

Whenne the wheles weren al yare,   *ready*
In the cyté were they set;
475   Many Sarezyn before hem ware.

---

[1] *You have never before heard tell of any such thing*

[2] Lines 459–60: *Very thickly studded all around / With opposing hooks, to kill her with*

The maydyn was ful gretly thret.[1]
Thanne bad the emperour hys men
That sche were out of presoun fet.   *fetched*
To ben awreke weel wende he then   *avenged; expected*
480   Of that maydyn withouten let.   *Against; hindrance*

They ledde here to that ylke stede   *place*
There sche scholde in hem gon.[2]
Many a modyr chylde ther yede   *mother's child*
For to loken here upon.   *to look at her*
485   Sche knelyd adoun that place amydde,
To God of Hevene sche bad here bone.   *request*
But lystnes now what hap betydde!   *listen; event happened*
Goddys help here com ful sone.   *came to her*

The whelys for to breke asundyr,
490   Aungelys were sent fro God anon.
On Sarezynys that were ther undyr
Venjaunse took He sone upon.   *Vengeance*
Among the folk they gunne to dryve —   *began to move forcefully*
Foure thousand there dede they slon.
495   Of hethene men were ded ful ryve,   *a very large number*
But evyl hadde the maydyn non.   *injury*

The Crystene men that there were
Of this myracle they were ful glad.
The kyng ne wyste what he dede there,
500   So sorweful was he and so mad.
The Sarezynys that ascape myghte
Hyyd hem faste — they weren adrad   *Hastened*
For that ylke perylous syghte;
Of sorewe were they nevere so sad.[3]

---

[1] Lines 475–76: *Many pagans gathered in front of the wheels. / Strong threats were uttered against the virgin [presumably by the crowd]*

[2] *Where she would have to go in among them (the wheels)*

[3] *They had never been so weary of (sated with) sorrow*

505   Soone aftyr this folk was flowe than,   *fled*
       Untyl hym sayde hys wyf, the qwene: *To him (the emperor)*
       "Weylaway, thou wrehche man!   *miserable*
       Wherof makys thou thee so kene?   *Why do you insist on being so obstinate?*
       He hath weel kyd that God is He,   *revealed, made known*
510   That born was of the maydyn schene.   *bright*
       I forsake alle thyne and thee
       And al thy myght forevere clene.[1]

       "Agayn the Lord that thou woldyst greve   *want to injure*
       Thy stryvyng is nought wurth a schyde;   *splinter of wood*
515   That these Crystene men on leve,
       Hys myghtynesse it goth ful wyde.[2]
       Crye Hym mercy of thy gylt!   *Beg Him for mercy*
       For yyf that thou to longe abyde,   *wait too long*
       When thou art ded thou schalt be pylt   *thrust*
520   In helle pyne for al thy pryde."

       He wex for wroth bothe wood and wylde,
       And to the qwene he sayde then,
       "Thou art dysseyvyd — the devyl thee hylde! — *deceived; may the devil skin you*
       Thorwgh wyhchecraft of Crystene men.   *witchcraft*
525   I swere thee be my goddys goode   *by my kind gods*
       And be al that I can sayn:
       But thou the sunnere chaunge thy moode,   *Unless; very soon (the sooner)*
       With wykkyd deth thou schalt be slayn.   *a cruel (savage)*

       "But thou forsake Jhesu ful prest,   *right now*
530   This schal be thy jugement:
       Fyrst thy pappys of thy brest   *breasts; upper body*
       With yrene hookes schole be rent;   *torn*
       And afftyrward withinne a thrawe   *moment*
       Thou schalt be hevedyd, ar evere I stent,   *beheaded, before I pause*

---

[1] Lines 511–12: *I renounce you and all your possessions / And all your power forever completely*

[2] Lines 515–16: *[The One] in whom these Christians believe, / His power extends far and wide*

535   With houndys and foules al todrawe,[1]
       Thorwgh myn owne comaundement."

       Whenne this emperour was war   *aware*
       That sche nolde nought turne here thought,   *would not at all change her mind*
       On alle maner than bad he thar
540   That sche schoolde out of towne be brought.
       Thenne lokyd sche to Kateryne,
       And myldely sche here besought
       To don here erende in that pyne[2]
       To God of Hevene, that al hath wrought.

545   Thenne sayde Kateryne, here trewe frende:
       "For sothe, dame, I telle it thee:
       Of the joye withouten ende
       Trust and sekyr may thou be,   *Confident; sure*
       Yif thou thy deth in Hys name has   *receive*
550   That spredde Hys body upon the Tree,   *extended; Cross*
       As Hys swete wylle was,
       For to maken oure soules free."

       Men drowen here pappys of here brest   *tore; breasts; upper body*
       And hedyd here, as I have told.   *beheaded*
555   Than bad the emperour ful feste   *strictly*
       That no man scholde be so bold
       For to beryyn here body —   *bury*
       For houndes scholde have it at wolde.   *in [their] control*
       The soule com ful hastyly
560   Before Jhesu, that it fore was solde.   *for whom it was given*

       Thenne aftyrward, whenne it was nyght
       Aftyr thys stronge passyoun,   *violent (cruel)*
       Com Purphurye, the goode knyght,
       And fond here lye withouten the toun.   *found; lying outside*
565   In Crystene beryeles with good entent   *burying-place*

---

[1] *[And] torn apart completely by dogs and birds*

[2] *To deliver her message (or intercede for her) in that ordeal*

He beryyd here with devocyoun,
Agayn the kyngys comaundement —   *Against*
To suffre deth he was ful boun.   *ready*

Thenne aftyr on that othir day
570   Men tolden the emperour ful rathe   *promptly*
That sche was beryyd, soth to say.
Than spak he wurdys grymme and wrathe:
"Enserches faste who this hath don,   *Search out*
My serjauntys that I clothe and fede!"   *officers*
575   Manye a man that gylt hadde non
Was flemyd and prysounnyd for that dede.   *put to flight; imprisoned*

Before this cruel emperour
Ful boldely com Sere Purphury
And seyde hym, there he sat ful sour,   *embittered*
580   Ryght ful of yre and felony,   *wickedness*
"I wole thee telle who dede this dede,
Siththe thou hast so gret desyr:
I, Goddys servaunt, withouten drede,
I have beryyd Hys martyr.

585   "Thou was ful wood wytles, sertayn,   *furiously irrational*
And lytyl thoughtyst thou on thy dede,
Aftyr that thou haddyst here slayn
The erthe whan thou here forbede.[1]
In helle pyne schal be thy playn   *complaint*
590   Withouten ende for thy qwed.   *evil deeds*
To Jhesu Cryst I take me ay   *forever*
And I forsake thy false red."   *counsel*

Thanne he began to crye and rore,
And often he callyd hymself "caytyf,"   *"poor wretch"*
595   As he hadde be woundyd thore   *As [if]*
With swerd, with spere, or with knyf.
Often he sayde, "Allas, allas,

---

[1] Lines 587–88: *When you forbade her [to be buried in] the earth after you had put her to death*

193

That evere I was born of wyf!   *from a woman*
Now Purphurye forsake me has
600   Wardayn of myn owne lyf!"   *Guardian*

He hadde sorwe and care most,
Wundyr woo he was in wede.   *in [his] madness*
He sayde, "Now I have hym ilost,
The beste knyght of al my lede!   *people (subjects)*
605   My beste help bothe fer and nere
Overal he was at my moste nede.
The wyhche schal it abye ful dere   *witch; pay for*
Thorwgh whom he hath don this dede!"

Hys knyghtys drowgh the knyght saunfayle   *led; without a doubt*
610   To and from in prevyté,
Thorwgh whom it was and whos counsayle   *[Asking] through whom*
That he wolde icrystenyd be.
When they hadde counsayllyd to and fram   *deliberated back and forth*
The knyghtys sayden, "Now so wil we!
615   We take us unto Crystyndam;
For drede of deth wole we nought fle."

Often he was in ful wroth plyte,   *wrathful state*
But nevere so wroth as he was thoo!   *then*
Here hedes he bad anon off smyte —   *Their heads*
620   But therof gaf they nought a sloo.[1]
Here bodyys he bad in feeld be caste
With houndys to gnawe and bestys thoo.[2]
Here soules come ful swythe in haste
There joye and blysse is everemoo.

625   Pray we now bothe fyrst and laste,
Lytyl and mochyl, I rede thertoo,   *I.e., everyone*
That whanne that we be hens ipaste,   *have gone (passed) hence*
That oure soules mowe do soo.

---

[1] *But they didn't give a sloe (a small, sour, worthless fruit) about that*

[2] *To be chewed up by dogs and [wild] animals then*

Thenne aftyr on that othir day
630   The kyng was set in hys chayere;   *throne (seat of authority)*
Sarezynys that heelden here lay   *had kept their own religion*
On ylke a syde they sat hym nere.
Kateryne he bad forth brynge;
To fetten here wente hys jayler.   *fetch*
635   Beforn hym com that holy thynge
With blythe mood and gladful cheer.

Wrothly on here than lokyd he
And spak to here with gret envye: *hostility (malice)*
"Mekyl woo hast thou do me,
640   Thou wyhche, ful of felounnye!   *witch; wickedness*
Thou hast maad my folk forlorne   *utterly lost*
And that thou schalt ful dere abye.   *pay for*
Ne schalt thou nevere eft me scorne,   *again*
Betraye me with thy sorserye!   *sorcery*

645   "But thou wylt leve on alle wyse   *believe completely*
Upon my goddys that al may weelde,   *govern*
And mekely don hem sacrefyze,
Knele and up thyn handes helde,   *raise (hold)*
This ylke day — and that als tyte —   *immediately*
650   Withowten the toun ryght in the felde
My men schole there thyn hed off smyte,
And so schole we thy servyse yelde."   *reward your service*

This mayde forbar hym nought that tyde.   *on that occasion*
Sche sayde, "Nay, thou teraunt, nay!   *tyrant*
655   That day ne schalt thou nevere abyde   *live to see*
That I schal leve upon thy lay.
Blessyd be Hevene Kyng above,
He hath me lent ful stable fay.   *granted; faith*
Blely wole I for Hys love   *Gladly*
660   Thole deth this ylke day.   *Suffer*

"Doo forth faste as thou began,   *Go on*
Thou fendes leme, thou fendes gaste!   *limb of the devil (fiend); spirit*
For al that evere thou thynke kan,   *All [the punishments] you can possibly devise*

	I wole hem suffre al in haste,	*without hesitation*
665	For Jhesu love, my Spouse gay,	*excellent*
	That born was of a maydyn chast.	*pure (chaste)*
	My soule to Hym beteche I ay,	*commit (commend) I ever*
	For I have lovyd Hym althermast."	*most of all*

	Thanne that Sarezyn bad hys men	
670	That they scholden lede that maydyn gent	*noble*
	Out of the burghe gates then	*city gates*
	And geven here there here jugement.	
	Ful blythe and glad that fayre may	*maiden*
	Out of the tounward sche went.	*away from the town*
675	With many a man that ylke day	*By; same*
	In the toun sche was bement.	*lamented*

	Whan sche was led to the place, for sothe,	
	There sche scholde ihedyd be,	*beheaded*
	Wyves fele and maydenys bothe	*Many [married] women*
680	Folewyd here of that cyté,	
	Makyng sorewe and wepynge harde	
	For that maydyn fayr and free.	
	Sche turnyd anon unto hemwarde	*toward them*
	And sayde as I schal telle thee:	

685	"I pray yow alle that ye gon hom,	
	Ye wyvys and ye maydenys bryght!	
	Dystourbles nought my martyrdom,	*Trouble (Disturb)*
	But bes ful glad: for He me hyght,	*be; has promised*
	That Lord that is over alle thynge,	
690	Soone aftyr when I martyryd be,	
	To Hevene blysse He schal me brynge."	
	Sche knelyd doun and up gan see,	*gazed*

	To heveneward, there sche hadde tyght.	*approached spiritually*
	Sche sayde, "Jhesu, my love fre,	
695	Of al that I leve in the ryght,	*believe rightly*
	Lord, this day I thanke thee.	
	I thanke thee, Lord, now ful of myght,	
	For thou hast maad me on of thyne,	*one of your own*

To wone among thy maydenys bryght
700   In Hevene, ther nevere schal be no pyne.

"Hevene and erthe, bothe lyght and derk,
Watyr and land, sunne and mone,
And al this world — this was thy werk,
That heyghe syttyst in holy trone.
705   I beseke thee today   *beseech*
That thou graunte me a bone   *boon (reward)*
Out of this world ar I go away —
For that I wot schal be ful soone:

"Alle that in the name of me
710   My passyoun wole here or rede,
Or have me in good memory
In ony lond or ony lede: *[among] any people*
Lord, yyf they praye in ryghtful case,   *righteous cause*
In poynt of deth or other nede,
715   Thou graunte hem for thyn holy grace
Of here prayer weel to spede.   *graciously to fare*

"To suffre deth I am here, loo,
Ful prest, Lord, for love of thee.   *eager*
This macegref is here alsoo   *executioner*
720   With drawen swerd, to hede me —   *behead*
My soule greve he ne may,
For therof hath he no pousté.   *power*
Tak it to thee now, I thee pray,
Into the blysse that evere schal be!"

725   Soone as sche hadde maad an ende
Of here orysoun and here prayer
For alle that here hadde in mende,   *remembrance*
And for hereself in this maner,
A voys fro hevene oure Lord dede sende,
730   That alle it herde that ther were: *So that all those who were present heard it*
"My gatys ben open, my leve frende.   *beloved*
Come to me, my doughtyr dere!

197

"To suffre the deth in the name of me,
Doughtyr, drede thou no wyght!   *not at all (no whit)*
735   Befor me schalt thou corownyd be,   *In my presence*
For hedyr hast thou longe ityght.   *journeyed*
The cumpany of aungelys schene   *glorious*
Schal come agayn thy soule bryght   *to meet*
And brynge thee to this place clene   *pure (shining)*
740   Ther evere is day and nevere nyght.

"Come, my doughtyr! come now smerte,   *quickly*
For herd is now thyn orysoun.
For alle that thee have in here herte
And blely here thy passyoun,   *gladly*
745   And alle that on thee calle in nede
With hertely devocyoun,   *sincere*
Of here prayer schole they spede   *They shall have their prayer answered*
And therto have my benysoun."   *also; blessing*

Of this answere, when it was herd,
750   Iwundryd was many a man.   *Amazed*
Sche stoupyd doun undyr the swerd —
Here swyre was whyt as ony swan.   *neck*
Swythe he smot here hed off there,
But for the blood the mylk out ran.
755   Above here stood that manquellere —   *executioner (man-killer)*
He was ful blak, he was ful wan.   *pale (pallid)*

Anon come aungelys from the ayr
And flowen awey with here body   *flew*
And beryyd it, that swythe was fayr,   *very much*
760   In the Mount of Synay,   *Mount Sinai*
There gaf the lawe God of Hevene
Unto the prophete Moysy.   *Moses*
The soule com to Jhesu evene   *directly*
With moche merthe and melody.   *rejoicing*

765   That day sche deyde — wetith weel it! —   *note it well*
Syxe aungelys deden here body lende   *bring*
Into the Mount, there it is yit

	And schal be to the worldes ende.	*until*
	Of syke folk were ther nevere so fele —	
770	Alle that evere wolde thedyr wende,[1]	
	Oure Lord sente hem boote and hele,	*health*
	That alle bales may amende.	*sufferings*

	The toumbe that sche was layd in ther,	
	It was al maad of marbylston.	
775	A strem of oyle fayr and cler	
	Sprong therof ryght ful good won —	*in great abundance*
	And so it hath don seththyn evere,	*ever since*
	Evere siththe that sche was slawe.	*slain*
	Alle Crystene folk that thedyr kevere	*make their way thither*
780	Here body wurschepith wundyr fawe.	*gladly*

	Here day it fallith in Novembre,	*occurs*
	In world as sche was martyryd here,[2]	
	On the sevynthe kalendes of Decembre,	
	As wreten is in kalendere.	
785	He that wrot here lyf thus,	
	And alle that it rede and here,	
	The joye of hevene hem geve Jhesus,[3]	
	For Maryes love, Hys modyr dere!	

	The heyghe Kyng of alle menkynne,	*high*
790	That spredde Hys body upon Tree,	*stretched out; Cross*
	Brynge us out of dedly synne	
	And sende us love and charyté,	
	That we mowe to that stede wynne,	*attain to that place*
	Withouten ende in joye to be,	
795	That Seynt Kateryne is inne —	
	Amen, amen, pur charyté!	*for the sake of God's love*
	[Explicit.]	

---

[1] Lines 769–70: *[To] all the sick people who went there, no matter how many there were*

[2] *[On the date] when she was martyred here in this world*

[3] Lines 785–87: *May Jesus give the joy of Heaven to him who thus wrote her Life and to all who read and hear it*

Explanatory Notes to Stanzaic Life of Katherine

Abbreviations: **A** = Auchinleck (National Library of Scotland MS Advocates 19.2.1), fols. 21r–24v; **G** = Gonville and Caius College, Cambridge MS 175/96, pp. 107–18 [base text]; **H** = Carl Horstmann; **R** = Bodleian Library MS Rawlinson poet. 225 (*SC* 15509), fols. 48r–48v, 46r–47v, and 1r–2r.

1–8   This text opens with both a blessing, recalling the invocation before a sermon, and the familiar call of the oral storyteller for the audience's attention.

10–15   These lines attempt to explain how the jurisdiction of Maxentius can extend to Katherine, who is the daughter of King Costus and living in Alexandria (lines 49–50). The historical Maxentius (Marcus Aurelius Valerius Maxentius) was a Roman emperor from 306 to 312 and controlled Italy and north Africa, including Alexandria. King Costus was not a historical figure.

17   *Mahoun.* See explanatory note to line 205 of the early *SEL* account of Mary Magdalen.

21   *Sarezyn.* See explanatory note to line 194 of the early *SEL* account of Mary Magdalen.

          tryst. The more usual form of this adjective is *thrist.*

25   *fyve and fyfty yer.* This version of the legend suggests, that is, that Maxentius was a very old man by the time of his confrontation with Katherine. A makes his previous reign even longer: 65 years.

66–67   *blyssyd . . . here tungge.* The gesture suggests that she is asking God to bless and guide her words when she confronts the emperor. Katherine's association with eloquent speech was so strong that medieval Christians sometimes invoked her aid to cure diseases and injuries of the tongue.

72   *They wente with here, that stood here by.* That is, she is accompanied by members of her own court or household.

93   *Jhesu, the welle of wyt.* It is appropriate for Katherine to call Jesus the wellspring or source of wisdom because the wisdom she will shortly display is portrayed as miraculous and divinely given (not merely the result of her excellent education).

102   *mawmettys.* See explanatory note to line 57 of Mirk's account of Mary Magdalen.

113–14   *Yyf thou were leryd.* Ironically, Maxentius argues that Katherine has been badly educated and should have studied with teachers like his own.

118   *Termagaunt.* See explanatory note to line 205 of the early *SEL* account of Mary Magdalen.

135–36   *Ther is no god but On of alle, / That . . . al hath wrought.* Katherine's reply echoes the beginning of the Nicene Creed ("I believe in one God, the Father Almighty, Maker of heaven and earth and of all things visible and invisible") — a good response to a polytheist and idolater like Maxentius.

139–48   This version of the legend places unusual emphasis on the secrecy and the personal sealing of Maxentius's letters to the philosophers, making one wonder what he fears.

166   *As Jhesu Cryst schal wysse thee.* An echo of Jesus's promise to His followers in Luke 21:12–15: "[you will be brought] before kings and governors, for my name's sake. And it shall happen unto you for a testimony. Lay it up therefore in your hearts, not to meditate before how you shall answer: for I will give you a mouth and wisdom, which all your adversaries shall not be able to resist and gainsay."

173   *In al wysdom and eke Latyne.* The philosophers' knowledge of Latin would not be worth mentioning, of course, except in a vernacular retelling of the legend for audiences who did not know it themselves.

183–84   The explicit mention of God's angel again at this point, together with the way Katherine "sees" her arguments as if they had been miraculously written in her heart, reinforces the message that she is successful in this debate because of divine inspiration, not her own learning.

205   *in fay.* Presumably intended as a mere asseveration, meaning "certainly." But it is an ironic choice, since its literal meaning is "in faith" and Maximus seems to be the only person present who has not been converted.

210   *Of ryche kynrede.* The idea seems to be that this scholar's family background makes him the natural spokesman for the others.

225–28   The martyrdom of the philosophers echoes the ordeal of Shadrach, Meshach and Abednego (Daniel 3), who refused King Nebuchadnezzar's command to violate their Jewish faith by worshiping his idols and were bound and cast into "a furnace of burning fire," from which they emerged unharmed (Daniel 3:6, et passim). Although the newly converted philosophers in the legend die, the miracle that preserves their bodies apparently untouched recalls the details recounted in Daniel 3:94 (3:27 in Protestant translations): "[All the witnesses] gathered together, considered these men, that the fire had no power on their bodies, and that not a hair of their heads had been singed, nor their garments altered, nor the smell of the fire had passed on them." There is also an important New Testament text on such miracles, when Jesus promises that His followers will be kept completely safe in the midst of persecution, even if they lose their earthly lives: "You shall be betrayed . . . and some of you they will put to death. And you shall be hated by all men for my name's sake. But a hair of your head shall not perish. In your patience you shall possess your souls" (Luke 21:16–19).

236   *par ma fay!* Literally, "by my faith" — another irony, when applied to Maxentius. See explanatory note to line 205, above.

239–40   A slightly veiled threat to have her beheaded.

242   *in boure and eke in halle.* Since *boure* in Middle English can mean "bedchamber," this line briefly recalls the familiar motif of the pagan suitor who attempts to seduce the virgin martyr away from her true bridegroom, Christ. The theme of sexual temptation, however, was never as important in the Katherine legend as in those of virgin martyrs like Margaret, and there is almost nothing else to suggest it in this particular retelling. The MED glosses *in bour and in hall* as meaning simply "in chamber and in hall, in cottage and mansion, everywhere" (see *bour* n. 4).

253–56   Maxentius offers Katherine a marble temple, within which she will be worshipped after death along with his gods. Instead, Katherine will be buried in a marble tomb, to which pilgrims will come forever to be healed and edified by the miraculous oil that perpetually flows from her remains (lines 773–80 below).

282   *whyt as whales bon.* A conventional image of beauty in Middle English poetry, meaning "as white as ivory." Ivory did not actually come from whales, of course,

but among its main sources were walruses and other animals that could be confused with whales. Interestingly enough, the corresponding line in A has *alpes bon* ("elephant's bone," another kind of ivory); R uses another image entirely, saying she was as white as milk foam.

289–96   In other versions of the legend, the emperor's temporary departure from Alexandria is attributed to other pressing business. In this version he is apparently so obsessed with the need to overcome Katherine that he can think of nothing else.

335–36   This seems to echo the promise in Matthew 10:32: "Every one therefore that shall confess me before men, I will also confess him before my Father who is in heaven."

349–52   An echo of 1 Corinthians 2:9 (and, somewhat more distantly, Isaiah 64:4): "That eye hath not seen, nor ear heard, neither hath it entered into the heart of man, what things God hath prepared for them that love him."

353–56   These lines echo several Biblical prophecies about the joy of the blessed in Heaven, most notably Revelation [or Apocalypse] 7:16–17 ("They shall no more hunger nor thirst, neither shall the sun fall on them, nor any heat. For the Lamb, which is in the midst of the throne, shall rule them, and shall lead them to the fountains of the waters of life, and God shall wipe away all tears from their eyes") and Revelation 21:4 (". . . and death shall be no more, nor mourning, nor crying, nor sorrow shall be any more, for the former things are passed away").

371   *pynk.* Either a minnow or a derivative of the verb "pinchen," suggesting a miserly portion.

375   *that.* In order to make the sentence parse, this word should either be construed as a demonstrative (that is, "the angels brought her that [as a] ration") or emended to *ther.*

392   *myn handwerk.* Referring to human beings as the work of God's hands recalls the poetic language used in the Psalms and some of the Old Testament prophets. See, for example, Psalm 138:8 [137.8 in Vulgate and Douay], Isaiah 29:23, 45:9–11, and 64:8.

398–400   These details about Maxentius's entourage have no equivalent in most versions of the legend. Their addition heightens his resemblance to a late-medieval monarch and also highlights the choice Katherine has made between earthly power and that of Jesus (whose own entourage of angels and saints has been mentioned just above, in lines 378–80 and 396).

426   *Sarezynys so blak.* The adjective here must be figurative rather than literally descriptive, referring either to their lack of enlightenment or more generally to their wickedness. On *Sarezynys*, see explanatory note to line 194 of the early *SEL* account of Mary Magdalen.

451   *Cursates* ("the cursed one"), the confederate of Maxentius who suggests, and in this version actually builds, the terrible wheel on which Katherine is to be torn apart.

456   *Another lessoun.* Continued play with the idea of Katherine's needing instruction from them: she will change her tune, predicts Cursates, once she sees this terrible torture device.

523–24 The only explanation Maxentius can imagine for his wife's conversion is witchcraft or sorcery by the Christians. He returns to this explanation below, in lines 640–44, calling Katherine a witch.

531–32 The cutting off of the queen's breasts has been interpreted as "a kind of metaphorical transference" which emphasizes her connection with Katherine, whose own body will bleed milk when she is beheaded, later in the legend (Wogan-Browne and Burgess, Introduction to *Virgin Lives and Holy Deaths*, p. xxxiv). It is more common in saints' legends for the virgin martyr herself to be mutilated in this way; see for example lines 441–44 of the Christina legend, below in this collection, and the accompanying explanatory note.

555–60 Although the queen's mutilated body is left unburied, to be eaten by dogs and other scavengers, her soul is immediately taken to Christ. In A lines 559–60 make this point even clearer: *The soule com bifor Jhesu, / Er the bodi were cold.*

574   *My serjauntys that I clothe and fede!* As he sends his officers out to find the unknown culprit(s), he arouses their zeal by reminding them of the loyalty and gratitude they owe him. Ironically, of course, it is the leader of his own officers who has chosen to follow Jesus Christ instead of the emperor.

583   *withouten drede.* The phrase probably means "without any doubt," but in this context it could also mean "without fear of the consequences."

593–608   Although modern readers might expect the emperor to mourn the loss of his wife more than that of his favorite lieutenant, medieval retellings of the legend nearly always skip over the former in favor of the latter. Indeed, the emperor's lament over Porphirius was obviously a favorite scene.

602   *in wede.* Perhaps "in [his] garments," but also "in [his] madness." See MED *wede* n. 3. This is also a handy formula to complete and intensify the alliteration on *w* and to supply a rhyme.

609–16   The sequence of events here is not entirely clear, but the idea in G seems to be that the knights assigned to guard Porphirius, their former leader, use their opportunities to talk with him privately while he is in their custody and are converted by what he tells them about his own decision to convert. A and R present a different scenario in which the emperor privately questions his knights about Porphirius's conversion (which they already know about) and they unanimously express their own faith (to which they have already been converted). One might logically connect these knights with the 200 whose conversion was mentioned earlier (lines 363–68), although A and R do not make that clear.

679–82   Compare Luke 23:27–28, in which Jesus is followed to His crucifixion outside Jerusalem by a multitude and specific mention is made of "women, who bewailed and lamented him." Jesus tells them to weep instead for themselves and their children.

709–16   Katherine's prayer for those who honor her memory. Note the similarity to St. Margaret's final prayer, in which that saint asked to be able to assist those who remember her martyrdom, give churches or alms in her name, or call on her in need. But unlike most versions of Margaret's prayer, which included petitions for women in labor and other particular categories of persons she wanted to help, Katherine just refers in a general way to the needs of people facing death or some other trouble and stipulates that her help be confined to those whose requests are *ryghtful* (line 713).

739–40   Again the legend refers to Heaven with details drawn from Biblical prophecies — for example, Revelation 22:5: "And night shall be no more: and they shall not need the light of the lamp, nor the light of the sun, because the Lord God shall enlighten them."

754   *for the blood the mylk out ran.* A miracle that is reported also at the executions of several other virgin martyrs and at least one male saint, the apostle Paul. In the cases

205

of Katherine and the other virgins, the miraculous substitution operates most obviously as a sign of the saint's physical and spiritual purity, suggesting that she has transcended the natural, sexual functions of her earthly female body. The connection with St. Paul reminds us, however, that milk was also a symbol of spiritual fruitfulness and nurturing that could cross gender lines — as it did in Paul's account of his own initial dealings with the new Christian community in Corinth: "And I, brethren, could not speak to you as unto spiritual [people], but as unto carnal. As unto little ones in Christ. I gave you milk to drink, not meat; for you were not able as yet. But neither indeed are you now able" (1 Corinthians 3:1–2).

756   *He was ful blak, he was ful wan.* Although there may be some word play here, in this context the principal meaning of *blak* is probably the opposite of the modern word it resembles — that is, it probably means pale, colorless, or dead-white (see the OED entry for the adjective *blake* and compare the word "bleak"). Paired here, the near synonyms *blak* and *wan* suggest the executioner's shocked reaction to the miracle that has just proved Katherine's sanctity and his own collusion in evil.

760–62 Mt. Sinai, on the Sinai Peninsula (now in Egypt), is believed to be the place where God gave Moses the Ten Commandments (see especially Exodus, ch. 19). Next to Mt. Sinai, where the legend says Katherine's body was taken by angels after her death in Alexandria, is Jebel Katherine, or Mt. Katherine. St. Katherine's Monastery, at the foot of the mountains, is the present site of Katherine's tomb. The monastery, built in 548–65 by Justinian I, originally commemorated the Burning Bush (Exodus 3:1–6), but was rededicated to St. Katherine in the tenth or eleventh century.

781–84 The anniversary of her death, November 25, was listed in medieval liturgical calendars all over Europe and commemorated every year in church services with special readings, hymns, and antiphons in her honor.

785–96 This version of the legend ends, as it began, with the invocation of a blessing that includes everyone who reads or hears it.

Textual Notes to Stanzaic Life of Katherine

Abbreviations: see explanatory notes.

6   *of.* The scribe of G regularly doubles medial and final *f*, writing *off* for *of*, *afftyr* for *aftyr*, and so on. Since this spelling quirk does not affect the pronunciation of the words in question, it has not been reproduced in this edition.

25   *he.* G: omits.

        hadde. G: *hadde ben*, with *ben* canceled.

45   *Glemen.* Emendation based on A. G reads *Alle men*, which does not make sense with the remainder of the line.

49   *that.* Inserted above the line in G.

50   G: *hys ryghte name*, with *ryghte* canceled.

52   *eightene wyntyr.* A gives her age as fifteen instead of eighteen.

        of. A, H: omit.

57   *in.* G: *i.*

59   *desport.* Somewhat conjectural, since the last three letters can no longer be read in G. "Coort," the rhyme word (line 57), helps, however. A ends the line differently.

64   *Maxeens.* H: *Maxcens.*

69   A has an easier reading: *Sche sayde sche wald thider wende*; R is similar but omits *thider*.

82   *as.* Inserted above the line in G.

112   *nothyng.* G: *no th thyng.*

133   *develys.* G: *develys alle*, with *alle* canceled.

141   *was.* G: *was ther*, with *ther* canceled.

146   *selyd.* G: *fe selyd*, with *fe* canceled.

150   *knyght.* G: *kyng knyght*, with *kyng* canceled.

151   *they.* G: omits. H's emendation.

164   *to.* G: omits. H's emendation.

185   *sayde.* The beginning of this word is too faint and worn to be read in G.

200   *it.* Inserted above the line in G.

205   *Maxcence.* G: *Maxcence hymself*, with *hymself* canceled.

215   *itold.* The *i* is inserted above the line in G.

218   *wende.* The last two letters are obscured in G.

222   *bad.* G: *bayd bad*, with *bayd* canceled.

224   *be.* G: omits. H's emendation.

227   *fax.* A, R: *flesche*; H proposed emending G's *fax* to *fay* ("face"), to avoid the apparent redundancy with *her*. But emendation is not really necessary, since the MED defines *fax* as referring specifically to the hair of the head, whereas *her* could mean facial hair (beard, brows, lashes) and body hair. The preservation of their hair is the most essential detail here because it shows the fulfillment of Jesus' promise to His followers in Luke 21:18.

228   *and.* G: *and and.*

235   *then.* The last letter is obscured in G.

240   *away.* The first *a* is inserted above the line in G.

251   *I.* G: omits.

261   *to Jhesu Cryst my love.* The sense is clear, but this phrase is not very idiomatic. A has *Ich have me taken to Jhesus Crist*, and R is very similar.

263   G also gives an alternative version of this line — *In hevene He schal me wedde above* — in what looks like the same scribal hand, with the Latin notation *elige* ("choose").

267   *my lyf.* G: *my my lyf.*

270   *thy.* H emends to *þy[s]*.

297   *iwent.* The *i* is inserted above the line in G.

305   *That ylke.* Inserted above the line in G, replacing an earlier reading, *Withinne the*.

307   *he.* Inserted above the line in G.

323   *up.* Inserted above the line in G.

329   *spak.* G: *be spak*, with *be* canceled.

344   *thou alsoo, I.* The *thou* and *I* are both inserted above the line in G. The original reading was *alsoo say I thee*, but the *I thee* in that clause has been canceled.

346   *joye.* The initial letter can no longer be read in G.

363–64 *here . . . hem.* In most versions of the legend, these two hundred men are Porphyry's converts, but here they seem to be the queen's. There is an initial confusion of the pronouns in G, however, which has *hym* both in line 363 (where it may have been meant to refer to Porphyry) and again in 364, where the sense clearly demands *hem*. A and R both have *hir* and *hem*, although neither of them repeats the language about being served at the table, which in G underlines the analogy between the heavenly servants who wait on Katherine in prison and the earthly ones who wait on the queen in her husband's court.

369   *drynk.* The last letter is obscured in G.

381   *ben.* The last two letters are obscured in G.

383   *thou.* Inserted above the line in G.

399   *dukes, eerlys.* G: *dukes and eerlys*, with *and* canceled.

404   *ful.* Inserted above the line in G.

449   *skypte.* Inserted above the line in G, replacing an earlier reading, *scypte* or possibly *stypte.*

455   *sche it seeth.* Inserted above the line in G, replacing an earlier reading, *it is wrought.*

489   *breke.* End of this word inserted above the line in G.

502   *adrad.* Inserted above the line in G, replacing an earlier reading, *dred.*

504   *sorewe.* The last two letters inserted above the line in G, which originally had *sore.*

513   *thou.* Inserted above the line in G.

523   *dysseyvyd.* Last three letters obscured in G.

545   *trewe.* Inserted above the line in G.

560   *it.* Inserted above the line in G.

575   *Manye.* The reading in G. H: *Many.*

589   *playn.* It may be that this word should be *play*, as in A and R, which would rhyme exactly with "ay" in line 591 instead of repeating the rhyme on "-ayn." H takes it that way; but the mark of abbreviation in G is clear, and *playn* makes better sense in this context.

625–28 An addition in G, not found in A and R, which briefly interrupts the narrative with a direct address to the audience, urging everyone to pray for the same reward after death that was won by the martyrs.

625   *Pray.* G: *And pray*, with *And* canceled.

626   *Lytyl and mochyl.* Written over an erasure in G.

627   G: *be be hens*, with *hens* written over an erasure.

635   *holy.* Inserted above the line in G, replacing an earlier reading, *swete.*

679   *fele.* G: *fele fele*, with the first one canceled.

698   *on.* Inserted above the line in G.

708   *soone.* G: *sone*, with a second *o* inserted above the line.

709   *me.* G: *my*, which makes a better rhyme but is ungrammatical in this context.

726   *orysoun.* G: *prayer orysoun*, with *prayer* canceled.

758   *flowen.* H reads *flowe*, but there is an abbreviation mark in G.

John Mirk, *Sermon on St. Katherine,*
from British Library MS Cotton Claudius A.ii, fols. 116r–117r

Gode men, suche a day ye schul have Seynte Katerine day, the whyche was an
holy martir. Than ye schul knowon that Seynte Katerine was a kyngus dowthur.
But thogh scheo were comon of so hygh blode, for Goddys sake scheo sette noghte
be the pompe of the worlde, but sette hur herte alle in oure Lorde Jhesu Criste.

5   Wherefore whan scheo hadde ben at scole, and was lerud at the fulle and cowde
spyton wyth any clerke that com to scole, whan scheo herde that Maxencius the
Emperoure was comyn to the cyté of Alysaundyr to make a solemp offering to hys
goddys of bollus and calveron and othur bestus, so that alle the cyté dynote of the
noyse of hem, than Katerine blessyd hur and yode into the tempul to the Emperoure

10   and baldely rebukyd hym, and sayde he dude foule to worcheppon fendys and
leve the worschep that he schulde do to God of Heven, that made alle thing and
send hym lyf and hele and alle thing to hys nede, and prevyd be very reson and
skylle that Criste was God and bouthe mankynde on the Crosse wyth Hys deth
oute of the fendes bandam. Than badde the Emperoure don hure into warde tyl he

15   mythe ben a lesur to heron hure; for than he was so bysy to pleson hys goddys that
he mythe not tende to hur.

    Than this menewhyle he made to fathe fyfty scole-maysteres of the wysest that
weron in any cuntré. And whan thei weron comyn, he badde hem gone and spyton
wyth Katerine and ovrecomen hur, and he wolde rewardon hem heyghly for hure

20   travayle. Than hadde the maysteres grete hokur that they caried were of so fere

---

1 suche a day, on such and such a day [to be inserted by the speaker]; **the whyche**, who.
2 kyngus dowthur, king's daughter. **3–4 sette noghte be**, cared nothing for. **5 lerud at
the fulle**, completely educated. **6 spyton**, debate/dispute. **8 bollus**, bulls; **calveron**, calves;
dynote of, resounded with. **10 baldely**, boldly; **dude foule**, did evil. **12 send**, sent; **hele**,
health. **13 skylle**, discernment; **bouthe**, redeemed (bought). **14 bandam**, power; **warde**,
custody. **15 mythe ben a lesur to heron**, could have time (be at leisure) to hear. **17 fathe**,
fetch. **18 spyton**, debate. **19 hure**, their. **20 hokur**, scorn.

cuntré to spyte wyth a womman, wyl the leste scoler of there hadde ben wyse inowh to have ovrecomyn hure. But whan Katerine hadde spokyn wyth hem a lytyl whyle, be helpe of the Holy Goste scheo convertyd hem, so that thei alle levyd on Cryste and wyth gode wille woldon take deth for Hys love.

25 Than anone Maxencius commawnded to makon a grete horribul fyre and bren hem alle therine. But God schewod there Hys miracul for hem, so that there was no cloth that thei hadde no none here of here heved tamyd wyth the fyre, bot alle lay dede be othor wyth as fayre chere os thei hadden ben on slepe. Than was the Emperoure wode for tene, and made to done Katerine nakyd and so to beton hur
30 fayre body wyth schoureges, that alle hur fayre body was ful of woundes and rennyng alle on blode, and made to putton hur into preson, to abyde there thritti dayes wythoute mete or drink til he com ageyne, for nedys he muste gone fro thennus.

Bot the quene hadde a grete longyng to speke wyth Katerine and toke wyth
35 hure on a nyght a knyte that was kallud Porphyrius, and yodon to the preson and spake wyth Katerine. And than see scheo an angel that hadde in eyther hande a crowne of schynyng golde, and sette that one on the quenes heved and that other on Porphyrius heved, and bad hem bene stedefaste in the beleve, for wythine the thridde day thei schulde bothe com to God be martirdam.

40 Than come this Emperoure hom and anone sende aftur Katerine and wende scheo hadde ben nygh dede for hungur, bot scheo was thanne alle thilk dayes fedde wyth a colvor from Heven, so that scheo was in bettur poynte than scheo was beforon. Wherefore this Emperoure was nygh wode and commawndyd to sette Katerine betwene tweyon whelus that weron wondurly makuth, so that too
45 turnyd upwarde and too dounwarde, ful of kene hokus, so that too schuldon have alle torasud hyre upwarde and othor too donwarde. But whan Katerine was sette

---

21–22 wyl the leste scoler . . . wyse inowh, when the humblest local scholar would have been wise enough. **27 cloth,** piece of clothing; **no none here,** nor any hair; **tamyd,** injured. **28 os,** as [if]. **29 tene,** anger; **made to done Katerine nakyd,** had Katherine stripped naked. **30 schoureges,** whips (scourges). **32–33 fro thennus,** from that place (thence). **35 yodon,** [they] went. **38 bene stedefaste in the beleve,** to be steadfast in the faith. **40–41 wende scheo hadde ben,** thought she would be. **42 colvor,** dove; **poynte,** condition. **44 tweyon whelus,** twofold wheels; **wondurly makuth,** cunningly made. **45 kene,** sharp. **46 torasud,** sliced.

in these weles, scheo prayed to God to helpon hur. And anone ther com an angel from Heven and smote alle the welys into pesus, os hit hadde ben a whyrwlewynde; thei ronnon on the pepul and slow anone foure thowsand of hem.

50 Than sawe the quene this miracull and anone com doune before hure husbonde and spak to hym boldely, rebukyng hym for he sagh Goddys myracul so oponly and yitte wol not levon on God. Than anone this tyrande commawnded to lede forth the quene and furste rason hur pappes wyth hokus from hur body and than smyton of hur hed; and so dudon. Then on the morowh, for Porphirius hadde 55 beried the quene, he was takon and an hundred knythes of hys felowes, and weron beheduth uchon for Goddys sake.

Than this Emperoure spake fayre to Katerine, and byhatte hure that he wolde weddon hure and done hur alle the worchep that he cowthe, if scheo wolde forsakyn Criste and levon on hys goddys. But for scheo sette noghte be hym ny be hys 60 goddys, he made to smyton of hure hedde. Than whan the hed was off, instede of blode ran oute whyte mylke. And anone therwyth com angellys and tokon hur body and bere it up into the eyre, and so forth twenti dayes jurney into the mounte of Synay, and there byried itte wyth grete worchep where God hath wrowte many grete miraclus, and yitte doth into this day.

65 For at the foot of this mount ther is an abbey of monkis whiche lyven in ful grete abstinens. And so this abbey is ful strong and high wallid and barrid bicause of wilde bestis. And in this abbey lieth Saint Kateryne in a rial tombe of alabastre. For here bonys were fett theder for more worship and reverence. And also in this abbey is the busshe whiche that oure Lord aperid inne what tyme that He spake to 70 Moises and what tyme that He delyvered to him the tablis of stone and of the commandmentis. And that busshe unto this daie is as feir and as grene as it was that same tyme that oure Lorde aperid therinne. Also in that same abbey is a grete merveile, which is this. Every monk in this abbey hath a lampe brennyng with oile. And what tyme ony of hem shal die, thaie shal have a knowelege by his

47 **weles**, wheels. 48 **welys**, wheels; **pesus**, pieces. 49 **slow**, killed (slew). 51 **oponly**, clearly (openly). 53 **rason**, tear; **pappes**, breasts. 54 **so dudon**, [they] did so. 55 **knythes of hys felowes**, fellow knights of his. 56 **beheduth uchon**, all beheaded. 57 **byhatte**, promised. 59 **sette noghte be**, cared nothing for. 63 **wrowte**, worked (wrought). 66 **barrid**, protected. 67 **rial**, royal. 68 **fett theder**, brought (fetched) there. 74 **a knowelege**, forewarning.

75 lampe. For evyn as he drawith to deethwarde, so his lampe will derke more and
more. And whan the abbot is deed, thaie shal singe a masse of the Holi Gost and
than bury him solemply. And by the tyme that the masse be done, theie shal finde
a lettre on the aultere and writen who shal be thair abbot.

Also another grete merveile ther is done there on Saint Kateryns daie, which is
80 this: that alle the birdis of the contrey as that daie comith thidir, and eche of hem
bringith a branche of olyve into the abbey. And pilgrimes sayn that the monkis
make hem oyle therof to serve her lampes all the yere, and the remanent they sille
for her sustynaunce.

[**Narracio.**] I rede of a man that furste servid Seynte Katerine and fast here
85 evyn, as many done, but aftyr he lafte of. Than in a vision he sagh a grete company of fayre maydenes comyng be hym, and among ham was one passing alle
othyr in bewté. Bothe whan sche com by this man, sheo hudde hure face and
wolde note lokyn on hym. Than askud he one of the hyndemaste whatte thei weron.
Than seyde scheo that thei weron alle seyntus of Heven, and that was Seynte
90 Katerine that hudde hure faas from hym and wolde note knowon hym, for encheson
that he hadde lafte the knalache of hur. Than this man repentut and turnid ageyne
to hys devociones as he hadde done before.

75 **drawith to deethwarde,** approaches death; **derke,** grow dim (darken). 78 **aultere,**
altar. 82 **the remanent,** the rest; **sille,** sell. 83 **her sustynaunce,** their livelihood. 84–85
fast here evyn, fasted [on the] eve of her feast day. 87 **Bothe,** But; **hudde,** hid. 88 **note,**
not; **the hyndemaste,** those coming behind. 90 **knowon,** recognize/acknowledge. 90–91
for encheson that, because. 91 **knalache,** recognition/honor; **repentut,** repented.

Explanatory Notes to Mirk's Sermon on St. Katherine

Abbreviations: **B** = Bodleian Library MS Gough Eccl. Top. 4 (*SC* 17680), fols. 156v–158r; **C** = British Library MS Cotton Claudius A.ii, fols. 116r–117r [base text]; **D** = Durham University Library MS Cosin V.III.5, fols. 152r–154r; **E** = Theodor Erbe [EETS edition]; **H 2371** = British Library MS Harley 2371, fols. 139v–141v; **H 2391** = British Library MS Harley 2391, fols. 131r–133r; **H 2403** = British Library MS Harley 2403, fols. 173v–175v; **U** = University College, Oxford MS 102, pp. 251–57 (on deposit in the Bodleian Library, Oxford).

2   *kyngus dowthur.* Katherine was the daughter of King Costus; see stanzaic Life, lines 49–50.

6   *Maxencius.* See explanatory note to the stanzaic Life, lines 10–12.

10   *to worcheppon fendys.* Katherine is speaking of the idols, which were commonly believed to harbor actual demons.

17   *scole-maysteres.* This term could conceivably mean university-trained experts in rhetoric or philosophy, but it could also mean just teachers in a grammar school. H 2403, which seems to belong to the same branch of the textual tradition as C, refers to them less ambiguously as *grete doctours.*

25–28 For Biblical parallels to this miracle, see explanatory note to the stanzaic Life, lines 225–28.

31–32 *thritti dayes.* In most retellings the length of this sentence is twelve days.

36–39 This vision of an angel with two golden crowns, betokening the impending martyrdom of the queen and Porphyrius, is not found in most versions of the Katherine legend. Readers of Chaucer will recall a similar vision in the Second Nun's retelling of the Cecilia legend, although there the crowns are made of roses and lilies, symbolizing both the saints' coming martyrdom and their virginity.

60   Notice that Katherine's final prayer is completely omitted in this version of the legend. See note on the *Speculum Sacerdotale* version, lines 28–36.

60–61 *instede of blode ran oute whyte mylke.* See explanatory note to the stanzaic Life, line 754.

62   *twenti dayes jurney.* This is a long time for the short journey from Alexandria to Mt. Sinai. On Mt. Sinai, see explanatory note to the stanzaic Life, lines 760–62.

69   *the busshe whiche that oure Lord aperid inne.* That is, the burning bush encountered by Moses (Exodus 3:1–6). The Burning Bush Chapel behind the altar of the monastery's church was a holy site as early as the fourth century. The burning bush is commonly associated with the Virgin Mary, who contained the fire of God without being consumed.

69–71 *what tyme . . . the commandmentis.* Although this text conflates God's first call to Moses from the burning bush and God's delivery to him of the Ten Commandments on Mt. Sinai (Exodus 19–20), they are separated of course by many momentous years in the history of Moses and the Israelites.

72–83 Miracles at the monastery. The great interest in oil from St. Katherine's Monastery ultimately stems from the belief that oil was miraculously exuded from Katherine's tomb which had healing properties. But that tradition, which is briefly described at the end of the stanzaic Life (lines 769–80), is conspicuously missing here, replaced by two miracle stories that would be much less likely to encourage pilgrimages to the monastery; the second one, in fact, can be read as debunking the usual claims for the monastery's oil by providing an alternative explanation of where it came from.

84–92 This *exemplum*, which underlines the importance of maintaining proper devotion to a patron saint, was told in connection with many saints, including the Virgin Mary, and with many variations in detail. A few MSS of Mirk's collection (including the base text for E's EETS edition) identify the inconstant devotee in this very story as a woman, and others give a fuller version of the story, as follows:

> I rede of a man whiche lovid Saint Katerine passing wele, and for the grete devocioun that he hadde to hir, he fastid every yere on hir evyn brede and watir. And so it happid him at the last that he felle into the company of rechlesse peple, and left his fasting by comforte of hem and did as thaie didde. And than, on the night folowing, as he laie in his bed him thought he sawe a grete company of maidens comyng by him, and oon of hem was passing faire above al other. And so eche of hem had a crowne, and the feire maiden had a passing

crowne above all other, whiche was Saint Kateryne. And as she come by this man, she hid hir face fro him and wolde not loke upon him. And than he askid oon of the maideny[s] what thaie were. And she answerid and saide, "We be virgins whiche sufferid martirdome for oure Lorde Jhesu Crist. And the chif of us that thoue seest look awaiward fro thee is Saint Kateryne. And bicause that thou leftist thie devocion and fastinge, that is the cause that she wil not loke on thee." And than this man was sorie and repentid him that he hadde so done amisse, and turned ayene to his devocion, and was aftirwarde a ful holy man. [text transcribed from D again; this version also in U and H 2371and H 2391).

Textual Notes to Mirk's Sermon on St. Katherine

Abbreviations: see explanatory notes.

1   *Gode men.* Some MSS add *and women*; others omit this whole salutation.

15   *goddys.* C: *goddy.*

28   *wyth.* C: omits.

37–38   *the quenes heved and that other on.* Words omitted from C, obviously because of an eyeskip, and supplied from other MSS.

41   *scheo₁.* C: omits.

47   *helpon.* C: *helpn.*

51   *rebukyng.* Emendation from H 2403 and E's EETS edition; C has the less grammatical *rebukyd.*

59   *goddys.* C has *god*, but Maxentius worships multiple gods and the other MSS have plural forms.

61   *angellys.* C: *an angellys.*

65–83   These paragraphs are omitted from C, H 2403, and E's EETS edition, but found in a number of other MSS, including D (from which the text here has been transcribed), U, H 2371, and H 2391.

68   *For here bonys were fett theder for.* Words omitted from D; supplied from U.

89   *scheo.* C has *he*, but H 2403 and E have forms of *she*, which the context seems to demand.

92   Conclusion added in H 2371: *. . . and went to blisse as God graunte that wee may, Amen.*

St. Katherine, from Speculum Sacerdotale,
from British Library MS Addit. 36791, fols. 137r–137v

In siche a day ye schul have the feste of Seynt Kateryne, virgine and marter.

Sires, this holy and blessid virgine, Seynt Kateryne, was ibore in the cité of Alexandre and doughtur of a kyng namyd Costus. And this yonge holy dameselle was experte, wyse, and discrete bothe in Godis wysdom and in the prudence of
5   man, and wele was ilettryd. And sche overcome and concludyd fifty wyse philosophers that sputyd with hire at the commaundment of the emperoure. And when sche hadde overcomen hem alle, sche convertyd hem to the feithe of Crist. And sche convertyd the queene with Porphorie, the mayster of the knyghttis, with two hundred knyghtis that were under hym fro here infidelité unto the feith of Crist.
10   And alle they suffrid marterdom, for conversion of whome the emperoure was highely wroth and dide commaunde the virgine to be bete with scourges and for to sytte in prison by the space of twelve dayes. But Crist refresshid hire and fedde hire yche day in the same prison by a white dowve. And oure Lorde aperide unto hire Hymself with a grete multitude of aungels and comfortyd hire ageyn hure
15   passiones and turmentis.

And at the counsel of the emperoure and his juge it was ordeyned thus for hire passion — *scilicet*, that two wheles schulde be sette togeder and renne acordyngly togedre, and other two as cruel as they rennynge in another maner contrarily ageyn hem, and alle these wheles were daggyd alle abowte outeward with scharpe nayles
20   made like to hokys so contrarily sette that when the mayde schuld be sette amonge

---

1 In siche a day, On such and such a day [to be inserted by the speaker]. **3 Alexandre**, Alexandria. **5 ilettryd**, educated ("lettered"); **concludyd**, defeated by arguments. **6 sputyd**, disputed. **8 mayster**, commander. **9 infidelité**, unbelief. **11 bete with scourges**, beaten with whips. **12 sytte**, remain; **by**, for. **15 passiones**, sufferings. **17 *scilicet***, namely; **acordyngly**, in harmony. **18 other two**, two others; **contrarily**, in the opposite direction. **19 daggyd alle abowte outeward**, made to project outward all around their rims. **20 contrarily sette**, set against each other.

hem that sche schulde amonge hem be rent upward and downeward in the moste cruellyst maner. But God dide save His spouse in alle these, for anoon He dyde sende downe His aungel to the turmentis, the whiche smote hem asundre with dynte of swerde everychone, that the fallynge of the wheles dyde kylle and sle ten
25 thousande men.

And then the tyrant dyde commaunde the virgine to be hedid. And when sche was ibrought to the hedynge, sche prayed hem for a litel tyme to make certeyne prayers. And then sche dide praye God in this maner: "O Lord God and Helethe of the trowynge in thee, O good Jhesu, hope and joye of alle virgines, I beseche thee
30 and thy mercy that whosoever in tyme to come doth make mencion or memorie, praysynge or worschepynge of my passion, that he mowe have his askynge igraunted of thee, whether that it be made in the ende of his lyf or in eny other angre or tribulacion in his lyf. And I beseche thee that no maner of pestilence, venjaunce, famyschynge evel, and evel eyre do noye hym ne dwelle with hym,
35 but I beseche thee that his londe be to hym plenteuous, the eyre to hym heleful, and that he have plenté of fruytes."

And unnethe sche hadde makyd hire prayers or there come a voys to hire and sayde, "Virgine, God hath grauntyd to thee thyne askynge."

And then the virgine was hedid, and mylke instede of blode ranne fro hire necke.
40 *Eius ergo festum, et cetera.*

21 rent, torn. **22 in alle these**, i.e., in the midst of these perils. **23 turmentis**, instruments of torture. **26 hedid**, beheaded. **27 hedynge**, [place of] beheading. **28–29 Helethe of the trowynge**, Savior of those who believe. **30 memorie**, commemoration. **31 worschepynge**, honoring; **askynge**, petition. **33 angre**, affliction. **34 famyschynge evel**, the danger (punishment) of famine; **evel eyre**, unwholesome air; **noye**, injure. **35 plenteuous**, fertile; **eyre**, air; **heleful**, healthful. **36 fruytes**, crops/profits. **37 unnethe**, scarcely. **40 *Eius ergo festum, et cetera***, Therefore her feast, etc.

Notes to St. Katherine, from Speculum Sacerdotale

16–22   This detailed description of the menacing wheels, which is even fuller and more vivid than the one in the stanzaic Life of St. Katherine (lines 450–64), stands in sharp contrast to the extreme brevity of almost everything else in the *Speculum Sacerdotale*'s retelling of the legend. Presumably the wheels receive such emphasis because the author of this account wanted to explain the familiar emblem for Katherine, the wheel that was traditionally used in the visual arts to identify her and distinguish her from other virgin saints.

24–25   *ten thousande men*. Most versions of the legend, including the other two in this collection, use the somewhat less extravagant number of four thousand.

28–36   Compare the petitions in this version of Katherine's final prayer with those in the stanzaic Life (lines 709–16). Surprisingly, this otherwise restrained account of Katherine's life makes the most extreme, magical-sounding promises for the benefits her devotees will receive. Mirk's account completely omits Katherine's prayer and its response, perhaps out of uneasiness with the tendency to over-emphasize this aspect of the legend. The references to *pestilence, venjaunce, famyschynge evel*, and *evel eyre* (lines 33–34), however, remind us of the severe food shortages and visitations of plague which must have created an unusual demand in the late fourteenth and fifteenth centuries for such promises of supernatural protection. Air was believed to be a carrier of disease, including plague; hence the fear of *evel eyre*. The term *venjaunce* could refer to any tribulation or series of tribulations inflicted as a punishment for sin, including fatal epidemics, floods, and other large-scale disasters.

39   *mylke instede of blode*. See explanatory note to the stanzaic Life of Katherine, line 754.

40   *Eius ergo festum, et cetera*. A fuller version of this closing formula, at the end of the *Speculum Sacerdotale* chapter on St. Stephen, calls on the faithful to keep the saint's feast day (by refraining both from earthly labors and from sins and by coming to church) and to pray for God's forgiveness and grace through the merits of the saint.

221

Christina of Bolsena

Introduction

Like Margaret and Katherine, Christina is an early virgin martyr with a legend too fanciful to have much historical credibility. The existence of Christina herself, however, is relatively well attested. Although some versions of her legend place her in Tyre (Phoenicia), the most credible evidence points to Bolsena: an ancient town in central Italy, near an Etruscan site called Volsinium, with catacombs in which archeologists have found the remains of an early Christian church and the tomb of a female martyr. Inscriptions found on the site confirm that this martyr had a name like Christina and that the local community was venerating her as a saint by the end of the fourth century. Some corroborating evidence is provided by a sixth-century mosaic in the basilica of St. Apollinare Nuovo at Ravenna, which includes in its procession of virgins a saint named Christina, wearing a martyr's crown. Her name also appears on July 24 in several early martyrologies, beginning with the one by pseudo-Jerome.

Despite the early beginnings of Christina's cult, she never became as popular a saint as Margaret and Katherine did. Although she was honored as the patron saint of Bolsena itself, her cult does not appear to have been very strong elsewhere. Thanks to the influence of the martyrologies, her name was included in many liturgical calendars — especially monastic and Italian ones, initially, and later in the standardized calendars of the Franciscans and the "Roman curia," which helped to spread it all over Europe. But her feastday seems virtually always to have been observed as a low-ranking feast with just three lessons at Matins (Margaret and Katherine tended to have nine or twelve, the maximum) and no special music or ceremonial. In England the Latin legend of St. Christina was found in monastic libraries as early as the ninth century, and detailed episodes from it were included in the *Anglo-Saxon Martyrology*, but there is no evidence that any English church was ever dedicated to her. Similarly, although she sometimes appeared alongside other virgin martyrs in paintings, she was not one of the female saints most frequently depicted on rood screens and church walls in England, and even in Italy she was not often chosen as the central saint in a work of art.

Like the legends of many other martyrs from the Roman calendar, Christina's legend became widely known in the late Middle Ages through the influence of compilations like the *Speculum historiale* of Vincent of Beauvais and the *Legenda aurea* of Jacobus de Voragine. Such compilations, which abridged older legends from a wide variety of sources, tended to increase the legends' accessibility and their appeal to potential translators by presenting them in versions that were efficient, dramatic, and full of colorful details. The abridged Latin versions subsequently gave rise to scores of vernacular versions, including at least seven retellings of the Christina legend in Middle English: the anonymous verse adaptations in the *South English Legendary*, *North English Legendary*, and *Scottish Legendary*, the prose versions in the 1438 *Gilte Legende* and Caxton's *Golden Legend*, and the longer and more elaborate verse retellings by William Paris and Osbern Bokenham.

The plot of the Christina legend — the young saint's persecution and torture by three successive judges, her miraculous rescues along the way, the swift punishments meted out to her judges and their supporters, and her final execution — is so full of improbabilities that some modern readers have found nothing good to say about it. In their updated edition of Butler's *Lives of the Saints*, for example, Herbert Thurston and Donald Attwater dismiss it impatiently as "a collection of unconvincing and pointless marvels" and lament that the martyr Christina is known only through this "inheritance of childish fables."[1] But medieval readers and writers obviously reacted to the legend differently, and there is something to be learned from trying to see it through their eyes. As Karen A. Winstead has suggested in *Chaste Passions*, Christina is probably the most aggressive and indomitable of all the legendary virgin martyrs. Her example of female courage and outspokenness clearly appealed to her namesake Christine de Pisan, for one, who retold Christina's legend and claimed her as both patron and model in Part 3 of the *Book of the City of Ladies* (1405). Nor was it only to women that late-medieval readers applied Christina's example. Osbern Bokenham developed the legend as a kind of general parable about salvation and damnation, adding a number of new speeches and other details that emphasize both Christina's constant awareness of her dependence on God's mercy and the contrasting blindness of her persecutors, who stubbornly refuse to repent even when God gives them chance after chance, miraculous sign after miraculous sign.

William Paris' verse retelling of the legend, which is presented here, is even more interesting than Bokenham's because his purpose is subtler and less explicit. Paris tells us in his epilogue (lines 497–520) that he was the squire of Sir Thomas Beauchamp, Earl of Warwick (c. 1345–1401), and translated this legend while sharing his master's imprisonment on the Isle of Man. Both the date and the immediate context of his translation can thus be known with some precision. Warwick, one of the Lords Appellant who had led the brief rebellion against Richard II in 1387–88 and apparently been pardoned for it thereafter, was suddenly arrested and accused of treason in July 1397. By the time he came to trial that autumn, another of the former appellants had been murdered and a third, Richard, Earl of Arundel, had been summarily tried and executed. Warwick, who evidently confessed to the charges, was convicted and sentenced

---

[1] *The Lives of the Saints, originally compiled by the Rev. Alban Butler*. Ed., rev., and suppl. Herbert Thurston, S. J., and Donald Attwater, 12 vols. (London: Burns Oats and Washbourne Ltd., 1932), vol. 7 (July), pp. 337, 338.

to perpetual prison on the Isle of Man. He remained there until King Richard's overthrow in 1399 — deserted, Paris laments, by all his former retainers except William Paris himself.

During this period of his life, Paris evidently found special meaning and consolation in the legend of St. Christina. His account has a number of distinctive characteristics which seem to be connected with the ordeal he was sharing with his master. For example, as Mary-Ann Stouck has noted ("Saints and Rebels," p. 84), he portrays Christina's handmaidens explicitly as spies whom she cannot trust (lines 37–40), thus heightening her resemblance to a political prisoner. He repeatedly emphasizes the theme of imprisonment itself. He makes Christina even ruder and more outspoken than usual, and Winstead suggests that he seems to cheer when she strikes back at her persecutors. He is also unusually insistent about her invulnerability to tortures and threats, even dismemberment.

Select Bibliography

Indexed in

Brown-Robbins, # 2877

Manuscript

London, British Library MS Arundel 168, fols. 2r–4v.

Previous edition

Horstmann, Carl, ed. *Sammlung altenglischer Legenden*. 1878. Pp. 183–190.

Translation into modern English

Winstead, Karen A., ed. and trans. *Chaste Passions*. 2000. Pp. 61–69.

Important sources and analogues in English

Bokenham, Osbern. *Legendys of Hooly Wummen*. Ed. Mary S. Serjeantson. EETS o.s. 206, 1938. Pp. 58–86.

Christine de Pizan. *Book of the City of Ladies*. Trans. Earl Jeffrey Richards. New York: Persea Books, 1982. [Christina's legend is retold in 3.10, pp. 234–40.]

Jacobus de Voragine. *The Golden Legend*. Trans. William Granger Ryan. 1993. Vol. 1. Pp. 385–87.

Historical background and criticism

Brownlee, Kevin. "Martyrdom and the Female Voice: Saint Christine in the *Cité des dames*." In *Images of Sainthood in Medieval Europe*. Ed. Renate Blumenfeld-Kosinski and Timea Szell. Ithaca: Cornell University Press, 1991. Pp. 115–35.

Gerould, Gordon Hall. "The Legend of St. Christina by William Paris." *MLN* 29 (1914), 129–33.

Stouck, Mary-Ann. "A Poet in the Household of the Beauchamp Earls of Warwick, c.1393–1427." *Warwickshire History* 9 (1994), 113–17.

_____. "Saints and Rebels: Hagiography and Opposition to the King in Late Fourteenth-Century England." *Medievalia et Humanistica* n.s. 24 (1997), 75–94.

Winstead, Karen A. *Virgin Martyrs*. 1997. Pp. 83–85.

William Paris, *Life of St. Christina*
from British Library MS Arundel 168, fols. 2r–4v

Seynte Cristyn was a maide bryghte,	*beautiful*
As clerkis in bokes hath rede and seen;	
Sche served God both daye and nyghte	
As martyr shuld and virgyn clene.	*pure*
In Itayle she was borne, Y wene,	*I believe*
And come of kynne were grete of myghte,	*family [who] were exalted in power*
But she forsoke them all bedene	*completely*
And holle hir herte to Criste she highte.	*entirely; promised*
She was so faire, that maiden myld,	
That every wighte that ones hire see,	*person; once; saw*
If it were man, woman, or child,	*Whether*
She wan theire lofe with hir beauté.	*won; love*
Suche grace of God forsoth had shee	
To flee all vice and werkes wilde,	*wanton behavior*
And fully purposed hir to be	*wholeheartedly resolved*
Goddes owne servaunte and maide unfylde.	*unsullied virgin*
Urban hight hir fader, ywisse,	*Her father was named Urban*
A wykked tyrande and a wode.	
It was of hym as of moo is:	*It was [true] of him as [it] is of others*
A sherew may gete a child righte goode,	*evil-doer; beget*
And so did Urban, be the Rode.	*by the Cross*
If he were man that dide amysse,	*Even though*
Yit gate he Cristyn, myld of mode,	*Yet fathered; gentle of heart*
That is with Criste in heven blysse.	*Who*
Many men desired that may	*maiden*
And wolde hafe wedded hir if thei myghte;	
Whan thei mighte se hir on a daie,	*one day*
Thei ferd the better a full sevennyghte.	*fared; a whole week*
Hir chere was suche in all mens sighte,	*demeanor*

5

10

15

20

25

227

30   It made ylke man to other saye,   *each*
        "Truly, this is the gentileste wighte
        That ever we see — this is no naye."   *there is no denying it*

        Hir kynne wolde gife hir to righte non,   *no one at all*
        For she shulde lyfe in mawmentrye;   *was supposed to live in idolatry*
35   But in a tour of lyme and ston   *tower*
        Hyr fader ordeyn hir to lye,   *directed; remain*
        And twelfe maydens to be hir bye,   *ladies-in-waiting*
        Of whiche she myght triste never on: *not a single one*
        For thei were ordeyn for to aspie   *assigned; observe*
40   How that she lyved and made hyr mon.   *complaint*

        Goddes of golde and silver bright
        That may hade with hir in hir toure,   *maiden*
        That she shuld wurchipe daie and nyghte,   *was supposed to worship*
        And when hir liste to do them honour.   *it pleased her*
45   But sodenly ther com socour
        Fro God, that is moste of myghte: *greatest*
        He made that maye to have savour   *delight*
        To brynge hir soule to heven lyghte.

        The Holy Goste in Cristyn is,
50   And he hath tawghte hir to forsake
        Hir fals goddes ilkon, ywisse,   *every one*
        That are but stonys and stokkes blake,   *blocks of wood*
        And full purpose now will she take
        To drede no ded, but think of blysse.   *death*
55   Thus God can of uncrystyn make   *from non-Christians*
        Right holy martirs to be His.

        Thus som have grace or thei borne be,   *before*
        As had the Baptiste, goode Seint John;
        And some in tendre age, pardé,   *certainly*
60   As Cristyn had, that faire woman;
        And some in elde when youghte is gon,   *old age; youth*
        As in Poules lyfe we may see;   *Paul's*
        And some when thei shall die anon,
        As Barabas thef, that honge so hye.

65	Encens she had, and sho it hyde	*incense; hid*
	Up in a wyndowe prevyly,	*secretly*
	And with goode hert she it dyde,	*did*
	For she thoughte never to sacrifiee	*intended*
	To no fals goddes of mawmentrie,	*idolatry*
70	For drede of non that wold hir byde;	*bid (command)*
	She prayed to Criste that she myght dye	
	And martire be, or that betyde.	*before that occurred*
	To it befelle upon a daie	*Until; on a certain day*
	That Urban wold his doughter se;	
75	And Cristyn maydyns all thei saie,	*Christine's*
	"Urban, sir, we telle thee:	
	Thi doughter and our lady free	
	Dispice our goddes and thaire araie	*Despises; ceremonies*
	And sais truly that she wille be	
80	A Cristen woman, if that she maye."	
	Urban saide, "Late me alon,	*alone*
	For I will to my doughthire goo;	
	With faire wordes Y shall anon	
	Make hir to lefe, if she saie soo.	*desist*
85	And truly, but she sacrifice doo,	*unless*
	She shall be wrouthe or I — the ton —	*grieved; one of the two*
	For it will breke myn herte in too	*two*
	To witte my doughter so begoon."	*deceived*
	Urban went with sobere schere	*expression*
90	To Cristyn chambir alle on hye	*Christine's; in haste (aloft)*
	And saide, "Cristyn, my doughter dere,	
	Se — I am comme to sitte thee bye	
	And als to se thee sacrifie	
	To all our goddes of grete powere.	
95	That was the cause sekyrly,	
	My faire doughter, that I sitte here."	
	"Thi doughter, Urban, clepe me noght,	*call*
	For fadere will Y never clepe thee;	
	For on Jhesu is all my thoughte	

100   And His child, sir, will Y be.
      And therfor speke no more to me
      Of maumentrie, of metall wrought,   *idols*
      But speke of God in magesté,   *majesty*
      For He alone me made and bought."   *redeemed*

105   "My faire doughter," Urban said,
      "Wurchup noght on god alon,   *one god alone*
      Un happe the other be evyll paid   *Lest the others might be displeased*
      For thou will do them wurchupe non,   *Because*
      But gete thank of them ilkon;
110   Than nedes thee noght be afrayed.   *you will not have to*
      And think how all thi kinne has don.
      Do thou thus, as I hafe thee prayed."

      "Thou wenes thou speke right well, ywisse,   *think*
      But as a fole thou spekes me to   *fool*
115   That knew no trueth nere thought of blysse.   *nor*
      But here, Urban, how I will do: *hear (listen)*
      The Fadire in hevyn, the Son also,
      The Holy Goste — the thirde He is;
      To this Y wille, and to no moo,   *these*
120   With all myn herte do sacrifice."

      "Sen thou will wurchipe goddes three,   *Since*
      Whi wurchups thou noght other also?"   *others*
      Cristyn said, "Fole, I tell it thee: *Fool*
      Thies three are on Gode, and no moo."   *one*
125   Thus Urban went away hir froo,
      Als wrothe as he myght be;   *could*
      Hym thought his herte wold breke in too   *two*
      For Cristyns lofe, his doughter free.   *the love of Christine*

      Anon after, wen he was gon,   *when*
130   Seint Cristyn went the mawmentes to   *idols*
      And caste them down everylkon
      And byrste ther legges and armys in too.   *broke; two*
      The plates of silver and gold also   *thin sheets*
      She pekyd all of, that was them on,   *stripped off entirely*

135   And caste it oute away hir froo
       To pore Goddes men that had right non.   *poor Christians (men of God); none at all*

       Urban com another daie
       And wold have wurchupe his goddes alle;   *worshiped*
       He fonde right non — thei were awaye.   *none at all; gone*
140   On Cristyns maydyns he dyd calle:
       "What hath Cristyn, my doughter small,
       Don with our goddes? Telle me, I saye!"
       Thei sai, "Thi doughter made them falle —
       Oute at the wyndow all are thei."   *Gone out the window*

145   Urban said, "So myght I thee,   *So may I prosper [on my life]*
       My doughter is a cursyd wyght!
       Maidons," said Urban, "how durste she
       Thus breke our goddes so myche of myght?"   *great*
       Thei answerd all with wordes on hight: *out loud*
150   "She auntred hir, as ye may see;   *took a risk*
       Now are thei all in peces dyght.   *fallen*
       Sir, make them hole! Late se, can ye?"   *whole; [if] you can*

       "Have of hir clothes," quod Urban thoo,   *Take off*
       "And bring hir faste me her before!   *firmly (quickly)*
155   And ye twelfe men shall to hir goo
       And bete hir, nakyd as she was bor!"   *born*
       Thei bete hir to thei myght no mor;   *until*
       Thei stent, as men that myght noght do.   *stopped; could do nothing*
       It semyd bi hir she felt no sor,   *concerning her; pain*
160   For thus she said hir fadire to:

       "Withoutyn honour and shame, I say,
       Abhomynable to God arte thou!
       Se, thi mens myght es all away;   *is*
       Ther strenghte is gon, thei wot noght how.
165   Aske helpe to them of thi goddes now!   *for them*
       If thei may do owght, now assay!   *anything; try and see*
       More betynge than thou ordeyn now   *order*
       For my Goddes lofe abyde I may."   *love of my God; endure*

Bownden in cheynes that mayden swete,
170 Cristyn, was in depe prisoun.
Hir modire herd tell that, where she sete.   *sat*
She tere hire clothes and felle in swoun,   *tore*
And after she hyed to that dongioun;   *afterward; hurried*
She had so wepped, hir chekes were wete.   *wept*
175 Whan she se Cristyn, she felle downe
Anon to hir doughter fete.   *daughter's*

She said, "Crystyn, my doughter dere,
Of bothe myn yen thou arte the lighte.   *eyes*
Alas, that evyre I se thee her
180 In such disease as thou arte dyght!   *pain (distress); placed*
Thou wote thou may make us light —   *glad*
Urban, thi fader, and me in fere.   *together*
Have mercy on me, gentill wight
And faire doughter — amende our cher!"   *lift our spirits*

185 Seinte Cristyn said hir modere to,
"Wherto thi doughter clepes thou me?   *Why*
Wote thou not wele that I hate soo   *am called so (i.e., Christina)*
After my God in magestie?
Criste, Godes Son, forsothe highte He.   *was called*
190 For thee and me He suffird woo;
Therfor His servaunte will I be —
Iwisse, I wille non other do."   *nothing else*

Hir moder se she had no myght
With no faire speche to turne hir mode;   *change her mind*
195 She wente oute as a sorye wighte,
That mete ner drynke myght do hir goode.   *Whom neither food nor drink could help*
Than Urban aste hir woo it stoode,   *asked; how*
And Cristyn answers she told right;
Therfor he fared as he were wode,   *insane*
200 And for his doughter sor he sight.   *bitterly he sighed*

"Do feche hir forthe!" said Urban.   *Have her fetched*
"Befor the barre that she were ibrouth,   *Let her be brought into court*
And I shall assay if I can

To make hir turne hir wikked thought.   *change*
205   She said my doughter was she noghte.
Thus coppid the kene, on me began;[1]
She braste my goddes so richely wrouth —   *broke; made*
What wondur if I were wrothe than?"

Befor the barre now Cristyn is —
210   God graunte hir grace right wele to saie!   *speak*
Urban bade hir, "Do sacrifice
To our goddes, that moste may.   *have most power*
For truly, if thou ous say nay,   *defy us*
Grete peyne shall make thee leve thi mysse, *abandon your offense*
215   Ne clepe thee doughter never I may
Ne never will do, but thou do this."   *unless*

Than said Cristyn, that maydyn bryght,
To hir fadire, that sate so hye,
"Se, suche grete grace thou has me hight: *promised*
220   The devels doughter no mor to be.
What child commes of the devele," said she, *Whatever; from*
"The devele may be his name oryght.   *rightly*
Thou arte fadir, Y tell it thee,
Of Satan fende, that cursyd wyght."

225   Urban commaunded than anon
Hir flesch, that was so white and shene,   *radiant*
It shuld be scraped of bi the bon   *off near*
With hokyd nayles, sharpe and kene.   *hook-shaped spikes*
He bad that all hir lymmes bedene   *completely (immediately)*
230   Thei shuld be brokyn, on be on.   *one by one*
It was grete peté, wo had it seen,   *pity, [for] anyone who*
Of such a mayde, be Seinte John!   *With regard to*

When Seint Cristyn hir flesch se,
She toke a pece that was of kytte,   *cut off*
235   And even she caste at Urbans eye;   *straight; threw [it]*

---

[1] *Thus the disobedient one argued, began against me*

	And he had not blenchyd, she had hym hitte.	*If; turned aside*
	Thus said the maydyn, full of wytt,	
	To hym that shuld hir fadir be:	*was supposed to*
	"Have here a morcell, teraunt — take it! —	*tyrant*
240	Of the flesche was getyn of thee."	*that was begotten by*
	Than Urban, full of ire so wode,	
	Upon a whele he layd that maye.	
	Full grete fyer, to chaunge hir mode,	
	He bad make under, as she lay;	*ordered to be kindled underneath*
245	Full of oile the fier powred thei.	*poured*
	Fro hir it wente — she felyd but goode.	*[Away] from; only well-being*
	It brent of men to ded that day	*death*
	Fyften hundrith, about that stode.	*who were standing nearby*
	Hir fadir wende that she had wrought	
250	By wichecrafte or sorcerrie;	
	Therfor had he myche thought.	
	He couthe not sytt ner stande ner lye,	*i.e., he could not rest*
	But bad his men agayn in hye	
	That she shuld be to preson brought.	
255	Now Criste hir help, and our Ladie,	
	As He on Rode that mayden bought!	*on the Cross; redeemed*
	Whan daie was gon and comme was nyght,	
	Aboute hir neke thei honge a ston —	*millstone*
	It was right hevy and nothinge lighte;	*not at all*
260	Thai caste hir in the see anon.	
	When thei that dulfull dede had don,	*sad (doleful)*
	Ther com aungels fro hevyn so bryght,	
	And held hir up the water anon,	*upon (on top of)*
	Thorough Goddes grace and His grete myght.	
265	Than Criste com downe Hymself, iwysse,	
	And baptyste Cristyn in the see,	*baptized*
	And in hir Lyfe writen is	*Vita*
	That thies same wordes to hir said He:	
	"In My Fadir and als in Me,	
270	Jhesu Criste, Goddes Son of blisse,	

And in the Holy Goste, Us Three,
I baptise thee in watire this."

      Criste cristynd Cristyne with His honde —
      He was godfadir and preste that nyght,
275   And after Criste, I understonde,
      Cristyn may be hir name orighte: *rightly*
      Than after hir godfadir so she highte,   *is named*
      Criste, that in the see hir fonde.   *found*
      Hir muste nedis be on holy wight   *She must necessarily be a*
280   That Criste thus baptiste in the stronde!   *sea*

      Criste hir betaughte Seint Mighell to,   *entrusted to St. Michael*
      And he to londe brought hir anon.
      Hir fadir herd tell that it was soo;
      He wiste in world what he myght don.
285   For ire he smote himself right sone
      In mydis the fronte — he was so woo.   *In the middle of his forehead*
      Whan he hir se, he lokyd hir on   *gazed at her*
      And thus he spak that mayden to:

      "What whichecrafte is this that thou can,   *witchcraft; know (have skill in)*
290   That see ne londe may make thee dye?"   *neither sea nor land*
      She said, "Full unhappy man,   *unfortunate (miserable)*
      Of Criste this grace resceyved have I."
      "Do have hir up anon in hye   *Have her carried off*
      In depe prison," quod Urban than;
295   "Hir hed shall of full sekyrly   *She shall be beheaded certainly*
      Tomorne, if I be lyvand man!"   *Tomorrow; a living*

      Yit if he said all in play,   *Even if*
      Yit said he sothe, that cursyd wight;   *he spoke truly*
      For he was ded, or it was daie,   *before*
300   And Cristyne lyved, that mayden brighte.
      Thus he thrette hir over nyghte   *threatened*
      That she shuld on the morne away;   *must depart (die) the next day*
      Yit was he ded, for all his myght,
      And Cristyn lyved a merye maye.   *joyful maiden*

305   Than cam Dyons with evyll spede   *misfortune*
           To make an ende of that virgyne.
           For he ordeynd as hote as glede   *burning coal*
           A grete vessell of hyrne fyne,   *pure iron*
           Full of oile, pyche, and rosyn —
310   It welled so hote all men myght drede;   *boiled*
           And therin caste thei faire Cristyne,
           But she lay still and toke non hede.

           Four men roked hir to and froo,
           To make hir payne mor violente
315   And als for Cristyn shuld also   *in order that*
           The soner be to pouder brente.   *sooner; burned to dust*
           Ther she laye als innocente   *like a little child*
           In credyll rokked, that felyd no wo.   *cradle*
           She thanked God she was not shente   *harmed*
320   With tourmentynge that thei couthe doo.   *knew how to do*

           She said, "I thankyd Thee, hevyn Kynge,
           That Thou has ordeynd thus for me:
           As twys-borne child that were right yonge,   *twice-born*
           Twys in credell rokked to be."
325   Dyons lokyd on hir and see
           How that she lay and felt nothinge;
           For sorow and care so wrothe was he,
           He thought he wold himself hynge.   *hang*

           Ther said Dyons to Cristyne thoo,
330   "Sen thies tormentes greves not thee,
           Thai are our goddes that help thee soo,   *I.e., the source of this help is our gods*
           For thei wold thou convertyd shuld be.   *Because they desired [that]*
           Therfor, Cristyn, goo with me;
           Forthink that thou has don hem too.   *Repent what; to them*
335   For thei woll have of thee peté   *pity*
           And mercy, if thou thus will doo."

           She said, "Dyons, the devels own son,
           Thi tormentes truly drede I noght.
           And syn thou have thus begon,

340	Let noght, to thi malice be wroght	*Do not stop, until your malice is carried out*
	Or thou me to dethe have brought.	
	Urban and thou togedire shall wone	
	In dyrnesse grete and sorow unsought,	*darkness; untold (immeasurable)*
	And both togedir to drynk of a tonne."	*from the same barrel*

345	Than Dyons: "Kytt of hir tresse!	*Cut off her hair*
	Let noght if hir here be bright,	*Do not desist*
	And shave hir hede yit neverthelesse.	
	Do nakyn hir in all men sighte.	*Have her stripped naked*
	Thorought-oute all the cité lede that wyght	
350	To Apolyn; late hym redresse!	*Apollo; correct [her]*
	So grete, I wote, is his myghte	
	He may amend hir wikkednesse."	

	Thai lede hir forthe in that araye	
	Thorought-oute the ceté longe and wyde.	*Throughout the city*
355	When wyfs and wemen se that may	*maiden*
	That all was bar, both wombe and syde	*stomach and flank*
	(She had no clothe, hir with to hyde),	*with which to cover herself*
	Therfor on Dyons all cried thei,	*against*
	"Vengeaunce, Dyons, on thee betyde!	*May vengeance fall on you, Dyons*
360	Thou dos all women shame this daie!"	*You cause*

	When she was broughte, that maydyn free,	
	To Apolyn, sche said full sone,	
	"In Cristis name Y commaunde thee:	
	In poudre thou fall downe anon."	*Into dust*
365	Apolyn felle ther downe on the ston	*pavement*
	In poudre, ther alle men myght see;	
	Thoroughte this miracle, whan it was donne,	*By means of*
	Thre thowsand Sarzyns converted she.	

	Whan Dyons herde that it was soo,	
370	That Cristyn had Apolyn schent,	*destroyed*
	For ferde his hert it braste in too.	*fear*
	Thus Dyons died and never repent.	
	Such grace God to Cristyn sent	
	That she of peyne felt no woo;	

237

| 375 | Bothe hir enmys now ere thei wente, | *are they gone* |
| | Thei may no more do hir too. | *do to her* |

	Urban and Dyons are now paste;	*passed (dead)*
	Of Cristyn have thei no more myghte.	*Over*
	Than com the thirde schrew at the laste:	*villain*
380	Julyan, wele Y wote, he highte.	
	Thus began that cursid wighte:	
	He bade his men do orden faste	*to prepare at once*
	An oven als hote as fier so brighte,	*as hot as fire*
	And therin Cristyn shulde thei caste.	

385	When it was hote, it shone as shene	*bright*
	As any fier that ever myght be.	
	Than Julyan said, that was so keene,	*fierce*
	"Do put hir inne anon, late see!"	*let us see [what happens]*
	Thei caste hir inne withoute peté;	
390	Thei wende thei shuld hir never have sen,	*would never see her again*
	But of that hete no more felte she	
	Than sche in a bathe had been.	*Than [if]*

	Fyve daies togedir, daie be daie,	
	Sche welkid therin to and froo;	*walked*
395	She songe ther as a mery maye,	
	Aungels and she togedir also.	
	All that Julian did hir to	
	Of grete tormentes and paynes alway,	*always (progressively)*
	She feled no grevaunce ne no wo,	
400	For all turnyd hir to aungels playe.	*everything turned to angels' play for her*

	When Julyan herd it greved hir noght,	
	But that sche songe with aungels bright,	
	He wende by wychecrafte that sche had wrouthe —	*worked (acted)*
	He had no grace to know the righte.	*truth*
405	But sone he called another wighte	
	(To slee Cristyn was his thoughte);	
	I have herde telle Marces he highte,	*[that] he was called Marcus*
	And sexté serpens he with hym broughte.	*sixty*

238

	Marces crafte, for soth, was this:	*skill*
410	That he couthe charme his serpens so,	
	What beste hym liste to do mys,	*Whatever animal; to harm*
	Anon to deth thei wold it do.	*they would put it to death*
	Now are thei put Seint Cristyn to.	*placed on St. Christine*
	She hath no drede of theym, iwysse,	
415	But loke upon them, who thei goo;	*looks; how they move*
	Abowte hir nek ther playinge is.	
	For swett hir nek was wondre wete —	*extremely*
	Too wormes lykkyd it clene away.	*Two serpents*
	Too wente downe unto hir fete;	
420	Thai lykkyd them clene, and ther thei lay.	
	At hir pappis too honge to play,	*breasts*
	As thei wold soke that maydyn swete.	*As [if]; suck [milk from]*
	To do hir harme no myght had thei;	
	This saw Julyan, ther he seete.	*where he sat*
425	Julyan said to Marces than,	
	"Thou said thi bestis wold slee hir sone.	
	Make tham to smyte hir, if thou can!	*strike*
	Thou wote well yit thei have not don."	*know; they have not yet done so*
	Marces beganne his charme anon,	
430	To make tham byghte that blissed woman;	*bite*
	But thei lefte Cristyn everychon	*i.e., every one of them*
	And slow hym that the charme began.	*slew him who*
	Seinte Cristyn loked who Marces lay,	*saw how*
	That shuld have made the wormes to byghte.	*was supposed to*
435	She bade the serpens voyde awaye	*depart*
	Into deserte, no man to smyte.	
	She bade Marces ryse up tyte,	*quickly*
	And he stode up before that may.	*maiden*
	Than Julian had so grete dispyte	*resentment*
440	Hym thought his herte schuld breste that day.	*burst*
	Hir paps were als rounde, ywysse,	*breasts*
	As an appill that growes in feld;	
	Thai kitte them of — the more dole is,	*cut; off; cause of sorrow*

When she was twelve yer of elde.   *age*

445 The mylke stremyd oute — all men behelde,

And some were sory that se this;

But Julian wold hym never yelde   *give in (yield)*

Ne never ones forthink his mys.   *regret his evil deeds*

Seint Cristyn saide, "With herte and thought

450 I thanke Thee, God in magesté,

Of alle that Thou has for me wroughte   *For everything*

To make men knowe the myghte of Thee.

In alle my peynes Thou has kept me,   *protected*

That fiere ne watir grevyd me noght.   *[So] that; fire*

455 Therefor me thinke right longe to Thee,

To Thi faire blisse, that I were broughte."[1]

Julian wondrede who she myghte   *how*

In hir grete tormentes jangill so.   *chatter*

Therefore he bade a wykkyd wighte,

460 "Kytte oute hir tonge! It dos me woo."

And whan hir tonge lay at hir too,   *toe(s)*

She spake als wele, that maydyn brighte,

As never it had be kytt hir froo.   *As [if]*

Thei herd and seye, all men, with sight.   *saw; with their own eyes*

465 She toke hir tonge upe, where it lay,

And even sche caste it at Julian eye,   *straight; Julian's*

That aftir nevermore alway   *never again afterwards*

On that syde myght he noght see.

For she hym hit, softely smylid she;   *Because*

470 He for wrethe lyste nothinge playe;   *fury had no desire to joke*

He said, "Vengeaunce com on thee!

Thou arte a wyche, Y dare wele say."   *witch*

With his on eye he lokyd asyde,   *one*

And thus he spake the tonge unto: *to the tongue*

---

[1] Lines 455–56: *Therefore it seems to me very long [that I wait] to be brought to you [and] to your perfect joy*

475	"Whiles thou waste in hir mouthe so wyde,	*While; were*
	Than with thi wordes thou wrought me woo.	
	Thi stroke greves me mor than soo,	*I.e., being hit by you is even worse*
	For it hath made myn eye out glyde;	*go*
	Thi wordis as wynde flyed too and froo,	*flew*
480	But strokes ar sor and evyll to byde."	*blows; painful to endure*
	For ire and wreth he was so woo	
	He wiste in world what he do myght:	
	But thre arraws he shett hir to,	*shot toward her*
	And too ageyn hir herte thei lyght;	*two reached her heart*
485	The thirde hit in hir syde full righte.	*directly*
	But when Cristyn was smyten so,	
	Hir soule wente up to heven so brighte,	
	Where she shall feele of peynes no moo.	
	Hir bodye lyeth in stronge castyll —	*remains*
490	And Bulstene, seith the boke, it highte —	
	Wher many seke men have had hele	*sick; health (healing)*
	And blynde also have had her sighte.	*their*
	Truly Y trowe: if any wighte	
	Praye hertely to that damesele,	*earnestly; young lady*
495	She will hym helpe with alle hir myghte,	
	If theire desire be goode and leele.	*loyal*
	Seint Cristyn, helpe thorought thi prayere	*by means of*
	That we may fare the better for thee,	*because of thy help*
	That hath ben longe in prison here,	*[We] who have*
500	The Ile of Man, that stronge cuntré.	*rugged (fortified) place*
	Sir Thomas Brawchaump, an erle was he;	
	In Warwikshire was his power.	*seat of power*
	Now is he of so pour degré,	*such low status*
	He hath no man save on squiere.	*servant except one*
505	Where are his knyghtes that with hym yede	
	Whan he was in prosperité?	
	Where are the squiers now at nede,	*in his need*
	That sumtyme thoughte thei wold not flee?	*formerly*
	Of yomen had he grete plenté	*retainers*

510	That he was wonte to cloth and feede;	*clothe*
	Nowe is ther non of the mené	*company*
	That ons dare se ther lorde, for drede.	*once [would] dare*
	In prison site ther lorde alone.	*sits*
	Of his men he hath no moo,	
515	But William Parys, be Seint John,	*Except*
	That with his will woll noght him fro.	*will not leave him voluntarily*
	He made this lyfe in Ynglishe soo,	
	As he satte in prison of ston,	
	Ever as he myghte tent therto	*Whenever he could work on it*
520	Whan he had his lordes service don.	
	Jhesu Criste, Goddes Son of myghte,	*God's powerful Son*
	As Thou com down to mende our mysse	*remedy our sinfulness*
	And in a clene virgyne Thou lyghte,	*alighted*
	Marie, that now Thi modir is,	
525	Thou graunte all grace that hath herd this,	*grace to everyone who*
	In Heven of Thee to have a sighte,	
	To se Thee sitte there in Thi blisse	
	With Seint Cristyn, Thi maydyn bright.	

Explicit vita sancte Cristine virginis.[1] Amen.

---

[1] *Here ends the life of the virgin Saint Christine*

Explanatory Notes to Paris' Life of St. Christina

33–34   Evidently her family has decided to keep her unmarried so that she can serve their gods as a temple virgin. Some retellings of the legend suggest that her father has incestuous designs on her.

34   *mawmentrye.* On this term see the explanatory note to Mirk's account of Mary Magdalen, line 57.

58   *As had the Baptiste.* According to the Gospel of Luke, the blessedness of John the Baptist was foretold by an angel even before he was conceived (Luke 1:13–17) and confirmed in the sixth month of his mother's pregnancy when he leaped for joy in her womb at the greeting of her kinswoman, the Virgin Mary, who had herself just become pregnant with Jesus (Luke 1:39–44).

62   *As in Poules lyfe.* The dramatic acts of grace which converted St. Paul from a persecutor of the early church to one of its chief missionaries are related in Acts 9:1–30.

64   *As Barabas thef, that honge so hye.* Presumably a reference to the thief who was crucified alongside Jesus and repented as he was dying, receiving forgiveness and the promise of Heaven (Luke 23:39–43). The name traditionally given to that thief, however, was Dismas or Demas. The criminal Barabbas, who seems to have gotten confused with him in this text, was the condemned prisoner whom Pilate released in place of Jesus (Mark 15:6–15; Luke 23: 17–25).

141   *my doughter small.* Either a reference to her slender body or to her extreme youth. Although this text does not mention her age until line 444, it follows the tradition which envisioned her as a child of twelve.

150–52   Although they are supposedly on Urban's side, Christina's handmaidens seem to be mocking him. The verb *auntred* (line 150) answers the question "how durste she" (line 147) with a simple assertion: she did dare to defy him. The term *dyght* (line 151) is ironic when used to describe the broken idols because it ordinarily refers to a constructive activity like building, adorning, or putting in order. But it also can

243

have negative connotations. See MED *dighten* v. 5 ("fall"), and 2c ("condemn"). And the question in line 152 sounds more like ridicule of Urban's pretensions to power than like faith in that power.

170   *in depe prisoun.* In this context, *depe* might refer either to the severity of her imprisonment or to its location; in the latter case, we should envision a dark dungeon below the ground or in the innermost part of a tower.

202   *Befor the barre.* The term *bar*, in this sense, refers to the barrier in front of the judge's seat in a court of law.

206   *Thus coppid the kene, on me began.* A difficult line to translate. *The kene* ("The haughty, obstinate, or rebellious one"?) looks like the subject of the verb *coppid* ("accused," "argued," "quarreled," or "tilted with"); but *coppid* could also be a past participle modifying *the kene* ("Thus accused, the haughty one"?). The phrase *on me began* could mean either "began [to quarrel] against me" or "began [her life] in dependence on me." It is even conceivable that the first half of the line is a description of the way Urban is speaking, rather than part of his accusation against Christina.

223–24   *fadir . . . / Of Satan fende.* This sounds reversed. We would expect Christina to be saying that Urban is the devil's son, not the devil's father; and at least one Middle English version, that of Bokenham, has her say just that. But William Paris is accurately translating the usual Latin version of this line. The point seems to be that Christina is glad to be disowned by Urban because Urban is a devil and she could only be his daughter if she were a devil too. Her real father, as the legend keeps suggesting, is Christ.

239–40   What is "full of wytt" (line 237) about this response is the way it accuses Urban of devouring the flesh of his own offspring. This act can be seen as a proof of God's anger against Urban, since it fulfills a dire curse with which God threatened in Leviticus to punish the most incorrigible transgressors against Him: "But if you will not for all this [preceding series of chastisements] hearken to me, but will walk against me: I will also go against you with opposite fury, and I will chastise you with seven plagues for your sins, so that you shall eat the flesh of your sons and of your daughters" [Lev. 26:27–29]. The connection between Christina's legend and this Biblical curse is confirmed by the fact that the very next verse, Leviticus 26:30, corresponds with the saint's victory over her second judge: "I will destroy your high places and break your idols. You shall fall among the ruins of your idols, and my soul shall abhor you." (See below, lines 361–72.)

269–72   Christ's words echo the standard baptismal formula, in which the priest says, "I baptize you in the name of the Father and of the Son and of the Holy Spirit."

274   *godfadir and preste.* That is, Christ had filled the role of her godparent and sponsor, bringing her to the ceremony and conferring her baptismal name, as well as the priestly role of administering the sacrament itself.

280   *in the stronde!* The noun *stronde* generally refers to land bordering a sea or river, but it can also mean the waters near a coast.

281   *Seint Mighell.* Michael the Archangel, mentioned in Revelation 12:7–9 as the leader of the angelic host that defeated Satan's army and drove them from Heaven, was generally associated with mountains and other high places rather than with rescues from the sea, and was the protector of soldiers in particular. His introduction into some retellings of Christina's legend (including the *Legenda aurea,* as well as William Paris's version) may have been intended to emphasize the resemblances between this intrepid young virgin and the archetypal Christian warrior.

284   *He wiste in world.* Obviously this must be an idiom which, like the modern "could care less," means the opposite of what it literally says.

294   *depe prison.* On this term see explanatory note to line 170, above.

305   *Dyons.* The name of Christina's second judge is generally given as "Zyon" in English sources. In the *Legenda aurea* tradition, on the other hand, he is usually called "Elius."

323   *twys-borne child.* That is, born again with baptism and enjoying the luxury of a second childhood, safe in the protection of her real father, Christ.

344   *tonne.* Drinking from the same tun — i.e., from the same barrel of wine or ale — was a proverbial expression for sharing the same fate.

350   *Apolyn.* That is, to a large statue of the Roman god Apollo, which must stand in a public place in this city.

245

353   *in that araye.* An ironic choice of words, since Christina is naked and the term *araye* usually refers to clothing.

355   *wyfs and wemen.* Married women and women in general.

368   *Sarzyns.* On this term, see explanatory note to line 194 of the early *SEL* Life of Mary Magdalen.

441–44   Kirsten Wolf discusses the possible implications of such mutilation of female saints in "The Severed Breast: A Topos in the Legends of Female Virgin Martyr Saints," *Arkiv for Nordisk Filologi* 112 (1997), 97–112.

445   *The mylke stremyd oute.* A miraculous sign reported at the deaths of several other virgin martyrs, including Katherine of Alexandria. For possible interpretations, see explanatory note to line 754 of the stanzaic Life of Katherine.

474–80   This complaint by the persecutor represents a surprising departure from most versions of the legend, which have Christina miraculously continuing to speak, and thus affirm the powerlessness of violence to silence the martyr's defiant witness. Stouck suggests that William Paris may have reversed the usual message at this point in order to reduce the embarrassing contrast between Christina and Warwick, who was said to have capitulated and confessed all too easily ("Saints and Rebels," p. 87).

482   *He wiste in world.* On this idiom, see explanatory note to line 284 above.

489–90   *stronge castyll . . . Bulstene.* The *Legenda aurea* identifies Bolsena as a fortified place between Orvieto and Viterbo.

501–02   *Sir Thomas Brawchaump.* That is, Sir Thomas Beauchamp, Earl of Warwick. See Introduction to this text.

505–12   Notice how the "Ubi sunt" motif in this stanza is used both to lament the absence of Sir Thomas' other followers and to suggest their cowardice and ingratitude. Christina was braver than any of them, which may be a reason for William Paris' retelling of the legend.

Textual Notes to Paris' Life of St. Christina

Abbreviations: **A** = British Library MS Arundel 168, fols. 2r–4v [base text]; **H** = Carl Horstmann.

8	*highte.*A: *toke highte*, with *toke* dotted for deletion.
68	*sacrifiee.* Corrected in A from *sacrifice*, presumably for the sake of the rhyme.
96	*My.* Conjectural reading; A damaged at this point.
97	*Thi.* Conjectural reading; A damaged at this point.
127	*wold.* Emended from A: *wild.*
216	*this.* Emended from A's reading, *thus*, to restore the rhyme with "is" (line 209), "sacrifice" (line 211), and "mysse" (line 214).
234	*toke.* Corrected in A from *to.*
250	*sorcerrie.* Emended from A: *socerrie.*
251	*Therfor.* Corrected in A from *Ther.*
258	*thei.* Emended from A: *thi.*
302	*away.* Emended from A: *al way.*
306	*To.* Emended from A: *Tho.*
321	Corrected in A, which originally omitted *thee.*
323	*yonge.* The text must originally have been composed in a dialect that could use the form *yinge*, rhyming in this stanza with "kynge" (line 321), "nothinge" (line 326), and "hynge" (line 328).
344	*tonne.* Emended from A: *towne.*
345	*Than Dyons.* H suggests emending this line by inserting the verb *bad.*
353	*forthe in that.* Corrected in A, which originally omitted *in.*
387	*keene.* Corrected in A from *kiene* or *kuene.*
399	*no grevaunce.* Corrected in A, which originally omitted *no.*
428	*well.* Emended from A: *will.*
438	*And he stode.* Corrected in A, which originally omitted *he.*
441	*ywysse.* Emended from A: *ywyse.*
450	*Thee.* A: omits. H's emendation.
460	*tonge! It.* There is a canceled letter between *tonge* and *It* in A.
465	Corrected in A, which originally omitted *toke.*
476	Corrected in A, which originally omitted *thi.*

500   *The Ile of Man, that stronge cuntré.* An emendation suggested by Gerould. A has
        another *of* after *Man.*

513   Corrected in A, which originally omitted the verb *site.*

521   *Goddes.* Emended from A: *goddeste.*

Legends of St. Anne, Mother of the Virgin Mary

Introduction

Although the canonical books of the New Testament never mention the parents of the Virgin Mary, traditions about her family, childhood, education, and eventual betrothal to Joseph developed very early in the history of the church. The oldest and most influential account of this kind is the apocryphal gospel called the *Protevangelium of James*, first written in Greek around the middle of the second century. The high status of the *Protevangelium* in the Eastern Church is attested by the survival of numerous manuscripts not only in Greek but also in Coptic (Sahidic), Syriac, Armenian, Georgian, Ethiopic, Old Church Slavonic, and Arabic translations. In the West, on the other hand, the *Protevangelium* fell under a cloud in the fourth and fifth centuries when it was accused of "absurdities" by St. Jerome and condemned as untrustworthy by Popes Damasus, Innocent I, and Gelasius. Jerome's most explicit complaint was that it explained the brothers of Jesus, mentioned most prominently in Mark 6:3 and Matthew 13:55–56, as Joseph's sons by an earlier marriage. In the interpretation preferred by Jerome and the Western Church, the so-called brothers are interpreted as cousins of Jesus, sons of Mary's sisters, thus allowing both Joseph and Mary to be envisioned as lifelong virgins.

The dubious reputation of the *Protevangelium* in the wake of these condemnations evidently delayed the development of Anne's legend and cult in the West by several centuries. But the stigma was not passed on to the Latin retellings and elaborations of the same narrative that began to circulate under different titles in the early Middle Ages; ironically enough, some of them even buttressed their credentials with prefatory letters supposedly written by Jerome. The most popular of these accounts was the Gospel of Pseudo-Matthew (sometimes called the History of the Birth of Mary and the Infancy of the Savior), which survives in several distinct recensions and at least 130 manuscripts, the earliest of which date to c. 800. The various recensions of Pseudo-Matthew gave rise in their turn to dozens of later works, in both Latin and the vernacular, that retold the story of Mary's birth and early life, adapting it to new audiences and purposes.

Anne was initially just a minor character in the legend derived from the *Protevangelium*. But her role was capable of great significance because of what it could imply about the Virgin Mary and about the workings of God in this world. Christians were obviously curious from the start about when and why God had selected Mary for her unique position as the mother of the Redeemer. The legend attempts to answer such questions by borrowing from Biblical stories about other long-awaited children, including Isaac (Genesis 15–18, 21:1–8), Samson (Judges

249

13), John the Baptist (Luke 1: 5–25, 57–80), and especially Samuel (1 Samuel 1–2); thus Mary becomes both a child of destiny, heralded before birth as a chosen instrument in the redemption of God's people, and a sign of God's favor toward her parents, a virtuous couple who had long been barren. With the growth of Mary's cult in the twelfth century, a harder and more controversial question began to be raised about her conception and birth. Was she subject to sin like other human beings, making her redemption dependent on Christ's sacrifice, or had she been "immaculate" (unspotted, free from original sin) from the start? The Council of Basel endorsed the latter position in 1438, and Pope Pius IX approved it definitively as a doctrine of the Roman Catholic Church in 1854. During the late Middle Ages, however, belief in Mary's immaculate conception was strongly opposed by many theologians, including most Dominicans. Since sexual intercourse was understood as the means by which original sin was transmitted from one generation to another, the legend about the separation of Mary's parents during the year before she was born took on new importance in the context of this dispute. Some versions of the legend support the "immaculist" position, suggesting that Mary was miraculously conceived at the moment when the angel appeared to her mother or (more often) when her parents were reunited at the Golden Gate in Jerusalem and chastely embraced. In versions preferred by the Dominicans and other maculists, on the other hand, there is no suggestion that she was conceived in anything other than the normal biological fashion, after her parents' reunion.

Anne also played a useful role for medieval commentators on the Bible when they attempted to explain the extended family of Jesus. As mentioned earlier, Jerome had argued successfully that the "brothers" mentioned in the Gospels were Jesus's cousins, sons of Mary's sisters. Biblical commentators in the early medieval West went on to identify those sisters with two other Maries mentioned in the Gospels (John 19:25 and Mark 16:1), to take Anne as the mother of all three, and to explain the names of her second and third daughters by creating the theory of the *trinubium,* or three marriages of Anne. According to the trinubium, Joachim must have died soon after the birth of the Virgin Mary, so that Anne could marry a second husband named Cleophas, by whom she bore Mary Cleophas, and (after Cleophas's death) a third husband named Salome, by whom she bore Mary Salome. From these three daughters, the theory continued, came Jesus and all six "brothers" or cousins named in the Gospels. James the lesser or younger, Joseph or Joses, Simon, and Jude were explained as the sons of Mary Cleophas, who had married Alpheus; James the Greater and John the Evangelist, as the sons of Mary Salome, who had married Zebedee. Thus Anne became the grandmother of some of the most prominent apostles, as well as Jesus himself. The trinubium theory was condemned in the twelfth century and later by a number of theologians, who felt that multiple marriages and additional children were incompatible with the purity and holiness that must have characterized the Virgin's mother, and some Biblical scholars rejected it on the grounds that it depended on misinterpretations of particular names and details. But the theory had a certain amount of internal logic on its side, given the way the legend equated fertility with blessedness and connected Anne with Hannah, the mother of Samuel, who was granted three more sons and two daughters after she dedicated her firstborn to God's service. The idea of the holy family as a large and powerful kinship had another advantage in medieval culture, of course, because it conformed so well with that culture's assumptions about family and class. The theory was incorporated into later recensions of Pseudo-Matthew and repeated in the *Legenda aurea*, and by those means became generally known and widely accepted in the later Middle Ages as part of Anne's life story.

Like her legend, the cult of St. Anne was so closely connected with that of the Virgin Mary, especially at the beginning, that it is not easy to tell where the one leaves off and the other begins. In the Eastern church the cult of Anne herself may go back as far as c. 550, when Justinian built a church in Constantinople in her honor. The earliest sign of her veneration in the West is an eighth-century fresco in the church of Santa Maria Antiqua, Rome, which shows her with a halo, holding the infant Mary. But not until the twelfth and thirteenth centuries is there unmistakable evidence that the Western church was honoring St. Anne in her own right, rather than just an adjunct to Mary. During those centuries returning crusaders and pilgrims from the East brought relics of Anne to a number of churches, including most famously those at Apt, in Provence, Ghent, and Chartres. By 1300 at least five important English monastic foundations were also claiming to have relics of Anne, and dozens of additional shrines, altars, and chapels had been dedicated to her, both in England and on the Continent.

Liturgical commemorations of Anne in the West seem to have followed a similar course of development, except that monastic houses in England played a more central role. The story of Joachim and Anne received at least passing mention in the liturgy for one of the oldest annual feasts of Mary, the Nativity of the Virgin (September 8 in Western calendars), which was included in the Sacramentary of Gelasius (c. 700) and firmly established in Anglo-Saxon England by the ninth or tenth century. Anne's role tended to take on more importance when an annual feast was added to celebrate the Conception of the Virgin (observed exactly nine months earlier — i.e., December 8). There is good evidence that the Conception was being commemorated at Winchester, Exeter, and Canterbury before the Norman Conquest, and this feast day was revived in the twelfth century through the efforts of Benedictine writers like Eadmer of Canterbury and Anselm of Bury, although it became generally established in England only after 1328 (when it was made obligatory for the whole Province of Canterbury) and was not clearly mandated for the Church as a whole until 1476 (when Pope Sixtus IV confirmed the Council of Basel's ruling on the matter). England also preceded most of the Continent in instituting a separate feast day for Anne herself (July 26). The date traditionally associated with the adoption of this feast is 1382, the year in which Pope Urban VI authorized its celebration throughout England, but it was already being celebrated in the twelfth century in some of the great English monastic churches, most notably those at Worcester and Evesham.

The great flowering of Anne's cult among the laity occurred between about 1300 and the Council of Trent in the mid sixteenth century. By 1540 there were at least 40 medieval churches and chapels under her patronage in England, the majority of which had been dedicated or rededicated to her during the previous two centuries. She also had major shrines at Buxton (Derbyshire) and Wood-Plumpton (Lancashire), and was frequently chosen by prosperous laymen and women as patron saint of their guilds and recipient of special bequests and offerings. As Gail Gibson has shown, such devotion to her seems to have been unusually strong in East Anglia. Many churches had cycles of paintings or tapestries illustrating key scenes from her legend, or portraits of the Holy Kinship that showed Anne surrounded by her daughters and grandsons. Another popular late-medieval image of Anne was the grouping known in German as the *Anna Selbdritt* ("herself making a third") — a maternal version of the Trinity, in effect, often with Anne seated in a position recalling God the Father on His throne, with the young Virgin Mary on her knee, holding the infant Jesus.[1]

Anne appealed in a number of different ways to various groups and classes within the late-medieval church. As has already been suggested, some theologians found material in her legend to support their arguments about the Immaculate Conception and other issues related to the Incarnation of Christ. Some religious orders, most notably the Carmelites, claimed a special relationship with her and other members of the holy family, which they used to lend prestige to their own institutional history. To many members of the laity, on the other hand, Anne obviously represented an attractive alternative to the standard equation of female saintliness with virginity, persecution, and early death. Envisioned as a holy mother and grandmother, contentedly presiding over a family of well-brought-up daughters and grandsons, she naturally became a patron saint of marriage and the family. A wife whose virtue was ultimately rewarded with fertility, she seemed an appropriate guardian against both lechery and barrenness. In addition, as Ton Brandenbarg has noted, the prominence of genealogies in her legend led to her association with "dynastic sanctity," an ideal with great attractiveness both to aristocrats and to members of the middle class with ambitions for their families. She was also associated with other bourgeois values, including prosperity, diligence, generosity to the poor, married chastity, and harmonious family life, and (since she was often portrayed with a book, teaching the young Virgin Mary to read) with education, especially for women. But her potential appeal extended even to illiterate peasants, especially insofar as she recalled the figure of the powerful grandmother in folklore, and indeed to anyone who simply needed an intercessor with Jesus and believed in the power of family connections.

---

[1] Numerous illustrations of these medieval images can be found in *Interpreting Cultural Symbols*, ed. Ashley and Sheingorn. On the theological and social implications of the medieval images of the Holy Kinship and their less matrilineal replacements during the Reformation, see especially Sheingorn's essay in this collection, "Appropriating the Holy Kinship."

The Middle English versions of her legend edited here suggest that the cult of Anne developed quite unevenly in different regions or segments of society in England. The two chapters by Mirk remind us how recently she had been added to the calendar in many English churches — and that the impetus for her cult sometimes came from above, not from the grass roots. Mirk's sermon on the Conception is really about Mary, as the final miracle stories show, and Anne receives less attention than Joachim does in the narrative leading up to Mary's birth. Even in his sermon for St. Anne's feast day, Mirk does not present Anne as a saint with her own cult and identity. The opening section, in which he distinguishes Anne from several women in the Bible with similar names, suggests that he didn't expect his audience to have much prior knowledge of her. When he gives a family lineage, it is the lineage of Anne's husband Joachim, rather than that of Anne herself. And although he repeats the legend of her later marriages, the sermon does not actually focus attention on Anne herself except at the end, and even there the account of her holy lineage in lines 65–71 is taken to prove her potential usefulness as a derivative or subordinate saint, a means of access to Mary, her daughter.

The fifteenth-century verse retelling of Anne's life by Osbern Bokenham (1393–1464?), in contrast, shows much more interest in Anne's own character and virtues, and in her human experience. Bokenham, an Austin (Augustinian) friar at Clare Priory in East Anglia, dedicated most of his accounts of female saints to laywomen from prominent families in the vicinity. In the case of St. Anne, he wrote for Katherine Clopton Denston, daughter and sister of wealthy cloth merchants whose family portraits survive in the parish church of nearby Long Melford, where they were major donors. Katherine and her husband John Denston, a local landowner and civil servant, had just one child, a daughter named after St. Anne, and Bokenham spells out one purpose of his account in the closing lines, when he invokes the saint's help in fulfilling their desire for a second child, a son.[2] But it is clearly not just St. Anne's role as an intercessor that makes her life relevant, in Bokenham's view, to women like his friend Katherine Denston. His account goes well beyond its sources in its sympathetic attention to the marriage between Anne and Joachim — adding passages, for instance, which emphasize how well matched they are in age, rank, and virtue (lines 229–50), how dearly Anne loves her husband (336–49), and how joyful she is when he returns from his long absence (567–73). Thus Bokenham reassuringly suggests through St. Anne that laypeople can have a good and loving marriage without forfeiting the possibility of holiness.

---

[2] Gail McMurray Gibson writes eloquently about this aspect of the legend in "The Religion of Childbed," pp. 104–07.

Select Bibliography

Indexed in

[Bokenham]   Brown-Robbins, #1414.

Manuscripts

[Mirk]   London, British Library MS Cotton Claudius A.ii, fols. 11v–13r, 95v–96v.

[Bokenham]   London, British Library MS Arundel 327, fols. 27r–39r.

Previous editions

Mirk
Mirk, John. *Mirk's Festial*. Ed. Theodor Erbe. EETS, e.s. 96 (1905). Pp. 15–18, 213–16.

Bokenham
Horstmann, Carl, ed. *Osbern Bokenham's Legenden*. In *Altenglische Bibliothek*, vol. 1. Ed. Eugen Kölbing. Heilbronn: Henninger, 1883.

Bokenham, Osbern. *Legendys of Hooly Wummen*. Ed. Mary S. Serjeantson. EETS o.s. 206. 1938. Pp. 38–58.

Translations into modern English

Delany, Sheila, trans. and intro. *A Legend of Holy Women*. 1992. Pp. 29–41. [For full reference, see Bokenham in General Bibliography, p. 15.]

Important sources and analogues in English

Gospel of Pseudo-Matthew. Chs. 1–5. In *The Ante-Nicene Fathers: Translations of the Writings of the Fathers down to A.D. 325*. Ed. Alexander Roberts and James Donaldson. Rev. and arranged A. Cleveland Coxe. Edinburgh: T. & T. Clark, 1867–72. Rpt. Grand Rapids: Wm. B. Eerdmans Pub. Co., 1989. Vol. 8. Pp. 368–71.

Jacobus de Voragine. *The Golden Legend.* Trans. William Granger Ryan. Ch. 131, "The Birth of the Virgin." 1993. Vol. 2. Pp. 149–58.

Meredith, Peter, ed. *The Mary Play from the N. town Manuscript.* London and New York: Longman, 1987. Pp. 30–48.

Parker, Roscoe E., ed. *Middle English Stanzaic Versions of the Life of Saint Anne.* EETS o.s. 174. London: Oxford University Press, 1928.

Protevangelium of James. Chs. 1–7. In *The Apocryphal New Testament: A Collection of Apocryphal Christian Literature in an English Translation.* Ed. J. K. Elliott. Oxford: Clarendon Press, 1993. Pp. 48–60.

Historical background and commentary

Ashley, Kathleen, and Pamela Sheingorn. "Introduction." In Ashley and Sheingorn, *Interpreting Cultural Symbols.* Pp. 1–68.

Bishop, Edmund. "On the Origins of the Feast of the Conception of the Blessed Virgin Mary." In *Liturgica Historica: Papers on the Liturgy and Religious Life of the Western Church.* Oxford, Clarendon Press, 1918. Pp. 238–49. [Originally published in *The Downside Review*, April 1886.]

Brandenbarg, Ton. "Saint Anne: A Holy Grandmother and Her Children." In Mulder-Bakker, *Sanctity and Motherhood.* Pp. 31–65.

Charland, Paul V. *Madame saincte Anne et son culte au moyen âge.* 2 vols. Paris: Alphonse Picard, 1911–1913.

Gibson, Gail McMurray. "The Religion of Childbed: Some East Anglian Texts and Talismans." In Ashley and Sheingorn. Pp. 95–110.

Sheingorn, Pamela. "Appropriating the Holy Kinship: Gender and Family History." In Ashley and Sheingorn. Pp. 169–98.

John Mirk, *Sermon on the Conception of the Virgin Mary,*
from British Library MS Cotton Claudius A.ii, fols. 11v–13r

Suche a day ye schul have the Concepcyon of oure Lady, the whech day Holy
Chyrch makuth mensyon of the concepcyon of hure for thre specyal poyntes: for
hure fadur holynes, for hure modur goodnes, and for hure oune chesen mekenes.
Heo hadde a fadur that was kallud Joachym, that was of such holynes that, when

5   he was fyftene yere old, he departed his good in thre partyes: on to wydewes and
faderles chyldren and othur that weren pore and nedful; that othur part to ham that
servet God day and nyght in the temple; the thryd part he kepte to his houshold.
And when he was twenty yere old, for the gret gudnes that he herde and knewe by
Seynt Anne, he weddet hure, and weron yfere twenty yere. The whech tyme, Anne

10   never dysplesyd hym, by nyght ne by day, for the grete gentelnes that was with
hure. But thagh they were bothe good and holy, God gaf ham no frut of hure
body; but were bareyn bothe. Wherfore they maden a vow to Godde, yef He wold
gev hem a chyld, they wold offren hyt in the temple, that shulden serve God day
and nyght.

15   Then upon a day as Joachym with hys nexbores yod to the temple to don hys
offryng, the byschop, that hette Ysacar, rebukud hym opunlych and sayde,
"Joachim," quod he, "hyt falluth not to thee, that art bareyn, for to offren in company with othur that God hath geve frut in Israel." Then was Joachym so aschomot
with thus rebuk that he went hom wepyng, and privyly tok hys schapardes with

1 **Suche a day**, On such and such a day [to be inserted by the speaker]. **2 poyntes**,
reasons. **3 chesen**, blessed. **5 departed his good in thre partyes**, divided his property
into three parts; **on**, one. **6 and othur**, and others; **that othur part**, the second part. **8
gudnes**, goodness; **by**, about. **9 weron yfere**, [they] were together. **10 gentelnes**, gra-
ciousness/nobility. **11 thagh**, although. **12 were bareyn**, [they] were barren; **yef**, if. **13
that shulden serve**, so that it would serve. **15 nexbores**, neighbors. **16 byschop**, high
priest; **hette**, was called. **17 hyt falluth not**, it is not fitting. **18 othur that God hath geve
frut**, others to whom God has given children; **aschomot**, ashamed. **19 thus rebuk**, this
rebuke; **schapardes**, shepherds.

257

20   his schep, and yod forth in fer contré among hulles, and purposed hym to have lyved there all his lyf-dayes, and never eft have seyn Anne, hys wyf.

    Then was Anne sory, and prayed to God and sayde thus, "Lord, that me ys woo, for I am bareyn and may have no fryt, and now more: myn hosbond ys gon fro me, I wot never wydur. Lord, have mercy of me!"

25   Then, as scho prayed thus, an angel com to hure, and conford hure, and sayde, "Anne, be of good conford. Thou schal han a chyld such was never non lyk ne never schal bee." Then was Anne aferd of thys angel word and of the syght of hym, and lay al daye in hure prayeres, as heo hadde be ded. Then went this same angel to Joachym, and sayde the same word, and bad hym taken a lombe and

30   offren hit to God in sacryfyce. And so dude. And when he hadde so ydon, fro mydday tyl evensong he lay upon the erthe in his preyeres, thonkyng God with al hys myght. Then, on the morwen, as the angel bad, he yode homward a softe pas with his schep.

    And when he com nygh hom, the angel com to Anne, and bad hure go to the

35   gate that was kalled the Gyldon Gate, and abydon hure husbond there. Then was heo glad, and toke hure maydenes wyth hire, and yode thydur, and mette there with Joachym, hure husbond, and sayde, "Lord, I thonk thee heyly, for I was a wydewe and now I am a wyf; I was baren and now I schal have a chyld; I was in woo and wepyng, and now I schal ben in joye and lykyng."

40   And so conseyvet oure Lady. And when heo was boren, heo was kalled Marya as the angel bad byfore. Then aftur heo was wenet, they broghton hure to the temple, and laften hure among othur maydenes to serve God day and nyght. Then was heo so meke among alle othur vyrgines in al hure dowyng, that othur virgines

---

20 hulles, hills; **purposed hym**, intended. **21 eft**, again. **22–23 that me ys woo**, how unhappy I am. **23 fryt**, offspring. **24 I wot never wydur**, I have no idea where. **25 conford hure**, comforted her. **26 a chyld such was never non lyk**, such a child that there was never any like it. **27 angel word**, angel's message. **28 as heo hadde be ded**, as if she were dead. **29 lombe**, lamb. **30 so dude**, [he] did so. **31 evensong**, vespers (the early evening service). **32 morwen**, next day; **a softe pas**, quietly/slowly. **35 Gyldon**, Golden. **37 heyly**, fervently. **40 so conseyvet**, so [she] conceived; **boren**, born. **41 wenet**, weaned. **43 meke**, humble/gentle/gracious/full of loving kindness; **al hure dowyng**, everything she did.

kalled hure quene of maydenes, so that yet heo ys the mekest seynt in Heven, and
45 most redy ys to helpe alle that kalle to hure in nede.

[Narracio.] I rede that ther was a lord that hade a peny-reve, the whech hadde
gedred his lordes rent, and yode to beren hit to hym. Then were thefys set for hym
in a wode that he most nedus goo thorgh. But when he come into the wode, he
bythoght hym that he hadde not sayde oure Lady Sauter that he was woned to say
50 uche day. Then anon he kneled dount, and bygan to say. Than anon com oure
Lady lyke a fayre mayden, and set a garlon on hys hed; and at uch "Ave," heo
sette a ros in the garlond that schon as bryght as a sterre. So by that he hadde
sayde, the garlon was so bryght, that alle the wode schon therof. Thus when he
hadde don, he cussed the erthe and yode his way.

55 Thenne weren the thefus redy, and broghton hym to here mayster that had seyen
alle thys doyng. Then sayde the theff to hym, "I wot that thou art soch a lordus
servant, and hast hys money with thee. But telle me what woman that was, that set
this garlon on thy hed."

"For soth," he sayde, "I sagh no woman, ne have no garlond that I know. But
60 for I hadde forgeton to say oure Lady Sauter and was adred of yow, I kneled
adoun and sayde hit, prayng to hure to helpe me at my nede."

Then sayde the theff, "For hyre love, now go thy way, and pray hure for us."
And so yede hys way saf and sounde by sokur of oure Lady.

[Narracio.] But now schul ye heren how thus fest was furst yfonden. Ther was
65 in Englon a kyng was kalled Wylyam Conquerour; he sende the abbat of Ramesey
to the kyng of Denmark on messager. But when he was in the see, ther come a
darknes upon hym and suche a tempest with that, he and alle that weren with hym

44 yet, even now. 46 peny-reve, manorial official with authority to collect rents. 47
gedred, collected; thefys set for hym, thieves lying in wait for him. 48 most nedus goo
thorgh, necessarily had to pass through. 49 bythoght hym, remembered; oure Lady
Sauter, our Lady's Psalter (the rosary); woned, accustomed. 50 dount, down. 51 garlon,
garland; uch "Ave," each "Hail [Mary]." 52 ros, rose. 52–53 by that he hadde sayde, by
the time he had said [it all]. 53 schon therof, shone with its light. 54 cussed, kissed. 55
thefus, thieves; mayster, leader; seyen, seen. 60 for, since; adred, afraid. 63 yede hys
way, [he] went his way; sokur, help. 64 how thus fest was furst yfonden, how this feast
day was first established. 65 abbat, abbot. 66 on messager, as an envoy; in the see,
enroute by sea.

wende to have be spyllyd anon. Than uch mon prayed bysyly to dyverse seyntes of Heven, to helpe and sokur ham in hure grete nede. Then as the abbot prayed devowtly to God, ther come to hym a fayre mon and sayde to hym thus, "Yef thou wolt halwe the Concepcyon of oure Lady, that ys the secunde day aftur Seynt Nycholas Day, heo wol sokur thee and alle that ben with thee in thus nede."

"Syre," he sayde, "with ful good wyll, and thou woldest telle me what schal be the servyse of this fest."

Then sayde he, "The same that ys in hure Nativité, save turne the *nativité* into *concepcyon*."

"Ful gladly," sayde he, "schal thus be don." And then anon the tempest sesed, and the wedur clered. He went forth and dude his message, and cam ageyn to spede wel in al hys doyng. And when he hadde told the kyng of thus vysyon, the kyng mad to prechen hyt alle the reme. And so was halwyt in Holy Chyrch.

[**Narracio.**] Also ther was a seculer chanon that went over a watur to have don advowtry. As he was in a bot, he bygan to saye Matenes of oure Lady. Whyl he sayed *Invitaterium*, "Ave Maria," the devel cast hym doun and drouned hym and hadde hym to peyne. Than oure Lady cam and sayde, "Why have ye tak this mon?" They sayde he was in here servyse. Oure Lady sayde, "Nay, he was in myn houres," and anon restoret hym to lyve and bed he schulde no more don avoutri and also halwe hure concepcyon. And so he dede and was a ful good mon aftur.

68 wende to have be spyllyd anon, expected to be killed at once. **70–71 Yef thou wolt halwe**, If you will hold sacred. **72 thus nede**, this need. **73 with ful good wyll, and**, [I will do it] gladly, if. **74 servyse of this fest**, prescribed liturgy for this feast day. **75–76 The same . . . nativité into concepcyon**, The same [liturgy] as for her Nativity, but replacing the word *nativity* with *conception*. **77 thus**, this; **sesed**, ceased. **78 wedur**, weather. **79 spede wel**, succeed. **80 mad to prechen hyt alle the reme**, had it preached throughout the kingdom; **was halwyt**, [it] was consecrated. **81 seculer chanon**, a clergyman not living under the rule of a religious order; **a watur**, a [body of] water. **81–82 to have don advowtry**, to commit adultery. **82 bot**, boat; **Matenes of oure Lady**, the Matins portion of the Little Office of the Virgin. **82–83 Whyl he sayed Invitaterium**, While he was saying the *Invitatory* (just beginning the service). **84 hadde hym to peyne**, took him to be tortured [in hell]. **85 in here servyse**, in their service; **in myn houres**, performing the liturgy in my honor. **86 restoret hym to lyve**, restored him to life; **don avoutri**, commit adultery. **87 halwe**, hold sacred.

[**Narracio.**] Also I rede that ther was a clerk that was wonot every day to say Matenes and servyse of oure Lady. Hyt fel that by consel of hys frendes he schulde

90   han a wyf, and when he schulde be weddet he hadde a mynde that he hadde not sayde the servyse of oure Lady that day, and he made alle that ther were to gon out of the chyrch. And when they were gon he kneled and sayde hys servyse tyl he com to the antyme, "*Quam pulcra es et quam decora.*" Then oure Lady appered to hym and sayde, "Whyl thou sayst that I am fayre and onest, why wyl thou leve me

95   and taken anothur?" Then anon he sayde, "Lady, what wol thou that I do?" Heo sayde, "And thou wolt leve thy flesly wyf and serve my Sone and me, I wyl be thy spose and thou schal have with my Sone a crowne in kyngdom of Heven. And also that thou wol worschep the Concepcyon of me."

88 **wonot**, accustomed. 89 **fel**, happened. 89–90 **shulde han a wyf**, was about to get married. 90 **hadde a mynde**, remembered. 93 **antyme**, antiphon. 94 **onest**, honorable/ virtuous/decorous. 96 **And thou wolt**, If you will; **flesly wyf**, earthly/carnal wife. 97 **spose**, spouse.

Explanatory Notes to Mirk's Sermon on the Conception of the Virgin Mary

4–7   Compare Bokenham's Life of St. Anne, lines 251–57. The details Mirk gives here conform with the version of the legend in Pseudo-Matthew, ch. 1, which attributes the division of the property entirely to Joachym himself, beginning at the age of fifteen, rather than to Joachym and Anne together after their marriage (as in the version given by the *Legenda aurea* and Bokenham).

8–9   Joachym's age at the time of the marriage is another detail from Pseudo-Matthew.

25–33   This part of the story is drastically abbreviated in Mirk's version (by comparison with Pseudo-Matthew, Bokenham, and even the *Legenda aurea*, which entirely omits Anne's lamentation and the angel's first appearance to her).

37–39   Anne's expression of thanksgiving here is somewhat expanded from the version found in Pseudo-Matthew (ch. 3) and elsewhere. Compare Bokenham's Life of Anne, lines 572–79.

42–45   The Pseudo-Matthew gives a much longer account of the virtues of the young Mary as she grows up in the temple (ch. 6) and has a very different explanation of how she came to be called the queen of virgins (end of ch. 8). Bokenham's Life of Anne has nothing similar to these lines at all.

46   *Narracio.* Strictly speaking, this Latin term just means "narrative," but in the Mirk MSS it seems to identify self-standing anecdotes that might easily be detached from their present context and used when writing or preaching on other topics.

49   *oure Lady Sauter.* The MED explains that the series of prayers recited on a rosary acquired the name "our Lady's Psalter" because there were fifteen decades of *Ave*'s, corresponding to the 150 Psalms (see *sauter* n. 1. [f]).

65   *Ramesey.* Ramsey Abbey, founded in 969, was one of the largest and best-endowed Benedictine monasteries in medieval England. It was located in Huntingdonshire, about 10 miles southeast of Peterborough.

71–72   *the secunde day aftur Seynt Nycholas Day.* That is, December 8 (exactly nine months before the Feast of the Nativity of the Virgin, which was already well-established on September 8).

73–74   *what schal be the servyse of this fest.* The question would apply primarily to the Daily Office, which had an elaborate set of special readings, antiphons, responsories, and hymns for each important feast day in the calendar, rather than to the Mass, which was changed relatively little on such occasions. The answer attributed to the heavenly messenger in this story — that the liturgy to be used for the Conception of the Virgin should be exactly the same as that for her Nativity except for the replacement of one word — agrees with the directions given in most English breviaries written after about 1350, but earlier breviaries give several competing versions of the liturgy for the Conception, showing that there was considerable diversity of opinion at the start.

82   *Matenes of oure Lady.* This was not part of the Daily Office that was required of all clergy, but a much simpler and briefer set of private readings, prayers, and hymns that was added by those members of the clergy who wished to express special devotion to the Virgin Mary and was also used by devout members of the laity. The Little Office of the Virgin (which begins with the hour of Matins) was one of the principal items in books of hours.

85   The joke in this story depends on the two possible meanings of the word *service.* The devils say the sinful canon was in their service because he was "doing the devil's work," or preparing to, when he set out on his journey with the purpose of committing a grave sin. The Virgin Mary trumps their claim with the clever and truthful reply that he was actually engaged in her service (that is, performing the liturgy of the hours in her honor) at the time of his death.

88–98   There is a slightly different version of this anecdote in the *Legenda aurea* chapter on the Nativity of the Virgin (Jacobus de Voragine, trans. Ryan, 2.156).

93   *"Quam pulcra es et quam decora."* The antiphon begins, "How fair you are and how worthy of honor" — that is, with the same adjectives the Virgin Mary will recite back to the clerk when she remonstrates with him for being unfaithful to her. If she has the qualities of a perfect bride, why is he about to marry another woman in her place?

Textual Notes to Mirk's Sermon on the
Conception of the Virgin Mary

Abbreviations: **C** = British Library MS Cotton Claudius A.ii, fols. 11v–13r [base text]; **H 2403** = British Library MS Harley 2403, fols. 10r–12r; **H 2417** = British Libary MS Harley 2417, fols. 15v–17r; **G** = Bodleian Library MS Gough Eccl. Top. 4 (*SC* 17680), fols. 8v–10v; **Dd** = Cambridge University Library MS Dd.X.50, fols. 9r–11r.

6	*that₃*. Inserted above the line in C.

6   *that*₃. Inserted above the line in C.

16   *hym*. Inserted above the line in C.

18   *aschomot*. The letter *h* inserted above the line in C.

19   *tok*. Inserted above the line in C.

27   *syght*. C: *sygh*. The other MSS have either *syght* or *lyght*.

32   *a softe pas*. C omits *a*, but the other MSS have *a* or (less frequently) *on* and the idiom seems to demand it.

41   *aftur*. Inserted above the line in C.

43   *alle*. Inserted above the line in C.

45   *ys*. Inserted above the line in C.

       to₂. Inserted in margin in C.

46   *whech*. Inserted above the line in C.

47   *thefys*. C: *there thefys*, with *there* canceled.

       set. Preceded in C by the prefix *y*, erased.

50   *dount*. Preceded in C by the prefix *a*, erased.

51   *and₁*. C: *a*.

54   *don*. Preceded in C by the prefix *y*, erased.

58   *hed*. Followed in C by another letter (*d*?), erased.

62   *now*. Inserted above the line in C.

64   *heren*. C: *hren*.

73   *schal*. Inserted above the line in C.

80   *so was halwyt in Holy Chyrch*. Some MSS add the words *for evermore* to this sentence and then continue with a claim that the influence of this vision and the men who responded to it have extended far beyond England: *and so, out of the reme, hyt ys now cananyset* [canonized] *yn the courte of Rome, and halowet throgh all Crystyndome* (quoted from G; similar wording in Dd and H 2403).

81–98   These two anecdotes are omitted from some MSS, including G, on which the EETS edition is based.

97–98   *And also . . . the Concepcyon of me.* Not a very conclusive note on which to end, but many MSS stop here. A few add *Amen.* H 2417 follows this anecdote with a closing formula: *Now shull ye knele [adown?* (conjectural)*] and praye to the blessed mayden owre Lady Seynt Mary that hoe woll be your meene bytwyne here sone Jhesu Crist and yow, that He wol sende yow grace to kepe yow owt of all deedly synne.* G (which omits the last two anecdotes) ends with a different closing formula: *Now pray we to oure Lady wyth good entent of oure lyvyng to have amendement, and pray for us to hure Sonne that we may [be] wyth Hym yn Heven. Lady, we pray that hit soo be. Amen, amen pur charyté.* H 2403 ends with *Now, etc.,* apparently a reference to the same formula just quoted.

John Mirk, *Sermon on St. Anne,*
from British Library MS Cotton Claudius A.ii, fols. 95v–96v

Gode men, ye schul suche a day have the fest of Seynt Anne, that was modur
to oure Lady. Wherefore in worschep of oure Ladi Mari, ye schulde come that day
to holy chyrch and worchepon hur modur, Seynte Anne. Thanne schul ye knowen
that we redyth of fyve holy wommen that weren kalled Anne. And lest any
5   unkonyng man toke one for another, therfore I wil telle yow of thys wommen, to
knowen one be another.

    The forme Anne was modur to Samuel, Goddys holy profetthe, that was bischop
aftur Heyly and governod the pepul of Israel fele yerus. This Anne hadde ane
husbande that was called Elchana and mythe have none schyldren be this Anne,
10   for scheo was bareyne. But at the laste, be gevyng of grete almus and wyth devoute
preyer to God, God grauntid this Anne a sone that was called Samuel, os I sayde
beforon.

    Anothour Anne was wyf to a man that was callyd Raguel, and haddon a doghtur
that was callyd Sara, the wyche Sara hadde seven husbandys and evre the fende
15   the forme nyghte strangeled hem, for thei wolde have cowpled wyth this womman,
Sare, for grete lust of hur flesse and not in reverens of God ne in purpos to geton
chyldron to do Goddys service. Wherefore God gaf the fende power to sclene hem
or thei hadde defowlyd the womman. Bot aftur com Tobye the yonge, the wyche

1 suche a day, on such and such a day [to be inserted by the speaker]. **2 worschep**, honor.
4–5 lest any unkonyng man toke one for another, to prevent any ignorant person from
mistaking one for another. **5–6 to knowen one be another**, [to help you] distinguish one
from another. **7 forme**, first; **profetthe**, prophet; **bischop**, high priest. **8 Heyly**, Eli; **fele
yerus**, several years. **9 mythe**, could; **schyldren**, children. **10 bareyne**, barren; **be gevyng of
grete almus**, by generous almsgiving. **13 haddon**, [they] had. **14–15 evre the fende the
forme nyghte strangeled hem**, the devil always strangled them the first night. **15–16 for
thei wolde . . . hur flesse**, because they wanted to have sex with this woman, Sara, out of
sheer lust for her body. **16–17 in purpos . . . Goddys service**, with the intention of begetting
children to serve God. **17–18 sclene hem or**, slay them before.

an angel browth to Raguel hous. And so, be tysyng of this angel, this Tobye
20 weddyd this Sare, and thre dayes and thre nythes he forbare hys wyfe, and weron
in here preyeres, and so the ferthe nyght yode to hur bedde and haddon schyldren.

The thrydde Anne was Thobyes wyf the elder, the wyche was fadour and modur
to this Tobye that I have spokyn of beforen. The weche Tobye the elder was an
holy man and dud besyly the werkys of mercy and of charité. And yete God, to
25 previn hys meke suffraunce, made hym blynde. Thus on a day, whan he hadde
beryed so many dede bodyes that weryn slayne that he was wery of travayle, he
lay downe in hys hows by the wowe to reston hym, and so os he lokud up the
fyntyng of swalowes fel upon hys eyen, and so was blynde. Bot for he toke hys
desese paciently and evre thankyd God of hys visitacioun, therfor God sende hym
30 hys syght ageyne.

The ferth Anne was in the tempul of Jerusalem whan Joseph and our Lady
broghton Criste into the tempul on Candelmes Day. And than cam this Anne and
prophesyed of Cryste how it fel aftyr of Hym. This Anne was so holy that whan
scheo hadde ben wedde seven yere and hur husband dyed, than scheo yode into
35 the tempul of Jerusalem and was ther servyng God day and nyght tyl scheo were
foure score yer olde. And than scheo hadde suche a grace that scheo see Criste er
scheo dyed and handled Hym wyth hyre handys.

The fyfte Anne is oure Lady modur and fostred hyr of hur brestes. And whan
scheo was of age, scheo browte hur into the tempul of Jerusalem and lafte hyr
40 thare among othur virgynes of hur age to lerne Moyses lawe and to serve God

---

19 browth, brought; **Raguel hous**, Raguel's house; **be tysyng**, by the urging. **20 forbare
hys wyfe**, left his wife alone. **20–21 weron in here preyeres**, [they] spent the time in
prayer. **21 yode**, [he] went; **haddon schyldren**, [they] had children. **22 Thobyes wyf the
elder**, wife of Tobias the elder; **the wyche was fadour and modur**, who were the parents.
24 dud besyly, diligently performed. **25 previn his meke suffraunce**, prove/test his
humble patience. **26 wery of travayle**, tired from the labor. **27 wowe**, wall. **28 fyntyng**,
excrement. **29 desese**, suffering; **visitacioun**, adversity imposed on a human being by
God. **32 Candelmes**, Candlemas (February 2). **33 how it fel aftyr of Hym**, what would
happen to Him later. **34 wedde**, married; **yode**, went. **36 see**, saw; **er**, before. **37 handled**,
touched. **38 Lady modur**, Lady's mother; **fostred hyr of**, fed her from. **39 of age**, old
enough; **browte**, brought. **40 Moyses lawe**, the law of Moses (i.e., the religion of Israel).

bothe day and nyght, and so scheo dude. This Anne hadde an husbande that was called Joachym, the whyche cam of the lyne and of the kynde of David the kyng. But for cause that prophetes toldyn long beforen how that the kyngdam of David schulde decende to Criste, and so dydon wryton in bokys, the wyche bokys weron kepte in the tresurye of the tempul in mynde of this thyng, Herode, kyng of Jerusalem, thoght to turne this kynde of lynage in hym and hys eyres aftyr hym. Wherefore he toke these bokys oute of the tresurye and made to brenne hem, so that whan thei weryn done away the mynde of Cryste schuld a ben forgeton and he myght so conveyon be sleytys the lynage of Kyng David doun into hym and to hyse. Wherefore ther ben bot few bokys that tellon openly how that Joachim cam be descende from David. But whan this Herode hadde done this fowle dede, yete were there gode men and wyse that hadde copyes of these bokys wyth ham at home, the wyche tellyth how Joachim cam of the kynde of David. For David hadde mani childron, and among alle he hadde on that was callyd Nathan, of the whyche was ther on Levi, and of this Levi was ther on Panther, and of Panther was ther on Barpanther; the wyche Barpanther was Joachymes fadur, and he was fadur to Mary, Cristis modur, the whech he hadde be Anne hys wyf, and aftyr gaf hyr in mariage to Joseph. And than dyed aftur Joachym, and Anne toke another husbande was called Cleophas and hadde be hym another doghtur was callud Mari Cleophe, and aftur he dyed. And than sche toke the thridde husbande, that was callyd Salome, and be hym scheo hadde the thridde doghtur, and scheo was callyd

42 kynde, family. **43 for cause that**, because. **45 in mynde of**, as reminders of. **46 thoght to turne this kynde of lynage in hym**, planned to apply this family lineage to himself. **48 the mynde of Cryste schuld a ben forgeton**, the mention of Christ would be forgotten. **49 conveyon be sleytys**, transfer by deceptions. **49–50 into hym and to hyse**, to him and to his [family]. **50–51 cam be descende**, descended (came by descent). **54 on that was callyd Nathan**, one who was called Nathan. **54–55 of the whyche was ther on Levi**, from whom came one [called] Levi. **56–57 the wyche Barpanther . . . fadur to Mary**, the same Barpanther was the father of Joachim, who was the father of Mary. **57 the whech he hadde be Anne**, whom he had by Anne. **58 dyed aftur Joachym**, afterwards Joachim died. **59 husbande was called**, husband [who] was called. **59–60 doghtur was callud Mari Cleophe**, daughter [who] was called Mary Cleophas.

Mari Salome. And so, whan scheo hadde geton hyr thre schyldren in worchep of the Trenité, scheo wolde have no mo, bot aftur alle hyr lyve scheo gaf hyr to chastité and to holynesse.

65   And so of these three doghtyres ther com an holy lynage. For the forme doghtur, Mari, scheo bare oure Lorde Jhesu Criste. The secunde, Mary Cleophe, was weddyd to a man that was callud Alpheus and hadde foure sonnes: James the Lesse and Joseph that was callud Barsabas, Symon, and Judas. The thrydde Mary was weddyd to a man that was callyd Zebedeus and hadde be hym to sonnus, Jamus the More

70   and Seynt John the Evangelie. Thus, as God sayde Hymself, of a gode tre comyth a gode froyte, so of theis holy womman, Seynt Anne, com an holy ofspryng. Wherefore ye schal pray to Seynt Anne to pray for us to hyr holy doghtur, oure Lady, that scheo wyl pray for us to hyr dere Son, to gef us hele bothe in body and soule, etc.

62–63 **geton hyr thre schyldren in worchep of the Trenité**, obtained for herself three children in honor of the Trinity. **63 aftur alle hyr lyve scheo gaf hyr**, for all the rest of her life she devoted herself. **65 the forme doghtur**, the first daughter. **69 hadde be hym to sonnus, Jamus the More**, had by him two sons, James the Greater. **70 Evangelie**, Evangelist. **70–71 of a gode tre comyth a gode froyte**, from a good tree comes good fruit. **73 gef us hele**, give us health.

Explanatory Notes to Mirk's Sermon on St. Anne

7–12   The story of this first Anne, or Hannah, is found in 1 Samuel [1 Kings in Vulgate and Douay] 1:1–2:21.

13–21   This story and the next one are based on the Book of Tobit or Tobias, one of the texts from the Septuagint that are accepted as a canonical part of the Old Testament by the Catholic Church but not by most Protestants. (For a somewhat fuller account of these texts, see explanatory note to line 238 of Bokenham's Life of St. Anne.) The plight of Raguel's daughter Sara is recounted in Tobit 3:7–25; the angel's advice and young Tobit's success in Tobit 6–8.

22–30   The virtues and tribulations of Tobit the elder are recounted in much more detail in chs. 1 and 2 of the Book of Tobit; his healing, in ch. 11.

27   *wowe.* An obsolete word for "wall" that comes from OE *wāg* or *wāh* rather than the more usual *weall.*

31–37   The Bible gives only a very brief account of this prophetess Anna (Luke 2:36–38).

32   *Candelmes Day.* Candelmas, also known as the Feast of the Purification of the Virgin, was celebrated on February 2 to commemorate Jesus' presentation in the temple by Mary and Joseph 40 days after His birth. The *Legenda aurea*'s chapter on this feast day gives several explanations of its connection with candles; see Jacobus de Voragine, trans. Ryan, 1.147–49.

43–53   This ingenious explanation for the dearth of evidence concerning Joachim's lineage (and the Virgin Mary's) is found in the *Legenda aurea*'s chapter on the Nativity of the Virgin (Jacobus de Voragine, trans. Ryan, 2.150), where it is attributed to the *Ecclesiastical History* (presumably meaning Eusebius) and Bede's *Chronicle.*

53–58   Bokenham presents this same genealogy for Joachim, also derived from the *Legenda aurea*, in lines 120–24 and 140–45 of his Life of St. Anne. The obvious differences here are that Mirk shows no interest in the more complicated genealogy of Joseph and that he goes on, where Bokenham does not, to recount the traditions about Anne's later marriages and their offspring.

58–70   Mirk may have derived this account of Anne's own "holy lineage" — her two additional husbands, two additional daughters, and six additional grandsons — from the same chapter of the *Legenda aurea* as the preceding material on the genealogy of Joachim. But the details were given in many other medieval sources as well. In fact, all but two of the grandsons were included in the original formulation of the *trinubium* theory by Haymo of Auxerre in the mid-ninth century, and those two were added by Peter Lombard when he wrote about the theory in the twelfth century. By the end of the Middle Ages the completed theory had been discussed and debated by other prominent theologians, popularized in later recensions of the Pseudo-Matthew (the source from which the *Legenda aurea* itself probably derived it, according to Ashley and Sheingorn), and circulated further in sermons and vernacular adaptations based on those sources.

Textual Notes to Mirk's Sermon on St. Anne

Abbreviations: **C** = British Library MS Cotton Claudius A.ii, fols. 95v–96v [base text]; **Dd** = Cambridge University Library MS Dd.X.50, fols. 133r–134v; **H 2403** = British Library MS Harley 2403, fols. 137r–139r; **H 2417** = British Library MS Harley 2417, fols. 59v–61r; **G** = Bodleian Library MS Gough Eccl. Top. 4 (*SC* 17680), fols. 122r–123v.

1	*Gode men.* Other MSS have *Good men and wommen*, or *Dere frendes*.
5	*thys wommen.* C: *thys womman*, but the context obviously demands a plural.
7	*was bischop.* The reading of virtually all the MSS except C, which has *is schef*.
23	*was.* C: *was was*.
30	*ageyne.* C: *agyne*.
36	*er.* C omits, but the other MSS all have some form of it.
41	*scheo.* C: omits. The other MSS either have it or omit the whole clause, ending the sentence with *nyght*.
61	*scheo₂.* C has no pronoun at this point, but the other MSS have either *she, which*, or *that*.
74	*etc.* Some MSS continue with wording that is clearly designed for an audience of laymen and lay women: *and grace to kepe your ordyr of wedlok and gete such chyldyrn that byn plesant and trew servandys to God, and so com to the blys that Saynt Anne ys yn. Amen* (quoted from G, the source of the EETS edition; same lines with minor variants in Dd and H 2417 and H 2403).

Osbern Bokenham, *Life of St. Anne,*
from British Library MS Arundel 327, fols. 27r–39r

Prologue

	If I hadde cunnyng and eloquens	*knowledge*
	My conceytes craftely to dilate,	*ideas artfully to expand*
	Als whilom hadde the fyrsh rethoryens	*once; fresh rhetoricians*
	Gowere, Chauncere, and now Lytgate,	
5	I wolde me besyn to translate	*attempt*
	Seynt Anne Lyf into oure langage.	*Anne's*
	But sekyr I fere to gynne so late,	*truly; fear; begin*
	Lest men wolde ascryven it to dotage.	*ascribe; senile folly*
	For wel I know that fer in age	*far*
10	I am runne, and my lyves date	*the end of my life*
	Aprochith faste, and the fers rage	*fierce*
	Of cruel Deth — so wyl my fate	
	Inevytable[1] — hath at my gate	
	Set hys carte to carye me hens;	*carry; hence*
15	And I ne may ne can, thau I hym hate,	*although*
	Ageyn hys fors make resistens.	*power (force)*
	Wherfore me thinkyth, and sothe it ys,	
	Best were for me to leve makynge	*It would be best for me to give up writing*
	Of Englysh, and suche as ys amys	*whatever*
20	To reformyn in my lyvynge.	*way of life*
	For that ys a ryght sovereyn cunnynge:	*most excellent knowledge*
	A man to knowen hys trespasce,	*misdeeds*
	Wyth ful purpos of amendynge,	
	As ferforth as God wyl grawnte hym grace.	*To the extent that*
25	For whil a man hath leysere and space	
	Here in this wordlys abydynge,	*world remaining*

---

[1] Lines 12–13: *as my inevitable fate decrees*

	Or than that Deth his brest enbrace,	*Before*
	To ransake his lyf in alle thynge	*thoroughly examine (ransack)*
	And wyth his conscience to make rekenynge	*[an] accounting*
30	And ryhtyn ageyn al that wronge is,	*[to] correct*
	He may not fayle, at his partynge	*departure*
	Owt of his lyf, to gon to blys.	
	Neverthelesse, onto the sovereyn goodnesse	*unto; highest*
	Of Jhesu I truste and of Marie,	
35	His moder fre, thow I my besynesse	*although; task*
	Do diligently to claryfye	*set forth clearly*
	Her moderes lyf and hyr genalogye,	*genealogy*
	To excyten wyth mennys devocyon,	*With which to stir up*
	Aftyr th'entent of the storye,	
40	They wyl accepten myn entencyon.	*purpose*
	For treuly I make a protestacyon	*solemn affirmation*
	To Seynt Anne and to hyr dowter Marye,	*daughter*
	That yf eythyr errour in myn opynyon	
	Geyn good maners or heresye	*Against*
45	Ageyn the feyth I cowde aspye,	
	Wythe alle diligence and besynesse	
	Alle my wyttes I wolde applye	
	It to reforme and to redresse.	
	But ere than I ferther forthe procede	
50	In this matere, I lowly beseche	*humbly*
	Alle that schul thys story rede	
	That they loke aftyr no coryous speche,	*expect; ingenious*
	For Tullyus wolde me never non teche,	*Cicero; teach me any*
	Ner in Parnase wher Apollo doth dwelle	*Parnassus*
55	I never slepte, ne never dede seche	*did seek*
	In Ethna flowrs, wher, as Claudian dothe telle,	
	Proserpina was rapt; nor of the sugird welle	*carried off by force; sweet*
	In Elicona, my rudnesse to leche,	*Helicon; cure*
	I never dede taste, to me so felle	*hostile*
60	Wher ever the Muses; and the cruel wreche	*Were; scoundrel*
	Orpheus, whiche hys wyf dede seche	*who; sought*
	In Helle, of me wolde never take hede	

Nor of his armonye oo poynt me teche *harmony [even] one*
In musical proporcyon rymes to lede. *utter*

65 Yet notforthan I wyl not blynne, *nevertheless; cease*
For youre sake, my frende Denston Kateryne,
Lyche as I can this story to begynne, *As well as*
If grace my penne vochesaf to illumyne. *graciously consent (vouchsafe)*
Preyth ye enterly that blyssed virgyne, *Pray; wholeheartedly*
70 Whiche of Seynt Anne the dowter was, *daughter*
That she vouchesaf som beem lat shyne *beam [of light]*
Upon me of hyr specyal grace,
And that I may have leyser and spaas,
Thorgh help of influence dyvyne,
75 To oure bothe confort and solace *To the comfort of us both*
This legende begunne for to termyn, *declare*
Or than Deth the threed untwyne *Before; unravel the thread*
Of oure fatal web, whiche is ryht thynne, *thin*
And save us bothe from endles pyne, *torment*
80 And here us kepe from shame and synne.

O perles Prencesse, of virginyté *peerless Princess*
Synguler gemme, whiche in eche nede *Unique*
Art ever redy helper to be
To them that thee for grace to grede! *call to you for grace*
85 Entende, Lady, of thy womanhede *Give heed*
To my prayer, and me soccour, *help*
Whiche purpose of thy kynrede
Sumwhat to seyn, thorghe thy favour,[1]
And specyally onto the honour *for (unto)*
90 Of thy modyr; whiche as I rede *who; read*
Rote was of thee, o most swet floure, *Root; sweet*
And wyth hyr mylke dede foster and fede *nourish*
Thee ful thre yer, and aftyr dede lede *led [you]*
Onto the temple and ther offerde thee.

---

[1] Lines 87–88: *Who intend to say something about your family, through your favor*

95   Now, Lady, graunt to me mede   *[the] reward*
        In blysse eterne yow bothe to se.

[The Life of Anne]

Aftyr the reulys of interpretacyon,   *According to; rules*
Anne is as myche to seyn as "grace."   *has the meaning*
And worthyly thys appellacyon   *name*
100   To hyr pertenyth, for wythin the space   *pertains*
        Of hyr wombe sche dede enbrace
        Here that is of grace the welle,   *Her who; source*
        Lady of Erthe and Empresse of Helle.

        I mene that blyssed and holy virgyne,
105   Modyr of Jhesu oure Savyour,
        Marye, of synners sovereyn medycyne   *most excellent medicine*
        And in alle dystresse synguler soccour   *special help*
        Aftyr hyr Sone; and of this floure
        Whiche is so redolent and so soote   *fragrant; sweet*
110   This gracyous Anne was stoke and rote.   *stem; root*

        The whiche is commendyde, as I do rede,   *She (Anne) is praised*
        Of thynges thre most syngulerly: *especially*
        Ferst of hyr nobyl and royal kynrede,   *ancestry*
        Conveyede from David down lyneally;   *in the direct line*
115   Of perfyht levynge also; and fynally   *manner of life*
        Of plenteuous fruht; and Ysachar hyr fadyr *plentiful offspring*
        Was clepyd, and Nasaphath hyht hyr modyr.

        As for the fyrst, I wil ye knowe
        Be doctryne of Scripture, whiche wyl not lye, *By [the] teaching*
120   David in Jerusalem hade on a rowe   *in succession*
        Fowre sones be oon cleped Bersabee,   *by one [woman]; Bathsheba*
        Whilom the wyf of wurthy Urye.   *Formerly; Uriah*

But to oure purpoos, the thryde hyht
Salomon, and the fowrthe Nathan be ryht.[1]

125   Moreovyr I wyl ye know also,   *want you to know*
      As Jerom and Damascen do testifye,
      The custome of Scripture not usyth, lo,
      Of wymmen to wryte the genealogye;[2]
      Wherfore, as the lyne of Marye   *lineage*
130   Is knowe be Joseph and non othyr wyse,   *known through*
      So is Annes be Joachym, as they two devyse.   *set forth*

      Also for more cler undurstondynge
      Of this genealogyal descencyon,   *family descent*
      I wil ye wyte that for nothynge   *want you to understand*
135   The Olde Law wold suffre permixtyon   *allow intermingling*
      Of sundry kynredes, for whiche conclusyon
      Joachym toke Anne of hys ny alye,   *close relative*
      And Joseph was streyned to wedde Mary.   *constrained*

      These thyngys knowen, lyst what I mene:[3]
140   Of Nathan longe aftyr descended Levy,
      Whiche of his wyf Estha, seyth Damescen,
      Too sones gat, Pantar and Melchy.   *Two; begot*
      Pantar gat Barpantar, and he lyneally   *he in the direct line [begot]*
      Joachym, whiche that husbonde was
145   To Anne, the moder of oure solas.

      On that other syde down descendynge
      From Salomon even unto Mathan,
      Cam Jacob, aftyr Matheus wrytynge,   *Matthew's writing (Gospel)*
      But, as Damascen wyl declare can,   *well*
150   Melchy (of the lyne of Nathan,

---

[1] Lines 123–24: *But for our purposes [what matters is that] the third [son] was called / Solomon and the fourth Nathan in truth*

[2] Lines 127–28: *The custom of Scripture does not ordinarily / Record the genealogy of women*

[3] *[Now that you] understand these things, listen [as I continue]*

Pantars brother and the sone of Levy)
Weddyd Jacobes modyr and gat Ely.

So Jacob and Ely were brethern uteryne,	*having the same mother*
Thow Jacob of Salmon and Ely cam of Nathan,	*Although; Solomon*
155 And whan Ely issules his lyf dede fyne,	*childless; ended*
Jacob, to reyse his brother seed, dede tan	*restore; brother's line, took*
Hys wyf, as comannded the Lawe than,	
And gat Joseph, spouse to Marye.	
Lo, thus endyth this double genealogye.	

160 And yf yt lyke onto moralyté	*If it pleases moral interpretation*
To draw the names of the progenytours	*translate; ancestors*
Of Marye, chef gemme of virginyté,	
Of helful doctryne ful redolent flours	*wholesome; fragrant*
We schul fynde, of ryht swete odowrs,	
165 Yf we hem dewly kun applye	*them properly can bring together*
And ordenelly, aftyr the ethimologye.	*in order*

Aftyr the sentence of the holy doctour	*teaching*
Seynt Austeyn, David dowth signyfye	*Augustine; means (does signify)*
"The sovereyn hevenely progenytour,"	*most excellent; ancestor*
170 And Salomon, "pesyble," aftyr ethimologye	*peaceful*
"The prince of pees" betoknyth sothly,	*peace*
Whom the Fadyr down sent pees to make	
Perfyth, oure kynde whann He dyde take.	*Perfect; nature*

Be Nathan, David sone also,	*David's*
175 "Gyfth" or "thynge govyn" is signyfyed,	*Gift; given*
Be whom descens Levy is made to,	*Through whom the line descends to Levi*
And "taken up" betoknyth, or "applyed,"	*Who (whose name)*
Wherein we be mystyly certyfyed	*By which we are spiritually assured*
That be hem oure nature assumpt shul be	*taken up [into heaven]*
180 To the secunde persone of the Trinité.	

But yet had it not ben sufficyent,	
The uptakyng of oure frele nature,	*raising; frail*
Whiche wyth synne was almost schent,	*destroyed (lost)*
But recuryd had ben oure brosure	*Unless our wound had been cured*

185	And he venguyshd that causyd the lesure;	*defeated; injury*
	Wherfore in the ordyr of oure reparacyon	*restoration*
	Descens is to Jacob, toknynge "supplantacyon."	*[The] descent; meaning "usurpation"*
	Jacob supplanted hys brother Esau,	
	Whiche toknythe "row" or ellys "hery,"	*means "rough"; "hairy"*
190	And it signifyeth that oure Lorde Jhesu	
	Supplanted the devyl, oure ruggyd enmye,	*shaggy-haired*
	Whan He on the crosce ful schamfully	*shamefully*
	Heng nakyd, fastnyd wyth nayles smerte	*sharp*
	And wyth a scharpe spere stunge to the herte.	*pierced*
195	Aftyr Jacob, Joseph (as seyth the text)	
	In descence of the genealogye,	*Descending through*
	Whiche toknyth "encres" stondyth next,	*means "increase"*
	Spouse of Annes doughter Marie,	
	Modyr of Jhesu, whiche is to sygnyfie	
200	"A byttyr see" and "salvacyon";	*"A bitter sea"*
	Whereof, lo, a bref moralizacyon:	*moral interpretation*
	Joseph, encrescynge in goodnesse,	*increasing*
	Must wedde Marye, the bytter see	*sea*
	Of penaunce, be constant stabylnesse;	*steadfastness*
205	And yf Anne penaunces modyr be,	*mother of penance*
	Whiche toknyth "grace" and "charyté,"	
	He schal conceyven be the humble vertu	
	Salvacyon, tokned be this name, Jhesu.	*signified by*
	Now have I shewed more compendyously	*briefly*
210	Than it owt have ben, this noble pedegré,	*ought [to]*
	But in that myn auctour I folow sothly,	
	And also to eschewyn prolyxité	*avoid long-windedness*
	And for my wyt is schort, as ye may se.	
	To the secunde part I wyl me hye	*hasten*
215	Of my processe, and Annes lyf descrye.	*task; recount*
	Thys blyssud Anne of the blode royal,	
	As toforn is seyde, of David the kynge,	*before*
	In a cyté that Bedleem men calle	*Bethlehem*

281

	Was born and hade hyr fyrst fostrynge	*bringing up*
220	In alle that myht to vertu hyr brynge,	*bring her to virtue*
	As diligently as hyr fadyr cowd do,	
	Isachar, and Nazaphat hyr modyr also.	

	And whan she to yeris of dyscrescyon	*years of discretion*
	Was comyn, aftyr ther lawes guyse,	*custom*
225	Not over yonge aftyr myn estymacyon,	*overly*
	But what yer of age I ne can devyse,	*tell*
	Wedded sche was in ful solenne wyse	
	Into a cuntré clepyd Galylé	*region; Galilee*
	And to a man acordyng to hyr degré,	*social rank*

230	I mene to Joachym, in the cyté	
	Of Nazareth dwellynge and of David hows,	*the house of David*
	A ryche man and of gret dignyté	
	Whos lyf of youthe was ever vertuous,	*from youth on*
	Symple, ryhtfulle and eke petous,	*just; also merciful*
235	Aforne God and man ryht comendable,	*Before*
	To whom Anne was wyf ful covenable.	*suitable*

	For aftyr the doctryne of philosophye	*philosophical teaching*
	In Jhesus Syrach, whoso it rede can,	*whoever can read it*
	Lyche to lyche evere doth applie,	*Like is always conformed to like*
240	As scheep to scheep and man to man,	
	Pertryche to pertryche and swan to swan,	*Partridge*
	So vertu to vertu is agreable;	*suited*
	Werfore Anne to Joachym was wyf ful able.	*For which reason; fitting*

	For liche as they in ther yunge age	*just*
245	Were bothne forthe browthe vertuously,	*brought up*
	Ryght so, conjoyned be maryage	*united by*
	Whan they were, more diligently	
	In vertus they grew; and cause is why —	
	For, as longe toforne be a poete was tolde,	
250	What newe shelle taketh it savouryth olde.[1]	

---

[1] *An old container preserves the scent of what it held when it was new*

And for they wolde lyven conformely   *in conformity*
To Goddes plesaunce, here possessyoun   *their property*
They devyded on partes thre treuly.
The ferst they goven wyth devocyon   *gave*
255 To the temple, the secunde to sustentacyon   *support (sustaining)*
Of pylgrimys and pore men seek and olde;   *sick*
The thrydde they kept for her howsholde.   *their houshold*

Thus ryhtful to God and to man petous   *righteous; compassionate*
Twenty wynter they lyved wythout issw,   *children (issue)*
260 In chast maryage and not vycyous.   *full of vice*
And thow of here seed no fruht grew,   *although*
Yet to God for grace they dede pursew   *petitioned*
At Hys temple thryes in the yere
Wyth offrynge and wyth devouht prayer,

265 And maden vowes wyth holy entent
That yf God wolde of His specyal grace
Ony fruht hem sende, they wolde it present,   *Any child*
Were it man or woman, beforn Hys face,   *male or female*
Even in the temple, that holy place,
270 Ther hem to sence bothe clene and pure[1]
As longe therof as they had cure.   *provided for [it]*

Long aftyr, upon a festful day,   *feast day*
Clepyd of the temple the dedycacyon,   *the Dedication of the Temple*
Joachym in his best aray
275 To Jerusalem went wyth devocyoun
To make his ofrynge as he was woun,   *accustomed*
Wyth other burgeys of hys cyté,   *citizens*
Eche man as longyd to hys degré.   *befitted his rank*

At that tyme byschop was Isakar   *high priest*
280 In the temple, as tellyth the story.
And whan he amonge other was war   *the others; aware*
Of Joachym, stondynge ful sturdyly,   *resolutely*

---

[1] *To purify them with smoke from burning incense*

He hym rebukyde, and askyde why
He that bareyn and frutles was   *childless*
285   Presumyde to apperen in that plas.

"Thy giftes," quod he, "ben unworthy
And to God nothinge acceptable.
For this I wyl thou knowe pleynly —   *want you to know*
That bareynesse to God is reprovable,   *reprehensible*
290   And cursed is yche man and condempnable,
As Holy Scripture us doth telle,
That no fruht forth bryngthe in Israele.

"Werfore, Joachym, I charge thee,   *For this reason*
Nevere aftyr use this presumpcyon
295   Here to offre, tyl assoylled thou be   *until absolved*
Of this legal malediccyoun.   *condemnation/curse*
And whan thou hast get an absolucyon
Of this curs and hast fecundyté,   *curse; become fertile*
Than shul thy giftes acceptable be."

300   Whan Joachym thus rebukyde was
Of the byschop in the temple opynly,   *publicly*
He was so aschamyd of that caas   *event*
That agyn hom he nolde goon pleynly,   *That he would not return home openly*
Ne hap his neybures which dwellyd hym by   *Lest; neighbors*
305   Hym wolde repreve anothyr day.
And therfore he toke al another way,   *a completely different road*

And to his herdemen he dede hym hye,   *herdsmen*
Which in wyldernesse fer dede pasture   *far-off pastured*
That tyme his schep ful diligently,
310   Which in thoo dayes were his most cure,   *greatest concern*
For wyth that encrecyde of here genderure   *the increase; engendering*
He and his wyf were wonte to fede   *accustomed to feed*
Pore folke whiche God dede love and drede.   *who loved and feared God*

Whyl Joachym hym thus dede ocupye
315   Abought his scheep in wast wyldyrnesse,   *solitary*
And Anne his spouse cowde non aspye   *learn*

Of hym tydynges, neyther more ne lasse,   *news*
Ful monythes fyve, wyth gret trestesse   *sadness*
Oppressede and prostrat she gan to preye,   *Distressed; overcome*
320   And in here prayer she thus dede saye:

"O soverayne everelastynge Majesté,
Whiche hast been evere and be schal
Regnynge in stable eternyté,   *Reigning*
Whos regne may neyther bowe ne fal,   *decline nor fail*
325   To whom eeke eche creature mortal   *also each*
Must obey — now, Lorde, in this nede,
Upon me rew for Thy nobylhede!   *have pity; nobility*

"A, Lorde of Israele most myhty,   *Israel*
Syth Thou no chylderne hast gove me to,   *given*
330   What have I trespascyd geyn Thy mercy,   *How; against*
That thus my spouse Thou takyst me fro?   *take from me*
For ful fyve monythes be passyd and go   *gone*
Syth I of hym had no tydynge,   *any message*
Wether he be dede or ellys lyvynge.   *Whether*

335   "Now help me, Lorde, I Thee beseche,
And graunte me grace to have knowynge
Were I myht my husbonde seche;   *Where; seek*
For yf I knew where, wythowt letynge   *delay*
I wolde hym seke, yf he were lyvynge,   *seek; alive*
340   And yf he ded were, his sepulture   *tomb*
I wolde enbelshyn wyth besy cure.   *adorn; careful attention*

"For, Lorde, Thou knowyst how affecteuously   *affectionately*
I hym now love and evere have do,
Syth we fyrst knyt were lawfully,   *joined*
345   Past alle creatures; Lorde, helpe me so!
And yf the knot be now undo   *undone*
Of oure spousayle, I noon but Thee   *marriage; no one*
Know, Lorde, that may my confort be."

Whan she thes wordes and many mo,   *more*
350   Which at this tyme I ne can expresse,

285

Had seyd, sobbynge for very wo
And sykynge for hertys byttyrnesse,   *sighing*
Into an herber she can hyre dresse   *arbor; went*
Besyden hyr hows, and ther certayn   *indeed*
355 Hyre prayer hertly she made ageyn.   *fervently; again*

And whan she roos from hyr prayer
And casuelly lyftyde up hyr eye,   *by chance*
In a fayr, fresh, and grene laurere   *laurel tree*
A sparow fedynge hyr bryddes she seye,   *young birds; saw*
360 In a nest made of mossh and cleye,   *moss; clay*
And anon she fel down sodenly
Upon hyr knees and thus gan crye:

"O Lorde Almyhte, which hast overe al
Soverenté, and to everé creature,   *every*
365 Fyssh, ful, and bestis, bothe more and smal,   *fowl; large and small*
Hast grauntyd be kyndly engenderure   *by natural procreation*
To joyen in the lykenesse of ther nature   *resemblance*
And in ther issu, iche aftyr his kynde,   *offspring, each; its nature*
To worshyp of Thy name wythowten ende!

370 "And I thank Thee, Lorde, that Thou to me
Hast don as it is to Thy plesaunce,
Fro the gefte of Thy benygnyté   *gift; generosity*
Me excludynge; swych is my chaunce.   *lot*
Yet if yt Thee had lykede me to avaunce   *if it had pleased You; favor*
375 Wyth sone or dowgter, in humble wyse
I wolde it han offrede to Thy servyse."

And whan she thus had hyr entent
Expressed wyth a ful mornynge chere,   *sorrowful (mourning)*
Sodeynly, or she wyst what yt mente,   *before she knew*
380 An aungel beforne hyr gan apere,
Clad in lyht than the sunne more clere,   *brighter than the sun*
And wyth debonayr chere and gret reverence   *gracious*
To hyr he shewyd thus his sentence: *revealed; message*

	"Be not aferde, Anne, thow unwarly	*afraid; though unexpectedly*
385	I thus appere in thy presence;	
	For from Heven down sent am I,	
	Of glad tydynges thee to encence:	*inflame*
	How the fruht of thi body in reverence	
	And honour schal be and in mennys mende	*mind*
390	Thorgh alle kynreddes to the werdys ende."	*families; world's*

Whan the aungel thus his ambacyat   *message (embassy)*
Had brefly doon, he vanysshed auay,
And she astoyned and so dysconsolat   *stunned; forlorn*
Was that she nyst what she myght seye.   *did not know*
395   And to hyr chaumbur anon she toke the way,
Wher wythowt bodyly confort or chere   *kindness*
A day and a nyght she lay in hyr prayer.

And aftyr what tyme she dyd up ryse,   *when*
Alle bywept from hyr prayer,   *tear-stained*
400   She clepyd hir mayde, to whom this wyse   *in this way*
She seyde, "Syth thou sey me here   *Since*
So longe lyenge wythowt confort or chere   *lying; kindness*
Of ony wyht, how mayst thee quyte   *From any creature; do your duty*
That lyst not onys me to vysyhte?   *[even] once; visit*

405   "Allas, Lorde, yf it schuld be seyde
Al mannys confort Thou hast from me   *human*
Wythdrawen, and also of myn handmayde,   *even from*
Which awt, me thynkyth, my confort han be!   *Who ought*
But al this Thou dost that only in Thee   *[so] that*
410   I schuld trust, Lorde, and syngulerly   *exclusively*
Al my hope puttyn in Thy mercy."

To whom this damysel grucchyng can sey,   *grudgingly*
"Thow God thy wombe wyth bareynesse   *Although*
Hath shet, and thyn husbonde takyn away,   *shut*
415   Wenyst thou these myschevs I myht redresse?[1]

---

[1] *Do you think I could repair these misfortunes?*

Nay, nay!" Than Anne for veray hevynesse   *sorrow*
Of this answere fel sotheynly down,   *suddenly*
And wepte wythowten consolacyon.

In this menetyme an aungel shene   *bright*
420   In lykenesse of a ful fayre yunglynge   *youth*
To Joachym apperyd in the mountes grene,   *hills*
As he was amonge his schepe walkynge;
And to hym he wsyde this talkynge: *used these words*
"What is the cause, telle it me pleyn,
425   Why thou gost not hom to thy wyf ageyn?"

"Yung man," quod Joachym, "I wyl trewly
Telle thee now even lyk as yt is.
I love my wyf as affectually,   *affectionately*
I dar wel seyn, as any man dothe his;
430   But this twenty wyntur whiche beforn this
We togedur han ben, or more I trow,
The seed is lost which I have sowe.   *sown*

"I wante the argumentes of a man;   *lack; qualifications*
And whan men be reknyd I am lefth behynde;   *counted*
435   For no maner isseu may I han,   *offspring; have*
Neythyr son ne dowghter lyke me in kynde.
And syth in my felde no fruht may fynde,   *field*
To telyn it lengur it were but veyne,   *cultivate (till); vain*
As me thynkyth, this is certayne.

440   "For he that sowyth his feld yerly   *sows; annually*
Wyth gret dilygence, and hys appyl tre
Eche day watryth by and by,   *one after another*
And nout therof growth, faryth as he   *nothing; behaves like the man*
To staunche his thrust which drynkyth of the se,[1]
445   Or betythe the wynde, or in gravel doth sowe,   *beats*
Or eryth the bank were nought wyl growe.   *plows; where nothing*

---

[1] *Who drinks salt water to quench his thirst*

288

"So have I longe, as it seyde before,
Labouryde in vayne, yf I xal not lye,   *shall*
Ful twenti yere; but I wyl no more.
450   And also whan I thynk on the vylany   *disgrace*
Whiche I hadde whan the byschop me hye   *high priest; to hasten*
Bad owt of the temple, and myn offrynge   *Bade*
Despysed, cause I have of mornynge.   *of grief*

"These thyngys peysed and other moo   *weighed; others in addition*
455   Thus avysede, whatevere betyde   *considered; happens*
Hom ageyn I wyl never more go,
But here wyth myn herdys I wyl abyde,
And wyth good avyhs I wyl provyde   *intention*
To sende the part whiche longethe hem to   *belongs to them*
460   Both temple and wyf and pore men also."

And whan he thus declaryde had his menynge,   *intention*
This yunglyng answerde ful demuerely: *youth; gently*
"I am an aungel of the hevenly Kynge,
Whiche han apperyde this day sothly
465   To Anne thy wyf, wepynge contenuely,   *[who was] constantly weeping*
And now am Y sent to declaren thee
How youre prayers and almes of God herd be.   *have been heard by God*

"I have also seyn thy gret schame   *seen*
And the hatful reprof of bareynesse,   *hateful reproach*
470   To thee objectyd wythowt thy blame.
And this I wyl thou know for sekyrnesse   *want you to know; certainty*
That God ys wenger of wyckydnesse,   *avenger*
And whan He the wombe of His wel-belovyde, sothly,
Schettyth, He it opnyth the more mervelusly.   *Shuts; opens*

475   "Sare, the princes of youre kynrede,   *Sara; princess; ancestors*
Tyl foure score yer sche was baren.   *Until the age of 80*
And thanne she had Isaac, in whoos seede
The blessynge of folk promyssed was certeyn.
Bareyn was Rachel, the sothe to sayn,
480   Tyl she hade Joseph, of Egipt governour,
And of many folk from hungur the salvatour.   *savior*

"Who amonge dukys was myghtyere   *princes (leaders)*
Than was Sampson? Telle thou me.
Or who amonge juges was holyere   *judges; holier*
485   Than Samuel? Whos modres bothe perdé   *indeed*
Were bareyn. Thy wyf stant in lyke degré;   *stands in the same position*
For a doughter she shal have, sothlye,
Whos name clepyd shal be Marye.

"She shal be offred from hyr nativyté   *birth*
490   To Goddes temple, of youre bothens vow,   *by the vow of you both*
And wyth the Holy Gost fulfyllyd schal sche be   *filled*
From hyr modir wombe. Wherefore thou   *mother's*
Hom to thi wyf go hastely nowe,
For blessyd is hyr seed, whos dowghter shal be
495   Modyr of blysse everlastynge, perdé."

Of thes tydynges Joachym affryht   *frightened*
Worchyped the aungel and thus can sey,   *Bowed down to*
"Ser, yf I have fownde grace in thy syht,   *Sir*
Com and suppe wyth me, I thee pray,
500   In my tabernacle her besyde the wey,   *tent; road*
And blesse thi servaunt." Onto whom ageyn   *To him in response*
Thus this aungel benygnely gan seye: *graciously said*

"Conservaunth, not servaunth, I wyl thou me cal,   *Fellow-servant*
For of o Lorde above bothe we servauntes be;   *one*
505   And for my mete is invysible and my drynk celestyal,
It may not be seyn in this mortalyté;   *mortal life*
Werfore to thy tabernacle compelle not me,   *Wherefore; tent urge*
But swiche as thou schuldest gyf to my servyse,   *would have given*
To God do offren it up in a brent sacrifice."   *burnt*

510   As sone as this worde was seyd, Joachym can renne   *ran*
Unto the shepys folde and brought a lamb clene,   *sheepfold*
And at the aungels byddynge he it gan to brenne,   *burn*
And anon, otherwyse than Joachym dede wene,[1]

---

[1] *And at once, in a way that Joachim did not understand*

This aungel, whiche was both bryht and shene,   *shining*

515   Or than he awar was, even beforn his syht,   *Before*

Wyth the fume he toke to Heven his flyht.   *smoke*

Than Joachym fel down sodenly

Grovelynges and abasshed ful sore,   *Prostrate*

And so from sext tyl nyht, sothely,   *midday (the sixth hour)*

520   On the yorth he lay as he dede were;   *earth*

And than hys herdys had purposyde hym bere   *herdsmen decided to carry him*

To his grave, wenynge he dede had ben,

And than to hymselfe he cam ageyn.

And whan he thus ageyn com was   *returned [to his senses]*

525   And wel adawed of his swouwnynge,   *recovered; fainting*

He tolde his servantys al the cas   *everything that had happened*

And what was cause of his fallynge,

And anon thei hym conseled for anythynge   *advised*

Al that the aungel dyde to hym seye

530   Wythowt taryeng he it shulde obeye.   *delay*

Aftyr this, as Joachym gan thynk

In his hert what best was to do,

Slepe aftyr hevynesse made him to wynke,   *sorrow; doze*

And anon this aungel, evene ryht so

535   As he had uakynge, appered him to   *when he was awake*

Whyl that he slepte, and on this wyse

His massage to hym thus he dede devyse: *message; tell*

"I am the aungel the whiche at assignement   *[the] order*

Of God am comaundyde thy kepere to be;   *guardian*

540   And of my comynge, lo, this is the entent —

In hasty wyse that thou home hye thee.

Youre prayeris ben harde, and therfore ye   *have been heard*

Swich a chylde shul have as never tofore   *before*

Ne never schal aftur of woman be bore."   *born*

545   And whan Joachym of his slepe awoke,

He made hym redy wythowt lettynge,   *delay*

And thankyd God, and aftur that he toke

Homward his weye, wyth hym ledynge
Bothe herdemen and bestys, forthe softe goynge;   *at an easy pace*
550   And ever be the wey as they dyde walke,   *along the way*
Of Goddes goodnesse they dede speke and talke.

And whan they had ful ner spent
Thryes ten dayes in here journey,   *Three times (thrice)*
An aungel from Heven to Anne was sent,
555   Whiche bad hyr goon to the hy cyté   *great city*
Of Jerusalem, wher she shulde ce   *see*
At the gate whiche hath name of golde
Hyr spouse, the joye of hyr housholde.

Owt of hyr prayers anon dede ryse
560   Thys blessyde Anne, and on hyr ueye   *way*
To Jerusalem-warde, as dede devyse   *Toward*
The auungel, she gan hyr fast conveye;
And whan at the goldede gates she sey   *golden (gilded)*
Hyr dere spouse comyn wyth his herdemen,
565   As fast as she myhte she gan to ren.   *run*

She toke heed of non other thynge
But of hym alone, for in veraay blysse   *true*
Here thowte she was for his comynge.   *It seemed to her*
And anon she gan hym halsen and kysse,   *embrace*
570   No joye wenynge that she myht mysse   *thinking; lack*
Syth she hym hadde, and thus she gan crye,
"Welkecome, dere spouse, and God gramercy!   *Welcome; thanks to God*

"I was a wedowe, now I am non.   *widow*
I was also bareyn and reprevable,   *blameworthy*
575   But nowe bareynesse is from me gon,
And to conceyvyn I am made able   *conceive*
Be Goddes providence eterne and stable;
And for His goodenesse shewyd unto me   *shown*
Magnyfyed mot evere His name be."   *Glorified*

580   Whan this miracle abowte was blowe   *carried*
Be the trompet of fame in that cuntré,   *trumpet*

292

To alle tho that hem dede love or know
Ful gret joy was of that novelté,   *news*
And specyaly to alle ther offynyté.   *relatives (affinity)*
585 And after this hom they went, sothly,
The promysse abydynge of God mekely.   *awaiting; patiently*

After the nyhnte monyth, as I remembre,   *ninth*
Whan Phebus in Virgine had his curs ny runne,   *Virgo; course*
I mene the eyghte day of September,
590 To the werd appered a newe sunne,   *world*
And of Annes wombe sprange the oyle-tunne[1]
Of gracyous helthe to alle that beth seke,   *are sick*
Wyth a devouht hert if they wyl it seke;   *seek*

This is to seyne, that this day was born
595 The glorious gemme of virginyté,
Syche as never non was beforn,
Nor never aftyr other lyke it shal be;
Whos singuler privylege was this, that she   *unique*
Shulde mayde be and modyr eke of Myssye;   *the Messiah*
600 And hyr name they dede clepe Marye.

This lady to preysen as it were skyl   *reasonable*
Aftyr the meryte of hyr worthynesse,
Fer pasyth my wyt, thow not my wylle;   *surpasses*
I pleynley knowleche myn owne rudnesse.   *acknowledge; clumsiness*
605 But whoso wyl knowen, as I do gesse,
In Englysshe here laudes, lat hem looke   *praises*
Of owre Ladyes Lyf Jhon Lytgates booke.

And who in Latyn have luste to know
This ladyes praysynge retorycally
610 Expressed, ten bookes on a row
He muste seke, entytlyd sothly
"Of the weddynge dytees," metryd coryously.   *" . . . songs," finely wrought in verse*
In which tow werkys he shal inow fynde   *two; sufficiently*

---

[1] *And from Anne's womb sprang the vessel that held the Savior (the oil of salvation)*

293

Al that of me is now lefth behynde.

615	Aftyr this, whan Phebus (whiche every day	
	Chaungith his herberwe, nowher stabylly	*resting-place*
	Usyd to abyden, for he mevyth alway)	*remain; moves*
	The twelve signes thryes by and by	*three times*
	In the Zodyak cercle had passyde coursly,	*in due order*
620	And in the ende of Virgo taken his hostayge,	*lodging*
	Than was blessyd Mary ful thre yer of age	

And Joachym dysposed hym, and his wyf   *resolved*
Anne, devowthly her vow to fulfille,
To offren hyr dowgthter to the Lorde of lyf,
625   In the temple ther to dwelle stylle   *continuously*
As long as it plessyd His blessyd wylle;   *pleased*
And to Jerusalem for the same entent
At the next feste both two they went.   *feast day*

Toforn the entré of the temple than   *entrance*
630   Were fiftene grees of marbyl grey and brounn,   *steps*
As olde scriptures wel declare can,
Be whiche to the temple was the ascencyon,   *ascent*
And at the netherest was Maria set down,   *lowest*
And she anon ryht up ovyr on alle dede pace   *climbed (passed)*
635   Wythowt ony help saf only of grace.   *except (save)*

A wondurful thyng it was to see
That of alle the while of hyr passage,
Whil she stey up from gre to gree,   *mounted; step to step*
Notwythstondynge hyr tendyrnesse of age,
640   She never ofbak turnyde hyr vysayge,   *backwards; face (visage)*
Nor after fadyr or modyr onys dyde calle,   *[even] once*
Tyl she had clomben up the grees alle.

Ryht up also and nothynge stoupynge   *leaning over*
Al the tyme she went, and evere hyr eye
645   On the temple she was lyftynge,   *lifting*
And never hyr syht kest other weye.   *cast*
And whan Anne hyr modyr this marvel seye,

294

Fulfyllyde wyth the Holy Gostes grace,
Thus gan to seyn in that same place: *[she] said*

650   "Owre Lorde God, most of puysshaunce   *power*
      Past alle other, evere blessyde mot be,
      Of His holy worde wich hathe remembraunce,   *who remembers*
      And of His hy grace hathe vysedetyd me   *visited*
      That I no lengere reprevyd shal be,   *blamed*
655   Whil that I lyve, of bareynnesse,
      Ever worshype to Hym for His goodenesse!

      "And not only from shameful bareynesse
      I am delyverde thus singulerly,   *individually*
      But eke Hys peple which was in dystresse
660   He hathe vysyted so marcyfully,   *mercifully*
      That thoroghe my fruht — Lord gramercy —   *thank the Lord*
      Not I alone but al mankynde
      Shal comforth fynde wythowten ende."

      Aftyr this wyth an holy entente
665   Joachym and Anne bothe two in fere   *together*
      In the temple dede up presente
      Mayde Marye wyth ful humble chere,
      Preynge to God wyth herte entere   *whole heart*
      That He vouchesaf of Hys mercy
670   Here present to acceptyn benyngly.   *kindly/graciously*

      Whan this was doun they lefte hyr ther,   *done*
      Joachym and Anne, and hom ageyn
      To Nazareth went, wher they dwelled er,
      And holyly lyvedyn, this is certayn.   *lived in a holy manner*
675   But how longe aftur I cannot seyn
      Joachym lyved, but wyl know I   *well*
      Anne had thre dowghters, and iche hyht Mary;   *each [was] called*

      But whether be oon husbonde or ellys be thre,
      At this tyme I wil not determyne,   *specify*
680   For in this mater what best plesyth me
      I have as I can declaryd in Latyn

295

In balaade-ryme. Wherfore here to fyne   *end*
Seynt Annes Lyf I fully me converte,   *turn*
Thus hyr besechynge wyth ful louly herte: *humble*

685   "O gracyous Anne, wich hast worthyly
      Of grace the name, outh of whom dede sprynge   *out*
      She that of grace most mervelously
      And of lyf eterne the welle dede forth brynge   *source*
      Into this worlde, graunt at my partynge   *departure*
690   Be the fatal cours from this mutabilyté,   *fated path; [place of] change*
      Me in blysse eterne stablisshed to be.

      "Provide, Lady, eek that Jon Denstone
      And Kateryne his wyf, if it plese the grace
      Of God above, thorgh thi merytes a sone   *son*
695   Of her body mow have or they hens pace,   *before they pass away*
      As they a dowghter han, yung and fayre of face,
      Wyche is Anne clepyde in worshyp, Lady, of thee,   *called in honor*
      And aftyr to blysse eterne convey hem alle thre."
      A.M.E.N. Lorde, for charyté.

Explanatory Notes to Bokenham's Life of St. Anne

1–96   Although Bokenham begins this poem with professions of poetic incompetence, he obviously does not expect the reader to believe him. The Prologue in particular is full of classical allusions, echoes of earlier English poets, and other literary conventions (including the pretense of incompetence itself), and it is written in a conspicuously elaborate and demanding stanza form that rhymes sixteen lines on just three sounds (ababbcbccbcbbaba).

3   *rethoryens*. A term used in the fifteenth century for excellent or eloquent writers, not just masters of rhetoric in the modern sense. The modifier *fyrsh* is probably a form of "fresh" (meaning something like "new," "vigorous," or "fertile"), but it could conceivably be "first," referring either to the preeminence of the poets named in line 4 or to their reputation as the originators of courtly poetry in English.

4   *Gowere, Chauncere, and now Lytgate*. The three most famous English poets of the late fourteenth and early fifteenth centuries. John Gower and Geoffrey Chaucer had both died several decades before Bokenham began to write, but John Lydgate (author of the elaborate verse Life of Margaret in the present collection) was still alive; hence the *now* in line 4.

9   *fer in age*. Bokenham mentions elsewhere in this collection that he was 50 when he began it in 1443. Despite his repeated suggestions of poor health and decrepitude, he evidently lived another two decades.

25   *leysere and space*. A pair of near synonyms meaning "time and opportunity." Bokenham evidently liked this phrase, since he uses it again at line 73.

36   *claryfye*. A word meaning not only "reveal, set forth, declare," but also "illuminate, brighten" and "glorify, exalt."

41   *For treuly I make a protestacyon*. An unmistakable echo of Chaucer, who used slight variants of this line on three occasions: "But first I make a protestacioun" (*CT* I[A]3137), "Therfore I make protestacioun" (*CT* X[I]59), and "And here I make a protestacioun" (*TC* 2.484).

49–64   More echoes from Chaucer, most obviously the modesty formulas used by the Franklin (*CT* V[F]717–22), who also claimed to know nothing about rhetoric because he had never slept on Mt. Parnassus or learned any Cicero.

66   *Denston Kateryne.* On Katherine Denston, see above in the final paragraph of the Introduction to this legend. The reversal of her two names here is presumably done for the sake of the rhyme.

77–78   One expects a reference to the thread of life, the length of which was determined in classical mythology by the three Fates who spun it, measured it, and finally cut it off; but the *fatal web* (line 78) here seems to be a flimsy woven fabric that Death will unravel.

85   *of thy womanhede.* A common late-medieval definition of ideal *womanhede*, or "womanliness," made it almost synonymous with mercy and tender-heartedness. One of the clearest examples is the passage in The Knight's Tale that relates the noble ladies' reaction when Theseus angrily sentences Palamon and Arcite to death: "The queene anon, for verray wommanhede, / Gan for to wepe, and so did Emelye, / And alle the ladyes in the compaignye. / Greet pitee was it, as it thoughte hem alle . . ." (*CT* I[A]1748–51).

92–94   A reference to the tradition that Mary was consecrated to God in the temple at the age of three and remained there for the rest of her childhood. Mirk alludes to it in his sermon for the Conception of the Virgin, lines 41–42, and Bokenham himself gives a fuller account below at lines 615–74.

103   *Lady.* I.e., female ruler.

          Empresse of Helle. Delany explains this title, which is also used by Lydgate, as a reference to a tradition in the Eastern church in which the Virgin Mary herself "descends into the underworld to witness the punishment of sinners [and then] intercedes with Jesus to gain a period of respite for the damned" (Bokenham, *A Legend of Holy Women*, p. 201).

118–59   Although the immediate source for this discussion of Anne's noble ancestors is the *Legenda aurea* of Jacobus de Voragine, it draws on a long tradition of efforts by Christian commentators to deal with two problems in the Gospels: their failure to give any genealogy whatever for the Virgin Mary, and the fact that they give two conflicting genealogies for her husband, Joseph. The list of Joseph's ancestors in

Matthew 1:1–17 agrees with the longer list in Luke 3:23–38 on most of the sequence from Abraham to David, but after David they diverge radically. Matthew traces a line of descent through Solomon to Joseph's father, whom he calls Jacob, son of Mathan; Luke, a line through Nathan, another son of David, to Joseph's father Heli (or Eli), son of Mathat, grandson of Levi, and great-grandson of Melchi.

121–22   *Bersabee . . . Urye.* A very cautious reference to the greatest sins in David's life, as related in 2 Samuel [2 Kings in Vulgate and Douay] 11–12: an adulterous affair with Bathsheba, whose husband Uriah was serving loyally in David's army, and David's concealment of the adultery by contriving the death of Uriah. 1 Chronicles 3:5 names the four sons born to Bathsheba and David after he married her. But 2 Samuel 12:13–28 mentions an additional son: a nameless infant whose life was taken by God to punish David's crimes against Uriah.

        The form of Bathsheba's name here is not unusual in medieval sources. Manuscripts of the Vulgate used many different spellings, and two of the most common were *Bethsabee* and *Bersabee*.

126   *Jerom and Damascen.* That is, St. Jerome (c. 347–420?), who translated much of the Bible from Hebrew and Greek into Latin and wrote important commentaries on a number of books as well, and St. John of Damascus (c. 675–750), a Greek theologian, polemicist, and commentator.

131   *they two.* I.e., Jerome and John of Damascus.

134–36   *for nothynge . . . kynredes.* Probably a reference to Numbers 36:1–10, which directed the children of Israel to marry within their own tribes so that family property would not be scattered. Modern translators tend to interpret this rule as applying only to women who would actually inherit property, but the wording in the Vulgate could be taken as applying to everyone.

138   *streyned.* According to the *Protevangelium of James*, which shaped the view of Joseph until the end of the Middle Ages, Joseph was divinely chosen to be the husband of the Virgin Mary, although he protested that he was too old and would become a laughing-stock if he took such a young wife.

150   *Melchy.* Mentioned above in line 142.

156–57   The rule about marrying a childless brother's widow and designating her first son to perpetuate the dead brother's name is found in Deuteronomy 25:5–10.

158   *And gat Joseph.* The *Legenda aurea* adds another sentence at this point to underline the conclusion reached by John of Damascus: "Joseph therefore was by birth the son of Jacob of the line of Solomon, and by law the son of Heli of the line of Nathan: in other words, the son born according to nature was the son of the father who begot him, but, according to the law, the son of the deceased" (Jacobus de Voragine, trans. Ryan, 2.149–50).

188   *Jacob supplanted hys brother Esau.* The story is told in Genesis 27.

213   *my wyt is schort, as ye may se.* Echoes the naively apologetic stance of Chaucer's narrator in The General Prologue to *The Canterbury Tales*: "My wit is short, ye may wel understonde" (I[A]746).

223–26   Delany resolves the apparent confusion in these lines with this translation: "And when she had arrived at the age of discretion — I don't know what age that was, according to their laws, but probably not too young . . ." (p. 33).

238   *Jhesus Syrach.* Ecclesiasticus, also known as "Wisdom of Jesus Ben Sirach," is one of some fifteen books in the Septuagint, the ancient Greek version of the Hebrew Bible, that are generally either omitted from Protestant translations of the Bible or relegated to a section called "Apocrypha" because they were not included in the final canon of Jewish scriptures. The Roman Catholic Church has always accepted these books as canonical, and some of them (including Ecclesiasticus) were important sources of texts for liturgical use and preaching during the Middle Ages. For the "like to like" passage cited by Bokenham, see Ecclesiasticus 13:19–20 (Douay) or 13:15–16 (more recent translations).

249–50   The quotation comes from Horace, *Epistles* I.2.69–70: "*Quo semel est imbuta recens servabit odorem, testa diu*" (Loeb Library translation by H. R. Fairclough, quoted by Delany: "The jar will long keep the fragrance of what it was once steeped in when new," p. 202n33$_2$.)

289–92   As Delany notes, p. 202n34, the Old Testament contains no such explicit, general curse on childless persons as these lines suggest; but a number of passages can be taken as implying that fertility is a sign of God's favor and barrenness a sign of His disapproval. See for example Deuteronomy 7:14, Isaiah 54:1, and Leviticus 20:20–21.

475–78   The story of Sara's long barrenness begins in Genesis 15:1–5, with Abraham's lament and God's promise that he will have countless descendants, and does not conclude until Genesis 21:1–8, when the promise is finally fulfilled with the birth of Isaac.

479–81   The story of Rachel's barrenness until the birth of Joseph is given in Genesis 29:28–30:24. For Joseph's later role in saving his people from starvation, see Genesis 39–47.

482–86   For the story of Samson's birth to Manoah and his barren wife, see Judges 13; for Samuel's birth to Hannah, the barren wife of Elkanah, see 1 Samuel 1:1–2:21. Both stories are worth comparing in detail with the legend of Joachim and Anne, for which they obviously served as models.

557   *gate whiche hath name of golde.* The Golden Gate, on the eastern wall of the ancient city, was believed in the Middle Ages to be the same gate through which Jesus entered Jerusalem on Palm Sunday. For further information, see Richard M. Mackowski, *Jerusalem, City of Jesus: An Exploration of the Traditions, Writings, and Remains of the Holy City from the Time of Christ* (Grand Rapids: Wm. B. Eerdmans Pub. Co., 1980), p. 135.

588   *Whan Phebus . . . ny runne.* That is, the sun had nearly finished its annual passage through Virgo, the sixth sign of the zodiac (which ran from August 12 to September 11 in Bokenham's time). Chaucer frequently uses similar astronomical references to specify dates and times, as did Boccaccio and Dante (among others) before him.

591   *the oyle-tunne.* Although this looks from a modern perspective like a very odd metaphor for Mary, it would presumably have made much more sense in an era when oil was most closely associated with healing, comfort, light, and (because of its use in the sacraments) salvation.

607   John Lydgate's *Life of Our Lady* is available in a critical edition by Joseph A. Lauritis et al. (Pittsburgh: Duquesne University, 1961).

610–12   No one has yet identified a work conforming to Bokenham's description (a 10-book collection of Latin "wedding songs" in praise of the Virgin Mary).

612   *dytees.* Although this word would become "ditty," in Bokenham's time it had not yet taken on its modern English connotations of brevity and simplicity. It comes

from the Old French *dité* or *ditié*, and could apply to a literary composition of any length, either in verse or prose, whether intended to be read, recited, sung, or even performed as a drama.

615–20   For the astronomical reference, see explanatory note to line 588 above.

675–82   Bokenham's reluctance to say anything more definite here about Anne's later life might suggest that he himself was uncomfortable with the tradition of her three marriages, but it might just mean that he thought it tactless to bring up the possibility of widowhood and remarriage in a poem addressed to a married couple like the Denstons. Curious readers might well wish to consult the Latin poem in *balaade-ryme* (line 682) in which he claims already to have expressed *what best plesyth [him]* (line 680) on the subject of Anne's other husbands and daughters, but unfortunately that work seems to have been lost.

Textual Notes to Bokenham's Life of St. Anne

Abbreviations: **A** = British Library MS Arundel 327, fols. 27r–39r [base text]; **H** = Carl Horstmann; **S** = Mary Serjeantson.

3	*hadde*. A's reading; S: *dede*.
11	*faste*. A's reading; S: *fast*.
60–61	*the cruel wreche / Orpheus*. My emendation. A reads *cruel wreche / Of Orpheus*, but the *of* looks like a scribal error, probably induced by the ambiguity in ME of the form *wreche*, which could mean "punishment" (from OE *wræc*) as well as "miserable person, outcast, villain" (from OE *wrecca*).
66	*youre*. A's reading; S omits the final *-e*.
76	*begunne*. Corrected in A from *begynne*.
91	*floure*. Corrected in A, which originally omitted the *o*.
96 ff.	There is no subtitle in the manuscript at this point, but the beginning of the Life itself is marked by a blank line and a large initial *A* in line 97. The stanza form also changes at this point, with the 16-line stanzas of the Prologue giving way to the more familiar 7-line stanzas called "rhyme royal."
101–2	The order of these two lines is reversed in A.
119	*not*. Corrected in A from *no*.
134	*ye*. Inserted in margin of A to replace *the*, which has been cancelled.
135	*Olde*. Corrected in A from *wolde*.
	wold. Corrected in A from *wol*.
141	*Damescen*. Corrected in A from *Danescen*.
145	*of*. Inserted above the line in A.
161	*the₁*. A has *þe*, with the thorn only partly closed at the top. Here and throughout, I have silently converted this ambiguous form to *the* except when it obviously means "ye."
168	*Austeyn*. A's reading; S: *Austyn*.
178	Line inserted in margin of A.
187	*is*. S's emendation; A: *it*.
197–99	Lines inserted in margins of A.
199	*is*. My emendation, supplying a grammatically necessary word that A omits.
217	*As*. A's reading; S: *Als*.
	seyde. S's emendation; A: *syde*.

225   *aftyr.* My emendation; A: *astyr.*

227   *in.* Emendation as in S and H; A: *and.*

231   *Of.* A: *Off.* Scribes often doubled *f*, writing *off* for *of* or *ffrom* for *from*, for example. Since such spellings do not affect the pronunciation, and often cause confusion, they have not been reproduced in this edition.

238   *In.* Emendation as in S and H; A: *And.*

248   *vertus.* My emendation; A: *vertush.*

259   *wynter.* Corrected in A from *wyntout.*

264   Line inserted in margin of A.

273   *Clepyd.* Corrected in A from *Clepud.*

283   *hym.* S's emendation; A: *hem.*

293   *charge.* Corrected in A, which originally omitted the *r.*

299   *thy.* My emendation; A: *they.*

305   Line inserted in margin of A.

310   *thoo.* Emendation as in S and H; A: *too.*

311   *genderure.* The reading of A, with the final *-e* added above the line; S: *genderin[g]e.*

330   *Thy.* Corrected in A from *hym.*

331   This line follows lines 332 and 333 in A, with letters added in the margin to show the correct order.

363   *which.* A's reading; S adds a final *-e.*

372   *Fro.* S's emendation; A: *For.*

384   *unwarly.* Corrected in A from *unwardly.*

390   *Thorgh.* Corrected in A from *Thogh.*

393   *astoyned.* Corrected in A from *astouned.*

403   *quyte.* Emendation as in S and H; A: *guyte.*

404   *onys.* Corrected in A from *wonys.*

409   *only.* Corrected in A from *ondly.*

451   *byschop.* The end of this word is unclear in A.

464   *Whiche.* A's reading; S omits the final *-e.*

466   Line inserted in margin of A.

477   *in.* S's emendation; A: *and.*

478   *blessynge.* A's reading; S omits the final *-e.*

481   *the.* Word inserted above the line in A.

482   *Who.* Emendation as in S and H; A: *Tho.*

486   *Were.* Emendation suggested by H, supplying a necessary verb which A omits.

487   *shal have.* Emendation suggested by H; A: *hath.*

489   *She.* Initial letter erased in A.

491–93   Lines inserted in margin of A.

496	*thes.* Corrected in A from *the.*
511	*shepys.* A's reading; S: *schepys.*
520	*as.* A's reading; S adds a final *-e.*
521	*bere.* S's emendation; A: *bore.*
524	*com was.* S's emendation; A: *was com,* ruining the rhyme.
533	*him.* H's emendation; A, S: *hem.*
535	*him.* H's emendation; A, S: *hem.*
558	*housholde.* Emendation as in S and H; A: *husbonde.*
560	*blessyde.* Corrected in A from *blessude.*
563	*goldede.* A's reading; H emends to *goldene.*
566	*She.* Corrected in A from *The,* but the initial *T* left uncanceled.
572	*Welkecome.* H emends to *Wellecome.*
592	*alle.* A's reading; S omits the final *-e.*
601	*to.* Inserted above the line in A.
606	*Englysshe.* A's reading; S omits the final *-e.*
616	*Chaungith.* S's emendation; A: *Chaumgith.*
643	*Ryht up.* A: *Ryht up on,* with *on* canceled.
644	*went.* Emendation as in S and H; A: *wet.*
656	*worshype.* Corrected in A from *worshupe.*
658	*singulerly.* Emendation as in S and H; A: *singulery.*
673	*dwelled.* Emendation as in S and H; A: *dwelle.*
685	*gracyous.* A's reading; S: *grasyous.*
695	This line follows line 696 in A, with letters added in the margin to show the correct order.

Glossary

a, an *one; a certain one; in, on*
ac, ak(e) *but*
aferd *afraid*
after, aftur, aftyr *afterwards, then; after, according to; about*
agayn, agen, agein, ageyn(e) *again, back; against, toward*
als, also *also, as*
an *and*
and *and, if*
anon(e), anoon *at once, immediately*
ar(e) *before; until*
arered, arerde *built, erected*
as, ase *as if, as*
assay *try, test*
away(e) *gone*
ay *forever, always*

bad, badde, bed(e) *asked, prayed; invited; told, ordered; promised*
bare, bere(n), bore, born(e) *carried, lifted; wore*
be, bi, by(e) *by, with, near, for*
bedene *completely, immediately, indeed*
belyve ⟿ **blive**
beo, beon (infinitive) *be*
bespak(e) *spoke, spoke up*
betake, beteche, bitake *give, assign, entrust, commit;* **betaughte, betoke, betokyn** (p.t.) *gave, etc.*
betydde *happened*
bi- unstressed prefix, also spelled **be-** and **by-** in Middle English

bidde, bede, bydde *ask, pray*
bihete, bihote *promise;* **byhatte** (p.t.) *promised*
bileve, bilefe *remain; leave, abandon; cease*
binyme, bynyme *remove, deprive, take away;* **bynome** (p.t.) *removed,* etc.
biside(n) *near at hand; beside*
bivore, byvore *before*
blely *gladly*
blive, blyve, belyve *quickly, at once, eagerly*
bone *prayer, request, favor;* **bonene** (pl.) *prayers,* etc.
bote, boote *remedy, help*
bote, bothe, but *but; unless; only; except*
bought *redeemed*
bour *private chamber, bedchamber, bower*
brend, brent *burned*
bright, bryght *beautiful*
but ⟿ **bote**
by- ⟿ **bi-**
bymene *complain*

can *know, know how to, have skill in*
careful, kareful *full of care, worried, anxious*
cas *event, occurrence*
certayn, serteyn *certain, sure; certainly, indeed*
certes, sertys *certainly, assuredly, truly*

chere, schere *face, expression, demeanor; spirits*

clene *pure; splendidly, completely*

clepe, cleope *call, address*

com(e), cam *came*

comyn of *descended from*

cors *body*

coude, couthe *knew, knew how to; could*

counseyl *advice*

cunnyng(e) *skill, knowledge, understanding*

cusse *kiss;* **custe, cussyd** (p.t.) *kissed*

ded *death*

deighe, deie, dye *die;* **deide, dyod** (p.t.) *died*

dere *dearly*

devel(e) *devil;* pl. **develene**

doen, don(e), doone, do *put, place; inflict on; do, cause; act;* **dede, dydde, dud, dude(n)** (p.t.) *put, placed,* etc.

dorste, durste, derst *dared*

dowter, doghtor, doghtyr *daughter*

drede *doubt, fear*

drunch *drink*

dyghte, dyghten *dispose of, put, place*

echon *each one, every one*

eft, efft *again*

eke *also*

eode ⟫ **yede**

eou, ou, yeou *you*

er, ere than *before*

everiche, everychon, everylkon *every, every one*

eyghen, eien, heyen *eyes*

faste, vaste *firmly, securely; eagerly, immediately*

fax *hair*

faye, fey *faith*

fele *many*

fende *devil (fiend)*

fer, ferther *far, further*

in fere *together*

fest(e) *feast, feast day*

fetten *fetch;* **fet, fette** (p.t.) *fetched*

fol(e), foule *fool; foolish, sinful*

fol ⟫ **ful**

folie *folly; wrongdoing, sinfulness; harm, damage; lechery, fornication*

fond(e) *found; provided*

for, for that *because; because of, for fear of*

fous, vous(e) *eager*

fre, free *gracious, noble*

fruht, frut, fryt *offspring, descendants*

ful, full, fulle, fol, vol (intensifier) *very, exceedingly*

gan *began, did*

gart(e) *caused*

gaste *spirit (ghost)*

gayler *jailer*

gent *noble, beautiful, excellent*

gete *beget, conceive [a child];* **gat, gate, gotten** (p.t.) *begot, conceived*

geve, give, gif, gef *give;* **gaf, gafe, gev(en), goven** (p.t.) *gave*

grede *cry, call to;* **gradde** (p.t.) *cried*

guod, goud, gode *good; goods, possessions*

habben, han *have*

hede *behead;* **hedyd, ihedyd** (p.t.) *beheaded*

heighte ⟫ **het(e)**

hele *health; healing*

hem, heom, ham *them*

hende *gracious*

hens *hence*

hent(e) *seize, take, get*

heo *she*

heore, her(e), hor, hur, hyr *their; her*

heorte *heart*

Heove, Heovene *Heaven*

het(e), hette, heighte, hight(e), hyghte, hyht *was called, was named; promised; ordered;* **hoten, ihote** (p.p.)

heved *head*

heyen ⟫ **eyghen**

heygh(e), hey, hye, hegh, hyghe *high*

hi, hii, huy *they*

hight(e) ⟫ **het(e)**

hire, ire, hur(e), hyr(e), here *her*

hondene *hands*

hor, hyr ⟫ **heore** and **hire**

hoten ⟫ **het(e)**

hou *how*

hurste *hill*

huy ⟫ **hi**

hwane *when*

hware *where*

hwodere *whither*

hwyle *while*

hye, on hye *haste, in haste*

hye *hasten* (also refl.)

i- prefix descended from OE *ge-*; also spelled **y-** in ME

ibeo, ibeon, ibe *been*

ibore, ybore *born; carried*

ic, ich, Y *I*

ichulle *I shall*

icleoped, yclyped *called*

ihedyd ⟫ **hede**

ihote ⟫ **het(e)**

ilke, ylke *each, every; same*

ilkon *every one*

in *in, on*

inome, ynome *taken, seized*

inou, inough, ynowe *enough, plenty; very, exceedingly*

irad *advised*

is *his*

isei, isaigh, iseighen *saw*

isseu, issw, issu *issue, offspring*

iwis, iwisse, ywisse, ywys *certainly, indeed*

kareful ⟫ **careful**

kunne, kynne *family; kind*

kynde *nature; family*

kynrede *family, birth, ancestry*

kytte *cut*

lavedi ⟫ **levedi**

lay(e) *law, religion*

lefe, leve *leave off, cease, desist from; leave, abandon*

lemman *lover, mistress; darling, beloved*

leof, leove, leve, leeff *dear, beloved*

lese *lose*

let(e), liete *cause, allow; leave; leave off, abandon*

leve, lieve *believe*

levedi, lavedi *lady*

levyng(e), lyvynge *way of life, behavior*

light *easy, cheerful, glad*

like, lyke (impers. v.) *please;* **likez me, me lykith** *it pleases me*

liste, lyst(e) *desired, chose;* (impers.) *pleased;* **hir liste** *it pleased her, she wished to*

lofe *love*

lore *instruction, teaching, doctrine*
loverd *lord*
luste *desire, pleasure*
luther(e) *wicked*
luytel, luyte, lute, lyte *little*
lye *remain, dwell*
lyst, lyst(e)nes *listen*
lyst ⟫ **liste**

magesté, magestie *majesty*
man, men, me *people, one*
mawmentes, -is *idols*
mawmentrye *idolatry*
may(e) *maiden, virgin*
may *can, is able, avails*
mekyl, meche, myche(l), muche,
  muchel(e), mochyl *much, great;*
  many; greatly
mete *food, dinner, supper*
mid, myd *with*
mod(e), moode *heart, mind; temper,*
  mood
mo, moo *more*
morne, morowon, morowh, morwen
  morrow, morning
moste *must, might, was allowed, could*
mote(n) *be allowed, be obliged*
mowe(n) *may, be strong, have power,*
  prevail, be able
muche, muchel(e), myche ⟫ **mekyl**
myght(e), mythe *strength, power;*
  could, was able

nadde *did not have*
nam, nom, nome *took*
namely *especially*
nas *was not*
nei, neigh, ny(e), nygh *near; nearly*
nelle, nele *will not, do(es) not wish*

neod(e), nede *need; necessary;* **nedys**
  necessarily
nere, ner *nearly*
noght *not; nothing*
nolde *did not wish, would not*
nom, nome ⟫ **nam**
non other *nothing else*
nother, nothur *neither, nor*
nothing, nothyng (adv.) *not at all*
nouthe, nogh, nou *now*
nuste *didn't know*
ny(e), nygh ⟫ **nei**
nyme *take, seize*

of, off *of, from; off*
ofdrad *afraid*
on, oon, oo *one*
onto *unto, to; for the sake of*
ony *any*
op *up*
opbraid *condemned*
opon, oppon *upon, on; in*
or, or than *before*
ore *our*
orighte, oryght *right, rightly, properly;*
  exactly; indeed
os *as, as if*
other, othur, othor, othyr *others;*
  another; second, next; otherwise
othur, othour, other *or; either . . . or*
ou ⟫ **eou**
ous *us*
overal *everywhere*

pardé, perdé *certainly, to be sure* (lit.,
  "by God")
peté *pity*
pleyn(e) *open, plain; openly, frankly*
posté, pousté, pousty *power*

povere *poor*

prest *ready, prepared; quick(ly)*

preste *priest*

prevyly, priveliche *secretly*

pruyde, prute *pride; proud*

puyr *completely*

pyne, peyne, payne *pain, suffering, torment; effort*

quelle, qwelle *kill*

rad *quick, eager, ready*

rede *counsel, advice; advise; instruct; read*

rere *build, erect; raise*

resoun *argument*

right(e) *true, proper; very, completely; exactly, directly; properly*

right(e) non *none at all*

rode *cross*

schal, schalt(e), schulle(n) *will; must*

schene *shining, bright*

scheppe, schippe, scip, schyppe *ship*

schewe, ischewe *show*

schipeden *embarked, set sail*

scho, sho, scheo, sche *she*

scholde, shuld(e) *should; must; owed; was supposed to, was obliged to*

schonde *disgrace*

schrof *confessed, absolved (shrove)*

se, see, seen, sei, sai, sagh(e), sey(e), seygh, seighe(n) *saw*

seche, seke *seek, search for*

segge, seighe *say*

sekyr *sure, confident, certain; surely, truly*

sen, syn *since*

sende *sent*

sere *sir*

serteyn ⇛ **certayn**

sertys ⇛ **certes**

seththe, sethen, sithen, sythen, suth *then, afterward; since*

sewe *follow*

siche ⇛ **swuch**

skile *reason*

soccour, sokur *help*

softe, softeliche *gently*

somdel *somewhat*

sonde *message, messenger; favor, dispensation (sending)*

sone *soon*

sor(e) *pain, grief; sorrowful; bitterly, grievously*

sory(e), sori *woeful, sorrowful, wretched; evil, accursed*

sothe *truth, truly;* **for soth(e)** *truly, indeed, certainly*

sovereyn *highest, most excellent*

stude, stede *place*

stynte, stent *cease, ceased*

sunful(e), sunfole, sunvol *sinful*

sunne *sin*

suth ⇛ **seththe**

swote, soote, suete *sweet*

swuch, siche, syche *such*

swylk(e) *such*

swythe *very, exceedingly*

synguler *unique, special*

syngulerly *especially; solely*

teone, tene *sorrow, suffering; vexation, anger*

than *then*

thau, thagh, thei, thof, thow *though, although*

thedyr ⇛ **thuder(e)**

Glossary

ther(e), theras *there; where*
thies, thes, this *these*
thinke, thynke *think;* me thinkith, me
thencth (impers. v.) *it seems to me;*
thoght hym, hym thought *it seemed
to him*
tho, thoo *then; when; those*
thole, tholie *suffer, endure*
thore *there*
thorgh, thorwgh, thoru, thorw
through
thuder(e), thidur, thydor, thedyr
thither
thulke *that same; the same one*
to *to; until; as*
toknyth *betokens, means*
too, tuo *two*
trowe *believe*

uche *each*
uchon *each one*
untyl *to, unto*

vair *fair, beautiful*
vaste »» faste
vertu(e) *power, strength; virtue*
vol »» ful
vor »» for
vorth *forth*

war(e) *where*
wel, weel, wyl *well; very*
welle *fountain, spring, source*
wende *go; turn; went*
wene *believe, think, suppose; expect;*
wende (p.t.) *believed, etc.*
weop *wept*
werfore, wher(e)fore *therefore, for this
reason; why*

wex *become, grow;* wax, woxen (p.t.)
became, etc.
which(e), wyche, whiche that, the
whiche, the whylke *who, which*
whilom *once, formerly*
wight(e), wyght *person, creature*
wille, wol(le), wyl(le) *will, wish, want
[to];* p.t. wold(e)
witte, wytte, wot, waat *know;* wuste,
wiste, wyste (p.t.) *knew*
wo, woo *woe, sorrow, misery; miserable*
wod(e), wood *furious, mad, insane*
wondur, wonder(e), wondyr
exceedingly, amazingly
wone, wonie *remain, dwell*
wor(s)chep, worschip, wurschep
worship, honor
woun, wonte *accustomed*
wrought, wrouthe *worked, acted;
accomplished, achieved; made*
wunne *wealth, happiness*
wuste »» witte
wyche »» which(e)

y- Most words with this prefix are listed
under i-.
yare, yore *long; for a long time; ready;
readily*
yche *each*
yede, yod(e), yood, yeode, eode *went,
walked*
yelde *pay, repay;* yolden (p.p.) *paid, etc.*
yen, yghen *eyes*
yer(e) *year, years*
yerne *eagerly*
yif, yyf *if*
yuyt(e), yyt, yit, yytte, yut(e) *yet, still;
even*
yyng, yong(e) *young*

312

Volumes in the Middle English Texts Series

The Floure and the Leafe, The Assembly of Ladies, and *The Isle of Ladies*, ed. Derek Pearsall (1990)

Three Middle English Charlemagne Romances, ed. Alan Lupack (1990)

Six Ecclesiastical Satires, ed. James M. Dean (1991)

Heroic Women from the Old Testament in Middle English Verse, ed. Russell A. Peck (1991)

The Canterbury Tales: Fifteenth-Century Continuations and Additions, ed. John M. Bowers (1992)

Gavin Douglas, *The Palis of Honoure*, ed. David Parkinson (1992)

Wynnere and Wastoure and The Parlement of the Thre Ages, ed. Warren Ginsberg (1992)

The Shewings of Julian of Norwich, ed. Georgia Ronan Crampton (1993)

King Arthur's Death: The Middle English Stanzaic Morte Arthur and Alliterative Morte Arthure, ed. Larry D. Benson and Edward E. Foster (1994)

Lancelot of the Laik and Sir Tristrem, ed. Alan Lupack (1994)

Sir Gawain: Eleven Romances and Tales, ed. Thomas Hahn (1995)

The Middle English Breton Lays, ed. Anne Laskaya and Eve Salisbury (1995)

Sir Perceval of Galles and Ywain and Gawain, ed. Mary Flowers Braswell (1995)

Four Middle English Romances: Sir Isumbras, Octavian, Sir Eglamour of Artois, Sir Tryamour, ed. Harriet Hudson (1996)

The Poems of Laurence Minot (1333–1352), ed. Richard H. Osberg (1996)

Medieval English Political Writings, ed. James M. Dean (1996)

The Book of Margery Kempe, ed. Lynn Staley (1996)

Amis and Amiloun, Robert of Cisyle, and Sir Amadace, ed. Edward E. Foster (1997)

The Cloud of Unknowing, ed. Patrick J. Gallacher (1997)

Robin Hood and Other Outlaw Tales, ed. Stephen Knight and Thomas Ohlgren (1997)

The Poems of Robert Henryson, ed. Robert L. Kindrick (1997)

Moral Love Songs and Laments, ed. Susanna Greer Fein (1998)

John Lydgate, *Troy Book: Selections*, ed. Robert R. Edwards (1998)

Thomas Usk, *The Testament of Love*, ed. R. Allen Shoaf (1998)

Prose Merlin, ed. John Conlee (1998)

Middle English Marian Lyrics, ed. Karen Saupe (1998)

John Metham, *Amoryus and Cleopes*, ed. Stephen F. Page (1999)

Four Romances of England: King Horn, Havelok the Dane, Bevis of Hampton, Athelston, ed. Ronald B. Herzman, Graham Drake, Eve Salisbury (1999)

The Assembly of Gods: Le Assemble de Dyeus, or Banquet of Gods and Goddesses, with the Discourse of Reason and Sensuality, ed. Jane Chance (1999)

Thomas Hoccleve, *The Regiment of Princes*, ed. Charles R. Blyth (1999)

John Capgrave, *The Life of St. Katherine*, ed. Karen Winstead (1999)

John Gower, *Confessio Amantis*, Vol. 1, ed. Russell A. Peck (2000); Vol. 2 (2003)

Richard the Redeless and *Mum and the Sothsegger*, ed. James Dean (2000)

Ancrene Wisse, ed. Robert Hasenfratz (2000)

Walter Hilton, *Scale of Perfection*, ed. Thomas Bestul (2000)

John Lydgate, *Siege of Thebes*, ed. Robert Edwards (2001)

Pearl, ed. Sarah Stanbury (2001)

The Trials and Joys of Marriage, ed. Eve Salisbury (2002)

Other TEAMS Publications

Documents of Practice Series:

Love and Marriage in Late Medieval London, selected, translated, and introduced by Shannon McSheffrey (1995)

Sources for the History of Medicine in Late Medieval England, selected, introduced, and translated by Carole Rawcliffe (1995)

A Slice of Life: Selected Documents of Medieval English Peasant Experience, edited, translated, and with an introduction by Edwin Brezette DeWindt (1996)

Regular Life: Monastic, Canonical, and Mendicant Rules, selected with an introduction by Douglas J. McMillan and Kathryn Smith Fladenmuller (1997)

Women and Monasticism in Medieval Europe: Sisters and Patrons of the Cistercian Reform, selected, translated, and with an introduction by Constance H. Berman (2002)

Commentary Series:

Commentary on the Book of Jonah, Haimo of Auxerre, translated with an introduction by Deborah Everhart (1993)

Medieval Exegesis in Translation: Commentaries on the Book of Ruth, translated with an introduction by Lesley Smith (1996)

Nicholas of Lyra's Apocalypse Commentary, translated with an introduction and notes by Philip D. W. Krey (1997)

Rabbi Ezra Ben Solomon of Gerona: Commentary on the Song of Songs and Other Kabbalistic Commentaries, selected, translated, and annotated by Seth Brody (1999)

John Wyclif: On the Truth of Holy Scripture, translated with an introduction and notes by Ian Christopher Levy (2001)

Second Thessalonians: Two Early Medieval Apocalyptic Commentaries, translated with an introduction by Steven R. Cartwright and Kevin L. Hughes (2001)

To order please contact:

MEDIEVAL INSTITUTE PUBLICATIONS
Western Michigan University
Kalamazoo, MI 49008–5432
Phone (616) 387–8755
FAX (616) 387–8750

http://www.wmich.edu/medieval/mip/index.html